HUMAN SERVICES FOR
CULTURAL MINORITIES

HUMAN SERVICES FOR CULTURAL MINORITIES

Edited by
Richard H. Dana, Ph.D.
Professor
Department of Psychology
University of Arkansas–Fayetteville

University Park Press
Baltimore

UNIVERSITY PARK PRESS
International Publishers in Science, Medicine, and Education
300 North Charles Street
Baltimore, Maryland 21201

Copyright © 1981 by University Park Press

Typeset by University Park Press, Typesetting Division
Manufactured in the United States of America by The Maple Press Company

Library of Congress Cataloging in Publication Data

Main entry under title:

Human services for cultural minorities.

Bibliography: p.
Includes index.
1. Social work with minorities—United States—Addresses, essays, lectures.
I. Dana, Richard Henry, 1927–   .   HV3176.H85   362.8'4'0973   81-16464
ISBN 0-8391-1687-X   AACR2

CONTENTS

Contributors ix
Preface xi

Section I NATIVE AMERICANS

1 Editorial Introduction 3
2 The Persistence of Essential Values
   among North American Plains Indians 5
      Joseph Epes Brown
3 The Psychiatrist and his Shaman Colleague:
   Cross-Cultural Collaboration with
   Traditional Amerindian Therapists 15
      Wolfgang Jilek and Louise Jilek-Aall
4 Mental Health Services for American Indians:
   Neither Feast nor Famine 27
      Morton Beiser and Carolyn L. Attneave
5 Federal Mandates for the Handicapped:
   Implications for American Indian Children 43
      Bruce Ramirez and Barbara J. Smith
6 Family Behavior of Urban American Indians 55
      John G. Red Horse, Ronald Lewis,
      Marvin Feit, and James Decker
7 Suicide among the Cheyenne Indians 65
      Larry H. Dizmang
8 Cultural Perspective on Treatment Modalities
   with Native Americans 71
      Ronald Lewis
9 The Papago Psychology Service: A Community Mental
   Health Program on an American Indian Reservation 79
      Marvin W. Kahn, Cecil Williams, Eugene Galvez,
      Linda Lejero, Rex Conrad, and George Goldstein
10 Grief Counseling with Native Americans 95
      Wynne Hanson

Section II AFRO-AMERICANS

11 Editorial Introduction 103
12 Black Ecology 105
      Nathan Hare
13 The Emergence of a Black Perspective in Counseling 115
      Gerald Gregory Jackson

14 Stylistic Dimensions of Counseling Blacks 139
      Johnnie McFadden
15 Dimensions of the Relationship between the
      Black Client and the White Therapist:
      A Theoretical Overview....................................145
      Alison Jones and Arthur A. Seagull
16 A Course on Counseling Ethnic Minorities: A Model 157
      Roderick J. McDavis and Max Parker
17 The Interpersonal Orientation in Mental
      Health Consultation: Toward a Model of
      Ethnic Variations in Consultation 163
      Jewelle Taylor Gibbs

Section III   HISPANIC AMERICANS
18 Editorial Introduction 185
19 Counseling Latinos 187
      Rene A. Ruiz and Amado M. Padilla
20 Therapy Latino Style:
      Implications for Psychiatric Care........................207
      Melvin Delgado
21 The Role of Folk Healers in
      Community Mental Health Services.........................217
      Pedro Ruiz and John Langrod
22 The Dynamics and Treatment of the Young Drug
      Abuser in an Hispanic Therapeutic Community 225
      Herbert J. Freudenberger
23 Counseling the Chicano Child 239
      Wayne R. Maes and John R. Rinaldi
24 A Hispanic Foster Parents Program
      Melvin Delgado 245
25 Strategic Intervention: A Mental Health Program
      for the Hispanic Community 251
      Melvin Delgado and John F. Scott
26 Common Errors in Psychotherapy with Chicanos:
      Extrapolations from Research and Clinical Experience.......265
      Samuel Roll, Leverett Millen, and Ricardo Martinez

Section IV   ASIAN AMERICANS
27 Editorial Introduction 285
28 Asian Americans as a Minority Group......................287
      *Stanley Sue, Derald Wing Sue,
      and David W. Sue*
29 Counseling Asians: Psychotherapy in the
      Context of Racism and Asian-American History 295
      Elizabeth Sook Wha Ahn Toupin

30 Social Work with Asian Americans 307
          Man Kueng Ho
31 Asians as Individuals: The Japanese Community............317
          Amy Iwasaki Mass
32 Therapy for Asian Americans...........................323
          Joe Yamamoto
33 Identity Conflict and Acculturation Problems
        in Oriental-Americans 331
          Vita S. Sommers
34 Eliminating Cultural Oppression in Counseling:
        Toward a General Theory 339
          Derald Wing Sue
        Epilogue 353
        Index 357

Contributors

Carolyn L. Attneave
Professor of Psychology
University of Washington

Morton Beiser
Director of Psychiatry
Student Health Services
University of British Columbia

Joseph Epes Brown
Professor of Religious Studies
University of Montana

Rex Conrad
Private Practice
Riverside, California

James Decker
Assistant Professor of Social Work
San Diego State University

Melvin Delgado
Associate Professor
Boston University School of
   Social Work

Larry H. Dizmang
Chief, Psychiatric Services
St. Helena Hospital
Deer Park, California

Marvin Feit
Assistant Professor
School of Social Work
University of Tennessee-Memphis

Herbert J. Freudenberger
Independent Practice
   (Psychoanalysis)
890 Park Avenue
New York, New York

Eugene Galvez
Papago Psychology Service
Sells, Arizona

Jewelle Taylor Gibbs
School of Social Welfare
University of California-Berkeley

George Goldstein
Director of Program Development
   and Evaluation of Mental
   Health Programs
Indian Health Service
Albuquerque, New Mexico

Wynne Hanson
Native American Social Work Project
San Francisco State University

Nathan Hare
Private Practice (Clinical Psychology)
San Francisco, California

Man Kueng Ho
Professor of Social Work
University of Oklahoma

Gerald Gregory Jackson
President, New Arena Consultants,
   Inc.
East Orange, New Jersey

Wolfgang Jilek
Clinical Professor of Psychiatry
University of British Columbia

Louise Jilek-Aall
Mental Health Clinic
Chilliwack, British Columbia

Alison Jones
Psychology Department
Michigan State University

Marvin W. Kahn
Professor of Psychology
University of Arizona

John Langrod
Research Scientist
Albert Einstein College of Medicine

Linda Lejero
Papago Psychology Service
Sells, Arizona

Ronald Lewis
Program Director
American Indian Training Program
University of Wisconsin-Milwaukee

Roderick J. McDavis
Associate Professor of Counselor
  Education
University of Florida

Johnnie McFadden
Professor of Counseling
University of South Carolina

Wayne R. Maes
Chairman, Department of
  Guidance and Counseling
University of New Mexico

Ricardo Martinez
Counseling Psychologist
University of New Mexico-
  Albuquerque

Amy Iwasaki Mass
Social Work Program
Whittier College
Whittier, California

Leverett Millen
Clinical Supervisory Psychologist
Geriatric Screening and
  Outpatient Services
Detroit, Michigan

Amado M. Padilla
Professor of Psychology
Director, Spanish Speaking Mental
  Health Research Center
University of California-Los Angeles

Max Parker
Associate Professor of Education
University of Florida

Bruce Ramirez
Director, American Indian Special
  Education Policy Project
Reston, Virginia

John G. Red Horse
Associate Professor of Social Work
Arizona State University

John R. Rinaldi
Associate Professor of Guidance
  and Counseling
University of New Mexico

Samuel Roll
Professor of Psychology and
  Psychiatry
University of New Mexico-
  Albuquerque

Pedro Ruiz
Professor of Psychiatry
Baylor College of Medicine

Rene A. Ruiz
Professor and Head of Counseling
  and Educational Psychology
University of New Mexico-Las Cruces

Arthur A. Seagull
Professor of Psychology
Michigan State University

John F. Scott
Director, Worcester Guidance Center
Worcester, Massachusetts

Barbara J. Smith
Specialist for Policy Implementation
The Council for Exceptional Children
Reston, Virginia

Vita S. Sommers*
Veterans Administration Mental
  Hygiene Clinic
Los Angeles, California

David W. Sue
Associate Professor of Psychology
University of Michigan-Dearborn

Derald Wing Sue
Professor of Counseling Psychology
California State University-Hayward

Stanley Sue
Associate Professor of Psychology
University of Washington-Seattle
Director of Training
National Asian Psychology Training
  Center
San Francisco, California

Elizabeth Sook Wha Ahn Toupin
Associate Dean of Liberal Arts
Tufts University

Joe Yamamoto
Professor of Psychiatry
University of California-Los Angeles

Cecil Williams
Papago Psychology Service
Sells, Arizona

*Deceased

Preface

The provision of services for minority persons has become a major activity of rehabilitation and mental health professionals and paraprofessionals during the last 20 years. The 1961 Report of the Joint Commission of Mental Illness and Health stipulated comprehensive care for all persons including the minority one-sixth of the population. Rehabilitation and treatment was to entail more than services to individuals (tertiary intervention) but required early identification of problems (secondary intervention) and intervention in community structures and political actions to influence policy (primary intervention). Service delivery was envisioned to become the responsibility of the community, under local control, and available wherever people lived. However, in spite of this ideology, these human services have been articulated in the professional idiom of white, middle-class service providers and were suitable primarily for clients who were similar in socioeconomic class and race to themselves. As a result, the very population segment for whom these services were intended had little access to programs they could utilize and find relevant to their specific problems. These culturally different persons often neither understood nor could accept in-office procedures that were conducted by service providers with whom they could neither communicate readily nor experience the trust that comes from shared values and similar life experiences.

The purpose of this book is to expose some of the pervasive cultural values that affect utilization of human services by Native Americans, Afro-Americans, Hispanic Americans, and Asian Americans. Knowledge of these values, beliefs, and prevailing cultural practices suggests the form and contents of effective remediation programs and intervention strategies. The kinds of interventions, the conditions of service delivery, and the particular characteristics, behavior, and training of service providers are all culture-specific. Awareness of client values and practices, especially as they pertain to the acceptance of care-giving by service providers, is a necessary ingredient in training.

This book is intended for courses in counseling, rehabilitation, social work, psychology, and psychiatry as well as those designed for training mental health technicians, child care workers, and other paraprofessionals involved in service delivery to minority persons.

The 30 articles which compose this book are organized into four sections, each focused on one minority culture. The terms Black and Afro-American, and Latino and Hispanic American are used interchangeably. Appreciation is extended to the authors, all of whom are listed in the Contributors section with their current affiliations, and to the original publishers of the articles who are credited in the footnotes on the first page of each article. Special acknowledgment is due to Rodger Hornby and the South Dakota State Library for facilitating the acquisition of relevant articles. This book is a nonprofit project for the editor and contributors; royalties are waived in order to reduce the retail price of the book. Because some publishers would not waive permission fees for reprinting articles, grateful acknowledgment is made to the Marie Wilson Howells Fund, Department of Psychology, University of Arkansas, for partial funding of these fees.

HUMAN SERVICES FOR
CULTURAL MINORITIES

Section I

NATIVE AMERICANS

1

Editorial Introduction

While Native Americans share urban ghettos with blacks and Hispanics, they also live on reservations in isolated rural settings. Their rates of unemployment reach 80%, and their arrest rates, particularly for alcohol, drug abuse, and family problems, exceed rates for other groups. Historically, their human service needs have been dealt with by special government agencies, the Bureau of Indian Affairs and the Indian Health Services. Almost without exception, rehabilitation and treatment approaches extrapolated from white society have been ineffective.

A cultural rationale for these intervention failures is described in the first selection. Joseph Brown outlines the essential values of Plains Indians as documentation of the profound differences in belief systems between Native Americans and whites. Brown describes rites of purification, the Sun Dance, and individual spiritual retreat or vision quest as embodiments of spiritual realization for individual and social groups. He indicates how these rituals have helped to maintain traditional values intact in spite of the Indian history of defeat, trauma, and disintegrating lifestyles.

Wolfgang Jilek and Louise Jilek-Aall present a sympathetic history of the uses of these rituals in American Indian shamanism. Eurocentric whites accepted Western culture as the absolute norm and labeled any deviation from expectations for rational behavior as pathological. Since the practice of shamanism includes a ritualized, illness-like but nonpathological trance state, it was dismissed as aberrant behavior. At present, however, white human service providers are beginning to acknowledge and accept the therapeutic effects of shamanism. Case examples of soul loss and spirit intrusion are presented. The shaman experiences prolonged training and enlists the extended kinship and tribal network as sponsors and cohorts in decision-making for the afflicted person.

The third article by Morton Beiser and Carolyn Attneave describes the current status of service provision and the extent to which earlier deficiencies in services are being remedied. The history and policies of the Indian Health Services are outlined including the range of available services and innovative approaches. The next selection by Bruce Ramirez and Barbara Smith deals with the potential impact of recent legislation upon Indian children. Their emphasis is on implementation by the Bureau of Indian Affairs using cooperative interagency agreements, recruitment and training of personnel, and advocacy roles and practices.

The next selection deals with child problems, particularly as related to family structure. The essence of the dilemma here is that existing service guidelines do not adequately reflect the Native American family structure. John G. Red Horse and associates describe family behaviors among Indians with varying degrees of acculturation in white society. These family lifestyle patterns of traditional, bicultural, and pantraditional Native Americans provide for differential language usage, religious beliefs, and acceptance of white society activities. Nonetheless, Indian core values persevere and are constant regardless of lifestyle pattern.

Larry Dizmang's paper suggests combinations of existing tribal and nontribal resources for suicide prevention. He urges a mobilization of clergy, VISTA workers, and those in public health and practical nursing positions for case-finding. Sensitization to cries for help by persons who understand the culture can lead to referral and subsequent treatment within Public Health Service hospitals.

Ronald Lewis provides case examples in which Indians utilize their cultural concepts of healing power as well as their natural tribal helping systems, including medicine men, sorcerers, and mutual self-help groups. The relationship between belief in an unseen harmony between person and environment and these healing practices is emphasized.

The next selection by Marvin Kahn and associates documents the functioning of a reservation community mental health service program that is staffed largely by human service providers who are Papago Indians. The services provided and the service delivery system were designed for traditional Indians living on a reservation and the tribe controls funds and makes policy decisions. The result is a case example in which Indian cultural values and practices shape the treatment and rehabilitation practices of the program.

The final paper by Wynne Hanson specifies therapeutic techniques for dealing with grief that are effective with Native Americans. Since the expression of feelings of grief have cultural origins, the alleviation processes must include knowledge of how residents of the Indian community grieve for their loved ones. Advocate participation by the service provider in an aftermath of death, including funeral arrangements, is also described.

2

The Persistence of Essential Values among North American Plains Indians

Joseph Epes Brown

INTRODUCTION

The focus for this examination of the complex question of the persistence of essential traditional values among American Indian groups will be upon the Indians of the great plains of North America. This selection in a sense is arbitrary, for similar studies could well be extended to almost any of the American Indian groups scattered in reserves throughout the United States, many of whom still retain, underneath the more evident surface changes and adaptations, a world view and life-ways still deeply rooted in ancient values. Since my closest personal contacts, however, have been the Plains tribes such as the Sioux, Cheyenne, Crow, Blackfoot, Arapaho, and Shoshone, I have chosen to look to these cultures for evidences of persistence in essential traditional values.

The use of the term "essential values" in the context of this paper refers to transcendent metaphysical principles which have been central to the spiritual ways of the Plains Indian, and which, it is insisted by this writer at least, constitute for these original Americans a valid dialect of what has been called the *Religio Perennis*. The uniqueness, or possibly strangeness, to us of the Indian's ritual forms or symbolical language should never blind us to this universal quality of the underlying values themselves. Due to this nature of the values we are here concerned with, there is not called in question the survival of the values themselves, for being ultimately timeless and eternal they can never in themselves be qualified by the vicissitudes of the socio-cultural environment. The question being accounted for, rather, is the degree to which forced changes issuing from an alien and generally profane culture will allow these values to continue to be operative within a changing cultural matrix and thus within the human substance of the individual himself.

This report will present first a description of selected core indigenous values of the Plains Indian as they are conveyed through their ritual sup-

From a paper presented, with slight changes, to the International Congress of the Istituto Accademico di Roma, October, 1968.

Reprinted with permission from *Studies in Comparative Religion*, 1969, *3*, 216–225.

ports, and thus as they contribute to methods of spiritual realization. This necessarily synthetic treatment should provide a reference base for the second part of the report which will deal with several dimensions in the dynamics of contact, as the indigenous culture confronts the pervasive and disruptive influences issuing from a materially dominant Anglo-American culture. The report will conclude with a brief statement concerning essential values which have remained viable to this day despite the often excessive breakdown of many traditional life-ways. It will be noted, in fact, that certain rites and ceremonies among some groups have not only persisted, but are actually, through a number of complex factors, now undergoing a period of vigorous revival.

VALUES

Among the many sacred ceremonies of the Plains Indian I have selected three major rituals within each of which, and in their totality, there is provided all necessary dimensions of a true way of spiritual realization for the individual and for the social group as a whole. These rites are those of purification, the annual tribal Sun Dance, and the individual spiritual retreat.

The rites of purification, considered to be essential preparation for any important or sacred undertaking, are centered in a simple dome-shaped lodge made of intertwined willows and covered over tightly with bison robes. In the circular form of the lodge, and in the materials used in its construction, the Indian sees a symbolical representation of the world in its totality. Indeed, it has been expressed that the lodge is the very body of the Great Spirit. Inside this lodge of the world the participants submit themselves to intensely hot steam produced when water is sprinkled on rocks which had previously been heated in a special sacred fire always located to the east of the lodge. As the men pray and chant, the steam, actually conceived as the visible image of the Great Spirit, acts as in an alchemical work to dissolve both physical and psychic "coagulations" so that a spiritual transmutation may take place. The four elements, with the invisible spiritual Presence—or "fifth element"—contribute their respective powers to this purifying process so that many may become virtually who he is through first dissolving the illusory sense of separateness, then becoming reintegrated, or harmoniously unified, within the totality of the universe. In finally going forth from the dark lodge, leaving behind all physical impurities and spiritual errors, the men are reborn into the wisdom of the light of day. All the aspects of the world have been witnesses to this cycle of corruption, death, wholeness, and rebirth; indeed, the cosmic powers have all contributed to the process.

In the rites of the Sun Dance there is a shift in perspective and function. These dramatic and powerful rites, normally of four days duration, are generally performed only once annually, and should be participated in, directly or indirectly, by the entire tribal group. A major overt goal of this prayer dance is the regeneration or renewal not only of the individual directly participating in the rites, but also of the tribe and ultimately of the entire universe. The ritual dances take place within a large circular pole lodge, at the centre of which is a tall cottonwood tree representing the axis of the universe, the vertical link joining heaven and earth, and thus the path of contact with the solar power, the sun, symbol of the Supreme Principle or Great Spirit. Supported day and night by the powerful rhythm of a huge drum energetically beaten by many men, and by songs which are both heroic and nostalgic, the dancers hold eagle plumes and continually orient themselves either towards the sacred central tree, or towards one of the four directions of space. Blowing upon whistles made from the wing bone of the eagle, the men dance individually with simple and dignified steps towards the central tree from which they receive supernatural power, and then dance backwards to the periphery of the circle without shifting their gaze from the centre. The sacred forms and ritual actions are virile, dignified, and direct, and though the rites usually take place only once a year the power of the sacred centre, now realized within themselves, remains with each individual and contributes to the unity of the people.

The third quality of spiritual way is the solitary retreat known as the "lamenting," or the vision quest. In this quest the individual, naked and alone, and in constant prayer, endures a total fast for a specified number of days at a lonely place, usually a mountain top. In utter humility of body and mind, often emphasized by the offering of pieces of his flesh, or the joint of a finger, the man stands before the forms and forces of nature seeking the blessing of sacred power which should come to him through a dream, or preferably a vision, of some aspect of nature, possibly an animal, who offers guidance for the future direction of the man's life. These natural forms or forces, conceived as messengers or Agents, constitute for the Indian a well understood "iconography" in which forms, with their accompanying powers, are ranked according to their ability to express most directly the ultimate Power, or essence, of the Great Spirit. Essential to this metaphysic of nature is the Indian's belief that in silence, found within the solitude of Nature, there is ultimately heard the very voice of the Great Spirit. This quest for supernatural power, coming symbolically from the "outside," but in reality being awakened from within, has always been essential to the spiritual life of Plains Indian men and women, and its influence upon the quality of their lives should never be underestimated.

Mention must be made, finally, of that important ritual implement, the sacred tobacco pipe which is central to all the rites which have here been described. In carrying this portable altar the Indian has at all times access to an effective synthetic support for spiritual realization. The rites of the pipe express sacrifice and purification, they affirm the integration of the individual within the macrocosm, and they lead finally to the realization of unity, prefigured by the totality of the grains of tobacco becoming one with the fire of the Great Spirit.

Pervading these spiritual ways of purification, of the Sun Dance, the retreat, and the use of the sacred pipe, there may be discerned a pattern for which parallels may be found in virtually all legitimate methods of realization within the world's great religions. This universal pattern affirms the sequence first of purification, followed by an expansive process in the realization of totality, or the state of human perfection, leading finally to the ultimate possibility of contact and identity with the one transcendent Supreme Principle.

CONTACT: DYNAMICS OF THE ACCULTURATION PROCESS

It is necessary now to pose the very difficult question which for decades has plagued those with a serious concern for the future of the American Indian: Is it possible today for small minority groups within the United States, or anywhere for that matter, to retain the integrity of cultural patterns and spiritual ways similar to those just described; ways which are rooted in traditions of primordial origin, and which had their essential supports in a world of nature still virgin and unscarred by the hand of any man?

All the forces of historical contact between the American Indian and the materially dominant White-American civilization seem to be totally against the possibility of any traditional continuity for the Indian. The power of alien forces and the inevitable disruption of life-ways which have ensued must not be minimized. It should be recalled that the people's subsistence base, the bison, was brought to near extinction through commercial exploitation combined with an avowed policy of extermination by the United States Army. Freedom of movement was restricted through force to reservations often arbitrarily chosen. Governing techniques based on the accumulated wisdom of the elders were replaced by an imposed bureaucratic system which could never, even if it wished, understand the real problems of the people under its charge. In accord with White-American concept of ownership, the random distribution of parcels of land on the basis of individual family units shattered the cohesive unity of the Indian's own larger consanguinial groupings, and the prohibition of plural marriages disrupted the immediate family units. School systems were imposed which had as their avowed goals the suppression and eventual elimination of traditional values in order to hasten forcefully the process of total assimilation. This is a policy, with all too few exceptions, which is still basic to the reservation school system of today. Ill-conceived government attempts at economic rehabilitation again and again ended in total failure largely due to the fact that agriculture, then identified by the whiteman with civilization, was a practice contradictory to all Indian values which held the earth as sacred and inviolate and not to be torn up with a plough. Among the most difficult trials, however, were the hostile attitudes towards the Indian's religious practices. Sacrificial elements of the Sun Dance were prohibited, as were the rites held for the departing souls of the dead, and it is well known how participation in the much misunderstood Ghost Dance ended with the infamous massacre of Wounded Knee.

What is seen in the assemblage of these series of traumatic shocks received by the Indian is obviously not just the inevitable result of straight-forward military defeats, as devastating as these were, but rather we have the tragic drama of two cultures in conflict, each representing to the other diametrically opposed values on every possible level and in all domains. Such conflict between cultures was undoubtedly intensified by the fact that those segments of White-American society with which the Indian had the most contact were, with few exceptions, probably the least enlightened carriers of the more positive facets of "civilization." With the exception of some Christian missionaries of "good heart" the Indian found no segment of American society with which he could identify himself.

After more than a century of this quality of bitter confrontation with accompanying disruptions in the social, economic, political, and religious life, it is difficult to understand how the people have survived at all. Yet the Plains Indians, as well as other groups, have survived with such tenacity and even vitality that certain rites and ceremonies are today actually undergoing renewed affirmation. Much to the surprise of the social scientists, and the Bureau of Indian Affairs itself, the "vanishing American" has somehow not vanished at all. It had been incorrectly assumed, among other factors, that just as so many European immigrants had readily assimilated into the great American "melting pot," so too would the Indian. There was obviously the failure here to take into account the tremendous differences between the European and the American Indian. The result of this new awareness, on the part of the anthropologists at least, has led to a growing number of hypotheses to explain this phenomena of the tenacity of traditional values and cultures.

One such hypothesis has been the isolation of the reservations. This is undoubtedly a factor of importance, yet it must be recalled that with certain groups, the Mohawk for example who work in high steel in New York City, close and frequent contact has not resulted in total abandonment of ancient values. The sustaining power of culture-bearing indigenous languages has with validity been pointed to in the literature; certainly this is a factor which has been well understood by the reservation school systems which to this day often forbid children, under threat of punishment, to speak their own native language.

It has been suggested, with reason, that policies of forced or "directed" acculturation to which all Indian groups have been subjected, may lead to violent reactions which reject change and reaffirm traditionalism. A converse possibility which has been neglected by the specialists has been the role of the half informed, usually sentimental, "Indian lovers," the "do gooders," who would preserve certain of the "more noble" Indian values, albeit they should be incorporated with those "logical" modern innovations in such things as housing and hygiene. Paradoxically, such seemingly sympathetic approaches to Indian traditions may be far more corrosive to traditional values than the uncompromising ethnocentric attitudes of those agents of civilization who insist on total assimilation achieved through force if necessary.

Among the vast array of forces which may work for the persistence of traditional values is the often neglected psychological factor of the inherent stability of the basic personality structure which acts as a selective screen in processes of change. A dimension central to this complex question, but which is inaccessible to the quantitative experiential tools of either cultural anthropology or psychology, is the qualitative power of metaphysical, or cosmological, principles and the degree to which these become virtual or effective within the individual substance through participation in traditional rites and spiritual methods. Related to this entire question of the quality of personality is the fact that where Indians are still able to live within a world of as yet unspoiled Nature, potentially they have access to a vast array of transcendent values. It is essential to add, however, that for this potential source to become virtual for the Indian he must still possess, to a certain degree at least, the Indian's traditional metaphysic of nature. Where this metaphysic is still understood, and can be directly related to the supporting forms of the natural world, here the Indian has perhaps his strongest ally for the persistence of essential values; it is also in this metaphysic of nature that we find the Indian's most valuable message for the contemporary world.

A final factor relating to the persistence of values must be mentioned since it is crucial today to a multitude of problems deriving from attitudes in America towards minority groups of various ethnic backgrounds. White-American racial attitudes have historically so tended to devaluate physical types of other cultural traditions that these peoples generally have been relegated to positions of inferior status in the larger society. With the possibility of social or cultural mobility thus being denied, many of these groups have tended to seek retention of cohesion and identity through reaffirmation of their own traditional values. The resulting low index of intermarriage between these minority groups and the dominant majority has in addition tended to slow acculturation. This is a situation, incidentally, which has not occurred in Mexico where positive valuation has been given to the Indian heritage. Among the ramifications of negative racist attitudes is the fact that many Indians who do attempt to assimilate into segments of White-American culture tend to undergo a cycle of progressive disenchantment, a process often hastened by the slum conditions of cities, or by participation in foreign wars. When such persons then attempt to reintegrate back into their own traditional patterns they often serve as powerful agents for the preservation of traditional values.

This review of factors contributing to the holding power of indigenous values under conditions of extreme stress, is obviously very incomplete. Yet the sampling may be useful to an understanding of the final concern of this report which will be a brief assessment of the viability of rites and their values on the plains Indian reservations today.

CONTEMPORARY ASSESSMENT

Reactions of the diverse plains Indian groups to several centuries of directed contact with White-Americans has resulted in such a broad spectrum of adjustments, conservative reactions, or total changes, that it is obviously impossible to make valid generalizations in terms of the contemporary persistence of values. Ranged on this spectrum of multiple possibilities are examples, across groups as well as within particular groups, of near total retention of traditional values at the one end of the scale to near total assimilation at the other end. The vast majority of groups or individuals, however, probably lie in the midrange and generally represent a more or less synthetic reassemblage of Indian and White-American values, always with the retention, however, of a remarkable degree of traditional Indianness.

If the range of possibilities on this spectrum are to be evaluated in terms of the major concern of this study, it should be pointed out that available data indicates that concordant with a high degree of traditional persistence there is generally a quality of culture that has cohesiveness, direction, and affords personal dignity. Assimilation, on the other hand, can be a double-edged term since it often represents acculturation into the lowest and least enlightened segments of White-American society, and this can be the first step leading to such extreme limits of cultural disintegration that we have the dangerous phenomena of a decultured people living precariously in a vacuum wherein they are unable to identify either with Indianness or with any of the White-American values.

In viewing the degrees of cultural wreckage strewn today across the prairies, a most impressive and hopeful phenomena is found in the fact that so many of the core indigenous values, with their supporting rites, are generally persisting among most plains groups. In spite of the virtual disappearance of a host of minor rites, still being practiced are the rites of purification, the Sun Dance, the spiritual retreat, and the rites of the sacred pipe. Sacred arrows, the original sacred pipe, and sacred bundles in general, are still being kept with reverence and respect, even though some of the spiritual meanings of these forms may have been lost. One of the most notable aspects of these examples of traditional tenacity is the fact that those who today affirm these forms and values are not necessarily just the "long hairs," the old men, but rather there is a growing interest and participation on the part of the younger generations.

An outstanding example of the contemporary process of reaffirmation is the increasing participation throughout the plains generally in the Sun Dance. Among the complex factors contributing to this revitalization, which cannot be explained here in detail, is the example and stimulus afforded by a dynamic series of interpersonal and intercultural relationships between the Crow Indians of Montana and the Shoshone of Wyoming. The renewing interest among the younger generations may be partly explained by the fact that the youth have not been able to find channels in the whiteman's society for the expression of specific needs, personal qualities, or virtues, which had always been central, and which still are relevant, to the indigenous cultures. Public display of personal courage, sacrifice, and generosity, for example, are key Indian themes dramatically affirmed in the context of the Sun Dance.

Although the three or four day total fast required in the Sun Dance is still observed, the self-torture features have not been publicly participated in since the government prohibitions of 1890. Such tortures, however, are still engaged in secretly by certain individuals. Also little known to outside groups is the fact that the spiritual retreat is frequently used today not only by the old, but also by younger men. It is evident, although it has not been specifically mentioned, that crucial to the spiritual ways which have been mentioned is the presence of the shaman or "medicine man." Judging partly from the present frequency and popularity of "yuwipi" rites, which allow for the ritual demonstration of shamanistic powers, it is evident that shamanism still plays a meaningful role among the people, and that it continues to have mechanisms for the transmission of power. The high personal quality and magnetism of many of these men is a very strong contributing factor to the holding power of traditional values.

The true nature of a growing number of Pan-Indian movements, or what I call the "pow-wow syndrome," still remains questionable, for the stimulus behind many of these movements represents reactions to White-American attitudes towards ethnic minorities. In being rejected the Indian affirms his Indianness, yet in doing this he often seeks to identify with the whiteman's image of what an Indian is—or should be. The result is a complex of heterogeneous forms and practices which have popular appeal and commercial advantage, but which risk sacrificing true spiritual content. The phenomenal growth of the new Black Elk Sweat Lodge Organization, with membership cards and all, is undoubtedly a good example of this double-edged phenomena of Pan-Indianism.

In concluding, there are a few basic questions which must at least be referred to, for the issues are vital both to the continuing viability of essential values within Indian cultures, and also to the ultimate quality of the larger American culture itself:

Will educational policy, which for so long has been dictated to the Indian, honour and support indigenous values and life-ways so that the young may grow with a rightful pride in their own heritage? Or, must the schools continue in their efforts toward total assimilation, thus denying to the Indian his birthright, and robbing the larger American culture of the possibility of a spiritual enrichment which present crises indicate is so desperately needed?

May not Indian lands be allowed to remain inviolate, so that a unique religious heritage may continue to retain its supports in a world of sacred natural forms? Or, must policies for rapid termination of protective mechanisms continue so that remaining Indian-held lands will melt away under the pressures of often unscrupulous commercial interests?

But above all, and crucial to these and many other questions: Cannot it be affirmed that all peoples, regardless of skin colour, of ethnic background, or of religious affiliation, are rightful members of one family of man? Should not differences of appearance, of culture, or of religion, be affirmed as valid and even necessary expressions of a greater Reality, so that they may contribute to a richer world? Any alternative cannot but lead to drab mediocrity and ultimate chaos.

Whatever the outcome, we might well heed the words attributed to a great Indian after whom one of our cities was named, Seattle.

> We are two distinct races with separate origins and separate destinies. To us the ashes of our ancestors are sacred and their resting place is hallowed ground. You wander far from the graves of your ancestors and seemingly without regret...
>
> But why should I mourn at the untimely fate of my people? Tribe follows tribe, and nation follows nation, and regret is useless...
>
> But when the last Red man shall have become a myth among the White man...when your children's children think themselves alone in the field... or in the silence of the pathless woods, they will not be alone...your lands will throng with the returning hosts that once filled them and still love this beautiful land. The White man will never be alone.
>
> Let him be just and deal kindly with my people, for the dead are not powerless. Dead—I say? There is no death. Only a change of worlds.[1]

---

[1]From Frank Waters, "Two Views of Nature: White and Indian." *The South Dakota Review,* May 1964, pp. 28, 29.

3

The Psychiatrist and his Shaman Colleague
Cross-Cultural Collaboration with Traditional Amerindian Therapists

Wolfgang Jilek and Louise Jilek-Aall

In recent years psychiatric publications dealing with the role of traditional healing have increasingly shown a tendency to advocate cooperation with, or even utilization of, indigenous therapeutic resources in the mental health care of non-Western populations, without necessarily going as far as Fuller Torrey (1) who feels mental health professionals ought to apologize for not trying indigenous healers. Western psychiatrists and psychologists in contact with North American Indian traditional healers and ritualists have been impressed by their positive psycho-hygienic and therapeutic role in native cultures (2, 3, 4, 5, 6, 7, 8, 9).

In the present paper, "traditional therapist" will be used as a gloss to denote a cultural institution which we find in the most divergent societies under various names. This institution is defined by a common criterion of function and purpose which can be abstracted from ethnographic descriptions: the traditional therapist, in logical or alogical actions derived from the belief system of an indigenous culture but not from modern Western science, aims at the relief of distress, the alleviation of anxiety and the maximization of a feeling of well-being and security in his clients. It is important to stress that, in the realm of psychotherapy, the difference between modern Western and traditional therapist cannot be reduced to the difference between scientific vs. non-scientific action, for the exact scientific basis of much of modern Western psychotherapeutic, and a fair share of modern Western medical practices, would appear to be somewhat shaky indeed. Rather, the essential difference rests in the cultural premises of therapeutic action in tradition-oriented non-Western societies *ver-*

This paper was originally presented at the World Congress of Psychiatry in 1977 in Honolulu.

Reprinted with permission from *Journal of Operational Psychiatry*, 1978, *9*(2), 32–39.

sus modern Western, or Westernized societies. We discern that in tradition-oriented non-Western societies disease is frequently seen as phenomenon of the supernatural, full of moral implication, while in modern Western society it is seen as natural phenomenon, devoid of moral implication. Consequently, traditional acts of curing have sacred rather than profane aspects, and in the healing arts, emphasis is on supernatural inspiration and magic knowledge—*a*rational but not *ir*rational—rather than on scientific (or pseudo-scientific) information. In so-called primitive cultures no essential distinction is made between physical and mental illness; collective issues are considered most relevant; the incomprehensible is generally explained by supernatural powers. In modern Western culture in spite of the lip service paid to psychosomatic and social medicine, physical and mental illness are still seen as distinct entities; individual issues are considered most relevant and there is a tendency to explain the incomprehensible by psychopathology—an unwarranted generalization resulting from positive fallacies. Traditional therapists, as tradition-directed people in general, tend to believe in collective rather than individual solutions, and consider ceremonial functions indispensable; conversely, to modern individualistic Western or Westernized man few, if any, ceremonial functions appear indispensable.

Clearly, different ethical, ideological and semantic systems lead to a very different outlook on life in modern Western and traditional non-Western therapists. One might expect, nevertheless, that the recognition of these differences as culturally determined and of a relative nature would lead to an objective evaluation of the merits of traditional healing by Western psychiatry and facilitate collaboration. However, major obstacles arise from the old Western image of the medicine man as a psychopathological type manifesting sanctioned and rewarded deviancy. This was the prevailing view expressed in scientific treatises on the subject until well after World War II. A few examples will serve to illustrate this with regard to North American Indian healers. Hambly (10) advanced the general hypothesis that medicine men are afflicted with "fear neurosis," "anxiety hysteria," compulsions, obsessions, and hallucinations. He characterized the Blackfoot Indian medicine man's garb as "mummery relieving the neurotic temperament of the performer." Wissler (11), considered an authority in his day, seriously proposed that the shaman of American Indian tribes "may be a veritable idiot." An author as well known in psychiatry as George Devereux also contributed his share to the lunacy hypothesis of Amerindian shamanism. In 1942 (12) he wondered "how many Indian psychotics have turned into shamans" while hospitalized in State hospitals; in 1957 (13) he tried to prove that the Mohave shaman is a "fundamentally neurotic person" comparable with borderline psychotic cases in Western society, in 1958 (14) he again referred to the shaman's "insanity," and in his prestigious Smithsonian report of 1965 (15) Devereux advised that the "Mohave shaman of either sex is to be diagnosed either as a borderline case, or else as an outright psychotic."

While relatively unopposed in the past, the "crazy witch doctor" doctrine has become increasingly subject to correction by less prejudiced researchers. Already in 1942, Hallowell (16) in a careful investigation was unable to elicit any abnormal personality traits in Salteaux Indian conjurers. Opler (17) found it difficult to reconcile Devereux's "sweeping assertion" of the shaman's psychopathology with his own findings among Apache, Ute, and Paiute tribes. Since then Drucker (18) for the North Pacific Coast tribes, Handelman (19) for the Washo Indians, and other investigators elsewhere, have refuted the assumption that traditional Amerindian therapists were recruited from among the mentally disturbed, and have rejected as inadequate the interpretation of shamanic practices in terms of neurotic defenses against emotional instability. As Leighton (20) succinctly stated, "What in shamanistic behavior may appear hysterical or psychotic to the Western psychiatrist is, to the people concerned, a time honored ritual through which practitioners heal sick people or divine the future. Hence the 'symptoms' of the shaman may in fact be the result of learning and practice."

The psychopathology hypothesis of shamanic healing appears to have been derived mainly from confusing with mental illness the phenomenon called *initiatory sickness* by Eliade (21). In many aboriginal cultures, shamans-to-be have to undergo a two-fold initiation; a) didactic initiation, which is a process of formal training, and b) ecstatic initiation or *initiatory sickness* which can be defined as ritualized pathomorphic, i.e., illness-like, but not pathological, state. In aboriginal Coast Salish Indian culture, *spirit sickness* was such a state inevitably leading to initiation into the spirit dance ceremonial (9). Spirit dance initiation was, in the past, conceived of as obligatory test and confirmation of spirit powers acquired in the young Salish Indian's quest for an individual guardian spirit. In traditional Salish culture, the future shaman's quest for specific healing powers followed the pattern of the adolescent Indian's guardian spirit quest, but required more effort and self-sacrifice over longer periods. The shaman's vision experience was also of greater force and intensity. Old Pierre, a Coast Salish medicine-man of greatest reputation in the earlier decades of this century, related to Jenness (22) how at the age of 10 years he started training for the shaman's vocation at his mother's behest, roaming the woods for four winters, fasting, running, dancing, swimming in icy pools, exhausting himself in long vigils until he finally experienced his spirit power vision. Our esteemed friend, Mr. Isadore Tom of the Lummi tribe, one of the last still practicing traditionally trained "Indian Doctors" among the Coast Salish told us he was sent by his father and grandfather—both medicine men—to quest for healing power at age 12. When 13 years old he encountered his shamanic spirit power whose voice told him that he would in the future be called upon to help the sick. Three years later during a healing ceremony a well known Nooksack Indian shaman summoned the then 16 year old Isadore from the backbenches of the smokehouse to assist a sick patient. The shaman prepared Isadore for this task by "fixing water" and putting it on his arms and hands. Later, when under a regime of forced acculturation at the Indian Residential School where traditional lore and language was outlawed, the young candidate suppressed the memory of his vision and vocation. Not until he was a man of 52 did he experience another dream vision: the same spirit returned and the same voice bade him go out and help sick people. He has followed this calling ever since, travelling the Northern Washington and Southern British Columbia coast and islands for twenty years on healing missions.

Western observers often infer psychopathology from the initiate's altered state of consciousness with its oneroid visions, auditory hallucinations and seemingly bizarre behaviour, which is repeated in shamanic practice. For the adept shaman has learnt to re-live this trance experience at every curing seance, having acquired, as did the Kwakiutl Indian healer in Boas' text (23) "the ways of the one who wishes to be a shaman, the one who faints and who trembles with his body." The familiar Western notion of the "crazy witch doctor" fed on such obviously exotic behavior, equating it with psychotic, neurotic or even epileptic disorders. No less a celebrity in American anthropology than Kroeber concluded in 1952 (24) from observations he made mainly in American Indian cultures, that "socially sanctioned and distinguished individuals who exercise special powers, especially of curing, acquire their capacity through experiences which in our culture would be stigmatized as psychotic." By announcing that "not only the shamans are involved in psychopathology, but often also the whole lay public of primitive societies," Kroeber was on common ground with Devereux (15) who, carried away by psychoanalytic speculation, asserted that "primitive religion and in general 'quaint' primitive ideas are organized schizophrenia." These two positions exemplify the fallacious conclusions of some Western experts on Amerindian cultures and shamanism which have filtered down to the medical and lay public, contributing to the prejudiced misconceptions which impede cross-cultural communication and collaboration with traditional indigenous therapists in mental health care. We suggest that the classification of shamanic behaviour and of native ritual, in terms of Western psychiatric nomenclatures, constitutes both a eurocentric and a positivistic fallacy: 1) *eurocentric,* because it elevates modern Western culture to an absolute norm against which other cultures and their institutions may be judged as abnormal, 2) *positivistic,* because it considers behaviour which does not fit into the framework of logico-experimental explanatory theory, as a departure from rational norm due to ignorance or poor reality testing. Shamanic ritual, as all ritual action, including the rituals of Western therapy, cannot be judged by the criteria of positive science. As Pareto (25) has shown long ago, ritual acts are, above all, "manifestations of sentiments," and it is fallacious to equate them with irrational, illogical, or insane behaviour. Rather, ritual is alogical and exempt from logico-experimental explanation; it is part of what makes healing an art.

The current reappraisal by Western authors of the merits of indigenous healing reflects profound changes in the prevailing zeitgeist which have deeply affected social sciences and psychiatry: First, the breakdown of positivistic systems in psychology and their substitution by more comprehensive theories of human behaviour; Second, the abandonment of Western superiority claims in the geopolitical context of decolonization and global retreat of Western powers. These historical processes led to the deflation of a once glorious Western self-image and the concomitant upgrading of the Western image of non-Western cultures; in our case, of the American image of Amerindian cultures. Who would, for example, nowadays expect leading Americans to glorify the genocide of Indian tribes as progress, as did the distinguished President of the National Geographic Society in his annual address in 1890.[1] Today the same National Geographic Society presents "The New Indians" on television and young Americans listen to their soliloquies for cultural inspiration. It is in such a changing climate that mental health professionals, aware of their own limitations in treating Amerindian patients, now recognize the value of native therapeutic resources (4, 5, 7, 8, 27).

Obstacles are placed in the way of cross-cultural therapeutic collaboration by more than Western views and attitudes. If we look over the "buckskin curtain" (28) which in Canada separates the indigenous races from majority society, we become painfully aware that even today psychiatry in native view is often seen as an instrument of dominant society control acting in the interest of the "White Establishment." Psychiatrists who expose themselves to free discussions with Indian people outside the protective office and hospital walls will likely be confronted with an altogether distorted image of their profession, created by past experiences with psychiatric institutions, or by Hollywood's projection of snake-pit asylums. The traditional Amerindian feeling is well expressed in the advice given to one of our patients by his grandfather: "The white man has

---

[1] "In North America the Anglo-Saxon race has dominated, carrying civilization from the Atlantic to the Pacific, expelling and exterminating the aborigines. There has been no mingling of the Anglo-Saxon and Indian races, no backward step, but ever civil, religious and intellectual progress" (26).

two ways of getting rid of Indians who make trouble for him: he puts them in prison or in the mental hospital. Stay away from the mental hospital! In prison you know how much time you have to do, but you never know when they will let you out of the mental hospital!'' It is hardly surprising, therefore, that Indian people try to avoid contact with psychiatric treatment centers.

Inspired by the spirit of Amerindian renaissance, there is an increasing desire even among partly Westernized Indian people to turn for help to traditional resources. In this situation, an indifferent, condescending, or covertly hostile attitude of Western professionals toward traditional native approaches creates iatrogenic anxiety in Indian patients who realize their dependence on the Western health care system. Keenly aware of this, a growing number of mental health professionals is today seeking a cooperative relationship with traditional Indian therapists (4, 5, 7, 8). Such a relationship holds definite advantages also for the Western therapist: it reduces the cultural barrier between psychiatry and the native people, and renders Western treatment, whenever necessary, more effective (27). Obviously however, cross-cultural communication has to precede cross-cultural collaboration. A fruitful dialogue can be entered into on two levels: 1) on a collective level of organizational contacts between the health professions and the Amerindian community; 2) on an individual level of personal contacts between health professionals and traditional Amerindian therapists. To initiate such a cross-cultural dialogue on a representative collective level, the Canadian Psychiatric Association Task Force on Native Peoples' Mental Health in 1975 began to organize annual Transcultural Workshops aiming at a better understanding between mental health professionals and native political and ceremonial leaders, in a living-in encounter on Indian territory devoted to the formal and informal discussions of psycho-social problems as presented mainly by native participants. There has been a growing response both in the psychiatric and in the native community to the annual Transcultural Workshops held so far on the Stoney Indian Reserve, Alberta in 1975 (29), at Manitou College, Quebec, in 1976 (30) and at the Department of Native Studies, Trent University, Ontario, in May 1977.

Psychiatrists who have sought the cross-cultural dialogue on an individual level came to realize the importance of comprehending the sociocultural conditions before and under Westernization, and the system of mores and values based thereupon which determines criteria of behaviour in Amerindian cultures. Besides ethnographic literature, personal contacts with Indian elders provide the best source of information. Such contacts can be established through native patients, through attendance at cultural activities, feasts and ceremonials of the native community where an introduced medical doctor, showing genuine interest, is likely to be well received. At least this is the experience we had when over the years we were able to establish personal ties of mutual trust and respect with native leaders, traditional ritualists, and therapists throughout the Northwest Coast area, from which a consultation and referral relationship emerged. The personal character of this relationship is illustrated by the fact that one of us was ceremonially adopted into a Kwakiutl tribe and given the name of a famous ancestor healer, *Kas'lidi*, "The One Called Upon For Help." Our eyes were opened to the semantic implications of indigenous nosology which often condition the specific format of symptom manifestation, and we were eventually able to perceive the symbolic processes underlying Salish Indian ritual therapy (31).

As there are important analogies in the religio-medical systems of most Amerindian cultures, it may be of general interest to sketch briefly here some observations on the therapeutic interventions of our Salish shaman colleagues. Two basic disease concepts appear to have been brought from Central and Northern Asia to the Western Hemisphere by consecutive waves of paleolithic immigration: 1) soul or spirit power loss; 2) intrusion of a pathogenic object or spirit power into the patient. Before Westernization soul loss and evil-agent intrusions, as etiological theories and indications for shamanic soul recapture and evil-agent extraction, were widely represented in Amerindian cultures (32). In the contemporary *Indian Doctoring* we observed that the concepts of soul and spirit power are closely related, although the soul is a general property of living beings while personal spirit power had to be acquired in the guardian spirit ceremonial. Loss of soul and loss of spirit power call for the same therapeutic intervention: the shamanic therapist's travel beyond the world of the living to recapture soul or spirit power without which the patient would ultimately die. We learnt that the Salish term for *Indian Doctor* or shaman derives from "searcher of souls" and "on one's course of travel," for the shaman is the one who travels to search and find the patient's lost soul or guardian spirit and restores it to the rightful owner.

Presented here are brief descriptions of contemporary shamanic treatments of soul loss and spirit intrusion in patients we shared with a distinguished friend, one of the very few traditionally trained Salish *Indian Doctors* still alive.

1. *Soul Loss* A young Coast Salish woman showing a prolonged mourning reaction with despondency and apathy was referred to the *Indian Doctor* who treated her at the home of a senior member of her family. When called to attend to this patient the *Indian Doctor* announced that she was suffering from "soul loss sickness." He said that his special spirit power had let him see and find the lost soul "on the other side of the river," i.e., in the land of the dead (note the archetypal river Styx symbolism). He was going to return the lost soul

to her rightful owner; however, he also stated that his spirit power had advised that the patient should become a spirit dancer for her own future protection, or else ancestral spirits would again take hold of her soul and cause her serious ills. Drumming started and while the patient appeared to re-enter the trance state in which she had been put initially under the effect of continuous rhythmic chanting and drumming, the *Indian Doctor* made gestures as if capturing the lost soul from the air, holding it in his closed hands. He then transferred the soul back to its owner by rubbing it on the patient's chest and sides. The girl started to cry and wail while the *Indian Doctor* in front of her, his head lowered and his eyes closed, listened intensely for the emerging spirit song, sometimes placing his ear to her chest. Finally he was able to pick up the tune from her wailing and began to sing the newly found spirit song. Drumming was intensified and the helpers fell in with their voices, the patient now crying out loudly. He proceeded to "blow power" into the patient's body and continued to chant until the girl blurted out her spirit song, led and accompanied by the chorus. She was "stood up," held by her relatives while she clumsily made her first dance steps. After hours of crying and wailing, accompanied by rhythmic chanting and drumming, the patient had found her own way of expressing her guardian spirit power. She was led to a makeshift tent for seclusion to undergo the required process of initiation into spirit dancing.

2. *Spirit Intrusion*   The *Indian Doctor* was consulted in the case of a teenage Coast Salish girl admitted to the psychiatric unit in a dysphoric state with psychogenic paresis of both legs in the context of a school phobia apparently developed in response to experiences of discrimination. An *Indian Doctoring* session was arranged at the home of relatives during patient's hospitalization. While the young girl was wailing and crying, the *Indian Doctor* accompanied by the drummers, chanted rhythmically, trying to get in contact with his supernatural power which helps him to find out the cause of the ailment. Suddenly the drumming and chanting stopped. After a period of tense silence he declared that the patient's illness was caused by the intrusion of her deceased grandmother's spirit. He promised to cure her if she had complete faith in him, citing examples of such cures which were confirmed by witnesses in the audience. During the healing ceremony he explained each step of the forthcoming procedure to the patient who was held by female relatives. He was "fixing" water, handling it as a precious substance with which he splashed the patient. He then removed the pathogenic spirit by making grabbing movements with his cupped hands, "taking over the spirit" to his own chest in order to control it. Finally he let the spirit free with gestures as if free-

ing a captured bird. The girl's father was requested to hold a glass of fresh water while kneeling beside the *Indian Doctor* who transferred power into it. The *Indian Doctor* then instructed the patient to slowly drink this water while he was chanting. Pointing at her mouth and stomach, he pronounced: "The fixed water goes down here and takes all the rest of your illness away, you will be cured. Now smile and the world will smile at you." At these words the patient abandoned her rigid posture, got up smiling and embraced her healer who encouraged her to return to school "because education will be our weapon." Speechmaking by witnesses and relatives concluded the ceremony.

The nature of *Spirit sickness,* in aboriginal Coast Salish Indian culture a seasonally limited ritualized state identifiable on the basis of learned stereotyped symptoms, channelling the young Indian into the *rite de passage* of spirit dance initiation, has changed after the spirit dance ceremonial was revived in the 1960s. The ceremonial itself, in the past a ritual with psychohygienic aspects, has become an organized native effort at culture congenial therapy for a condition which we have described under the heading of *anomic depression* (9) and which is frequently seen in partly Westernized Amerindians. Today younger Indian people with *anomic depression,* showing either intrapunitive affective-psychophysiologic or extrapunitive-antisocial reactions to experiences of anomie, relative deprivation, and cultural identity confusion, are considered prime candidates for spirit dance initiation by Salish ritual therapists. They are seen as suffering from sickness and abnormal behaviour as a result of exposure to the pathogenic effects of the alien Western culture, whose medical, psychiatric, and social agencies are considered incapable of providing useful assistance to Indians thus afflicted. Only the traditional *Indian Doctor* and ritualist can offer effective help, and the therapeutic appoach then indicated is spirit dance initiation. Following the ancient myth of death and rebirth the candidate's faulty and diseased old self, alienated from Indian culture, is symbolically "clubbed to death." The initiate is made to regress to a state of infantile dependency in order to obtain his personal spirit "song" in a vision experience while passing through an altered state of consciousness, entered into under the effects of suggestion, psychic and physiologic stress, sensory deprivation and stimulation. With his newly acquired spirit power, the initiate grows into a healthier existence, having found a new Indian identity validated in a namesgiving ceremony at the conclusion of the initiation process. The revived spirit ceremonial provides the participants with an annual winter treatment program which in scope and duration is unparalleled in non-Indian society.

We have repeatedly referred to our shaman colleagues' Indian patients in whom *anomic depression* was revealed as primary pathology which appeared amenable to indigenous therapy but needed a sanctioning medical opinion. Some referrals were made while the patients were still hospitalized; they were given passes to attend healing ceremonials. Before such referral psychiatric assessment had suggested to us that the patient might benefit from traditional therapy. The patient's motivation can be gauged when this subject is introduced at an appropriate moment. Often the patient and his significant kin group, which has to be consulted, is relieved when the Western doctor discusses traditional rites as a fully acceptable therapeutic avenue. The selection of specific healing procedures has to remain the prerogative of the traditional therapist who advises the patient's relatives and friends. For, in contrast to most Western therapists, the *Indian Doctor* always works with and through the patient's extended kinship and tribal network. The step of initiation into spirit dancing, for example, is a decision to be made by this network rather than by the patient alone who will have to depend on supportive sponsors "standing behind him" in order to guarantee therapeutic success. Family and friends also have to lend their active support in such *Indian doctoring* sessions as we have sketched above. Thus even those indigenous treatment procedures outside the spirit dance ceremonial, in which an individual traditional therapist attends to an individual patient, are very much a collective affair and they usually take place in the patient's home. There is, in Salish Indian culture, no provision for a one-to-one psychotherapy in the seclusive atmosphere of a private office.

In this paper we have tried to point out historical and contemporary factors influencing the relationship between the Western psychiatrist and his shaman colleague. We have also tried to convey our own experience with traditional therapeutic resources in the care of Salish Indian patients. It was the demonstrated effectiveness of traditional therapeutic procedures comparing so favourably with Western medical and correctional management in cases of Amerindian *anomic depression,* which prompted us to actively explore and practice a cross-cultural collaboration with the traditional indigenous therapists of our area.

REFERENCES

1. Torrey EF: The case for the indigenous therapist. Arch Gen Psychiatry 20: 365–373, 1969.
2. Kluckhohn C, Leighton D: The Navaho. Cambridge, Harvard University Press, 1946.
3. Kaplan B, Johnson D: The Social meaning of Navaho psychopathology and psychotherapy, in Magic, Faith and Healing. Edited by Kiev A. New York, Free Press, 1964, pp. 203–229.
4. Beiser M, De Groat E: Body and spirit medicine—conversations with a Navaho singer. Psychiatric Annals 4:9–12, 1974.
5. Attneave CL: Medicine men and psychiatrists in the Indian Health Service. Psychiatric Annals 4:49–55, 1974.

6. Bergman RL: Navajo peyote use—its apparent safety. Amer J Psychiatry 128:695–699, 1971.

7. Bergman RL: Learning from Indian medicine. Paper presented at the Winter Meeting of the Oregon Psychiatric Association, Portland, January 27–29, 1977.

8. Jilek WG, Todd N: Witchdoctors succeed where doctors fail—psychotherapy among Coast Salish Indians. Can Psychiat Assoc J 19:351–356, 1974.

9. Jilek WG: Salish Indian Mental Health and Culture Change. Toronto, Holt Rinehart and Winston of Canada, 1974.

10. Hambly WD: Origins of Education among Primitive Peoples. London, Macmillan, 1926, p. 219.

11. Wissler C: The American Indian. New York, Oxford University Press, 1931, p. 204.

12. Devereux G: The mental hygiene of the American Indian. Ment Hygiene 26: 71–84, 1942.

13. Devereux G: Dream learning and individual ritual differences in Mohave shamanism. Amer Anthropologist 59:1036–1045, 1957.

14. Devereux G: Cultural thought models in primitive and modern psychiatric theories. Psychiatry 21:359–374, 1958.

15. Devereux G: Mohave Ethnopsychiatry and Suicide. Smithsonian Institution, Bureau of American Ethnology Bulletin 175. Washington D.C. U.S. Print. Office, 1961, p. 285.

16. Hallowell IA: The Role of Conjuring in Salteaux Society. Philadelphia, University of Pennsylvania Press, 1942, p. 13.

17. Opler MK: Culture and Mental Health. New York, MacMillan, 1959, p. 102.

18. Drucker P: Cultures of the North Pacific Coast. San Francisco, Chandler, 1965, p. 92.

19. Handelman D: The development of a Washo shaman. Ethnology 6:444–464, 1967.

20. Leighton AH, Hughes JH: Cultures as causative of mental disorder, in Causes of Mental Disorders—A Review of Epidemiological Knowledge 1959. New York, Milbank Memorial Fund, 1961, pp. 341–365.

21. Eliade M: Shamanism—Archaic Techniques of Ectasy. New York, Random House, 1964, p. 14, 33.

22. Jenness D: The faith of a Coast Salish Indian, in Anthropology in British Columbia Memoir No. 3. Edited by Duff W. Victoria, B. C. Provincial Museum, 1955, pp. 5–85.

23. Boas F: The Religion of the Kwakiutl Indians; part II, Translations. New York, Columbia University Press, 1930, p. 7.

24. Kroeber AL: The Nature of Culture. Chicago, University of Chicago Press, 1952, p. 317–318.

25. Pareto V: The Mind and Society, vol. I. New York, Harcourt & Brace, 1935.

26. Hubbard GG: South America—Annual address by the president. National Geographic Magazine 3:1–29, 1891.

27. Jilek WG, Jilek-Aall L: A transcultural approach to psychotherapy with Canadian Indians—Experiences from the Fraser Valley of British Columbia, in Proceedings of the V World Congress of Psychiatry, Mexico, part II, pp. 1181–1186. Amsterdam, Excerpta Medica 1971.

28. Cardinal H: The Unjust Society—The Tragedy of Canada's Indians. Edmonton, Hurtig, 1969, p. I.

29. Canadian Native Peoples' Mental Health—Transcultural Workshop of the Canadian Psychiatric Association. Transcultural Psychiatric Research

Review 13:193–194, 1976.
30. Jilek WG: Second Transcultural Workshop of the Task Force on Canadian Native Peoples' Mental Health, Report by the Chairman. Canadian Psychiatric Association Bulletin 10:24–30, 1977.
31. Jilek WG, Jilek-Aall L: Symbolic processes in contemporary Salish Indian ceremonials. Unpublished Ms, 35 pp.
32. Margetts EL: Canada—Indian and Eskimo Medicine, with notes on the early history of psychiatry among French and British colonists, in World History of Psychiatry. Edited by Howells JG. New York, Brunner/Mazel, 1975, pp. 400–431.

4

Mental Health Services for American Indians
Neither Feast nor Famine

Morton Beiser and Carolyn L. Attneave

In this report, we attempt to dispel a myth.

The myth, which asserts that few, if any, mental health services exist for American Indians (Torrey, 1970), is misguided at best, conducive of stereotyping and racism at worst.

This report, prepared by members of the American Psychiatric Association Task Force on Indian Affairs, documents the existence of such services over a period of years in the late 1960s and the 1970s. It is part of a series of evaluation studies carried out for the Indian Health Service, a federal agency responsible for providing health services for 500,000 Indian people. We have used the term "American Indian" in a broad generic sense and have included Aleut and Eskimo, cultures which are distinctly different from Indian, but people for whom the Indian Health Service assumes responsibility. The service's mental health program, a 13-year experiment in comprehensive mental health care, provides some insight for the larger society as it struggles to evolve a system of universal health coverage.

HISTORY OF THE INDIAN HEALTH SERVICE

Among the numerous treaties between the United States government and various Indian tribes which were signed in the late 1800s and the early part of this century, a typical formula prevailed. The tribe surrendered land. In exchange, the United States government furnished guarantees of sovereignty, and agreed to provide certain services to the reservations, particularly education and health.

Initially, the War Department administered Indian health programs. Later it was the Bureau of Indian Affairs, an agency of the Department of the Interior. Finally, in 1955, the Indian Health Service came into being as a division of the United States Public Health Service.

Reprinted with permission from *White Cloud Journal*, 1978, *1*(2), 3-10.

The formal Mental Health Program was inaugurated by a pilot project in 1965. Congressman Ben Rifel, himself an Oglala Sioux, initiated a congressional appropriation for a demonstration mental health program on the Pine Ridge Reservation in South Dakota. By December of that year, the Surgeon General's Advisory Committee on Indian Health recommended establishing a similar one for Alaska Natives.

Growth during the first five years was rapid; new areas were opened, new positions added, and the budget increased. Table 1 describes this growth in spare but telling terms: by the number of new staff positions (psychiatrists and other personnel) and budgets allocated on a year-by-year basis (see Table 1).

As Table 1 indicates, by 1969 the Indian Health Service mental health staff had grown to 26 persons, operating with a budget of $580,000. The pattern of rapid expansion has continued under the leadership of Dr. Emery Johnson, Director of the Indian Health Service since 1969. By 1977, Mental health staff numbered 232 and the budget appropriation was $4,200,000.

THE ORGANIZATION

In broad administrative outline, the Mental Health Program resembles the Indian Health Service, the parent organization to which it remains closely attached. Since it is impossible to understand the organization of the Mental Health Programs in isolation, we here sketch the total health program.

Most federally recognized Indian reservations and Indian Health Service programs are concentrated in the States west of the Mississippi River. Some Indian groups, for example those living in northeastern states, maintain treaties with individual states rather than the federal government. Other tribes, once federally recognized, have been "terminated," that is, in return for a settlement, they have relinquished claims to federal land reservations. In both cases, health services, in theory at least, fall under the jurisdiction of individual states. In 1970, three reservation groups—the Choctaw at Philadelphia, Mississippi, the Cherokee in North Carolina, and the Seminole/Miccosukee in Florida, plus a number of non-federally recognized or serviced tribal groups—formed the United South East Tribes (U.S.E.T.). Since 1974, U.S.E.T. has received contract funds from the Indian Health Service, which they have used to develop their own locally controlled programs. Since our evaluation did not include U.S.E.T. Programs, we do not cover them further in this report.

The Indian Health Service divides itself administratively into eight major areas and two subareas; headquarters for each of the areas and subareas is indicated in the map (see Figure 1). Table 2 lists the regions served by each area office.

Table 1. Original Funds for IHS Area Mental Health Teams and Additions for First Five Years

	FY 1966			FY 1967			FY 1968			FY 1969		
	Positions		Amount	Positions		Amount*	Positions		Amount	Positions		Amount
	New	Total	New	New	Total	New	New	Total	New	New	Total	New
Aberdeen	5	5	$100,000	—	5	—	5	10	$50,000	—	10	—
Albuquerque	—	—	—	—	—	—	2	2	$25,000	2	4	$40,000
Anchorage	—	—	—	5	5	$100,000	—	5	—	—	5	$17,000
Billings	—	—	—	1	1		—	—	—	1	1	$13,000
Navajo	—	—	—	—	—	—**	3	4	$75,000	3	7	$40,000
Oklahoma	—	—	—	—	—	—	—	—	—	—	—	—
Phoenix	—	—	—	—	—	—	—	—	—	4	4	$60,000
Portland	—	—	—	—	—	—	—	—	—	4	4	$60,000
Additions for each FY	5		$100,000	5		$100,000	10		$150,000	14		$230,000
Cumulative totals		5	$100,000		11	$200,000		21	$350,000		26	$580,000

*Once funded, positions and amounts were carried from year to year. Only additions are entered here, but cumulative totals for each fiscal year are entered below.

**The mental health position for this year was funded from another source.

One reads the table as follows in the Aberdeen Area five positions were funded in FY 66 at $100,000, and the same budget and staff continued in FY 67. In FY 68, 5 new positions were funded with an additional $50,000 (a total of 10 positions funded at $150,000). This continued to be the level in Aberdeen through the period recorded.

Figure 1.   Map showing eight IHS administrative areas and two sub-areas.

In each of these offices, a chief administrator, who is usually a physician and is titled Area Director, directs a staff consisting of deputy administrators who are responsible for overall planning, and chiefs for each of the following specialty services: nursing, medicine, environmental health, dentistry, social service, and mental health.

Hospitals, clinics, or health centers provide direct service in each area: the generic term used to cover all three is Service Units. Clinics limit themselves to outpatient services. Health centers may be established to care for children in federally administered (Bureau of Indian Affairs) schools or in remote locations where full scale clinic or hospital services are not justified by the population size but where part-time care is necessary. For specialized and surgical care which exceeds the capacities of Indian Health Service staff, contracts must be negotiated with local, non-Indian Health Service providers of service.

Tribal representatives constitute local advisory bodies in each of the Indian Health Service areas. Each board maintains a liaison with a national Indian Health Service advisory board. While the boards have, in the past, concentrated on giving advice, they are now assuming more responsibility for stimulating and initiating programs.

National headquarters for the Indian Health Service is in Rockville, Maryland; however, the Mental Health Program administrative center is

Table 2.   Area Offices

Area Office	States or Regions Included
Anchorage, Alaska	Alaska
Portland, Oregon	Oregon, Washington, and Idaho
Billings, Montana	Montana, Wyoming, and Brigham City Indian School, Utah
Aberdeen, South Dakota	South Dakota, North Dakota, Nebraska, Iowa
Bemidji, Minnesota (Sub-Area)*	Minnesota, Wisconsin, Michigan
Oklahoma City, Oklahoma	Oklahoma, Kansas (also included USET until 1970)
Albuquerque, New Mexico	All of New Mexico (except that portion lying within the Navajo Reservation) and extreme southern portion of Colorado and Utah known as the "4 Corners."
Window Rock, Arizona	The Navajo Reservation lying partly in New Mexico, partly in Utah and mainly in Arizona. Excluding the Hopi Reservation lying within its boundaries
Phoenix, Arizona	All of Arizona except the Navajo Reservation, but including the Hopi Reservation, Nevada, California and parts of Utah not allocated elsewhere.
Tucson, Arizona	The Papago Reservation in southeastern Arizona serves as a model for the Health Systems Program Information Center, and as such has autonomy from the Phoenix Area Office.

*Moving toward Area status, but under Aberdeen during the period covered by this report.

located in Albuquerque, New Mexico. Dr. Robert Bergman, head of the Mental Health Program since its inception in 1966, was succeeded in that position by Dr. H. C. Townsley in 1974.

The chiefs of mental health programs at the area level come from a variety of disciplinary backgrounds: Two are psychiatrists (in Anchorage and Albuquerque), three are social workers (in Aberdeen and Navajo), and three are nurses with public health and psychiatric experience (Portland, Billings, and Phoenix). Area chiefs report both to the Indian Health Service Area Directors in each area and to the national Chief of Mental Health Programs.

Following the model of the Service as a whole, the Mental Health Program provides services mainly as part of a service unit, responsible for a population in a geographically defined area. Staff composition varies greatly from service unit to service unit. All service units operate with paraprofessionals; psychiatrists, psychiatric social workers, and other disciplines are represented, but not in every setting.

SERVICES TO INDIANS

Operating through more than 90 service units, spread throughout 17 states, the Mental Health Program offers services to more than 400,000 federally-recognized reservation Indians. The enormous effort involved is complicated by the fact that the clientele represent more than 135 distinctive tribal groups.

A range of services is offered: Some familiar from community mental health work, some innovatively geared to this particular clientele.

Quantitative data are lacking for the early years of the program's existence. However, in 1974 the practice of service-wide automated record keeping was instituted. Figures describing service trends in this report derive from analyses of the 1974 data.

Outpatient Services

In 1974, about three percent of the total population of reservation Indians, 12,897 outpatients, appeared for assessment and/or treatment.

Inpatient Programs

There are two inpatient wards for referral from the more than 90 service units in the Mental Health Program. These two are located in Gallup, New Mexico, and in Anchorage, Alaska, where each occupies a wing of the Indian Health Service General Hospital. During 1974, the two units provided services for 1,872 inpatients.

In all other areas, if a patient requires hospitalization, one of two options may be taken. The first option, a bed in a general medical wing, is useful in short term crises such as detoxification. Violent, manic, and chronic patients tax the resources of the general hospital staff, leading to the use of another kind of facility. The second option, turning to private or state hospitals or to community mental health centers, is in keeping with a general drive to develop service networks and to integrate Indian peoples more closely with the surrounding community.

In some states physical, attitudinal, and other barriers interfere with Indian use of mental health services meant for the general population. South Dakota state hospitals, for example, require a $100 deposit before a patient can be admitted. For needy non-Indian patients, the county commissioner's office provides the $100 deposit. Since reservations are independent of counties, Indians do not have recourse to this option. In effect, then, the requirement prohibits access to the hospitals for needy South Dakota Indians.

Even when admission policies are more encouraging, other factors often limit access. In places like Arizona and New Mexico, state hospitals are located far from Navajo, Hopi, and many of the Pueblo reservations. When someone falls ill, his family has difficulty getting to a hospital because of its distance; then, if they succeed in having him admitted, contact becomes difficult to maintain. The patient's feeling of isolation will be intensified because he is now dependent on two foreign cultures: the hospital and the Anglo.

INNOVATIVE APPROACHES

Need, coupled with opportunity, has given birth to many innovative programs, only a selection of which can be described in this report.

Model Dormitory

Because of the scattering of population on many Indian reservations and the poor roads which make transportation difficult, many Indian children from the age of six and over attend government-run boarding schools. On the Navajo reservation alone, 25,000 children spend most of each year in a boarding school. Research has documented that a great deal of mental illness, social and learning problems characterize children who attend these schools. Authorities have identified neglect and disregard of Indian culture and language, student and parent powerlessness, overcrowding, and underfinancing as explanatory factors (Krush *et al.,* 1966; Hammerschlag, Alderfer, & Berg, 1973).

The Model Dormitory Project, begun in 1969 at a Bureau of Indian Affairs boarding school in Toyei, Arizona, is an experiment in preventive mental health. The design was simple; it called for hiring an extra complement of personnel who acted as additional houseparents for the children, lowering the ratio of students to personnel. Since the assumption was that Navajo children are best cared for by Navajo speaking people, the houseparents chosen by the school board were all Navajo. Personal qualities and work experience, rather than formal training, dictated the board's selections. Two elderly female employees spent their day weaving rugs in the school's public room and teaching this traditional skill to young girls who displayed an interest. They also recounted tribal legends to the children and taught them how to cook, Navajo style. An elderly silversmith performed the same function for boys.

Compared with the children in a control school, the children at Toyei performed better at intellectual tests, suffered less emotional distress, displayed more group cohesiveness, and were more willing to persevere at tasks (Goldstein, 1974).

Residential Treatment Center

Too often, when foster home placement becomes necessary, children are placed outside of their communities. Follow-up services, desperately needed by the children's families, are inadequate. Many Indian groups feel that removing children from the reservation also removes a family's motivation to solve the problem which led to the child's being placed away from home in the first instance; when this is coupled with a lack of adequate follow-up services, family dissolution often results (Unger, 1977).

In 1972, the Portland area established a group home offering therapy and rehabilitation. The aim was to provide an alternative to jail for known delinquents, to provide a shelter for the care of dependent children, to provide therapy for emotionally and behaviorally disturbed children, to provide counseling for parents and substitute parents, and to facilitate a successful return of the child to his family.

An interesting anecdote was told about the discussion surrounding this project during a tribal meeting. An interpreter, asked to explain the proposal, reminded the elder members that in former times the tribe used to select one of its wisest members to be the "whipper man" who administered proper discipline to those youth and children who showed disrespect for tradition and their elders. The interpreter suggested that the group home program was a modern equivalent. The project, thus brought under the sanction of tradition, became an acceptable and successful part of the community's life (Shore & Nicholls, 1977).

Traditional Medicine

Mental Health Program staff have become highly sensitive to the value of working with traditional Indian medicine persons and, in some areas, formal consultative relations have developed, with healers being eligible for consultation fees (Beiser & deGroat, 1974; Attneave, 1974). However, it was also becoming apparent that younger persons were not becoming apprentices to medicine people as they had in the past. The shift from a barter exchange economy to a wage economy made taking the time to become trained as a traditional healer increasingly difficult (training which may last from 10 to 20 years). By the late 1960s a real danger existed that unwritten liturgies would be lost forever and that medicine persons would not be replaced when they died. A training grant application to the National Institute of Mental Health was funded under the title "Navajo Mental Health Program." This program, still in existence, provides stipends for approximately 12 apprentices and 6 medicine persons to meet regularly in order to learn their difficult craft. Plans are underway to extend the program to other areas besides Navajo.

Paraprofessionals

The Indian Health Service employs close to 100 mental health paraprofessionals, men and women of Indian background many of whom have had years of experience in tribal government or in federal jobs.

Mental health workers do home visiting, and family and group psychotherapy, and they do it in such languages as Lakota and Navajo. Sometimes, Indian mental health workers function as cultural interpreters, sorting out misunderstandings. Once communications are clarified, it is surprising how often "uncooperative patients" suddenly become "cooperative."

A variety of training programs operate, including individual supervision by professional staff, lectures, discussions, trips to various institutions, and reading and writing assignments. In several different areas, mental health workers are now taking part in educational programs offered jointly by the Indian Health Service and local community colleges. Through the community colleges they can earn associate and bachelor's degrees; they may apply these credits toward advanced degrees elsewhere (Bergman, 1974).

Indian Leadership

Paraprofessionals are all Indians, whereas the top administrative positions tend to be filled by non-Indians, a stratification which is reminiscent of other minority programs. However, in this bureaucracy, Indian leadership is becoming increasingly prominent. When Dr. Bergman retired as Chief of Mental Health in 1975, he recruited Dr. H. C. Townsley, a Chickasaw psychiatrist from Oklahoma. Dr. Bergman also played an active role in recruiting Ellouise de Groat, M.S.W., a member of the Navajo tribe, to be Area Chief of Mental Health Services of the Navajo Reservation.

Indian advisory boards have already been mentioned. In some areas, local boards have gone beyond giving advice to assuming total responsibility for a mental health program. In these instances, the Indian Health Service awards health monies to tribal boards on a contract basis. The boards then develop their own programs, hire their own staffs and develop their own directions.

Alaska presents a unique situation. The 1971 Native Claims Settlement Act greatly affected the lives of the 55,000 indigenous people living in Alaska. The Act's three major provisions consisted of a money settlement of $900 million dollars for Native lands, a land agreement of 40 million acres, and formal recognition of 12 Alaska Native Regional Corporations. Each corporation has a profit-making branch, entrusted with receiving land and money as part of the settlement, investing this wealth and distributing the proceeds to indigenous persons who are stockholders. The nonprofit branch of each corporation, concerned with health, education, and welfare, works with existing federal, state, and local agencies to improve delivery of services. Integrating their own and government resources, the corporations have embarked on innovative mental health programs which include school consultation and training of indigenous persons as paraprofessional workers. The health programs, whose consumer boards consist of Native persons and which report directly to an organization in which Native persons are actual stockholders, represents an experiment in true community control of mental health services (Bloom & Richards, 1976).

POLICY

Within a short time, faced with enormously complex tasks, the Indian Health Service Mental Health Program has established an impressive record of achievement. Nevertheless, many issues remain unresolved, while, at the same time, new and specific questions are emerging.

Direct Service vs. Consultation

One old, tension-producing issue is deciding upon an optional balance of direct versus consultative activity. An emphasis on direct services results in an accumulation of acute and chronic cases and, eventually, the creation of long waiting lists. An emphasis on consultation, teaching, and community organizing, on the other hand, makes no provisions for individuals or families for whom preventive and early interventions prove insufficient or come too late.

National health insurance, coming under increasingly serious scrutiny in the United States, generates more and more discussion of the relative merits of fee-for-service reimbursement versus the model presented by a salaried staff working in a comprehensive medical health center. The Indian Health Service experience suggests that an integration of both may provide the best coverage, at least in the foreseeable future. The Indian Health Service uses the private sector for supplemental clinical services. This kind of supplementation makes particular sense where specialized services are required; some of these kinds of services are so costly and so infrequently called upon that it would make no sense for a service unit to develop them. In these instances, the service unit can call upon the resources of the surrounding community. On the other hand, the service unit team, equipped as they are with multidisciplinary skills, and employing people who can bridge the gap between the cultures of mental health personnel and Indians, possess an unique ability to deliver certain kinds of clinical service and to develop preventive programs. A comprehensive approach to mental health will probably need to incorporate both elements and to allow for a creative meshing of organizational methods.

Mental Health Programs and Traditional Practices

One of the particular strengths of the Mental Health Program stems from a tradition of adapting and integrating mental health services with traditional culture and practices. In the Navajo and Phoenix areas, this finds concrete expression in policies which permit paying consultation fees to traditional healers from the Indian Health Service budget, on the same basis as these are paid to other specialists. Resistance to this program, when it comes from Indian people, sometimes seems puzzling. However, one must recognize that many people,. having been coaxed and coerced over several generations to adopt Anglo attitudes (including a view of medicine as "science"), now see the subsidization and sanction of traditional healers as a step backwards along a road they and their families · have painfully travelled.

Obviously, the Indian Health Service must continue to recognize both the constraints which local cultures impose and the opportunities they provide for creative approaches to mental health. Emphasizing the former, however, while neglecting the latter—something which has characterized the general health literature (Paul & Miller, 1955)—means that opportunities will be overlooked.

Racism

When different cultures come into contact, misunderstandings often arise, some of which may be branded "racism." One form which racism assumes is "institutional racism," defined generally as a series of policies, actions, and regulations that oppressively discriminate solely on the basis of race or color, and which are rationalized as being for the good of the racial group they affect.

The Indian Health Service is generally freer of institutional racism than many government agencies but evidence of it occurs, even here.

For example, Indian preference, an official recruitment policy, means that if two equally qualified job applicants are available, the one with Indian descent will have preference. However, the qualifications for many positions in mental health are sometimes so poorly defined, and the method by which the Indian community—usually the advisory board— can have input into selection procedures so confused, that chaos ensues. As a result, a position remains unfilled and the Indian community ultimately suffers.

Career mobility geographically and vertically is as important as initial hiring. It appears that there has been within the Indian Health Service a policy that allowed Indian preference to operate to fill a position locally within an Area. However, as a hedge against the chance that this position might be filled by an unqualified person, the individual so hired was barred from full civil service status in relation to any other position within the Indian Health Service. In other words, transfers, promotions involving an increase of responsibility for more than the original unit, etc., were not to be the normal expectations of individuals hired under Indian preference rules. Although this policy seems to be changing, its effects were observed while gathering data for this project. Only Indian personnel are hired because they can work with their particular tribal group and then given highly technical training, but then are not given the opportunity to work with a more varied group of people. In contrast, non-Indian personnel are considered mobile geographically and vertically, according to their ability and skills.

Restricting trained Indians to particular projects becomes particularly significant as one looks at the long-range career prospects of the mental health paraprofessionals. In every instance these individuals are hired because of their ties with and expertise within a local community and tribal group. Their function as a link to the Indian community is extolled as the justification for the position and as one of its chief values when these positions are created and filled. However, on-the-job training, formal educational opportunities, and experience outfit many paraprofessionals with skills exceeding their original, limited roles. They become therapists, psychometrists, social workers, and administrators; however, they are immobilized by both the local preference policy described above and the job definitions and attitudes which tie them to specific localities and specific tribal associations. For some individuals the increase in pay and seniority in a home location may be sufficient substitutes for long range career plans, but for others blocked opportunity gives rise to frustration.

Differences in experience and perception also manifest themselves in the physical settings in which care is offered. Most clinics or hospitals have poorly lighted waiting rooms equipped with chairs arranged rigidly in rows and barely adequate restrooms. Accommodations for relatives, especially small children and mothers, or the elderly, are often makeshift. Mental health facilities, often located in "trailers" separate from the other health buildings are hard to find. Disgusted patients often conclude that the facility is designed and operated for the convenience of non-Indian staff rather than for the Indian consumers, interpreting this as a subtle but persuasive indication of relative status and often of lack of respect. There are exceptions, but the conditions described above tend to be the norm and the exceptions depend most often on the temporary presence of individuals with strong positive influence. With high turnover of personnel either through short tours of duty or frequent transfers at two year intervals, the exception of one year may revert to the norm the next.

Racism in reverse is demonstrated by some persons who are so afraid to intervene in a strange cultural setting that they abandon their sense of expertise and become impotent. They should be aware that non-Indian modes of intervention, ranging from psychotherapy to consultative intervention have proven to be of value, provided they are carried out with sensitivity and mutual respect for the parties involved (Stage & Keast, 1966).

Prejudice, to be sure, exists on both sides of the racial boundary. The Indian population is often skeptical of overtures which seem to offer status and recognition only in return for becoming so like the non-Indian that one is forced to give up parts of his or her own identity and culture. For these reasons, it is often difficult to develop free social exchanges; even discussions about shared problems may be misunderstood because they continue to be seen from different perspectives.

Institutional racism—from which no paternalistically founded bureaucracy can ever be quite free—retards the development of staff, interferes with patient care, and impedes the kind of collaboration among Indian and non-Indian personnel which the Indian Health Service at its best has been able to achieve. Awareness that these tendencies always pose a threat constitutes the best defense against them.

Today and Tomorrow

As with any busy health service, the Indian Health Service Mental Health Programs tend to become so involved in service activity that no energy remains for planning. A current saying captures the essence of this problem: "We are so busy mopping the blood off the floor today, that we haven't time to worry about tomorrow."

During the initial years of growth and expansion, program planning and evaluation did not assume a high priority. However, after several years of effort and pilot testing a service-wide automated record keeping system was introduced in 1974. Both mental health and social service staffs participate by using a problem-oriented check list to describe each service contact. The resulting data have proven useful in describing patterns of staff activity and in demonstrating areas where future development efforts need to be directed.

The automated record keeping system provides some data useful for planning. For example, some interesting trends emerge according to age. Currently, 45 percent of the total Indian population is under the age of 15 yet only about 12 percent of all mental health patient contacts take place with Indians from that age group. We do not wish to imply that, of necessity, children should receive 45 percent of the service's attention. The discrepancy does, however, raise some questions about service needs for this, the fastest-growing segment of the Indian population (Bloom, 1972).

CONCLUSIONS

In a highly condensed form, we have sketched the mental health services available to American Indians through the Indian Health Service. While the sketch has been based on close observation of the services in action, a cautionary remark must be made concerning the time lag between data collection and publication of its analysis. Change and evolution continue to characterize Indian Health Service Mental Health programs; expansions, shifts of personnel, and legislative and budgeting pressures affecting the field operations continue. The full impact of the Indian Health Care Improvement Act (Public Law 94.437) has yet to be felt. Under the provisions of this act, the resources of the Indian Health Service will expand over a 7-year period so that Indian people will receive care at the same level as that of the population at large.

Under Title 2, the mental health portion of the Act, the following are mandated:

The development of a diagnostic and treatment center for children
Four new inpatient facilities
The establishment of more model dormitories
Program expansion for training people in traditional medicine
Expansion of field mental health efforts by increased staffing

These developments remain the subject of ongoing monitoring and research both within the Indian Health Service and externally. The presence of these programs and their availability demonstrably refutes the quip so often encountered when describing this work to urban and academic colleagues: "Mental Health for Indians: they surely need it. It's about time somebody did something."

Information about ongoing and evolving attempts to meet these needs should now be shared, for the mutual benefit of Indian and non-Indian communities.

REFERENCES

Attneave, C. L. Medicine men and psychiatrists in the Indian Health Service. *Psychiatric Annals,* 1974, *4*(11), 49–55.
Attneave, C. L., & Beiser, M. Service networks and utilization patterns. Mental Health Programs, Indian Health Service (Report No. 110-73-342). U.S. Public Health Service, Indian Health Service, 1975.
Beiser, M., & Attneave, C. L. Analysis of patient and staff characteristics, presenting problems and attitudes towards mental health: Indian Health Service

mental health and social services (Report No. 240-75-0001). U.S. Public Health Service, Indian Health Service, 1977.

Beiser, M., & de Groat, E. Body and spirit medicine: Conversation with a Navajo singer. *Psychiatric Annals,* 1974, *4*(11), 9–12.

Bergman, R. L. Paraprofessionals in Indian mental health programs. *Psychiatric Annals, 4*(11), 76–84.

Bloom, J. D. Population trends of Alaska Natives and the need for planning. *American Journal of Psychiatry,* 1972, *128*(8), 998–1002.

Bloom, J. D., and Richards, W. W. Alaska native regional corporations and community mental health. In R. J. Shepard and S. Itoh (Eds.), *Circumpolar health.* Toronto: University of Toronto Press, 1976.

Goldstein, G. S. The model dormitory. *Psychiatric Annals,* 1974, *4*(11), 85–92.

Hammerschlag, C. S., Alderfer, C. P., & Berg, D. Indian education: A human systems analysis. *American Journal of Psychiatry,* 1973, *130,* 1098–1102.

Krush, T., Bjork, S., Sindell, P. et al. Some thoughts on the formation of personality disorder: Study of an Indian boarding school population. *American Journal of Psychiatry,* 1966, *122,* 868–876.

Paul, B. D., & Miller, W. B. *Health culture and community.* New York: Russel Sage Foundation, 1955.

Shore, J. H., & Nicholls, W. W. Indian children and tribal group homes: New interpretations of the whipper man. In S. Unger (Ed.), *The destruction of American Indian families.* New York: Association on American Indian Affairs, 1977, 79–83.

Stage, T. B., & Keast, T. A psychiatric service for Plains Indians. *Hospital and Community Psychiatry,* 1966, *17,* 131–133.

Torrey, F. F. Mental health services for American Indians and Eskimos. *Community Mental Health Journal,* 1970, *6,* 455–463.

Unger, S. (Ed.). *The destruction of American Indian families.* New York: Association on American Indian Affairs, 1977.

5

Federal Mandates
for the Handicapped
Implications for
American Indian Children

Bruce Ramirez and Barbara J. Smith

The enactment of Public Law (P.L.) 94-142, the Education for All Handicapped Children Act of 1975, has been hailed by advocates and others as the beginning of the final phase of the rights movement to assure each handicapped child the right to a free, appropriate education (Abeson & Zettel, 1977). As implementation of this landmark legislation proceeds for children in the general population with special learning needs, attention also must be directed toward groups of handicapped children who, due to their particular circumstances, may not benefit fully from the rights and protections assured under the Act. Such children often come from disadvantaged social and economic backgrounds and they include racially and culturally different children, children in juvenile corrections programs and foster care, abused and neglected children, and those who reside in sparsely populated and inner city areas. Not to be forgotten are American Indian, including Alaskan Native, handicapped children whose special education needs have, until recently, received little consideration.

According to the U.S. Bureau of the Census (1973), there were 827,000 people in the United States in 1970 who identified themselves as American Indians, including 34,000 Aleuts and Eskimos. The Bureau of Indian Affairs has reported further that there are an estimated 543,000 Indians residing on or near reservations in 26 states (U.S. Department of Interior, 1974). While Indians comprise a relatively small portion of the total U.S. population, the educational problems that have plagued them are enormous (Brophy & Aberle, 1966; Fuchs & Havighurst, 1973; U.S. Congress, 1969). Given the previous inadequacies and failures of Indian education, it should be no surprise that many Indian handicapped children have been denied access to school (Inter-Tribal Symposium on Men-

Reprinted with permission from *Exceptional Children*, 1978, *45*, 521–528.

tal Retardation, 1976) while those who are in school often are denied the specialized services they need (U.S. General Accounting Office, 1977).

Advocates for the handicapped will undoubtedly recognize these difficulties as analogous to problems encountered by parents and others seeking educational services for non-Indian handicapped children. While common problems do exist, resolution of these problems for Indian handicapped children often is more difficult due to the varying educational delivery systems (i.e., state, federal, community controlled, and private) that have evolved to serve these children. Basic to the difficulties in this area is the federal relationship with Indians which historically has caused confusion between the states and the federal government over responsibility for educating Indian children (Allen, 1976). With the passage of P.L. 94-142, this debate has extended to the education of Indian handicapped children (Boston, 1977).

In view of these factors, the requirements of recent federal laws for the handicapped need to be related to state and federal agencies with responsibility to provide educational services to Indian children. In addition to the provisions of P.L. 94-142 and Section 504 of the Vocational Rehabilitation Act of 1973, P.L. 93-112, this article explores what actions must be undertaken if the promise of these two federal mandates are to become a reality for all Indian children who are handicapped and in need of special education and related services.

INDIAN EDUCATION BACKGROUND

In order to better understand some of the problems that stand in the way of the implementation of P.L. 94-142 and Section 504 for Indian handicapped children, one needs to have some knowledge of Indian education as it presently exists.

Educational Delivery Systems

As a result of past governmental policies and practices, Indian children can be found attending several different types of schools. In this regard, the annual school census of the Bureau of Indian Affairs indicated that 72% of all Indian children enrolled in school on or near reservations for fiscal year 1976 attended public schools, about 23% attended federal schools, and 5% were in other schools (U.S. Department of the Interior, n.d.). A brief description of the most prevalent types of educational delivery systems serving Indian children follows:

State   States, through their respective local educational agencies, provide school services to Indian children in rural, urban, and reservation settings.

Federal   The U.S. Department of the Interior, through the Bureau of Indian Affairs, operates a system of 188 day and boarding schools for eligible Indian students on or near reservations in 17 states. These schools are maintained for children residing in areas with inadequate public school programs or who for social reasons require boarding services in addition to educational services. Indian tribes also have an option to contract with the Bureau of Indian Affairs for the operation of "contract" schools.

Community controlled   Tribal groups and Indian communities, through contracts and grants from the Bureau of Indian Affairs, the Office of Indian Education and other sources, operate independent schools for the benefit of Indian children.

Historical Development

These varied educational delivery systems have not evolved by chance but rather developed as a result of shifting governmental policy with respect to the education of Indian children. In addition, while these delivery systems represent differing and sometimes competing interests, they rely heavily upon the federal government for basic and supplemental program support.

Contrary to non-Indian children, the education of Indian children prior to the Indian Citizenship Act of 1924 was considered a federal rather than a state responsibility. This unparalleled situation can be traced to the U.S. Constitution, which gave Congress the power to regulate "commerce with foreign nations, among the several states, and with the Indian tribes" (Article I, Section 8, Clause 3) and the President the authority, subject to Senate approval, to negotiate treaties (Article II, Section 2, Clause 2). These powers have been interpreted as giving broad jurisdiction over Indian affairs, including education, to the federal government. In this regard, subsequent treaties and legislation contained education provisions for Indians. To meet this responsibility, the federal government first contracted with various religious orders to provide school services and later proceeded to develop its own school system for Indians.

With the passage of the Indian Citizenship Act, which accorded citizenship status to all Indians who were not already citizens through other legal means, the federal government began to urge greater state involvement in the education of Indian children. However, it was not until the enactment of the Johnson-O'Malley Act in 1934 that a more direct step was taken by the federal government to secure greater state participation in Indian education (Indian Education Task Force, 1976). This act authorized the Secretary of the Interior to contract with states and territories for education and other human services and remains the primary mechanism through which the Bureau of Indian Affairs provides funding to state and local educational agencies for educating Indian children. At the same time, the federal government, through the Bureau of Indian Affairs, has continued to operate schools of its own.

Although the Bureau of Indian Affairs traditionally has had the most prominent role in administering Indian affairs, Congress has allocated this responsibility particularly with respect to education to other federal agencies as well. In 1953 the federal Impact Aid Laws, P.L. 81-874, Maintenance and Operations, and P.L. 81-815, School Construction, were amended to provide financial assistance to public school districts who faced financial hardships due to the presence of nontaxable Indian land within their school boundaries. In addition, public schools as well as the Secretary of the Interior are eligible to receive funds for the education of disadvantaged children under Title I of the Elementary and Secondary Education Act of 1965 (P.L. 89-10). More recently, the passage of the Indian Education Act, P.L. 92-318 (1972), created the Office of Indian Education within the U.S. Office of Education to provide assistance to educational agencies for special programs and projects to improve educational opportunities for Indian children, youth, and adults.

Earlier federal policies that encouraged increased state responsibility in Indian education and more recent policies supporting greater Indian self determination in the operation of educational programs (P.L. 92-318; P.L. 93-638, the Indian Self-Determination and Education Assistance Act, 1975) have resulted in a diversified educational delivery system for Indian children, particularly on or near many of the reservations. In view of this situation, there is a danger that any number of Indian handicapped children in need of special education services may be overlooked and considered the responsibility of some other agency.

EDUCATION FOR ALL HANDICAPPED CHILDREN ACT

Public Law 94-142 requires that every state and its localities, if they are to continue to receive funds under the Act, make available an appropriate education to all handicapped children, ages 3 through 18, by September 1, 1978. (This requirement, with respect to handicapped children ages 3 through 5 and 18 through 21, does not apply if the provision is inconsistent with state law, practice, or court order.) Further, this education must be at no cost to parents. While responsibility for ensuring that all the requirements of the Act are carried out rests with the state education agency, there is a similar requirement for the Secretary of the Interior. The provisions of this Act as they relate to states have been detailed elsewhere (Ballard, 1977; Ballard & Zettel, 1977) and are, therefore, discussed only briefly with regard to Indian handicapped children. Greater emphasis is devoted to the role of the Bureau of Indian Affairs since under the Act this agency has similar responsibilities for assuring that the requirements of P.L. 94-142 are accomplished in schools within its jurisdiction.

State Education Agency / Local Education Agency

In addition to the requirement that the state education agency guarantee compliance with all of the provisions of the law, all educational programs administered within the state must meet state education agency standards and be under the general supervision of the state education agency (P.L. 94-142, Section 612(6)). These requirements reflect the desire of Congress for a central point of accountability for the education of handicapped children within each state.

Responsibility for administering P.L. 94-142 is shared between local educational agencies, state educational agencies, and the U.S. Commissioner of Education. Under this administrative arrangement, the U.S. Commissioner may not allocate funds to a state until its annual program plan has been approved. Accordingly, the state education agency may not permit the local education agency to receive its entitlement until it has approved the local application. Moreover, the local application must conform to the approved state annual program plan (P.L. 94-142, Section 614(a) (1)–(7)).

It is through these interlocking administrative responsibilities that handicapped children and their parents are afforded the rights and protections guaranteed under the Act. Hence, it is the duty of the state education agency and the appropriate local education agency to assure an appropriate education to all handicapped children within their jurisdiction. In this regard, Indian handicapped children within the service area of a local education agency are accorded all the rights and protections afforded their non-Indian counterparts.

Secretary of the Interior / Bureau of Indian Affairs

While the relationship of P.L. 94-142 to state and local education agencies is clearly defined by the Act, the participation of the Secretary of the Interior on behalf of the Bureau of Indian Affairs is less clear. Section 611 (f)(1) of the law recognizes the unique situation of Indian children who attend schools under federal jurisdiction and provides that

> the Commissioner is authorized to make payments to the Secretary of the Interior according to the need for such assistance for the education of handicapped children on reservations serviced by elementary and secondary schools operated for Indian children by the Department of the Interior. The amount of such payments for any fiscal year shall not exceed one percentum of the aggregate amounts available to all states under this part for that fiscal year.

This inclusion of the Secretary of the Interior assures that Indian handicapped children and their parents on or near reservations served by

Bureau of Indian Affairs schools are entitled to the same rights and protections guaranteed to other handicapped children served by state and local education agencies. In this regard, the Committee report (No. 94-168) accompanying the Senate version (S. 6) of P.L. 94-142 stated:

> It is the intent of the Committee that all requirements applied to state and local educational agencies respecting eligibility and application shall apply to the Department of the Interior, and that all benefits and protections provided for handicapped children served by state and local education agencies shall also be provided to handicapped children served by the Department of the Interior. (p. 14)

In keeping with legislative intent, the Secretary of the Interior must also comply with the requirements of the Act by the beginning of the 1978 school year, including the provision of a free, appropriate education to all handicapped children served by Bureau of Indian Affairs schools. As with the annual program plan requirements for the states, the Secretary of the Interior, in order to continue to receive funds generated by the Act, must submit the equivalent of an annual program plan to the U.S. Commissioner of Education for approval. In addition, the Department of the Interior is required to insure public participation throughout the development of its "annual application" (P.L. 94-142, Final Regulations, Section 121a.261). Other mandated provisions that must be complied with under the Services and Procedural Safeguards subparts of the Final Regulations for P.L. 94-142 include the following:

Ongoing child identification activities
Written individualized education programs
A comprehensive system of personnel development
Due process procedures for children and parents
Safeguards in evaluation materials and procedures
Least restrictive alternative placements
Confidentiality of information

To further insure that the rights and protections of the Act are met, the Secretary of the Interior must adhere to the requirements that a single education agency be accountable for the general supervision of appropriate special educational services. Other administrative responsibilities include monitoring and evaluation activities as well as the establishment of and consultation with an advisory panel (P.L. 94-142, Final Regulations, Section 121a.600-121a.650).

SECTION 504

Section 504 of the Vocational Rehabilitation Act is the basic civil rights provision with respect to ending discrimination on the basis of handicapping conditions. Section 504 provides that no otherwise qualified handicapped individual...in the United States shall, solely by reason of his handicap, be excluded from the participation, be denied the benefits of, or be subjected to discrimination under any program or activity receiving federal financial assistance.

While brief in language, this law represents a national commitment to protect the rights of handicapped persons. The regulations that accompany Section 504 contain provisions regarding preschool, elementary, and secondary education programs and activities, and, in almost all respects, these regulations conform to the requirements of P.L. 94-142. With respect to educational programs, the law basically requires recipients of federal financial assistance to afford a free, appropriate education to all handicapped children.

As mentioned earlier, the greatest danger resulting from the diverse educational delivery systems providing services to Indian children is the possibility that the handicapped may be overlooked. However, this possibility is lessened with Section 504, since almost all education agencies serving Indian children receive federal financial assistance through such programs as Johnson-O'Malley, Impact Aid, Title I, Title VII (P.L. 90-247, 1968) (Bilingual education), and Title IV of the Indian Education Act. Consequently, this civil rights law, with its broad scope and similar provisions to P.L. 94-142, will further insure that Indian handicapped children receive an education suitable to their needs.

WHAT NEEDS TO BE DONE?

As the September 1978 deadline for full services for the handicapped approaches, issues have emerged that, if left unattended, will further delay this goal for Indian handicapped children, particularly those on or near many of the reservations. In order to assure that these children receive suitable services, several modifications and/or expansions of current practice at all levels of government will be required. Areas requiring immediate attention include the following:

Policies and practices of the Bureau of Indian Affairs
Development of cooperative agreements
Recruitment and training of personnel
Advocacy needs and activities

Bureau of Indian Affairs

As previously mentioned, under P.L. 94-142, the Bureau of Indian Affairs is required to comply with the provisions of the Act. However, recent evidence indicates that Bureau services for the handicapped have been so lacking that compliance by the beginning of the coming school year is doubtful. In this regard, a recent U.S. General Accounting Office report (1977) found

> BIA was not operating its own program for providing special education for handicapped Indian children, even though BIA studies indicated that Indian children suffer from a higher-than-average incidence of hearing loss, vision difficulties, and other handicaps. Limited special education was carried out with some funds obtained from the Office of Education, Department of Health, Education and Welfare. However, such funds were inadequate to meet the needs of Indian students. (pp. 9–10)

This finding is startling, particularly in view of the progress that is being made by many of the states with respect to appropriate special education programming. Rather than arising as a result of policies and categorical funding, special education within the Bureau of Indian Affairs has developed as a consequence of available U.S. Office of Education flowthrough funds. Thus, at a time when federal mandates and good educational practice call for comprehensive services for the handicapped, the Bureau of Indian Affairs, due to its supplemental programming approach, must overcome such basic problems as a) a lack of policies requiring the appropriate education of handicapped children; b) no budget line item for initiating and sustaining special education and related services; and c) inadequate numbers of qualified permanent special education personnel (U.S. General Accounting Office, 1977).

These problems have not gone unnoticed by advocates and others concerned about improved services for the handicapped. During this past year's appropriations hearings, The Council for Exceptional Children (1977), joined by Indian advocacy groups, presented testimony concerning the need for the Congress to appropriate sufficient funds to permit the Bureau of Indian Affairs to comply with the requirements of P.L. 94-142. Moreover, the Senate Appropriations Committee, in its report No. 95-276 on appropriations for the Department of the Interior and Related Agencies (U.S. Congress, Senate, 1977), noted that the Bureau of Indian Affairs has been "remiss in providing special education services" to handicapped children. Accordingly, the joint Conference Report No. 95-461 (U.S. Congress, House of Representatives, 1977) accompanying the 1978 appropriations bill directed the Bureau of Indian Affairs to allocate from funds available for school operations $2 million for special education and submit a report on its unmet special education needs.

The action taken by the Congress has been hailed by advocates for Indian children as an important first step in assuring full services for the handicapped within the school jurisdiction of the Bureau of Indian Affairs. While some officials have expressed concern over this relatively low level of special education funding, the Bureau has an opportunity in its forthcoming report to the Congress to provide a description of and budget projection for the number and kind of activities, services, personnel, and facilities needed in order to fully implement P.L. 94-142.

Cooperative Agreements

While P.L. 94-142 places the responsibility for the education of all handicapped children with the states and their political subdivisions, the inclusion of the Secretary of the Interior has raised questions about who has responsibility to provide services to Indian handicapped children on reservations. This issue becomes particularly troublesome in Alaska, Arizona, New Mexico, North Dakota, South Dakota, Oklahoma, and other states where public, Bureau of Indian Affairs, and community controlled schools coexist. A means of overcoming the danger of handicapped children falling through service delivery gaps is the development of cooperative written agreements specifying respective educational responsibilities. While the need for such agreements can be seen most readily in state and Bureau of Indian Affairs child identification activities, problems can also arise during placement, particularly when Indian handicapped children are placed in state operated institutions by an agency other than a state agency.

In addition to cooperative agreements between state and federal educational agencies, attention also should be given to agreements between other federal service providers such as the Indian Health Services Bureau and the Bureau of Indian Affairs Social Services Program. An example of the benefits that can be realized in this area is the recent agreement between the Bureau of Indian Affairs and the Indian Health Services (Indian Health Services, 1977) regarding Bureau accessibility to the Health and Medical Records System maintained by the Indian Health Services. This system contains health and medical data concerning Indian children and will enable the Bureau to take advantage of existing data to meet their child identification and evaluation responsibilities under P.L. 94-142.

Recruitment and Training of Personnel

Recognizing the need to have available sufficient numbers of appropriately trained special education and related services personnel, the Congress saw fit to include personnel development provisions in P.L. 94-142. These provisions require state education agencies as well as the Bureau of Indian Affairs to develop and implement a comprehensive system of personnel development. To assure that sufficient numbers of teachers, administrators, and related services personnel will be available to work with Indian handicapped children, these systems need to give special consideration to the preparation of persons who are not only qualified to work with the handicapped, but who are also able to work effectively with culturally different children. The nondiscriminatory assessment, procedural safeguards, and individualized education program requirements of P.L. 94-142 further reflect the need to recruit and train persons knowledgeable in the fields of special education and Indian education.

The existing shortage of Indian educators in many areas combined with the relatively new emphasis of special education on or near many of the reservations indicates a need to expand personnel training opportunities for Indians in the fields of special education and related services. The Division of Personnel Preparation, Bureau of Education for the Handicapped, has several programs that have provided training opportunities for Indian paraprofessionals as well as undergraduate and graduate students. Similar training opportunities need to be undertaken by the Office of Indian Education as well as the Bureau of Indian Affairs.

Advocacy

In addition to strengthening existing educational delivery systems so that they can provide the appropriate educational services called for by P.L. 94-142 and Section 504, advocacy efforts are needed to insure that the legal rights of Indian handicapped children and their parents are protected. This is important especially at the grassroots level since many Indian parents, due to unique cultural, social, and economic factors, have had little experience in school affairs and, as a result, often are unaware of the availability of services or the administrative procedures necessary to secure such services. Moreover, there generally has not been a structured form of legal advocacy for the handicapped on or near most reservations.

In some instances parents, educators, and others have joined together to form advocacy groups such as the Sicangu Association for Retarded Citizens (Rosebud), Diné Association for Retarded Citizens (Navajo) and the Hopi Tribal Parents Association for Retarded Children and Adults. These local groups have been instrumental in helping to establish and maintain and monitor community services for the retarded (Ramirez, 1977). In addition, such groups can play a prominent role in educating parents of handicapped children about their rights and the availability of services as well as serve as a source of support and assistance to parents involved in due process proceedings.

At the same time, national advocacy groups such as The Council for Exceptional Children, the National Congress of American Indians, the North American Indian Women's Association, and the National Indian Education Association have begun to speak out on behalf of the Indian handicapped child. The most visible to date in the area of special education has been The Council for Exceptional Children who, in addition to monitoring federal policies, continues to disseminate information and provide technical assistance to those concerned about the education of Indian handicapped children.

As legal problems arise with regard to this group of handicapped children and the requirements of P.L. 94-142 and Section 504 as well as other legislation benefiting the handicapped, it is likely that advocates will have an increased need of some type of legal assistance. In this regard, consideration should be given to the establishment of a long term law project whose services would be available to parents, educators, advocates, and others. Such a project could be affiliated with an existing national law firm such as the Native American Rights Fund, which specializes in the protection of Indian rights.

CONCLUDING REMARKS

P.L. 94-142 and Section 504 reflect the nation's concern that all handicapped children have available a free, appropriate education in the least restrictive educational setting. In this regard, the full attention of policymakers, educators, parents, and advocates is required to assure that Indian handicapped children are afforded an equal educational opportunity.

REFERENCES

Abeson, A., & Zettel, J. The end of the quiet revolution: The Education for All Handicapped Children Act of 1975. *Exceptional Children, 44,* 114–128, 1977.

Allen, S. A. On educating Indians. *Compact,* 1976, *10*(4), 19–28.

Ballard, J. *Public Law 94-142 and Section 504—Understanding what they are and are not.* Reston, Va.: The Council for Exceptional Children, 1977.

Ballard, J., & Zettel, J. Public Law 94-142 and Section 504: What they say about rights and protections. *Exceptional Children, 44,* 177–185, 1977.

Boston, B. O. *Education policy and the Education for All Handicapped Children Act (P.L. 94-142).* Washington, D.C.: Institute for Educational Leadership, The George Washington University, 1977.

Brophy, W. A., & Aberle, S. D. *The Indian: America's unfinished business.* A Report of the Commission on the Rights, Liberties and Responsibilities of the American Indian. Norman, Oklahoma: University of Oklahoma Press, 1966.

The Council for Exceptional Children. Congressional Testimony to the Subcommittee on the Department of the Interior of the Committee on Appropriations, United States Senate, April 20, 1977.

Fuchs, E., & Havighurst, R. J. *To live on this earth: American Indian education.* New York: Anchor Press, 1973.

Indian Education Task Force. *Report on Indian education.* Report to the American Indian Policy Review Commission, Washington, D.C.: U.S. Government Printing Office, 1976.

Indian Health Services Memorandum. *IHS support of education for all handicapped children program,* November 31, 1977.

Inter-Tribal Symposium on Mental Retardation. Unpublished testimony. Window Rock, Arizona, May 5, 1976.

Johnson-O'Malley Act, enacted April 16, 1934.

Public Law 81-815, *School Assistance in Federally Affected Areas,* enacted 1953.

Public Law 81-874, *School Assistance in Federally Affected Areas,* enacted 1953.

Public Law 89-10, *Elementary and Secondary Education Act.* Title I, enacted 1965.

Public Law 90-247, *Education Amendments of 1968,* Title VII, enacted 1968.

Public Law 92-318, *Indian Education Act of 1972*, Title IV, enacted 1972.

Public Law 93-112, *Vocational Rehabilitation Act of 1973*, Section 504, enacted 1973.

Public Law 93-638, *Indian Self-Determination and Education Assistance Act*, enacted 1975.

Public Law 94-142, *Education for All Handicapped Children Act*, enacted 1975.

Public Law 94-142, *Education for All Handicapped Children Act*, Final Regulations, Federal Register, Vol. 42, No. 163, Tuesday, August 23, 1977.

Ramirez, B. A. Special education policy and Indian handicapped children. *Indian Education*, 1977, *7* (4).

U.S. Bureau of the Census. *Census of population: 1970 subject reports*. Final Report PC (2)-1F American Indians. Washington, D.C.: U.S. Government Printing Office, 1973.

U.S. Congress, House of Representatives, Conference Report, *Making appropriations, Department of Interior and related agencies for fiscal year 1978*. Report No. 95-461, 95th Congress, 1st Session, 1977.

U.S. Congress, Senate, Committee on Labor and Public Welfare, Special Subcommittee on Indian Education, *Indian education: A national tragedy, a national challenge*. S. Report No. 91, 501, 91st Congress. 1st Session, 1969.

U.S. Congress, Senate, *Education for All Handicapped Children Act, S.6.*, 94th Congress, 1st Session, June 2, Report No. 94-168, 1975.

U.S. Congress, Senate, Committee on Appropriations, *Department of the Interior and Related Agencies Appropriations Bill, 1978*, Report No. 95-276, 95th Congress, 1st Session, 1977.

U.S. Department of the Interior, Bureau of Indian Affairs. *The American Indians*. Washington, D.C.: U.S. Government Printing Office, 1974.

U.S. Department of the Interior, Bureau of Indian Affairs, Office of Indian Education Programs. *Statistics concerning Indian education: Fiscal year 1976*. Lawrence, KS: Haskell Indian Junior College Publications Service, n.d.

U.S. General Accounting Office. *Concerted effort needed to improve Indian education*. Washington, D.C.: Author, 1977.

6

Family Behavior of
Urban American Indians

John G. Red Horse, Ronald Lewis,
Marvin Feit, and James Decker

Ecological formulas are becoming increasingly popular as protocols for human service models. This trend represents a certain irony in the context of service provision to minority families. The function of American Indian families, for example, has long been disabled by social service personnel who appear insensitive to unique Indian family cultural and structural needs. Removal of children from American Indian families following a variety of social diagnoses is approaching epidemic proportion. William Byler cites that 25 to 35 percent of American Indian children are raised outside their natural family network.[1] If ecological standards are applied, American Indian families appear qualified for endangered species status.

This article examines characteristics unique to American Indian families and attempts to relate these to developing human ecology models in casework.[2] Attention is directed toward extended family networks which represent the interactive field in which caseworkers should conduct transactions.

Irving M. Levine's social conservation model serves as a theoretical orientation. This model assumes that individual mental health is linked to a sense of selfhood which is accomplished through adherence to an historical culture and is transmitted principally through family socializa-

Reprinted with permission from *Social Casework,* 1978, *59,* 67–72. Copyright Family Service Association of America.

[1]William Byler, "The Destruction of American Indian Families," in *The Destruction of American Indian Families,* ed. Steve Unger (New York: Association on American Indian Affairs, 1977), p. 1.

[2]This article was made possible by grant no. 90-C624 from the National Center on Child Abuse and Neglect, Children's Bureau, Office of Child Development, Office for Human Development, U.S. Department of Health, Education, and Welfare. Its contents should not be construed as official policy of the National Center on Child Abuse and Neglect or of any agency of the federal government.

tion.[3] Family structure and process, therefore, represent the cornerstone for individual behavior, cultural acquisition, and mental health.

FAMILY STRUCTURE AND CULTURAL BEHAVIOR

American Indian family networks assume a structure which is radically different from other extended family units in Western society. The accepted structural boundary of the European model, for example, is the household. Thus, an extended family is defined as three generations within a single household. American Indian family networks, however, are structurally open and assume a village-type characteristic. Their extension is inclusive of several households representing significant relatives along both vertical and horizontal lines.

Network structure influences individual behavior patterns because family transactions occur within a community milieu. This is important for professionals to understand so that mislabeling may be avoided. Normal behavioral transactions within the network relational field, for example, may appear bizarre to an outside observer.

Case Illustration

The following case illustration provides a typical example of this point.[4]

> A young probationer was under court supervision and had strict orders to remain with responsible adults. His counselor became concerned because the youth appeared to ignore this order. The client moved around frequently and, according to the counselor, stayed overnight with several different young women. The counselor presented this case at a formal staff meeting, and fellow professionals stated their suspicion that the client was either a pusher or a pimp. The frustrating element to the counselor was that the young women knew each other and appeared to enjoy each other's company. Moreover, they were not ashamed to be seen together in public with the client. This behavior prompted the counselor to initiate violation proceedings.

A Minneapolis American Indian professional came upon the case quite by accident. He knew the boy's family well and requested a delay in court proceedings to allow time for a more thorough investigation. It was discovered that the young women were all first cousins to the client. He had not been frivolously "staying overnight with them"; he had been staying with different units of his family. Each female was as a sister.

---

[3]Irving M. Levine, "Ethnicity and Mental Health: A Social Conservation Approach." Paper presented at the White House Conference on Ethnicity and Mental Health, Washington, D.C., June 1976.

[4]This case illustration and all subsequent cases are drawn from the files of Ah-be-no-gee, an innovative demonstration program in child abuse and neglect. Ah-be-no-gee is located in Minneapolis, Minnesota, and funded by the National Center for Child Abuse and Neglect, Office of Child Development, U.S. Department of Health, Education, and Welfare.

Moreover, each family unit had a responsible and obligated adult available to supervise and to care for the client.

A revocation order in this case would have caused irreparable alienation between the family and human service professionals. The casework decision would have inappropriately punished the youth as well as several members of his family for simply conducting normal family behavior. Moreover, its impact would affect people far beyond the presenting client and those members of his family who were directly responsible for his care. The young man had a characteristically large Indian family network consisting of over 200 people and spanning three generations.

Structural characteristics of American Indian family networks confront human service professionals with judgmental issues beyond that of labeling. Extended family often serves as a major instrument of accountability. Standards and expectations are established which maintain group solidarity through enforcement of values.

Single-parent and single-adult households do appear in American Indian communities. Professionals bound by nuclear family parameters point to this fact in planning service resources. Consequently, they are reluctant either to use or legitimate aunts, uncles, cousins, and grandparents as alternate or supportive service caregivers.

Other Case Illustrations

Nancy, for example, was an eighteen-year-old mother identified as mentally retarded and epileptic by the department of welfare officials. Although retardation was subsequently disproved, the department assumed control and custody of Nancy's infant child.

Nancy's parents insisted that the family network was available for assistance, if necessary. The welfare staff, however, considered this offer untenable. The grandparents were deemed senile and unable to care for an infant. They were in their early fifties.

The staff ignored the fact that the grandparents had just finished caring for three other young and active grandchildren without dependence on institutional social intervention. Moreover, these children appeared to be well-adjusted. The officials simply insisted in this case that standard placement procedures be followed; a foster home was obtained for Nancy's child.

The placement orders were eventually overruled in Nancy's case, but not without heroic legal intervention. It is unfortunate that such adversary strategies are necessary to prove competencies of natural family networks. Often, as the following case illustrates, family competency and responsibility evolve as a normal process of network accountability.

Anita was the elder within the family. She was a direct descendent of the most renowned chief of her band and enjoyed high status. She lived alone in a trailer. Shortly after her seventieth birthday, she became ill and unable to care either for herself or to perform routine household chores. A social worker arranged for Anita's admission to a rest home.

The family accepted this interventive plan without comment. Subsequently, however, the situation changed. Anita received regular visits, but these did not satisfy family needs. Anita become lonely for home and the family became lonely for her. A ritual feast was held which Anita attended. Family concerns regarding her absence were expressed and a decision was made that she should remain at home.

The family developed its own helping plan. Each member was given a scheduled time period to provide homemaker services for Anita. Through this shift system, the family network assumed service responsibility. In this case, the family in the immediate vicinity consisted of ten households. Service providers ranged from thirteen-year-old grandchildren to fifty-year-old children.

FAMILY NETWORK HIERARCHY

American Indian family network behavior also contributes to a very conservative cultural pattern. A vigorous network is both retained and developed for transmission of cultural attributes. Continually reinforced and enduring relational roles serve to illustrate this behavior.

Grandparents retain official and symbolic leadership in family communities. Both are active processes sanctioned by the children and their parents. Official leadership is characterized by a close proximity of grandparents to family. It is witnessed through the behavior of children who actively seek daily contact with grandparents and by grandparents who monitor parental behavior. In this milieu, grandparents have an official voice in child-rearing methods, and parents seldom overrule corrective measures from their elders. Symbolic leadership is characterized by an incorporation of unrelated elders into the family. This prevails during an absence of a natural grandparent, but it is not necessarily limited to, or dependent on, such an absence. It is witnessed through the behavior of children and parents who select and virtually adopt a grandparent. In this milieu, younger people are seeking social acceptance from an older member of the community. Symbolic grandparents will not invoke strong child-rearing sanctions. Because their acceptance is sought, their norm-setting standards are seldom ignored.

THREE DISTINCT FAMILY PATTERNS

Extended family networks represent a universal pattern among American Indian nations. Data from one American Indian family service program, however, point to significant variability among the networks. Specific family characteristics, therefore, serve as critical information in the development of methodological guidelines for casework practice.

Three distinct family lifestyle patterns serve for initial identification: 1) a traditional group which overtly adheres to culturally defined styles of living, 2) a nontraditional, bicultural group which appears to have adopted many aspects of non-American Indian styles of living, and 3) a pantraditional group which overtly struggles to redefine and reconfirm previously lost cultural styles of living.[5] Selected behavior variables for each pattern appear in Table 1.

Many observers of American Indian life tend to hold biases concerning which pattern is most legitimate or functional in contemporary American society. This judgmental behavior represents a luxury that caseworkers must avoid, because each pattern is legitimate within its own relational field and contributes to a family sense of selfhood.

Many observers assume that different family lifestyle patterns point to an ongoing erosion of cultural values. Studies suggest, however, that American Indian core values are retained and remain as a constant, regardless of family lifestyle patterns.[6] Pattern variables, therefore, do not represent valid criteria for measuring "Indianness."

The importance of family lifestyle patterns to human service professionals is that each pattern represents a different interactive field, that is, a different environmental context for social casework. As would be expected, family responses to intervention vary. Traditional families, for example, cannot relate to professionals and prefer to ignore mainstream social methodologies. Generally, these families are very courteous to strangers. They will politely listen to professionals, but seldom respond to any social prescriptions which depart from customary practice.

Conversely, bicultural families are able to relate to professional caregivers. They are able to accept and cope with contemporary social prescriptions. Pantraditional families denounce professionals and mainstream social methodologies. They are engaged in attempting to recapture and redefine cultural methodologies.[7]

---

[5]Data on family patterns were drawn from Ah-be-no-gee.

[6]See, for example, A. Irving Hallowell, "Ojibway Personality and Acculturation," in *Beyond the Frontier,* ed. Paul Bohannan and Fred Plog (New York: The Natural History Press, 1967); Thaddeus P. Krush, John W. Bjork, Peter S. Sindell, Joanna Nelle, "Some Thoughts on the Formation of Personality Disorder: Study of an Indian Boarding School Population," in *Hearings Before the Special Subcommittee on Indian Education of the Committee on Labor and Public Welfare United States Senate—Part 5* (Washington, D.C.: U.S. Government Printing Office, 1969); and Native American Research Group, *Native American Families in the City* (San Francisco: Institute for Scientific Analysis, 1975).

[7]Caution must be exercised in appraising the issues of "coping ability" and "openness to mainstream social methodologies." Staff at Ah-be-no-gee, for example, have witnessed an overwhelming preference by American Indians for self-determination and self-governed programs, regardless of differences in family lifestyle patterns.

Table 1. Some selected variables of behavior according to family lifestyle—patterns among Minneapolis Urban Chippewas

Variable of behavior	Family lifestyle pattern		
	Traditional	Bicultural	Pantraditional
Language	Ojibway constitutes conversational language of parents and grandparents. Children are bilingual and able to transact family affairs following Indian language.	English constitutes conversational language by parents, grandparents, and children. Grandparents are usually bilingual. Some Indian language is recaptured through formal classes.	Either English or Ojibway constitutes conversational language of parents, grandparents, and children. Indian language is recaptured through formal academic classes
Religion	Midewiwin remains as the belief system. It retains the characteristics of a very closed system, following family networks.	Anglo belief system prevails; is generally, but not exclusively, Catholicism. Some all-Indian congregations exist with culturally adapted canons.	A modified Indian belief system mixing several traditional forms; i.e., Midewiwin, Native American Church, etc. Unlike closed structure of traditionalists, proselytizing strategies are employed.
Family relational field	Extended network.	Extended network.	Extended network.
Social engagement	Some acceptance of dominant society's activities; i.e., bowling, etc. Cultural activities such as feasts, religion, and pow wows prevail and take precedence over all others.	Dominant society's activities prevail, i.e., bowling, baseball, golf. Relate to non-Indians well. Cultural activities remain of interest but not necessarily enacted through behavior, e.g., will sit and watch at pow wows and read about religion. Very active in Indian meetings and politics.	Openly eschew activities of dominant society. Cultural activities prevail. Those who are not expert try to recapture singing and dancing skills.

FAMILY NETWORK DYNAMICS

Diverse family network interlockings have emerged over time as a result
of geographic movements and intertribal marriages, and these complexities warrant scholarly investigation. Of critical significance to this discussion, however, is the fact that American Indian relational values have
remained intact through the years: Extended family networks remain as a
constant regardless of family lifestyle patterns.

Network behavior patterns clearly point to the emergence of a distinct, closed American Indian community. Outsiders, including representatives of agencies providing mandated service, do not gain entrance easily. This attitude has influenced the development of health and welfare
services. Ninety percent of the American Indians in Minneapolis responding to questions relating to health needs behavior, for example, indicated
a preference for receiving services from American Indian workers.[8] This
preference is clearly demonstrated by American Indian clients in the St.
Paul-Minneapolis "Twin Cities" metropolitan area of Minnesota who
rely upon American Indian service agencies. This contrasts with non-
Indian health programs located in the same community, which are continuously involved in strategies to recruit American Indian clients and are
unable to serve a representative number.[9]

Outside observers often cite this network behavior as fraught with
dangers, because many American Indian service providers are not professionally trained. American Indians, however, have a commendable history in medicine and in community mental health. American Indian families, for example, traditionally organize supportive networks for children
through a naming ceremony.[10] This ceremony actually reconfirms the responsibilities of a natural network, that is, aunts, uncles, and cousins.
The family emerges as a protective social fabric to provide for the health
and welfare of the children. Namesakes provide what professionals define
as "substitute services" if parents become incapacitated. Unlike similar
religions and cultural rituals, namesakes become the same as parents in
the network structure.

American Indian programs in the "Twin Cities" metropolitan area
formally incorporate aspects of ethnoscience, such as naming ceremonies,
into caregiving strategies. Traditional feasts represent a common activity.
Ritual feasts are held according to customary standards, for example, at

[8]Willy DeGeyndt, "Health Behavior and Health Needs in Urban Indians in Minneapolis," *Health Service Reports,* 88 (April 1973):360–66.

[9]John G. Red Horse and Marvin Feit, "Urban Native American Preventive Health
Care." Paper presented at the American Public Health Association Meeting, Miami Beach,
Florida, 18–22 October 1976.

[10]Frances Densmore, *Chippewa Customs* (Minneapolis, Minn.: Ross and Haines,
1970).

Table 2.   Individual seeking aid—numbered according to order of significance and sequential path followed by urban Indians seeking help

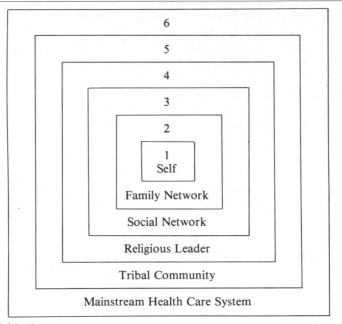

1. Individual
2. Goes to immediate family first
3. Goes to extended family (cousins, aunts, uncles)—social network
4. Goes to religious leader
5. Goes to tribal council
6. Finally goes to formalized health care system

the seasons' changes or at naming ceremonies. Preventive feasts are conducted to bring a family together whenever danger is imminent. Celebrative feasts are held during special occasions, such as Mother's Day observances. American Indian people, of course, feel comfortable in these surroundings. Moreover, they are secure in developing relationships with American Indian service providers who attend the feasts.

Ronald Lewis developed an interesting schematic through a tracking of Indian health behavior in Milwaukee, Wisconsin.[11] Table 2 identifies various resource levels and a sequence of behavior that emerged from his investigation. It confirms network behavior. Its prevailing characteristic is that the mainstream health care system is used only after network resources are exhausted.

[11] Ronald Lewis, "But We Have Been Helping Indians for a Long Time..." April 1977, p. 9, School of Social Work, University of Wisconsin, Milwaukee, Wisconsin. Unpublished research.

CONCLUSION

The objective of this article has been to identify important attributes of American Indian family network structure and cultural behavior and to inform professionals about the importance of culture as a variable in human services, especially as it affects understanding within an interactive field.

Because any health care is dependent upon client utilization, an understanding of American Indian network behavior appears critical to policy development and service planning efforts.

Using Levine's social conservation model, two critical human ecology imperatives emerge: 1) to identify traditional, long-standing cultural attributes, which have contributed to family cohesiveness and individual mental health, and 2) to develop human service systems which reaffirm a sense of family purpose.

An exigency specific to American Indians is that the cultural and structural integrity of extended family networks be revitalized and be supported. The authors believe that the adoption of a social conservation model by the human services would greatly improve service efficiency and, at the same time, vigorously enrich the quality of life of a currently alienated and underserved client population.

7

Suicide among the Cheyenne Indians

Larry H. Dizmang

Suicide among a number of tribes of American Indians has been recognized as a serious problem for many years. An urgent "cry for help" was made at the Los Angeles Suicide Prevention Center in June 1966 by a social worker asking for advice in handling a near epidemic of suicide attempts among the adolescents of the Northern Cheyenne. Over the next several months some of the problems began to unfold as the author consulted with various members of the tribe and members of the Public Health Service hospital staff.

The high incidence of suicide among the Indians seemed, upon study, to be caused by a breakdown in the ways of acquiring and sustaining self-esteem and a disintegration of the culturally evolved means of dealing with aggression. Suicide among Northern Cheyenne males is reported to have been rare in the early history of the tribe. When a man became depressed or lost face for some reason, the usual means of dealing with such a situation was to organize a small war party. During the ensuing battle, the warrior would either perform some feat of bravery which would renew his self-esteem or he would engage in a suicidally brave act in which he was killed (although this was not considered suicide). Suicide among the Cheyenne women, however, was a more frequent occurrence although still relatively rare. Suicide among the women, usually by hanging, seemed to stem most often from an unhappy, cruel, or childless marriage.

To relieve the tribe of bad luck caused by either suicide or homicide, the elaborate "cleansing of the arrows" was performed. Even though suicide created the same potential for ill fate as homicide, it was not taboo and the general feeling seemed to be that, if a Cheyenne chose to take his life, he must have good reason to do so. To provoke suicide in another individual, however, was considered homicide and punished accordingly.

Intragroup aggression of any kind was strictly forbidden. The Cheyenne child learned very early that the expression of aggression toward another Cheyenne child or adult was a serious offense. Punish-

Reprinted with permission from *Bulletin of Suicidology,* 1967, July, 8-11.

ment for violating this taboo among the children did not involve physical rebuff but verbal shaming. Thus, by the time the child had reached adulthood, he had very strong inhibitions concerning the expression of aggression toward any member of his own tribe. Consistent with later patterns in adulthood, the "approved" way a Cheyenne child could express his agression was to set up mock battles with an "enemy" or to enact a buffalo hunt. One of the major ways of handling aggression within the tribe, generally among the men, was by self-mutilative behavior, which was primarily ritualized in the Sun Dance, where one could engage in various degrees of self-torture. Participation in this ritual was as important in handling aggressive feelings as going into battle with an enemy.

After they were confined to the reservation, the Indians were forbidden to hold their Sun Dance or carry out any other "primitive and barbaric rituals." They could no longer hunt the nearly extinct buffalo, and of course fighting between tribes was outlawed. A Government program designed to improve health conditions forced the Indian men to cut their long hair, a prized symbol of their strength; and, because the Indian could no longer support himself or his family on the reservation, the Government was forced to set up welfare programs, which only added to the rapid downward spiral of increasing dependency and loss of self-esteem.

Two major symptoms of the present cultural deterioration are the high rate of alcoholism and the exceptionally high incidence of violent injuries, which include suicide, homicide, and accidents. On the basis of the background information, it seems far more than coincidence that, as the culturally derived ways of dealing with aggression and renewing self-esteem were systematically lost, the aggression began to manifest itself in culturally self-destructive ways. When the aggression was abruptly contained, it rapidly turned either on other members of the tribe or on self. The other alternative was to attempt to dissolve some of the unmanageable aggression in alcohol. The alcohol, however, only delays the aggression rather than dissolving it, for the individual dies from the chronic complications of alcohol intake, or he dies in an accident, or commits a homicide while intoxicated.

When an individual (or the culture) is denied means for dealing with instinctual feelings, it essentially boxes him in, and the result is a feeling of hopelessness and helplessness. This intolerable feeling results in a reflex-escape reaction. Escape can come in the form of intoxication, the development of a state of depressed uninvolvement with one's self and the world, or suicide. The constructive way of escaping an intolerable position is to leave the situation and move toward a more workable alternative. For the Cheyenne, this might be to leave the reservation and enter the white man's world or to evolve a new "subculture" on the reservation or elsewhere. For the Northern Cheyenne, neither of these has been a workable alternative. The reasons for the failure of these alternatives are complex, but they are the keys to unlocking the position in which the Indians find themselves.

A number of major obstacles block the Cheyenne from being able psychologically to synthesize his rich heritage with the present-day world. First, there is the problem of communication. The Cheyenne language is still the primary language; English remains the secondary language. Thus basically a Cheyenne still "thinks" in Cheyenne; he reads and speaks English but does not "understand" or think the same way we do . In reality, complex abstract communication with a Cheyenne is very difficult, even when both parties *speak* the same language.

The Cheyenne encounters a second problem when he endeavors to transfer from his own culture to that of the white man. As the child is growing up learning Cheyenne, he is simultaneously saturated with Cheyenneness; that is, the old Cheyenne legends and customs and the way of life of the Great Cheyenne are instilled into the child. As the child gains in awareness, he begins to find that his greatness is no more. The legends and stories of heroic deeds are only memories now, and he himself feels the defeat. As the child reaches adolescene, much of his normal rebelliousness is directed toward the white man, while the Cheyenne simultaneously feels contempt for his own people at having been defeated. The school and mass media only compound the problem as the boy learns what the outside and white world is like. At some point the white world usually becomes tempting, and as the psychological and physical move is made to leave the reservation the first real crisis occurs; for along with murder one of the worst crimes a Cheyenne can commit against his people is to desert them—and this boy has a *Cheyenne* conscience. There is a tremendous push to leave the reservation, but almost always a greater pull to stay. For those who do manage to leave, it is almost always temporary, for the guilt of having left is very powerful. The white man's world is not that well understood, and the built-in feeling of inferiority *plus* the guilt topple many who manage the initial "desertion."

The third major problem of the Cheyenne who decides to leave is that he has "no place to go." When a Negro breaks away from the South, for example, he almost always has a Negro community to which he can go as an initial stepping-stone before he eventually finds his own place in the larger community. This "stepping-stone effect" of a friendly community within a larger "unknown" or "hostile" community is almost a necessity for an immigrant of any kind. There are no Cheyenne "communities" outside the reservation for the few who are able to make the initial break.

The problems outlined above are among a few of the major obstacles that effectively thwart the Cheyenne from breaking away from his present situation and prevent his being assimilated into the white-man's world. The questions still remain: What can be done now to alleviate or interrupt the near epidemic of suicide and suicide attempts and what can be done on a larger range basis to resolve some of the underlying "social distruption" that is creating a cultural dead end for these people?

The answer to the first question is perhaps found in identifying individuals in trouble early enough to be able to offer them a more constructive alternative than suicide. An emergency mental health service or suicide-prevention program with a 24-hour telephone answering service is inappropriate because there are few telephones on the reservation. Who then are the "gatekeepers" of this community? Who would most likely come into contact with potentially suicidal persons or, conversely, who would most likely be sought out by a Cheyenne when he is in psychological trouble? From many conversations with the Public Health Service staff, the president and members of the tribal council, the clergy, the tribal judge, and the VISTA (Volunteers in Service to America) workers, it became increasingly clear that several key groups carry the major "gatekeeping" responsibility for this community. Two of the three adolescents who attempted suicide contacted two VISTA workers. The VISTA workers, the clergy, and a group called the Community Health Workers seem to be the major "gatekeepers" for this particular community. The Community Health Workers are Cheyenne who have received special training primarily in public health practices and practical nursing procedures and who are beginning to be seen by their people as "where you go for help."

One way to deal with the immediate problem of suicide and attempted suicide in this particular community is to alert the three primary "gatekeeping" groups—the clergy, VISTA, and the Community Health Workers—to become much more sensitive to cries for help. It is important to help the "gatekeepers" recognize the situations in which individuals need referral or consultation. It is likewise important for the "gatekeepers" to have a strong backup "team" to deal with individuals in crisis as they are identified. In this particular community, the backup personnel would be the Public Health Service hospital staff. Nothing would be more destructive than to set up a sensitive front-line defense and then not have readily available backup resources.

A series of training seminars could be set up for the VISTA workers, the clergy, and the Community Health Workers. Simultaneously, another series of seminars at the professional level could be offered to the hospital staff. Two psychiatrists 60 miles away at the Veterans Administration Hospital in Sheridan, Wyo., have already established a consultative relationship with the hospital staff and would be participants in the professional training seminars.

This overall plan would utilize three teams: 1) The "gatekeepers" of the community, who would do much of the primary case-finding, 2) the

Public Health Service hospital staff, who would take referrals of individuals needing intensive medical or psychological help and who would consult with the community workers on other cases that could be managed with support in the community, and 3) the psychiatrists at the Veterans Administration hospital, the backup team for the Public Health Service hospital staff who would take over cases requiring special management and would provide continuing education for the Public Health Service hospital staff.

The answer to the second question—how to resolve some of the "social disruption" that confronts the Indians—would seem to be in teaching those who deal with Cheyenne to undertand them historically as a people and the processes that lead to their cultural dead end. This holds the most promise in helping them find their own way out. If a Cheyenne wants to leave the reservation, he needs the tools to function in the white-man's world. Most specifically, he needs to develop a concept of the white-man's working habits, which are contrary to the Cheyenne's basic way of life. Presently, a Neighborhood Youth Corps program is being started for adolescents, and the response has been overwhelmingly positive. This is a story in itself. Unfortunately it is an extremely rare example of a program where adolescents can learn regular work habits, spend their time improving their reservation, receive money and satisfaction, and, most important, may gain approval of the tribe for their efforts.

If the Cheyenne chooses to stay on the reservation and not to integrate with the outside world, there is almost no way for him to support his family other than to accept welfare. Even if he can find a job, outlets for spending his leisure time are not available. Hence alcohol becomes a close friend and ally. Some efforts are being made to create jobs on the reservation and to provide some leisure-time outlets, but the efforts are small. In any case, these activities are being thrust upon the Indians in such a way as to provoke rejection and are thus relatively ineffective.

The larger problem is basically one of "community organization" in a broad sense. These terribly "beaten" people still hold on to a core of pride and self-respect: They are still basically an industrious and intelligent people. If these latent but dying internal resources could be tapped, a cultural process of self-renewal rather than self-destruction could be reinstated.

8

Cultural Perspective on Treatment Modalities with Native Americans

Ronald Lewis

INTRODUCTION

... I would like to invite you to look at mental illness through the eyes of the Native Americans. Although outwardly, there have been numerous changes among the Native Americans' traditions, their basic orientation toward mental health and physical health (which are not seen as separate entities) is the reflection of an unseen harmony between an individual and his environment. It includes three areas: the natural living world, relationships with fellow human beings, and the mystical. Mental illness indicates an imbalance between man and any of the three above areas or all the above areas (Native Americans approach this matter in an holistic manner). The illness is attributed to the breaking of societal norms, to a contact with mystical powers, or to malevolence on the part of others. If one adheres to this perspective of mental illness, one can view the Native Americans as a community of people, struggling valiantly, but caught between two life-styles, two cultures, and all the ensuing complexities.

To work with Native Americans, one must effect a blending of the Western philosophy and the Native American philosophy. Native Americans are often willing to accept new ideas if they fit into their culture. This paper represents one attempt at syncretizing the Western and Native American philosophies in order to develop styles of working with the Native Americans. Treatment modalities with Native Americans must include cultural understanding.

HEALING POWERS

In working with Native Americans, one must first recognize the cultural concept of healing power. To the Native American, healing power is evident in all of nature. Nature, the life process itself, offers people

From a paper presented at the NASW Professional Symposium, San Diego, California, November 1977. Reprinted by permission of the author.

numerous opportunities for healing power if they are willing to open themselves up to such awareness. For the Native American, the healing process is not compartmentalized, but is evident in all he does. This is an holistic approach and is done to validate an inwardness as a means to achieving insights as well as an experiential connection with the world of nature. For example, Native American religious celebrations are often a community effort to promote and share this very mode of healing. Here is a merging of social interdependency and inwardness in order to connect human beings with nature.

A creative mental health worker can blend Western philosophy with Native American healing events. In addition, the worker can time some of his or her efforts at insightful awareness with important positive experiences that emerge for the client or groups as a result of ceremonial happenings. For example, therapy was held after a ceremonial dance and at the patient's home [disguised cases]:

> Ben Dancewell is a thirty-four-year-old full-blooded Cheyenne-Arapahoe who was medically diagnosed as an alcoholic. He is married and has four children. He is an excellent dancer and has won several contests. The timing of the therapy was unique in that it was held after the ceremonial dances.

> The ceremonial dances served Ben in many therapeutic ways such as 1) helping him to ventilate his feelings; 2) helping him possess a unique sense of identity and pride in his culture; 3) giving him a great sense of belonging through being with other Native Americans. 4) As he danced, one could see other Indians giving him support; therefore, he gained a unique support system. 5) This experience enhanced his altruistic feelings and made him uniquely ready for therapy.

> In attendance was his entire primary family, as well as his parents. Each week, he began to ventilate, for example, about his pride at being an Indian but how he felt inferior when he was in the majority culture. After several sessions of ventilating and using the extended family as support, drinking diminished and he was able to hold a job.

A variation on this technique can occur when a client reports an individual experience with some power-revealing event in his life. If the social worker is able to appreciate the Native American's attunement with nature, he or she can make use of both positive and negative forces reported by the client in his or her personal dialogue with the vast and varied world of nature. This will help clarify directions and conflict that emerge in the client's awareness. Sometimes the social worker can help the client assess both meaning and potential actions to such events.

> Joe Nighthawk, a twenty-one-year-old full blooded Cherokee, severely depressed, came to the therapist very excited because a nighthawk (sacred bird to the Cherokee) had been found injured in his backyard and he had nursed it back to health. To him this was indeed a good omen. Instead of passing it off as pure superstition, the therapist stated that he was pleased because, with the appearance of the omen, improvement in all areas of life

might occur and that maybe this sign meant he should use the positive forces and strength in his life to cope. The patient appeared very encouraged and elated as he left the office.

At other times the worker will encourage the client to make use of a sorcerer or medicine man who can deal with such phenomena in ways available to the helping professional. The worker may ask the aid of the medicine man (or religious leaders).

> Ben Brown, a thirty-five-year-old full-blooded Creek Indian, came to the P.H.S. Clinic complaining, in Creek, of many psychosomatic complaints such as nausea, vomiting, and trembling. He was checked medically, and the doctors suggested that it was psychosomatic. The wife led the therapist aside and suggested a "curse has been put on him, and only the religious leader could cure him; could she use him." The therapist concurred. Once a week the medicine man met with the man. No information concerning the man's curse was discussed with the therapist or any members of the family. Sessions were dealt with secretly, but the psychosomatic manifestations began to diminish and the Indian returned to his job and family.

An important form of revealing power forces is that of dreams and visions. The worker needs to appreciate the Native American's way of perceiving such occurrences. Dreams and visions are commonly prophetic rather than revealing of historical conflicts. "Psychotic" phenomena will often have a similar positive meaning to the Native American.

> One Indian woman who was very depressed over her husband's death reported a dream in which her husband came back to her as a bird. In her husband's voice, the bird said that he was in a better place now and was waiting for her to join him. He said that she must be strong for the grandchildren. After talking about the dream the woman seemed happier and relieved about her future. The therapist expressed confidence in the message of the dream, but did not attempt to interpret it. This type of situation needs no interpretation to an Indian person—its meaning is quite clear.

What is of critical importance is the worker's attitude toward use of dreams, visions, and power forces. If he or she takes an unaccepting paternalistic stance toward such "superstitions," he or she will quickly lose whatever power of influence the Native American client may have given him or her. That is why the "Don Juan" experience of Carlos Castaneda has been so immensely important. One cannot look at the world through rational, pragmatic eyes. Daniel Noel's book, *Seeing Castaneda,* is an effort to understand Castaneda's writings as a valid although vastly different way of understanding reality.[1]

NATURAL HELPING SYSTEMS

When dealing with Native Americans, mental health work must take on a systems perspective. The worker must be able to analyze problem-solving networks that Native Americans follow. When the Native American has a problem, he or she first goes to the immediate family. If the problem is not resolved there, the social network is then contacted. This includes friends, neighbors, relatives, a bar, or anywhere else where one will listen. Next the person will go to the spiritual or religious leader. If the problem still is not resolved, the person may go to the tribal council. The last place the person will go for help after all else has failed or if he or she is dying or has done something drastic is a formal agency.

One reason for the failure of mental health work with Native Americans offered by mainstream society is that it has not established linkages with the natural helping system. Too often social workers have set up medical model mental health offices and have expected the Native Americans to come there for help.

Not only have mental health workers not established linkages with the natural helping systems, but they have also proved unknowledgeable in the traditional medicine and healings that are practiced in their area. In addition, the attitudes of the mental health workers have driven these practices underground.

Because it is so important to be able to use the natural helping system for the good of the Native American people, it is essential that the mental health worker understands the system with which he or she must work. Minuchin states:

> Like the anthropologist, the mental health worker joins the culture with which he is dealing. In the same oscillating rhythm, he engages and disengages. He experences the pressures of the cultural system. At the same time he observes the system, making deductions that enable him to transform his experience into a community map from which he derives therapeutic goals. To understand and know a system in this intimate, experiential way is a vital component of community therapy [p. 124].[2]

The community map approach was used by this psychiatric social worker and a paraprofessional in developing the first comprehensive mental health program for Native Americans in Oklahoma. Rather than hanging out a shingle and waiting for clients, the mental health workers used the first six months in a friendly professional outreach program. The workers began this outreach program by going to the families of known mentally ill patients whose names were obtained from the Indian Health Service. In informal discussions, it was discovered where the family went for help in crisis situations. After obtaining permission from the family, the mental health workers visited the social network, which contains significant others, such as cousins, aunts, uncles, and so on. It was found from the social network that the religious leaders were a very important aid in the care and treatment of the mentally ill. Finally, the mental health workers very quietly visited the tribal community meetings, explaining to the tribe that they worked with these people who had personal problems.

Within six months, through the use of this community map, the workers found more clients coming to the office than they could handle. They did not destroy the broader community health care delivery system but became a part of the natural helping system of the community (See Figure 1).

Too often in our service to the Native American people, inadvertently we bypass the natural helping system. We must learn to work with the community as it is, not as we would like for it to be.

The community helping system for the Native American represents a refuge in a highly hostile environment. It is a trusted source of aid rather than a suspected source of surveillance, which is the way most Native Americans view the health care delivery systems provided by the whites.

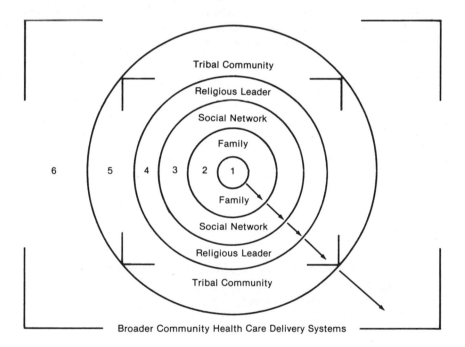

1. Individual
2. Goes to family first
3. Then to extended family (cousins, aunts, uncles, etc.) — social network
4. Religious leader
5. Tribal council
6. Finally formalized health care delivery system

Figure 1. Helping methodology must take on a system perspective. *Schema:* Individual seeking aid. Numbered in order of significance for Native American and path followed for seeking help.

Health care delivery systems must blend in with the community they are to serve.

SELF-HELP GROUPS

A third concept of treatment modality is that of peer or self-help groups. Self-help groups can be defined as voluntary associations among individuals who share a common need or problem and who seek to use the group as a means of dealing with that need or problem.[3] Although self-help groups have existed for a long time, mental health professionals are now beginning to look seriously at the self-help model.[4] Self-help groups have taken a variety of forms: Alcoholics Anonymous, Synanon, Seven Steppers, Take Off Pounds Sensibly, Recover, Inc., and cultural identity groups such as the Black Muslims. Self-help groups have traditionally avoided leadership from helping professionals.

The Native Americans have had a long history of attempting mutual self-help. They have tried to cope with life, however ineffectively, by the use of peer self-help groups, while relating very little to organizations that are imposed upon them—to be of aid, the mental health worker must become part of that self-help organization.

The self-help groups could be developed along these lines:

1. Assessment and counseling (group therapy, family planning)
2. Environmental arrangements (halfway houses, nursing homes, homemaker services)
3. Training, education, and equipment (work training, nutrition, home management)
4. Protective and legal (protective services for adults and children, legal aid)
5. Liaison (information and referral, resource mobilization-social change)
6. Transportation (escort service)
7. Social advocacy

My experience has taught me that regardless of where you start in a self-help group, you will come back to one major topic: the Native Americans' realistic rage at dehumanizing forces that have oppressed them for so long. This is a theme that will inevitably reoccur—that of dissatisfaction with the impersonal order of a contemporary society that does not adequately provide for the needs of its members. "Native Americans will not be helped by anybody or any policy which assumes that they are the problem that needs to be changed. It is the environment, the system, the bureaucracy that is the problem."[5]

Every self-help group, regardless of its stated goals, must give the Indian pride and dignity in who and what he or she is. Wilfred Pelletier, a full-blooded Indian, described his life as an Indian and the importance of this self-realization:

> The first step towards surviving in an alien environment is to feel proud of who you are. Being surrounded by an aggressive and confident majority has made me somewhat defensive; I have spent a lot of years trying to convince myself, after being told all my life that I was no good because I was an Indian, that I am really all right. That I am a human being like everyone else and that maybe we Indians did have something to contribute to society, something that was sadly missing in the dominant culture.[6]

The journey of the Indian people is not an outward journey to find good housing, plumbing, and so on, but the first journey is an inward one to regain pride and dignity in themselves. The mental health workers are in a unique position to help the Native Americans regain this pride and dignity in themselves.

CONCLUSION

Mental health and mental illness must be redefined so that this definition applies to all cultures. As long as we look at the individual as the cause of mental illness then we will continue to "blame the victim."

It was succinctly stated when Mary Richmond said that "the good social worker . . . does not go on helping people out of a ditch. Pretty soon she begins to find out what ought to be done to get rid of the ditch."[7]

Three types of treatment modalities have been discussed that have proved effective in the treatment of mental illness in Native Americans: healing powers, natural helping systems, and self-help groups. Each of these concepts is an integral part of the Native Americans' culture dealing with their basic belief in the unseen harmony that should exist between an individual and the individual's environment. These concepts then must become a part of the mental health worker's methodology in the treatment of mental illness.

We don't know how effective our therapeutic modalities are with Native Americans. Is it possible that some of our treatment modalities run counter to the community concept of mental health and mental illness? Do we really know from data available what constitutes a Native American community and its constituents? Is it necessary that the values of the therapeutic community take on the values of the community being served? These questions need to be asked and some attempt made to seek answers to them. Thus, I hope that this paper will encourage others to look in a different way at the psychopathological aspects of Native Americans and, in addition, to question basic therapeutic methods.

REFERENCE NOTES

1. Daniel Noel, *Seeing Castaneda* (New York: G. P. Putnam's Sons, Capricorn Books 1976), p. 5.
2. Salvador Minuchin, *Family and Family Therapy* (Harvard University Press, 1974), pp. 2 and 3.
3. *Journal of Applied Behavioral Science,* Vol. 12, No. 3, 1976, p. 433.
4. *The Journal of Applied Behavioral Science,* Special issue / Self-Help Groups, Volume 12. No. 3, July-August-September, 1976.
5. *Journal of Applied Behavioral Science,* Vol. 12, No. 3, 1976, p. 454.
6. Wilfred Pelletier, "For Every North American Indian Who Begins to Disappear, I Also Begin to Disappear," unpublished paper, p. 5.
7. Mary F. Richmond, *Social Diagnosis* (New York: Russell Sage Foundation, 1917) p. 13.

REFERENCES

Attneave, Carolyn. *Psychiatric Annals,* Volume 4, No. 1, November 1974.

Cafferty, Pastora San Juan, and Leon Chestang. *The Diverse Society: Implications for Social Policy.*National Association of Social Workers publication No.: CBC-072-C. Washington, D.C., 1976.

Capps, Walter Holden. *Seeing With A Native Eye.* New York: Harper and Row, 1976.

The Journal of Applied Behavioral Science. "Self-help Groups." Volume 12, No. 3, 1976.

Minuchin, Salvador. *Families and Family Therapy.* Cambridge, Massachusetts: Harvard University Press, 1974.

Richmond, Mary F. *Social Diagnosis.* New York: Russel Sage Foundation) 1917.

Thomas, Alexander, and Samuel Sillen. *Racism and Psychiatry.* Secaucus, New Jersey: Citadel Press, 1974.

9

The Papago Psychology Service
A Community Mental Health Program on an American Indian Reservation

Marvin W. Kahn, Cecil Williams,
Eugene Galvez, Linda Lejero, Rex Conrad, and George Goldstein

INTRODUCTION[1]

The Papago Psychological Service is run by the Papago Indian tribe and is staffed largely by Papago Indians who have been trained as mental health technicians. This clinic is unique among mental health services for Indians in several respects: 1) The Papago tribe has complete control of the funds for the service and sets its own policy and hires its own personnel. The clinic director is a Papago. 2) The service was developed for a rather traditional Indian group. Respect for the culture, traditions, and wishes of the Papago community was carefully considered in developing the clinic. In this connection, professional consultation with Papago medicine men was built into the program from the start. 3) Adaptations of current mental health techniques in assessment, therapy, and consultation have been and are being developed for the clinic's functioning.

The mental health needs of native American people are today largely the responsibility of the mental health program of the Indian Health Service. Basic to the program is the realization that indigenous people, both professional and paraprofessional, ultimately will be, as they should, the providers of that service. Therefore, the Papago Psychology Service is of great importance in that it is the prototype of a mental health delivery system for Indian communities.

Based on a symposium given at the Convention of the American Psychological Association in Montreal, Quebec, Canada, 1973, George Goldstein, Chairman. The papers have been edited by the first author.

Reprinted with permission from *American Journal of Community Psychology*, 1975, 3(2), 81–97.

[1]This part was written by George Goldstein.

Not only have the staff become sophisticated in traditional psychotherapy and consultation models but they have also managed to translate these techniques into traditional Papago life experiences. There is an open and meaningful two-way interaction between the staff of the Papago Psychological Service and traditional medicine men and healers within the Papago community. They have been able to bridge both cultures for the most meaningful form of psychological service to the Papago people. Traditional medicine men have united in themselves the three learned professions: theology, law, and medicine. Imagine a society in which there is no difference between a church and a hospital. Usually in ceremonies there is no way to tell what is healing and what is worship. Moral guidance and clinical judgments are inextricable elements in ceremonial practice. Today among many local healers, school boards, young Anglo-educated Indians returning to the reservation, and other indigenous authorities there exists a growing desire to reestablish traditional values which the white society has, under the guise of religion or education, replaced with its own. This need is being filled by the inclusion of medicine men in the Papago mental health program. It is for this reason that the program has become accepted by the older non-English-speaking Papago community as well as the young bilingual Papagos who have returned to the reservation.

While the Papago Psychology Service is a mental health program adapted for the traditions and culture of a rather traditional Indian group, the greater psychological community may have much to learn from the Papago approach.

TRIBAL PRACTICES AND TRIBAL HEALTH PROGRAMS[2]

One important aspect of Papago culture and tradition is that the Papago people shun individual glory or success. The tribe's approach to the overall development and management of tribal health programs reflects this. It has come to be known as the "Bith Haa" model, after the Papago term for cooking pot. The tribal mental health program is in the pot with other tribal programs. Cooking together with the other programs undoubtedly gives it a rather different taste than that of traditional programs.

The Bith Haa process is similar to the process traditionally used by Papagos as a functional means of defining problems, developing and selecting alternatives to resolve these problems, making decisions, and carrying out the necessary activities. This process develops human resources to their full potential by recognizing and utilizing the appropriate experiences and multi-skills of either an individual or a group when decisions are made or approaches taken to resolve problems.

---

[2]This part was written by Cecil Williams, Director of the Papago Psychology Service. Mr. Williams is a Papago Indian.

The evolution of the health programs did not follow that of typical Anglo organizational structures. In fact, without knowing it, the tribe has operated its health programs in a very traditional Papago way. The prototype of this is that whenever there is an event in a village there is a meeting or a series of meetings held to determine what is to be done. Once a plan evolves, the particular individuals with the needed skills do their part to make sure that the project is implemented. For example, if there is a dance or a feast, a cow is usually slaughtered. Those members of the village who are knowledgeable about livestock will go after the cow. A woman having overall experience with cooking will be selected to serve as head cook, and so forth.

The villages or communities as a rule have functioned in this fashion for hundreds and hundreds of years and still do today, so that every member of a community contributes and decisions are made as a group. Figure 1 is a graphic illustration of the Bith Haa model.

This concept, simple as it sounds, is being applied to a fairly large organization that includes seven health programs and is very complex in

Figure 1. Organizational model of the Papago tribal health programs (Bith Haa model).

nature. Close to a hundred employees are involved. The program operations are as effective as those of other agencies now on the reservation. Factionalization of programs and agencies is minimized. People are beginning to have a common goal and still retain their identity.

To exemplify how this concept was put into action recently, the tribal health organization started a project, known as the Diarrhea Control Project, to alleviate gastroenteritis among Papago infants. Diarrhea has been a major cause of death during the summer months on the reservation. Several programs and agencies participated. This effort was directed and coordinated for the tribe by one of the tribal health program directors, who is a Papago, as are all the tribal health program directors. The Diarrhea Control Project succeeded beyond expectations. For the first time that anybody can recall, there were no infant deaths on the Papago reservation. Such a coordinated, integrated attack on a health problem had never been previously attempted and the approach was entirely different from what had previously been known on the reservation. This coordinated project is now well known throughout the Indian Health Service.

Conceptually, mental health is considered an element of the overall health of a Papago individual. When a Papago speaks, he will say to another, "How are you?" It does not mean how is your mental health. It means how is all that is around you. The Papagos have translated that concept into a health goal: "to live as O'odham with the environment." The reservation environment is mostly desert, but the Papagos learned to survive on it a long time ago.

This philosophy of the Papagos has implications for the development and staffing of individual programs, and for the kind of financial support that programs obtain. It is also a central mechanism whereby the tribe sets its own priorities in terms of health and other related areas. The tribe is evolving its own way of dealing with these matters and is developing the expertise of its own people. Again, the mental health service within this tribal context promises to be different from the orthodox Anglo model. Perhaps it might even suggest a more effective one than exists in many places.

The tribe is moving toward control of its own health system. The Mental Health Program is one of the first, and perhaps will serve as a model and a test for other Indian tribes who attempt to move toward control of their own health systems.

The Papago health programs involve the use of the medicine man, who has been recognized by the Papago Council as a very important part of the culture and heritage. The Public Health Service has accepted him and cooperates fully in having him practice in the hospital. Finally, it is not particularly uncommon for physicians to make referrals to the medicine man.

At least on the Papago reservation it has been shown that, given the opportunity, Indian communities can work cooperatively in assessing their problems and reasonably synthesize efforts for their own well-being. This is inherent in the culture and traditions of Indian tribes as evidenced by thousands of years of survival.

THE PAPAGO COMMUNITY: ITS PROBLEMS AND THE TRADITIONAL PAPAGO MEANS OF TREATMENT[3]

The Papagos have lived in the same desert area continuously since long before the white man came to the New World. While they have not been physically displaced like some of the other tribes, their living area has been considerably restricted by the incursion of the white man. The traditional economy was that of gathering wild vegetation in season, hunting, and limited farming.

Anthropologists describe Papagos as being friendly, nonaggressive people whose culture supports noncompetitive approaches to most things (Joseph, Spicer, & Chesky, 1949; Spicer, 1941). Individual glory or success is avoided and traditionally tends to carry a certain degree of social stigma. Respect for age and elders is a very important factor in the culture.

The Current Papago Reservation Community

The Papago reservation is as large as the State of Connecticut, and the population on the main reservation is about 8000. Most of the people are concentrated in several large settlements, the largest of these being a community of about 2000. There are a number of small villages scattered about this vast region. A small village might consist of 3–7 houses scattered over an area of several miles.

Papagos tend to be traditional in terms of observing their culture and this is especially true in the more remote villages.

The older people are the ones who are most likely to carry out the customs and the traditions of the tribe. They make sure that the children are properly initiated into the traditional customs. They may try to pick the bride or groom for their children to make sure they marry someone from far off who is not related to the family.

Traditionally, Papagos weave and sell baskets, raise some cattle and very few horses, and make some general products such as cheese, leather, ropes, and pottery.

In most instances, the head of the household receives his financial support through the Tribal Work Experience Program (TWEP), which is

---

[3]This part was written by Linda Lejero, a mental health worker at the clinic. Mrs. Lejero is a Papago Indian.

essentially a form of welfare. However, the able-bodied recipients must put in an 8-hour day doing some jobs in and around their villages, such as fence repair and restoring homes. In the absence of a male head of household, the wife and children can receive various forms of aid to dependents. The fact is that there simply is not any real industry on the reservation, and the unemployment rate is something over 50%.

Men have gone with their families to relocate in some of the large cities and have learned trades and skills such as welding and auto mechanics. However, these are skills for which there are few jobs on the reservation. On the other hand, the skills that the women learn, often secretarial or nursing, tend to be in demand with various government or tribal bureaus and in the health services on the reservation. This, of course, creates the problem of the women being the breadwinners, having economic power and a kind of prestige.

When Indians relocate and work in a city, they feel very ill at ease with white people and in fact quite out of place in white society. Being noncompetitive, quiet, and shy with strangers, they have little or often no opportunity to meet and relate to others. For example, one couple relocated in a large California city. The husband trained as a welder and worked there for 4 years. The couple were unable to make friends with any of the Anglos during that period and avoided the few Indians who were available because they seemed just to want to go out and drink. They were very uncomfortable in public places. In fact, they would only go to the drive-in movies as they felt quite segregated and apart from the rest of society. These people commented on how they seldom saw Indians in any kind of a mixed group and how Indians were most often by themselves and appeared very sad and lonely.

Poor housing is one of the main living problems on the reservation. It is crowded and facilities such as running water or electricity are rare. Yet many Papagos are not that unhappy with their housing.

Alcoholism, depression, and suicide certainly are among the most visible social background problems and these seem related to the lack of employment. The woman works and the man feels uncomfortable about what he has not been able to contribute to his family.

Traditional Papago Healing

Before white man's medicine, when a condition that Papagos defined as sickness continued, the people would contact a medicine man. Gradually many Papagos have come to accept, at least in part, white man's medicine for certain kinds of physical disorders, but much less so for psychological disorders.

There are two specialties in medicine men's practice. Determining the cause is one, and curing particular disorders is the other. Different medicine men often perform each function separately. The diagnostic medicine man has the ability to determine what sort of cure will be used. Through using lighted cigarettes and carefully inhaling and blowing smoke over the patient, and waving the sacred eagle feathers, a diagnostic medicine man can determine the patient's sickness.

The cure usually involves a "Papago sing" in which the other type of medicine man chants out sacred healing songs. In addition to the ceremony, he may prescribe herbs for the patient to drink or administer them himself. Most often he will just restrict the patient's diet if he has chosen to give the sacred earth mixture. He may have the patient omit salt and grease from his meals, forbid him to eat meat, or restrict anything cold or red for at least 3-5 days.

While only a medicine man determines what the offending spirit is, there are some types of physical ailments which tend to be associated with different animals, birds, or insects. Mentioned here are a few of them:

1. Tarantula: pain in the ear
2. Bees: draining pus from ears
3. Quail: if eaten dims the eyesight
4. Turtle: difficulty walking
5. Ants: itchy eyes
6. Devil: person who is gifted at certain things such as crafts, horse management, music
7. Horned toad: pains in the joints
8. Deer: severe headaches
9. Rabbit blood: sores

The owl is feared as it is said to be a person returning from the dead, but owl feathers are sacred and are used as tools of the medicine man.

The older, more traditional Papagos routinely bring their problems of mental health to a medicine man. Younger people are becoming increasingly aware of mental health and are referred from the hospitals, schools, or the court, or are self-referrals.

Very often, however, our procedure requires that we understand where a patient is in terms of the things that he feels can help him, and for many individuals this necessitates the combination and cooperation of the medicine man and the mental health technician.

THE INDIGENOUS PAPAGO MENTAL HEALTH WORKER[4]

Emphasis on the training and development of the Papago mental health workers has been a central feature of the clinic since its beginning. The mental health workers, especially the first ones, were trained on a very close tutorial basis with the clinic staff, especially in connection with the

[4]This part was written by Eugene Galvez, a mental health worker at the clinic. Mr. Galvez is a Papago Indian.

Clincial Psychology Graduate student externs in the program (Kahn & Delk, 1973). The training has always been mutually interactive: the Papagos being trained were also training the Anglo consultants and student staff in Papago ways and in Papago culture. Training in interviewing skills and clinical evaluation was stressed at first. Once those skills were in hand, training moved to techniques of supportive treatment, marital and family counseling, and individual counseling. A formal training program for Indian mental health workers has since been developed by the Indian Health Service, and the latest members of the group have the advantage of having both types of training.

The mental health workers function as the basic service providers in the clinic and are backed up by the professional consultants with whom they may jointly work on cases or consult with in terms of other cases. The mental health workers have a very broad role in the program which is quite necessary in terms of the language and cultural factors. The important thing is that the mental health workers know when they need consultation.

I had first heard about mental health through a friend who was working as a Community Health Representative. She had asked if I would be interested in a position in the mental health field. Although I really didn't know much about mental health, it sounded interesting, so I applied and was surprised that I was hired.

I learned the job mainly from on-the-job training, dealing with cases at the same time that I was learning and getting experience. We started with an introduction from the mental health staff that included the professional staff and the one already trained Papago mental health worker.

We then paired up with the trained people and learned as we went along. We had a lot of training sessions in the beginning, which included role playing and explanations of things. The most important thing I think a mental health worker needs to learn is to develop a trusting relationship with people with whom he is working. Being honest with people about what you are trying to do and how you are trying to find ways to help them and maintaining confidentiality are important. Confidentiality is particularly sensitive on a reservation, where many people are related or know each other. The villages are very small and things can get around rapidly. Developing the interviewing skills is also quite important, as well as knowing what kind of information you need to have in order to understand the problem. Things like observing people's behavior and expression during the interview and getting them to talk about their feelings and to trust you enough to tell the details of the problem are other important skills. We had to learn about neurosis and psychosis, and how these conditions can be changed or helped.

Our program tries to build ongoing training sessions using the professional staff to have regular weekly sessions about different topics in the field. We spend a lot of time learning about abnormal psychology and having in-depth case conferences. We also try to have a training session for the whole staff at the University of Arizona at least once every several months, where we can take up a topic sometimes through a film and discuss it.

We have developed our skills in helping people, both in Anglo ways and in Papago cultural ways and sometimes with a combination of both. While we see a good variety of types of cases, I tend to work a lot with couples with marital problems and often these involve problems of alcoholism. I've learned it's important when I work with a couple that I also involve a female mental health worker so that I'm not biased for the man.

It's also important in many of the Papago marital situations to get the husband to show the wife some affection. Papagos aren't people who show others their feelings very readily and this is often a problem in marital situations. Take, for example, the case of a middle-aged couple I worked with recently. The case involved alcoholism, as do many cases on the reservation. The husband had been intoxicated for some time, seemingly ignoring his spouse's feelings. This came to our attention as a result of his spouse being admitted to the hospital because of acute depression. I worked extensively with the wife providing supportive therapy while attempting to contact the husband.

We finally managed to get the couple together. I then enlisted the aid of a female mental health worker to provide marital counseling. There was a misinterpretation by the couple that the other member did not wish to continue the marriage. Our first task was to get the couple together to assure that each wanted to continue the marriage. Our second task was to get the couple to express their feeling for one another. After many sessions the couple began to realize that their situation was not as hopeless as it seemed. Since then they have been able to resolve some of their problems.

There was one case where both members were agreeable to counseling. Usually the man will be reluctant or in some cases will not show up at all.

Another case which is not a marital case but has more cultural factors involved is one in which our clinic received a referral from a public health nurse about an elderly but well-respected Papago medicine man whose family was concerned that he was acting strangely. Our clinic has always taken the position that we would consult with medicine men about Papagos whose behavior seemed more related to Papago tradition than Anglos' definitions of mental health problems. This was the first time we were in the position of being asked to evaluate the mental health of a medicine man and possibly be involved in a treatment program.

The medicine man's problem was expressed in fairly typical Papago terms. He felt the voices and accusations he was experiencing were the result of a spell put on him by another medicine man, possibly a group of them. We understand that he had previously consulted other medicine men to remove the spell, but to no avail.

Interestingly, the information we had was that the other medicine men suggested that the spell had gone too far and that the victim should seek help from our facility. There are, of course, many interesting facets to this case, one of the most important being what this says about the acceptance and utilization of our clinical service by the Papago people.

In another type of treatment program, mental health workers are involved with a specially adapted group therapy procedure undertaken with 15 Indian high school youths who had been in trouble with the law. The effectiveness of the procedure was evaluated in terms of change in delinquent acts known to authorities, and school attendance before and after therapy (Kahn, Lewis, & Galvez, 1974). The specialized approach to group treatment was devised because, in addition to the usual problems of working in this mode with adolescent delinquents, for this group the difficulty was compounded by a culture, like many other Indian cultures, in which intimate or personal revelations to peers or others are simply not made.

The adaptations of group procedure included 1) presenting therapy as hard work for which the participants would be paid an hourly wage, 2) having an indigenous Indian mental health technician as cotherapist, 3) using didactic presentation of topics of presumed interest to the group, such as alcoholism, homosexuality, and venereal disease, and 4) developing much of the discussion in the third person, talking about "someone else."

The results were encouraging. The group continued through the entire school year and indicated a desire to continue the next year. A comparison of delinquent records from the year previous to therapy, the records of the therapy year, plus records for 3 months beyond the end of therapy showed the following: that during the year prior to therapy each of the participants had from 1 to 4 arrests, or a total of 22 for the group. During the year period from the start of therapy to several months after the end of therapy, a total of only 3 arests, involving 2 of the 15 group members, had been made. This represents a reduction of 86% in the number of arrests from the onset of therapy. School attendance comparisons from the year previous to the year during which therapy occurred also showed improvement. The average number of days per month absent from school dropped from 2.74 to 1.76.

This is an example of one of our projects. We feel it represents the kind of adaptation of techniques we have mentioned. Thus the Papago mental health worker must not only work with his own culture but also adapt Anglo techniques to his own culture.

TRADITIONAL PSYCHOTHERAPY
ADAPTED TO THE PAPAGO CULTURE[5]

Several factors have influenced the methods employed when providing psychotherapy to the Papago people. The most obvious, of course, is the use, in many cases, of indigenous mental health technicians as the primary therapists. The technicians bear primary responsibility in nearly all of those cases where the client is a traditonal member of the tribe or has not become highly acculturated. Mental health technicians are generally employed in such cases because only they can establish rapport and only they can understand the subtleties communicated by the traditional Papago. It might be added that most of the therapy in the Papago Psychology Service is provide by the technicians regardless of the nature of the case.

Much of what follows from here pertains to the therapy performed by Anglo members of the clinic. This is not to say that the mental health technicians do not use these therapy methods. In fact, many of the following ideas originated with the Papago members of the clinic.

The Papago client brings several attitudes with him which influence the mode of therapy utilized. Many of these attitudes are due to the influence of the traditional culture and, more specifically, due to the influence of the medicine man or Mai Kai. Only he possesses the knowledge to heal and only a brief diagnostic interview is required before the healing ceremony begins. Clearly, this is much different from psychotherapy, wherein the client is an active participant and has a great deal of responsibility for his improvement.

Another attitude the Papago brings to therapy is that of secrecy regarding personal matters. Most Papagos loathe discussing personal information with anyone, and doing so with strangers is certainly most uncommon.

The paucity of verbal communication (as compared to the Anglo) is another variable which has considerable influence on therapeutic methodology. Impressionistically, it seems the Papagos really aren't very verbose among themselves and certainly not with Anglo professionals or, if you will, authority figures. This brings us to another attitudinal factor of considerable importance when dealing with a Papago client.

Papagos treat age and social status with a great deal of respect. And respect within the Papago culture is often expressed by silence.

Avoiding eye contact can also be of considerable importance when dealing with Papagos in any social setting, and this includes psychotherapy. Establishing and maintaining eye contact are considered to be impolite among these desert people and may be interpreted as anger.

---

[5]This part was written by Rex Conrad.

On the desert reservation, time is treated much differently than what urban dwellers are accustomed to. Papagos may be an hour late for a meeting and think nothing of it. This, we will discover, has a considerable influence on therapy.

These several factors then are of central importance when doing therapy with the Papagos. They include the importance of the mental health technicians, the influence of the medicine man, personal secrecy, a lack of verbosity, respect for age and social status, avoidance of eye contact, and an informal orientation to time. How these variables influence the approach to therapy is considered next.

As a group, the variables just mentioned dictate that therapy done with Papagos would involve, for the most part, at least one indigenous mental health technician and that the therapy would nearly always be of a crisis intervention nature. The need for the mental health technician is obvious. Perhaps the reliance on a crisis intervention approach has reasons which aren't so obvious. First, although a medicine man often needs only one treatment session to effect a cure, this one treatment session could last several hours. The therapist must remain flexible regarding his own time orientation. Rigid adherence to the 50-minute session is simply of no value. As one graduate student extern recently pointed out when discussing marital therapy, the therapist should be willing to spend 2–4 hours with a couple and realize that this may be the only session there will be with them.

Not only does the variable of time orientation affect what will happen in one session, it also influences the execution of other sessions. That is, the client may be several hours late and the therapist must remain flexible and try to accommodate the client whenever possible.

The fact that the Papago client has had little to do when receiving other treatments (medicine man and physician) certainly affects what will happen in therapy. Quite often the Papago will present his problems (briefly) and ask "What is wrong with me?" and "What should I do?" A Rogerian reflection or question in return from the therapist may have little meaning. The therapist must be prepared to be directive—to make suggestions.

Confrontation in the therapeutic sense could be considered taboo with the Papago client. Socially, the Papago will religiously avoid confrontation. This is simply a matter of social courtesy. The therapist who confronts a Papago client in a manner that causes intense anxiety will lose the client.

Interviewing the Papago client has some unique features. The Anglo who attempts to establish direct eye contact with his client will make therapeutic rapport almost impossible. Similarly, an aggressive therapist with a loud voice will intimidate and perhaps anger the Papago client. The pace or tempo of the interview is also affected. That is, a longer period of time is needed to establish trust and rapport with the client. More time must be spent getting acquainted with the Papago client. Questions of a personal nature should be delayed. An opening question of "What brings you here?" could stimulate anxiety and defensiveness on the part of the client.

Because of language problems, interpretations and suggestions must be made crystal clear. A client may seem to understand but not understand at all. The pretended understanding and acquiescense are a result of trying to show respect and social timidity.

Group therapies have enjoyed considerable success in the Papago clinic. Every group has had at least one mental health technician and one university therapist. Different approaches have been used successfully, but with adaptation to the culture (Kahn, Lewis, & Galvez, 1974).

In summary, some factors which we consider to be important in providing psychotherapy for the Papago are as follows:

1. Relying on the mental health technicians
2. Using a crisis intervention approach
3. Avoiding eye contact
4. Approaching therapeutic topics slowly and cautiously
5. Avoiding confrontations
6. Making interpretations very clear
7. Utilizing directive techniques
8. Remaining flexible in regard to time
9. Talking less than usual

THE NON-INDIAN PROFESSIONAL CONSULTANT[6]

The Papago Psychology Service is unique in several ways beyond the fact that it serves an Indian population and is run by the Papago tribe. While several other Indian tribes run their own programs, they tend to hire or contract with professionals for clinic direction and policy. In the Papago Psychology Service, administration, clinical direction, and policy are the responsibility of the Papago Director, Mr. Cecil Williams. From its beginning, the Papago clinic was developed to make it a truly Papago Psychology Service, one which would respect and work within the Papago Indian culture and the wishes of the Papago people, and also a service which would be run by as well as for Papago Indians.

Ideally, trained Papago Indian professionals, instead of Anglos, should be in the appropriate roles in the clinic. Realistically, this is still some time in the future. It has been only in the most recent times that

---

[6]This part was written by Marvin W. Kahn.

there have been Papago graduates from college at the bachelor's level and advanced degrees are still something of a rarity. However, the times are changing rapidly in this respect. There is an increasing pool of Papagos going on for higher education. The Papago Psychology Service, as a matter of policy, makes a specific effort to recruit at least some of them into the mental health fields, in the hope that they will go on to receive professional training in this area. In the meantime, the need is present but it is being met quite ably with the means available.

Given this background and orientation, this non-Indian professional consultant's approach has emphasized several major points:

1.   Foremost in the role of consultant is that he must recognize, respect, and appreciate the spirit of the clinic—that of serving the Papago people with respect for their culture, their traditions, and their authority over the clinic. This includes respect for the Papagos' rights and the Papagos' ability to determine their own course with regard to their mental health program. In reality, the consultant is an employee of the tribe and works under the direction of the clinic director. The emphasis is on the Papago mental health workers as the primary deliverers of service. The consultant's job is to assist, support, and help train the mental health workers rather than to be highly involved in delivering service himself or to be involved in administrative issues.

It is here that professionals may experience hang-ups in terms of status in relationship to the authority of the clinic, in terms of responsibility for cases, in terms of control, and in terms of middle-class Anglo concern with detailed organization, routine records, etc. These problems are referred to here as hang-ups because working in a different culture and under nonprofessional directions requires flexibility and acceptance of doing certain things in ways different from what professional training would suggest.

2.   Within this context, however, the professional consultant must carry out the professional obligations of a psychologist, maintaining ethical and professional standards albeit adapted to the cultural circumstances of the clinic. As the primary professional backup for the clinic, the consultant provides information, advice, and recommendations with regard to the functioning and direction of the clinic. However, he should not expect that this will be readily, or even at all, accepted and put into operation. Training and supervising of the service staff in procedures, techniques, and professional case handling are done through conferences, both with individual workers and with the staff as a whole. These are accomplished by sitting in with staff members while on cases and by serving as a model to the workers in the professional delivering of service. Didactic presentation of subject matter such as types of psychopathology and psychotherapy is also important. Knowledge of the resources of the nonreservation community for mental health and other

services and sometimes being a bridge for the tribal program are important.

It is not a matter of any lesser professional standard for the consultant in this role, but rather more of an adaptive, flexible approach to the standard practices which will enable the program to be effective in this setting.

3. While a good share of the consultant's role is that of teacher, a perhaps equally large role, that of the student, is particularly necessary in this setting. Observing, listening to, and learning from the mental health workers, the patients, and the Papagos in general with whom he comes in contact enable the consultant to discover what is usable or can be adapted to working in the setting and what can't. Translation of mental health techniques that are available to the professional community so that they can be meaningful and applicable to the Papago culture is one of the most important things the consultant can do. This obviously can be accomplished only when there are knowledge and understanding of the people and how they perceive and go about things. Thus the consultant must always be a student, and to be effective perhaps must learn much more than he teaches.

4. Particularly for a psychologist, the orientation toward research in this setting requires some comment. Papagos have accepted the clinic and the few Anglos associated with it as a service to their people. For many years some academic disciplines have done studies on the Papagos without even informing them of the results. While the researchers wrote papers and books, the Papagos were not being helped. Research thus has a rather unsavory name on the reservation. It must be recognized that the clinic's commitment is to service. Even within this policy, however, the Papagos can recognize when a project might lead to better service for them and tribal committees do approve certain studies.

5. There are factors that can help the consultant develop and maintain acceptance and credibility. While it is a pleasant fantasy to think that successful consultation results from personal magnetism and skill, there are probably more than a few placebo effects in the case of this consultant. These include one important cultural factor, the Papago respect for age. My graying hair and "mature" appearance in this situation did no harm. Also, the status that a consultant might bring from other sources, such as being on the university faculty, and being a program director, may have some influence, at least initially, in the tribe's being willing to give him a chance. That factor perhaps was more useful with the Indian Health Service in obtaining their initial backing and financing of the program.

In the more tangible realm, the consultant's effectiveness ultimately depends on the acceptance and the trust of the Papago staff and, of course, the patients and the tribe. There is probably less immediate acceptance of a doctor title or professional credentials than in middle-class Anglo society. In fact, white skin and fancy degrees in some instances might be more of a hindrance than a help.

In working with this particular culture and Indian group, a relationship style that is low-key, accepting, and open to input is important. Assertive, pedantic directing styles, especially in any forceful and loud way, would be disastrous in this setting.

Within the low-pressure style, being able to show dedicated interest in the program and people on a sustained basis is important. The Papagos, like other Indians, have had their share of do-gooders trying to tell them what to do and how to do it and of those who have started things only to drop them and pull out when it was convenient. They want to feel that they can count on a consultant to be available, not only when he says that he will, but also for emergencies and for special meetings and programs. When the consultant is not physically available, availability by phone, even when he is out of town, has proved to be important. Of course, honesty and availability must be matched with competence. The clinic staff must feel that the consultant knows what he's doing, that he does it well, and that he uses the most appropriate and effective means available.

The human relationship between the consultant and those he consults with ultimately is the vehicle which carries those other attributes the consultant may have. Getting along with people as human beings together seems to be a basically sufficient approach. While gaining knowledge of the Papago people and their ways obviously enhances communication and relationship, it brings with it no necessity that in order to relate the consultant must try to be what he is not, that is, a Papago Indian. The non-Indian professional consultant should recognize that he can be good friends with the Papagos by being himself.

REFERENCES

Joseph, A., Spicer, R., & Chesky, J. *The desert people.* Chicago: University of Chicago Press, 1949.
Kahn, M. W., & Delk, J. L. Developing a community mental health clinic on the Papago Indian Reservation. *International Journal of Social Psychiatry* 1973, *19,* 299–306.
Kahn, M. W., Lewis, J., & Galvez, E. An evaluation of a group therapy procedure with reservation adolescent Indians. *Psychotherapy: Theory, Research and Practice,* 1974, *11,* 241–244.
Spicer, E. The Papago Indian. *The Kiva.* 1941, *6,* 6.

10

Grief Counseling with Native Americans

Wynne Hanson

As mental health programs for Native Americans are developed, there is an increasing need for mental health practitioners to understand the burial customs among Indian tribes if services are to be therapeutic (Ablon, 1971). It follows that any discussion of grief counseling must take into consideration the values of the Indian client, his philosophy of life, his attitude toward death, his cultural traditions, and his assumptive world (Kubler-Ross, 1969). This paper will discuss the complexities of grief counseling in the urban Indian community, encompassing behavioral steretypes, customs, and counseling techniques. Before this discussion takes place we first need to follow the migration of Indian people from the reservations into urban areas.

URBAN MIGRATION

Native Americans of over a hundred different tribes have migrated to the San Francisco Bay Area in increased numbers over the past two decades, beginning with the enactment of the Relocation Act of 1952 (Stuart, 1977). In reviewing the literature, the situation appears to be one where the Bureau of Indian Affairs hoped to assimilate the Indians into the mainstream of the population by encouraging them to move to the cities with the promise of training and jobs. However, the Indians, like other ethnic migrants, formed their own communities in the cities for emotional support and survival. Though assimilation did take place to a minor extent, many Indians chose to socialize only with their own people. The urban migration (relocation) program was started in the hope of providing the Indians with training and jobs to sustain them in the cities. To this day the comment made by Senator Watkins of Utah is repeated as representative of the attitude of the federal government: "The sooner we can get the Indians into the cities, the sooner the government can get out of the Indian business" (American Indian Policy Review Commission, 1976). From 1952 through 1968, some 67,522 Indian heads of household were

Reprinted with permission from *White Cloud Journal,* 1978, *1*(2),19–21.

relocated through this direct employment program. Today there are more Indians living in urban areas than on the reservations (U.S. Bureau of the Census, 1970).

Urban areas usually have more sophisticated social services available, particularly psychiatrists and other mental health resources. Unfortunately, most Native Americans do not receive these sophisticated services because they are largely irrelevant to Indians' emotional needs (Barter & Barter, 1974). During the past 10 years, urban Indian centers have been the primary providers of culturally sensitive mental health services to urban Indians (Ablon, 1971). Where no urban Indian centers exist, the Native American in an urban setting must rely on a service delivery system of western medicine that was designed for and by the White majority—a fact that Asians, Blacks, Chicanos, and other minorities have also pointed out repeatedly, to no avail. The result is that Native Americans do not use these services.

STEREOTYPES

Tribal affiliation is the Native American's most basic identification. The tribal teachings and experiences determine to a great extent the personality, values, and life goals of the individual, including the meaning of death and customs surrounding the burial of the dead. Because of extreme forms of discrimination toward Indians in certain parts of the country, many Indians have denied their tribal affiliation in fear of losing their lives or suffering physical harm.

The attitude of American society towards Native Americans is a strangely ambivalent one. The popular holistic health movement with its emphasis on the harmony of body, mind, and spirit embraces to a great extent the world view of Native Americans with their emphasis on the natural harmony of all living things. Native American speakers have been invited to holistic health seminars to share their philosophy on many occasions. Native American art and jewelry have never been more popular. People everywhere seem to be wearing turquoise rings, bracelets, and necklaces handcrafted by Indian silversmiths. Indian symbols and designs are found on the wallpaper, bedspreads, and rugs of plush Fifth Avenue apartments. Indian-designed sweaters are seen from coast to coast. It would appear that the Indian culture is to be admired and embraced.

On the other hand, social scientists, television, and the film industry portray a drunken Indian, suicidal and hopeless. Native Americans are either to be glorified and idealized as having mystical wisdom or ridiculed and stigmatized as being the shame of society. Mental health practitioners need to understand the self-image predicament Native Americans find themselves in when reacting to these extremely positive or negative sterotypes. The Indian client desires to be seen as a human being, with feelings of pride in his heritage and a desire for others to respect his beliefs and cultural traditions.

Negative sterotypes of Native Americans contribute to false impressions of behavioral adjustment (Shore, 1974). One commonly held assumption is that Indians as a group have many psychiatric problems and there is no hope for them (Beiser, 1974). After working with Native Americans of over a hundred tribes in the San Francisco Bay Area, I can recall a dramatic example of a young Hopi man experiencing auditory hallucinations after a family death. The local psychiatric emergency ward erroneously interpreted the hallucination as a psychotic symptom rather than part of the symptom complex associated with unresolved grief. Our agency intervened and this man was returned to the reservation to participate in a series of rituals and tribal ceremonies appropriate for the burial of the dead. Shortly after the ceremony he was free from the hallucinations. This man could have been hospitalized in a state mental hospital as a psychotic patient if Native American mental health personnel had not intervened on his behalf. In most instances practices that are difficult to understand are usually interpreted as indicators of psychopathology by the dominant society. There are other examples of a blending of healing and worship in the literature for the improvement of mental health as opposed to a diagnosis of pathology and long term treatment (Bergman, 1973).

BURIAL PRACTICES

At least some urban Indians migrate back to the reservations when old age approaches. Many who have lived most of adult lives in the city wish to be buried, when death comes, on their home reservation. This creates problems of a financial nature for the survivors, since to do so entails two funerals and additional costs to transport the deceased. Some tribal offices will give assistance in providing funds for travel for survivors and funeral costs depending on the amount of funds available. For some the desire to return to the homeland is indicative of a sacredness of the land. Some tribal cultures have been accustomed to having wakes for the family of the deceased. This is prevented in many urban areas as a violation of city and state laws. Thus the grieving process is sometimes interrupted and delayed until years later (Kubler-Ross, 1969). A few tribes have a specific number of days set aside for the mourner to grieve. During this time no work is done by the mourners. Friends of the family take care of the cooking and other necessary housekeeping chores. Other tribal beliefs require the deceased to be buried within 24 hours. This creates problems for the families in urban areas when funeral directors are insensitive to these beliefs and fail to cooperate.

THE LANGUAGE OF GRIEF

Nothing can begin to compensate for the loss of a loved one. Similarly, words cannot fully express our grief feelings. The loneliness, emptiness, and sadness cannot be adequately conveyed. Even the most eloquent C. S. Lewis wrote:

> "Grief feels most like fear. No one ever told me loss felt like fear. The fluttering in my stomach, the same yawning, and I keep swallowing. Perhaps, more strictly, it feels like suspense. Or like waiting, just hanging about waiting for somthing to happen. I can't settle down. I fidget. I smoke too much. Up until this loss I had too little time. Now there is nothing but time." (Lewis, 1961)

Colin Murray Parker saw grieving resembling a physical injury: "The loss may be spoken of as a blow. As in the case of physical injury, the 'wound' heals gradually. But occasionally complications set in, healing is delayed, or a further injury reopens a healing wound" (Parker, 1971). Edgar N. Jackson wrote, "Grief is a universal human experience. It is the strong emotion we feel when we come face to face with the death of someone who has been a part of our lives" (Jackson, 1961). Emotions cannot truly be described. In attempting to express our grief, the deepest and truest things about our feelings will stay unsaid. Words grow fewer. Touching or being touched "says" more than words. Memories from childhood remind us that a touch is the most comforting mode of communication available to us.

COUNSELING TECHNIQUES

It is important in grief counseling to assess the meaning of death, the customs surrounding funerals and the personal wishes of the client survivor. The treatment of the deceased after death is of utmost importance as is the participation for some Native American clients in certain rituals and ceremonies. Interruptions in these processes have a direct effect on resolution of the grief process of the survivors (Bergman, 1973).

In counseling Native American clients who are experiencing grief, I have found Ira Tanner's method most effective (Tanner, 1976). His method includes information on the facts of healing, validation, and confrontation. The client needs to know what feelings to expect in order to allow the grieving process to flow naturally. Clients need to hear from others that the loss has indeed happened. Funerals and tribal ceremonies help to validate the reality of a death. Responsible confrontation is also necessary for sound physical and emotional healing.

The client survivor should be encouraged to share his feelings and ventilate his anger. The bereaved may need help for months after the funeral to allow them to work through their feelings of guilt and anger (Kubler-Ross, 1969). It is important that the practitioner tolerate the client's anger, regardless of whether it is directed at the deceased, at God, or at the helping professions. In this way the bereaved takes a step toward acceptance of the loss without guilt. If we blame the client for feeling angry we may prolong the grief, shame and guilt, often resulting in physical and emotional ill-health.

Because of the cultural and communication barriers existing between some Native Americans and societal institutions it is sometimes necessary for the mental health practitioner to play an active role in the funeral arrangements and legal steps after a death. This may involve assistance with disposal of property, assistance with obtaining social security benefits, obtaining the death certificate, legal assistance, etc. Social workers at the Intertribal Friendship House in Oakland, California frequently act as advocates for clients with funeral arrangements, especially when the deceased is transported back to the home reservation. For this reason the social work profession plays an integral part in grief counseling of Native Americans.

When social workers and other mental health practitioners become aware of the cultural factors involved in the symptom complex associated with unresolved grief for Native Americans, the incidence of grief resolution should occur more frequently with these clients.

REFERENCES

American Indian Policy Review Committee. *Final report, Task Force Eight, urban and rural non-reservation.* Washington, D.C.: Government Printing Office, 1976.
Ablon, J. Cultural conflict in urban Indians. *Mental Hygiene,* 1971, *55*(2), 199–205.
Barter, E., & Barter, J. Urban Indians and mental health problems. *Psychiatric Annals,* 1974, *4*(9), 37–43.
Beiser, M. Indian mental health. *Psychiatric Annals,* 1974, *4*(9),6–8.
Bergman, R. L. Navajo medicine and psychoanalysis. *Human Behavior,* 1973,*2,*9–15.
Jackson, E. J. *You and your grief.* New York: Channel Press, 1961.
Kubler-Ross, E. *Death and dying.* New York: MacMillan Publishing Co., 1969.
Lewis, C. S. *A grief observed.* New York: Seabury Press, 1961.
Parker, C. M. *Bereavement. Studies of grief in adult life.* New York: International Studies Press, 1971.
Shore, J. H. Psychiatric epidemiology among American Indians. *Psychiatric Annals.* 1974, *4*(9),56–64.
Stuart, P. United States Indian policy. *Social Service Review.* Sept. 1977,451–463.
Tanner, I. *The gift of grief.* New York: Hawthorn Books, 1976.
United States Department of Commerce. Bureau of the Census. *Subject Report, American Indians.* Washington, D.C.: Government Printing Office, 1970.

Section II

AFRO-AMERICANS

11

Editorial Introduction

Articles in this section discuss the unique contributions of racism and a submerged racial identity to the problem of relevant human services for Black persons in this society. In the first selection, Nathan Hare depicts living environments that differ in degree and in nature according to one's race. As a result Blacks experience different survival problems which require unique approaches to amelioration. These problems are economic and political consequences of racism.

In a comprehensive article on Black counseling perspectives, Gerald Gregory Jackson describes the impact of racism on devaluation of Blacks—clients and human service workers alike. He posits that personality development of Blacks is always affected by racism and consequently racial identity is the crux of any rehabilitation or treatment process. Jackson indicts society as the locus of problems and as provider of inadequate and inappropriate training for human service workers. He argues for techniques based on Black culture that are proferred without racist, status quo, or middle-class attitudes. He enumerates the major techniques currently available that are culture-specific and calls for training programs that encourage participation by Black professionals and offer both information and opportunity for trainees to explore their own feelings about the culturally different.

The next selection by Johnnie McFadden presents a culturally relevant approach to service delivery. McFadden describes three stylistic dimensions that may be used for recontextualizing Black behaviors during counseling. A cultural-historical dimension includes racial discrimination, dynamics of slavery, and value systems. Psychosocial components are racial identity, psychological security, and self-concept or self-inspection. Scientific-ideological aspects are race relations, behaviors, and individual goals. The interrelationships across dimensions such as racial discrimination, racial identity, and race relations suggest the complex meanings of individual behavior and invoke awareness that can provide a relevant cultural context for understanding.

Alison Jones and Arthur Seagull and Roderick McDavis and Max Parker focus on training in the next two selections. First, the quality of the provider's experience in white-Black service delivery encounters provides a sensitive engagement with individual self-consciousness. Such experiences point toward planned training sequences for human service providers. Jones and Seagull have explored the complex relationship between Black client and white service provider. The worker needs to have examined his or her feelings about Blacks and be aware of possible countertransference, guilt, and power needs. Service provider and client may be dissimilar in living environment, values, and income as well as race. The provider must acquire experiential knowledge as a means for increasing awareness of interpersonal similarity as a basis for empathy, acceptance, and understanding. Service providers also need to make their services meaningful by actions designed to help Black clients cope with reality problems first, including an involvement in social activism as a primary intervention. Honest, mutual encounter with the Black client over the fact of race difference is presented as precursor to effective utilization of cultural knowledge by white service providers.

McDavis and Parker advocate a course on counseling minorities and describe the planning, goals, and content. Group experiences are designed to foster awareness of attitudes. The problems and mechanics of organizing interracial group experiences are stressed by literature review, videotape, feedback of feelings, and role playing. Videotaped panels of minority student discussions of counselors are viewed and their implications are discussed. Finally, instruction is provided in techniques that have been effective with culturally different persons.

Jewelle Taylor Gibbs documents Black-white differences in any communication process that may ultimately develop into a professional relationship. Five distinct stages describe the relationship process that leads to utilization of services. *Appraisal* finds Black clients aloof while whites attend to professional skills. *Investigation* involves Black clients in an inquiry into personal life while their white counterparts regard the professional task. *Involvement* for Black clients consists of a personal relationship with the service provider instead of a professional relationship. *Commitment* for Black clients is to the process via the person of the service provider as opposed to the goals of the service process. Ultimate *engagement* with the service is thus interpersonal for Blacks and instrumental for white clients. These stages are related to dimensions that are valued by Black clients as guarantors for each stage. Personal authenticity, egalitarianism, identification, and acceptance result in adequate engagement with the service provider and ultimate service delivery. Illustrative examples are provided. An interpersonal orientation for service delivery and training may be generalized to other ethnic minority groups, especially Hispanics who have a concept, *personalismo,* to describe a preference for trust in persons rather than services.

12

Black Ecology

Nathan Hare

The emergence of the concept of ecology in American life is potentially of momentous relevance to the ultimate liberation of black people. Yet blacks and their environmental interests have been so blatantly omitted that blacks and the ecology movement currently stand in contradiction to each other.[1]

The legitimacy of the concept of black ecology accrues from the fact that: 1) the black and white environments not only differ in degree but in nature as well; 2) the causes and solutions to ecological problems are fundamentally different in the suburbs and ghetto (both of which human ecologists regard as "natural [or ecological] areas"); and 3) the solutions set forth for the "ecological crisis" are reformist and evasive of the social and political revolution which black environmental correction demands.

In the realm of white ecology, pollution "closes your beaches and prevents your youngsters from wading, swimming, boating, water-skiing, fishing, and other recreation close to home."[2] And, "we want clear water, for boating, and swimming, and fishing—and clean water just to look at."[3]

Similar involvement includes the planting of redwood trees, saving the American eagle, and redeeming terrestial beauty. Thus it is seen that ecologists aimed at the hearts and purse strings of industrialists and hit the eyeballs of the white bourgeoisie.

Ecology accordingly has come to refer for the most part to chemical and physical or esthetic conditions only, while professional ecologists themselves have been known to differ in their definition of ecology.

> ...the concept is borrowed from biology, where it means the study of relations between organism and environment. In biological usage it includes relations between individual organisms and environment (autecology) and between groups and environment (synecology). In social science it is restricted to human synecology, that is, the study of relations between human groups (or populations) and their respective environments, especially their physical environments.[4]

Reprinted with permission from *The Black Scholar*, 1970,*1*,2–8.

A recent U.S. Department of Health, Education and Welfare report defines environment as "the aggregate of all the external conditions and influences affecting the life and development of an organism, human behavior, society, etc."[5] It is imperative therefore for us to understand how both the physical and social environments of blacks and whites have increasingly evolved as contrasts.

With the industrialization and urbanization of American society, there arose a relatively more rapid and drastic shift of blacks from Southern farms to Northern factories, particulary during periods when they were needed in war industries.[6] Moveover, urban blacks have been increasingly imprisoned in the physical and social decay in the hearts of major central cities, an imprisonment which most emphatically seems doomed to continue.[7] At the same time whites have fled to the suburbs and the exurbs, separating more and more the black and white worlds.[8] The "ecology crisis" arose when the white bourgeoisie who have seemed to regard the presence of blacks as a kind of pollution, discovered that a sample of what they and their rulers had done to the ghetto would follow them to the suburb.

But there is a greater degree of all varieties of pollutants in the black ghetto which also lies extremely exposed to the most final variety of environmental destruction imaginable—the "sneak atom bomb attack peril" this month reported by an authoritative study made by Great Britain's Institute for Strategic Studies.[9]

> Say Russia does drop a 10-megaton bomb on Washington, D.C. or Chicago, for example. Up to five miles from ground zero (the point of the explosion) nine out of ten of all inhabitants would be killed instantly and the rest seriously injured or victimized by radiation. All structure would be demolished. From 5 to 9.7 miles out, half of the inhabitants would be killed, a third of them injured, all others dazed, shocked, and sickened by radiation, and all buildings damaged beyond repair. . . . In other words, this would just about take care of the Negro community.[10]

But the ecological ordeal of the black race does not have to wait for a nuclear attack; present conditions are deadly enough. The environmental crisis of whites (in both its physical and social aspects) already pales in comparison to that of blacks.

In addition to a harsher degree of industrial pollutants such as "smoke, soot, dust, fly ash, fumes, gases, stench, and carbon monoxide"[11]—which, as in the black ghetto, "if there is no wind or if breezes are blocked dispersal will not be adequate"[12]—the black ghetto contains a heavier preponderance or ratio, for instance, of rats and cockroaches. These creatures comprise an annoyance and "carry filth on their legs and bodies and may spread disease by polluting food. They destroy food and damage fabrics and bookbindings."[13] Blacks also are more exposed to accidents, the number four killer overall and number one in terms of working years lost by a community.[14]

> ...poverty amid affluence, urban squalor and decay, and alienation of young people pollute the environment as much as garbage and industrial smoke. . . . A polluted political system which enables a handful of senile Southerners to dominate, through the seniority system, the law making body of a supposedly free people is a political system wich finds racism, poverty, and poisoned rivers equally congenial in its scheme of things.[15]

Moveover, "the ecological perspective directs attention to various kinds of phenomena. These include, among others: 1) the psychological behavior of persons (singly and in groups of various kinds). . . ."[16] Crime, insanity and other forms of social pathology pollute the central city environment.[17]

> It would be a tragic mistake to consider only the material costs of slums. The great expansion of slums in recent times has become a more serious social problem because the areas demoralize a large segment of the urban population.[18]

At the heart of this predicament, though not that alone, is the crowded conditions under which most black persons must live. Black spatial location and distribution not only expose blacks to more devastating and divergent environmental handicaps; they also affect black social and psychological adjustment in a number of subtle ways.

At certain levels of optimum density, flies in fruit jars have been known to die in droves and rats in crowded places to attack and eat their young and otherwise behave in strange and aberrant ways. Frantz Fanon and others have patiently charted the way in which oppressed people's so crowded turn upon themselves when, for whatever reason, they feel too weak to fight their oppressor.[19] Blacks accordingly are relatively more prone to be victims, contrary to popular belief, of all major crimes of violence as well as a number of other forms. Although it is true that blacks also exhibit higher rates of criminal activity, this merely stands in ecological succession to such groups as the Irish and Italians who in other eras inhabited the lower strata of the urban slums.[20] Only a minority of blacks are criminals; more are victims of crime. Due largely to existence in a criminally infested environment, blacks are about four times as likely to fall victim to forcible rape and robbery and about twice as likely to face burglary and aggravated assault.[21]

The social and psychological consequences of overcrowding are tangled and myriad in degree. To begin with, the more persons per unit of space the less important each individual there; also the noisier the place, other things equal, and the greater the probability of interpersonal conflict. Studies show that there is a greater hearing loss with age and that much of it is due to honking horns, loud engines and general traffic noise.[22] The importance of space to contentment also is suggested by the fact that in a survey of reasons for moving to the urban fringe, that of "less congested, more room" was twenty times more frequently given than the fact that the environment was "cleaner."[23]

The extent of black overcrowding may be seen in the fact that if population density were as great for the United States at large as it is for some blocks in Harlem; every person in the nation could live in one-half of New York City.[24] Using the yardstick of 1.5 persons per room, blacks are about four times as likely to be overcrowded as whites and they also are more often impelled to live "doubled up" with another family.[25] This necessity for doubling up imposes physical and psychological stress and affects self-perception and social behaviour.[26] A study of working class blacks in Chicago revealed that most of them, owing to a lack of space for beds, slept less than five hours in a given night.[27]

But the residential pollution of blacks rests not alone in overcrowding and the greater prevalence of unsightly and unsanitary debris and commercial units such as factories. The very housing afforded blacks is polluted.[28] This fact is crucial when we consider that the word "ecology" was derived by a German biologist from the word "aikos" meaning "house." A house, like the clothes we wear, is an extension of one's self. It may affect "privacy, child-rearing practices, and housekeeping or study habits."[29] Three of every ten dwellings inhabited by black families are dilapidated or without hot water, toilet or bath.[30] Many more are clearly fire hazards.

The shortage of adequate housing and money for rent produces high rates of black mobility which have far-reaching effects on the black social environment.[31] It means that blacks will disproportionately live among strangers for longer periods of time and, in the case of children, attend school in strange classrooms.

The household and neighborhood environments of blacks are perhaps of greater detriment to black health. The ability to control temperature and humidity at will—climate control—in homes can affect the incidence of respiratory infections. Its impact on comfort and productivity in all seasons is without doubt.[32] Health as a community resource is invaluable.

> ...health is, aside from the personal comfort or pain accruing to a given individual, a natural resource for the black community or any other. Health not only affects demographic composition and change; it also affects the ability of individuals—and therefore the community—to play their social, political, and economic roles. Tied in with this assumption is the fact that the advance in health since the eighteenth century may be attributed mainly to improvements in the physical environment. ... Not only are the rates of mortality higher for blacks by each cause of death; there are some significant variations in degree. Blacks also, of course, are subject to higher rates of ill-

ness. Much of the differential causes of mortality revolve around communicable diseases, the narrowing of which has been the major factor associated with the decline in differential mortality rates by race.[33]

Throughout a person's life, both his probability of dying and the type of death he meets may be in large part a product of the kind of community in which he lives.[34] It is no coincidence in this context that the high rates of death for blacks are in the area of communicable diseases and nonmotor-vehicle accidents, mainly in industry. Blacks are more than twice as likely to die from pneumonia and influenza.[35] In the case of syphilis the death rate for blacks is about four times as high. The same is true of tuberculosis and of dysentery; and blacks die more from whooping cough and other communicable diseases.[36] The effect of all of this for even those who do not die is relatively more activity limitations on the job than whites.[37]

The life expectancy of blacks is almost ten years less than that of whites, and black infant and maternal mortality rates are at the level which whites exhibited twenty years ago. Black women are more than four times as likely to die of childbirth, and black children are about three times as likely to succumb to post-natal mortality. This is because (among other factors such as dietary deficiencies) black births are about twelve times as likely to occur in a setting in which there is an "attendant not in a hospital and not specified."[38]

Moreover, poor nutrition during pregnancy and in early childhood can retard the brain's development. Illnesses and inadequate medical care combine with unsanitary conditions to effect physiological pollution. "The glazed eyes of children, legs that never grew straight, misshapen feet," and skin disorders are visible signs of this form of pollution.[39]

Yet there is alive today a neo-Malthusian fashion which blames "population explosion" for the ecology crisis.[40] Actually, the problem is not so much one of population explosion as population implosion, or "the increasing concentration of peoples on relatively small proportions both of the world's and America's land surface."[41] There is both an inadequate distribution of land and people and, more significatly, of people and resources. The United States accounts for only one-fifteenth of the world's population but controls at least three-fifths of its resources.[42] Within the United States three-fourths of the corporate wealth is controlled by about one per cent of the people. Hence one man's overpopulation is not so much a problem to him as is another man's overeating.

There is apparently something within the conditions of poverty that impels people to produce a larger number of children. Although the black birth rate is higher than that of whites, that is not true among women married to college trained men, where white women bear more children than do black women.[43]

No solution to the ecology crisis can come without a fundamental change in the economics of America particularly with reference to blacks. Although some of the ecological differentials between blacks and whites spring directly from racism and hence defy economic correlations,[44] many aspects of black environmental conditions are associated with basic economics. Blacks are employed in the most undesirable or polluted occupations,[45] lagging far behind their educational attainment.[46] About two-thirds work in unskilled and semi-skilled industries.[47] Aggravating, and associated with, the occupational effects on the black environment is the consistently low family income of blacks which must generally support larger families. Since the turn of the century, the family income of blacks has remained about half that of whites. Six in ten of all black children must grow up in poor families.[48] The figure is even higher for black families with a female head.[49] Unemployment is continually at least twice as high for blacks and has been shown to affect the rate of illegitimacy and marital separation, leaving many black families fatherless.[50]

In addition to unemployment, the same technology which defaces the general society also displaces a disproportionate number of blacks occupationally, into the throes of underemployment. At the same time, the black mother is more likely to be taken out of the home environment to work.[51] Today the war in Vietnam continues to send many of the most vibrant black males disproportionately to die in a foreign land in battle with fellow peoples of oppression. This means that five or ten years from now, assuming that blacks do not reject monogamy, an already depleted black sex ratio will drop considerably and there will exist even a greater shortage of young black males for black women to marry. The result will be increased marital and family disorganization.

Thus the reformist solutions tendered by the current ecology movement emerge as somewhat ludicrous from the black perspective. For instance, automobiles are generally regarded to be the major source of air pollution.[52] This is compounded in the case of blacks by the relatively smaller space in which they must live and drive amid traffic congestion and junked cars. On top of this, white commuters from the suburbs and the outer limits of the central city drive into the central city for work or recreation and social contacts, polluting the black environment further. In every region of the country there has been a direct parallel between the increase in the number of cars and the growth of the suburban and fringe population.[53] Although automobile manufacturers are the chief profiteers, the contradiction of alien automobile polluters who daily invade and "foul the nest" of black urban residents remains.

Some of these commuters are absentee landlords who prevail as "ghetto litterbugs" by way of corrupt and negligent housing practices. Thus blacks suffer the predicament wherein the colonizer milks dry the resources and labor of the colonized to develop and improve his own habitat while leaving that of the colonized starkly "underdeveloped."

> The problems of the ghetto are comparable to a colonized country. Middle city businesses and housing are owned and taxed by downtown and nothing is given in return except renewal programs that are determined by the needs of foreign interests and the transportation network that feeds downtown. . . . The job market is determined by the needs of foreign business geared to producing goods that middle city ghetto dwellers can't afford and often don't want.[54]

The real solution to the environmental crisis is the decolonization of the black race. Blacks in the United States number more than 25,000,000 people, comprising a kidnapped and captive nation surpassed in size by only twenty other nations in the entire world. It is necessary for blacks to achieve self-determination, acquiring a full black government and a multi-billion dollar budget so that blacks can better solve the more serious environmental crises of blacks. To do so blacks must challenge and confront the very foundations of American society. In so doing we shall correct that majority which appears to believe that the solution lies in decorating the earth's landscape and in shooting at the moon.

FOOTNOTES

1. For example, in a 760-page volume, "being the record of a conference convened by the Conservation Foundation in April, 1965, at Warrenton, Virginia," only one-fifth of one page was devoted to the black race. (*See* P. Fraser Darling and John P. Milton, ed., *Future Environments of North America.* Garden City Natural History Press, 1966.) Likewise, in a 286-page volume, "a Dial Report on the deteriorating quality of the American environment" the index contains no entry for "Negro" or "black." The book is entitled *Moment in the Sun,* but blacks received no "moment in the sun." Also, "suburbia" appears but there is no mention of the "slum" or the "ghetto." (See *Moment in the Sun.* New York: Dial Press Robert Rienow and Leona Train Rienow, 1967.)
2. Izaak Walton League of America, *Clean Water.* Glenview: February, 1970, p. 1).
3. Federal Water Pollution Control Administration, *A New Era for America's Waters.* Washington, D.C.: U.S. Government Printing Office, 1967, p. 4.
4. Julius Gould and William L. Kolb, ed., *A Dictionary of the Social Sciences.* Glencoe: The Free Press, 1964, p. 215.
5. U.S. Department of Health Education and Welfare, *Environmental Health Planning Guide,* Washington, D.C.: 1968, p. 1.
6. Nathan Hare, "Recent Trends in the Occupational Mobility of Negroes in the United States: An Intracohort Analysis." *Social Forces,* December, 1965. U.S. Bureau of the Census, *Statistical Abstract of the United States.* Washington, D.C.: U.S. Government Printing Office, 1969, p. 20, Table 20.

   In 1910 when whites were about twice as urban as blacks, only 27 per cent of blacks were urban. By 1960 blacks had grown more urban than whites, about four out of five of all blacks now live in urban places. See

Bureau of Labor Statistics, *op. cit.,* p. 67 and Karl E. Taeuber and Alma F. Taeuber, *Negroes in Cities,* Chicago: Aldine Publishing Company, 1965.

7. Bureau of Labor Satistics, *The Negroes in the United States: Their Economic and Social Situation.* Washington, D.C.: U.S. Government Printing Office, June, 1966, p. 69. *Statistical Abstract, op. cit.,* p. 18, Table 17. Scott Greer, *The Emerging City,* New York: Free Press, 1962, p. 82. Jeanne R. Lowe, *Cities in a Race with Time,* New York: Vintage Books, 1968, p. 283, George Schermer Associates, *More Than Shelter,* Washington, D.C.: U.S. Government Printing Office, 1968, pp. 20, 26, 51–53.

8. Bureau of the Census, *We the Black People of the United States,* Washington, D.C.: U.S. Government Printing Office, 1970. Taeuber and Taeuber, *op. cit.*

9. *San Francisco Examiner,* April 11, 1970.

10. Nathan Hare, "Can Negroes Survive a Nuclear War?" *Negro Digest,* May, 1963, p. 29.

11. Kenneth G. Bueche and Morris J. Schur, Air Pollution Control. Boulder: Bureau of Governmental Research and Service, University of Colorado, 1963, p. 5.

12. *Air Pollution: The Facts.* Christmas Seal Associates National Tuberculosis Association, 1967, p. 4.

13. Entomology Research Division, *Cockroaches,* Washington, D.C.: U.S. Government Printing Office, Leaflet No. 430, October, 1969, p. 2.

14. Ralph Thomlinson, *Population Dynamics: Causes and Consequences of World Demographic Change.* New York: Random House, 1965, p. 109.

15. The Editors, "Action for Survival," *The Progressive,* April, 1970, pp. 4, 5.

16. Harold and Margaret Sprout. *The Ecological Perspective on Human Affairs.* Princeton: Princeton University Press, 1965, p. 8.

17. Egon Ernest Bergel, *Urban Sociology.* New York: McGraw-Hill Book Company, 1955, p. 420.

18. *Ibid.,* p. 421.

19. Martin Oppenheimer, *The Urban Guerilla.* Chicago: Quadrangle Books, 1969, p. 64.

20. Office of Policy Planning and Research, U.S. Department of Labor, *The Negro Family.* Washinton, D.C. U.S. Government Printing Office, March, 1965, p. 25.

21. *Statistical Abstracts, op. cit.,* p. 140, Table 204.

22. Gary G. Smith, "Suggestions for the Schools," in Garrett De Bell, ed., *The Environmental Handbook.* New York: Ballantine Books, 1970.

23. Walter T. Martin, *The Rural-Urban Fringe.* Eugene: University of Oregon Press, 1953, p. 37. Svend Riemer, "Maladjustment to the Family Home," *American Sociological Review,* October, 1945, pp. 642–648.

24. Abram Kardiner and Lionel Ovesey, *The Mark of Oppression.* New York: Meridian Books, 1968, p. 52.

25. Division of Housing Research, *The 1950 Housing Situation in Charts.* Washington, D.C.: Housing and Home Finance Agency, June, 1952.

26. Alvin L. Scorr, *Slums and Social Insecurity.* Washington, D.C.: U.S. Government Printing Office, 1966, pp. 17, 18. George Schermer

27. Allison Davis, "Motivation of the Underpriviledged Worker," in William F. Whyte, ed., *Industry and Society.* New York: McGraw Hill, 1946, pp. 84-106.

28. Lowe, *op. cit.,* p. 237.

29. Scharr, *op. cit.*, p. 8
30. *We the Black People, op. cit.* See also Bureau of Labor Statistics, *op. cit.*, pp. 39, 40, 209.
31. Scharr, *op. cit.*, p. 86.
32. Thomlinson, *op cit.*, p.92.
33. Nathan Hare, "Does Separatism in Medical Care Offer Advantages for the Ghetto?" in John C. Norman, ed. *Medicine in the Ghetto.* Appleton-Century-Crofts, 1969, p. 44.
34. Wilbur Zilensky, *A Prologue to Population Geography.* Englewood Cliffs: Prentice-Hall, 1966, p. 42.
35. Marshall B. Clinard, *Sociology of Deviant Behavior.* New York: Holt, Rinehart and Winston, 1963, p. 42.
36. Bureau of Labor Statistics, *op. cit.*, p. 223.
37. *Ibid.*, p. 227.
38. *Ibid.*, p. 222.
39. The President's Commission on Income Maintenance Programs, *Poverty Amid Plenty: The American Paradox.* Washington, D.C.: U.S. Government Printing Office, 1969, pp. 17, 18.
40. Paul R. Ehrlich, *The Population Bomb.* New York: Ballantine Books, 1970.
41. Patricia Leavey Hodge and Philip M. Hauser, *The Challenge of America's Metropolitan Population Outlook—1960 to 1985.* Wash. D.C.: U.S. Government Printing Office, 1968, p. 1.

    Two-thirds of the people in the United States now live in 212 metropolitan areas comprising only one-tenth of the total land area; 53 per cent are crowded into less than one per cent of the land area.
42. Rienow and Rienow, *op. cit.*, p. 3.
43. Bureau of Labor Statistics, *op. cit.*
44. Taeuber and Taeuber, *op. cit.* Robert H. Connery, ed. *Urban Riots: Violence and Change.* New York: Vintage Books, 1969, p. 112.
45. Scharr, *op. cit.*, pp. 68-69. Bureau of the Census. *Nonwhite Population by Race,* PC (2)-1C, Table 39.
46. Bureau of Labor Statistics, *op. cit.*, p. 31.
47. John Sirjamaki, *The Sociology of Cities.* New York: Random House, 1964, p. 247.
48. Schermer Associates, *op. cit.*, pp. 22, 34. President's Commission, *op. cit.*, pp. 14, 30. *Statistical Abstracts, op. cit.*, p. 324, p. 477.
49. Nathaniel Keith, Housing America's Low—and Moderate—Income Families, Washington, D.C.: U.S. Government Printing Office, 1968, pp. 1, 2.
50. Office of Policy Planning and Research, *op. cit.*, p. 22.
51. President's Commission, *op. cit.*, p. 36.
52. Ralph Nader, "The Profits in Pollution," *Progressive,* April, 1970, p. 19. Kenneth P. Cantor, "Warning: The Automobile is Dangerous...", in Garret De Bell, *op. cit.*, pp. 201, 202. Gary G. Smith *op. cit.*, p. 303.
53. Cantor, *op. cit.*, p. 201. William E. Cole, *Urban Society.* Cambridge: Riverside Press, 1958, p. 167.
54. Berkeley People's Architecture, *op. cit.*, p. 240.

13

The Emergence of a Black Perspective in Counseling

Gerald Gregory Jackson

Scholarly concern with the process of counseling the Black client can be traced readily to the 1940s when, for example, workers in the field were disturbed and uncertain about specific aspects of counseling Black youth and adults (Williams, 1949). Specifically, need was expressed for special information in counseling such youth. Today, concerned counselors have expressed a similar need for special techniques to use with minorities or asked if it is better for minorities to be counselors to other minorities, since racial and ethnic barriers are so threatening and difficult to penetrate (Vontress, 1973). The difference today, however, is that the volume of data on counseling Blacks is greater, as is the tolerance for discussion of those related issues, such as racism. This increase in attention was predicted by one researcher who found three studies on the subject at the time of his review but asserted that in the ensuing years considerably more research would be reported (Island, 1969). The plethora of publications since the initial review tends to confirm the prediction. Ironically though, while the quantity and quality of articles waxed, the number of reviews remained conspicuously low. To illustrate, using the term "review of the literature" in the most liberal sense, only six such "reviews" could be uncovered (Island, 1969; Sattler, 1970; McGrew, 1971; Banks, 1971; Carkhuff, 1972; Denmark & Trachtman, 1973). This finding is particularly striking when one considers both the attacks on the profession in terms of the practices of its professionals toward Black clients (Williams, 1949; Barney & Hall, 1965; Washington & Anderson, 1974) and Black professionals (Jones, M.C. & Jones, M.H., 1970; Smith, 1970; Smith 1971a; Daley, 1972) and the perennial admonishments by Black people that they are not receiving adequate services (Himes, 1948; Manley & Himes, 1948; Russell, 1949; Waters, 1953; Brazziel, 1958; Hypps, 1959; Record, 1966; Russell, 1970; Tolson 1972).

As limited as the number of reviews may be, the genuine need is not for still another summation of contemporary publications but, more im-

Reprinted with permission from the *Journal of Negro Education,* 1977, *46,* 230–253.

portantly, a synthesis of the emerging Black perspective in counseling. Briefly stated, this outlook is derived from a sense of Black culture and focuses on means of liberating Black people. This acknowledgment and ensuing description does not suggest, however, that a concern by Black professionals with their profession has not been historically manifested; this viewpoint suggests a new genre of expression, one that emerged from the civil rights throes of the 1960s which exposed many of the shibboleths of the profession. For example, one long-standing barrier to innovation was the notion that everyone should be regarded as the same. More specifically, the individuality of the counselor should not affect the techniques used and the psychosociological background of the client, though probably different, should not affect the techniques which he will use or his role (Trueblood, 1960). Under the aegis of this notion, which has been referred to ironically as the doctrine of color-blindness (Fibush, 1965), consideration of the differential services rendered to Black clients, problems basic to Blacks because of racial discrimination and changes in the training of personnel based upon the preceding were kept at an ineffectual minimum.

Conversely, the Black perspective demands that the construction of counseling theories take into account the factor of culture (Stikes, 1972) and that the ultimate objective of counseling entail more than the development of academic skills. Counseling, from this point of view, should give instruction in Black ideology and cultural identity which embraces the social and political realities involved in existing symbiotically with the larger culture (Toldson & Pasteur, 1972). Any other posture, it is viewed, is merely another means of perpetuating the slavery of both Blacks and whites—Blacks to their victimized status, and whites to their illusions of superiority (Barnes, 1972). Similarly, training institutions located at colleges and universities, it was felt, should transfer experiential learning activities from their academic settings to indigenous community centers, street academies, or store front schools so that students can gain practical skills in assisting Black clients (Smith, 1971b). To grasp the meaning of the roles, techniques, and stances advocated by this new perspective, one has to be cognizant of the historical struggle preceding its development, and its clash with traditional outlooks.

STRUGGLE FOR POSITIVE RECOGNITION

Tolson's (1972) charge, "We try so hard not to see black or poor that we end up seeing nothing," suggests that recognition of the Black client and professional may apparently be the crux of the problem, but upon closer inspection it is evidently only a symptom. Acts, for example, which are now a part of history cogently demonstrate how both groups were dissected from the benefits to be accrued American citizens. Frank Parsons, one of the founders of the guidance movement, who was paradoxically concerned with matching people with their appropriate job, favored European immigrants, over native born Blacks, in allocating his services (Smith, 1971b). Similarly, Black professionals found little kinship with the professional organization of the American Personnel and Guidance Association until the inception of the National Defense Act and its training institutes. Moreover, Black professionals were denied a modicum of political prominence in the professional organization until the 1970's, after over twenty years of its existence as a body (Daley, 1972). These forms of discrimination could not have transpired without acknowledgment of a separate racial group and as a consequence, support the contention that Black people were not only seen but viewed in a negative light.

This negative perception of Black people is largely the result of the conceptual framework employed by the vast majority of professional counselors who unwittingly subscribe to the deficit hypothesis (Hayes and Banks, 1972). To elaborate, rather than searching in the environment for causal explanations of observed behavior, it is postulated that Black people have underlying deficiencies which are attributable to genetic and/or social pathology, which in the context of this reality, limits the probability of achieving successful academic and/or social adjustment. The implications for practitioners are facile; rather than critically observing their own behavior, the assumption of the hypothesis eliminates such a need and minimizes the likelihood of counselors considering important psychosocial factors which determine Black behavior. More importantly, since the onus of the problem is on the client, the professional's mission is oppressively one of getting the client to adjust to the status quo, while the behavior of those in power and the role they perform in creating and maintaining psychologically oppressive environments, in which Blacks must function, are ignored. In short, professionals alternately espouse the doctrine of color-blindness on the one hand, but practice discrimination on the other because acknowledgment of the latter implicitly demands affirmation of racial difference and discrimination which is too painful for many of them to bear. Clearly, it is the recognition of their passivity in the face of manifestations of racism, coupled with the guise of the notion of a melting pot, which instinctively encouraged them to adhere to certain reactionary principles. To illustrate, Williams (1949), in reaction to the cry for special information in counseling Blacks, responded that there was no need for special information. Deceptively for some, Rousseve (1965) added that while the environment of Blacks and whites can be differentiated because of racist patterns still prevalent in America, no essential distinction exists as far as behavioral or adjustive processes are concerned. Myopically, educators have interpreted such statements as meaning that the white middle-class can therefore serve as a model. Frequently overlooked or repressed is the condition of racism resulting from skin color differences. Williams added, for example, that while Blacks have the same basic needs, the frustrations, defeats, and conflicts are intensified and faced more frequently because of their color. She observed that in counseling Black students, counselors too often, either directly or indirectly, have discouraged vocational interests and choices and added that counseling for maximum adjustment does not attempt to adjust them to accept barriers of the status quo, but prepares them to cope with the barriers, find ways around them, and even to master techniques for removing them. This belief that Black clients should be assisted in learning how to negotiate in all senses of the term is one of the pillars of the Black perspective which is frequently minimized in the general literature and often overlooked in counseling contacts with such individuals. To return again to the significance of color, Boykins (1959) asserted that to counsel the Black college student effectively, one had to proceed on the assumption that the personality development of the youth was affected both by participation in the culture of the larger society and by membership in the caste to which Blacks in the U.S. are subjected by their minority position and status. Being a Black, she noted, had many implications for ego development that were not inherent in lower class membership. Here again is another important point which is frequently misconstrued by researchers and professionals in their haste to disregard how Black people are treated because of their color. Lumping Blacks with lower-class whites is a more convenient and face-saving alternative than understanding and dealing with the American contradiction of discrimination. More recently, Siegel (1970) expressed the view that in counseling the non-white student today, counselors must be aware of that student's identity because in her estimation, there lies the key to a proper approach to him, that is, does he see himself as a Negro American or an American Negro, colored person or Black man? White counselors in particular it has been shown are uniquely vulnerable in this regard (Vontress, 1971; Jackson & Kirschner, 1973); and Cross (1971) postulated five identifiable psychological stages black people undergo in moving from a self perception of Negro to a more liberated one of Black. Yet, the professional band continues to play the tune of "see no evil."

It is apparent from the references alluded to that the case for viewing Blacks in unique ways is not a recent issue and the same holds true for proposals to correct the problems engendered by the profession. Trueblood (1960), as others have similarly reported, felt that a counselor should explore the personality adjustment of the Black student and the possible influence that being Black, with the attendant social, educational, and economic restrictions has on his personality adjustment. He based his belief on the idea that there are possible problems of behavior and attitude which are related to the fact that the student is Black. Where he, in addition, digressed appreciably from conventional wisdom was in his view that while the process or techniques employed in assisting the student remained basically the same as those used for other population groups, the role of the counselor must be affected by his special knowledge of the student's needs. This special knowledge, he felt, could be gained only by studying the psychological and sociological background of Blacks. Presumably, such a professional understanding would be gained in graduate training where, theoretically, the opportunities are given and the insights gained. Yet, those who are trained in counseling, those who teach it and those who write it, do not have the instinctive, internalized knowledge of the ghetto culture, nor has a realistic opportunity to learn been provided them (Jones, M.C. & Jones, M.H., 1970). The student or counselor who wished such knowledge had to find his own way of acquiring it, which took unusual determination and initiative. To illustrate, Mickelson and Stevic (1967) also felt that counselor educators were not meeting the special needs of trainees in preparing them for work with the disadvantaged. They even conceded that many times the fault may reside within the counselor; however, in the opinion of these authors, "in all too many cases the root of the problem may well be traced to the preparation program of the counselor" (p. 77). Similarly, the Lewises (1970) noted that present programs of counselor education did not provide the basis for inner-city counselors to understand their students and their culture, or provide them with knowledge of the processes of social change and their potential contribution. Finally, Boxley and Wagner in their 1971 publication of a survey of APA approved psychology training programs reported that while many of the schools responding indicated an interest in recruiting more minority students, the available sites (clinics and counseling centers) were centered on the white middle-class client and minority faculty members at these schools were underrepresented. In their replicative study reported in 1973, they found no significant changes in the representation of minority group faculty, significant changes in the representation of minority peoples in the graduate student population but training programs which remained limited in breadth. Proposals to correct this deficit in training have been largely ignored. Vontress (1969a) for one, proposed pre-professional training which was undergirded in anthropology, sociology, and psychology, and the removal of counselor training from educational settings. He saw it within the purview of training programs to also provide opportunities for trainees to explore their feelings about the culturally different, live in the ghetto, and have a respresentative from the community be employed by the training institute to help counselors relate to the culturally different (Vontress, 1969b). Rousseve (1965) proposed that such trainees be exposed more extensively to updated scientific findings in cultural anthropology and related fields as these findings relate to intergroup prejudice and discrimination. Moreover, he felt that they should be required to sample and analyze some of the recent literary expressions of minority group authors.

In spite of these proposals, training programs in general showed little imagination in practice or in developing attitudes toward the preparation of counselors to work in settings focused primarily on urban Blacks (Smith, 1971a). Even those programs, however, which have been designed, in theory at least, with the preceding recommendations in mind still err because the Black perspective demands even greater allegiance. A brief description of some of these programs will illustrate the significant difference between the two points of view. Mickelson and Stevic (1970) recommended that counselor educators think beyond the rather traditional approach which had been taken in preparation programs and think in terms of a two-year integrated program. The first year of such a program would entail an introduction to the various theoretical, cultural, and philosophical foundations of the profession. The second year would involve placement in the ghetto school or in a federally sponsored program such as the Neighborhood Youth Corps. In addition, the second year would include courses in Black sociology and psychology and seminars which would bring in prominent local Black leaders and students at the university. This curriculum they believed would enable counselors to be of service to teachers which would further the rights of the pupil since the counselor would be promoting appropriate classroom behavior and understanding. They concluded that counselor educators could continue to ignore the need, but if they did others would institute programs to replace the school counselor "who is now charged with various guidance and counseling responsibilities but who because of lack of preparation and/or commitment had fallen far short of the goal of providing assistance to all youth (p. 77)." The Lewises (1970) proposed that students be paired with an experienced counselor and placed full-time for a year in an inner city school. During this stay he would be expected to provide direct counseling with students, attempt to involve the community in the operation of the school and the school in the operation of the community and spend a good deal of time working in a consultative capacity with teachers. Didactic course work was viewed as a bridge between theory and practice and included courses designed to enhance the trainees' awareness of the school's total milieu and the sociology of the school and the community. Their model counselor would be recognized as a consultant and an agent of change; however, they envisioned a training program that would specifically prepare the counselor for the role rather than assuming "that he will learn these functions later in some mystic manner" (p. 37). In terms of criticisms, George Banks (1971), after reviewing the literature in counseling, psychotherapy, testing, information-gathering, social casework, and education regarding the effects of race on the outcome of the interview situation, concluded that the task was no longer to analyze the Black man, but to reexamine the training and experiences of those involved in working with Blacks. He advocated that professionals should be concerned with selection and training based on the set of facilitative and action-oriented variables found to make a constructive difference in one-to-one relationships in general. One step further, the argument was advanced that even training programs which encouraged the perception of differences still may produce helpers who are a part of the problem rather than the solution. Accordingly, the comprehension of alienation divorced from a Black perspective, was deemed insufficient because the propensity of the formidable majority of professionals constrained them to center on what they considered as problems of personal disorganization within the Black client (Banks, W., 1972a), that is, the deficit hypothesis. More specifically, others cautioned against the use of certain approaches. Counselors were cautioned against subscribing to psychoanalytic models in general and classical psychoanalysis in particular when providing assistance to Black counselees (Harper, 1973a). The criticism was that the original theory of Freud was based upon middle- and upper-class white Europeans of the 1800's which had little, if anything, to do with a Black ghetto child. In addition, it was viewed as a post-dictive therapeutic approach which explained the why of behavior and not how to get food to quell hunger. As a more appropriate objective, it was felt to be the moral duty of the counselor to recondition the behavior of the counselee in helping him to learn new ways of meeting his needs and new ways of relating to the world, since he had been conditioned not to achieve such an end or even predestined by the dehumanizing conditions into which he is born. In contrast with the psychoanalytical approach, the use of behavioral principles was advanced as being progressive since they went beyond the deficit hypothesis (Hayes & Banks, 1972). Once again, from the Black vantage point, it was added that behavioral theory would be useless if the counselor did not understand what constitutes reward or punishment for a Black client, or if he failed to perceive the particular environmental conditions that effect a reward or punishment to his client (Banks, 1972a). This is an extremely important consideration, but an even more important one is that the counselor using such an approach should not confine himself to remedying the individual's lack of skill or inappropriate response repertoire because to do so is to inherently accept the notion that the problem is solely within the individual and encourages one to lose sight of the parameters of the problem.

The Alternatives

To counteract the unrelenting negative view of Black people, the Black perspective reordered some fundamental tenets. First, the locus of problems was shifted from the individual to society. Termed systemic counseling, this model assumed that most of the problems that had heretofore been labeled client problems were in actuality system problems. The role of the counselor in such an arrangement would be to treat the system for its problems which, when appropriate, would ultimately bring about a corresponding change in individuals (Gunnings & Simpkins, 1972). A word of caution must be added because of the tendency of some to use the concept of the culpability of the system as a justification for doing absolutely nothing. They ascribe all problems to the operation of the system and postulate that since they cannot correct the system through their individual assistance they cannot assist the Black client (Thomas, 1962). Such an approach is not systemic counseling but systemic racism and should not be confused with the view that Blacks are not disadvantaged but are placed in situations where they are at a disadvantage (Simpkins, Gunnings & Kearney, 1973).

Second, techniques and approaches evolved which were based upon Black culture. Mitchell (1970), for one, attacked what he perceived as the traditonal posture of counselors to attempt to be nice guys by just listening. He felt that such a stance was not enough because Black students needed tools for dealing with their problems. The counseling process itself, in his estimation, should deal with the present as well as with the "hereafter." Those counselors, he charged, who dwelled only on early childhood experience often turned off Black students, because the latter do not see how such early experiences are relevant to their current crises. Moreover, the Rogerian trilogy of congruence, empathy and positive regard had to be combined with definite techniques through which the student could acquire desirable skills or attitudinal change. Toldson and Pasteur (1972) saw the use of soul music as an appropriate way of achieving positive counseling ends when working with Black students. Stikes (1972) advocated the use of modeling and simulation techniques, verbal reinforcement and contracts as culturally specific counseling devices for assisting Black clients. In addition, he felt that advising Black students was appropriate because they expected authority figures to do so and did not result in expected dependency, and he suggested the use of the environment as a means of teaching the client appropriate attitudes and skills for dealing with the environment. In line with this approach, the counselor would provide psychologically safe experiences by reducing threat and removing barriers and helping the client understand and actualize his personal perspective in the Black social movement. Toldson (1973) analyzed the human potential movement and concluded that all Black groups were the most appropriate vehicle for Black liberation. Finally, Edmund Gordon (1970) not only challenged the individual psychological model still regnant today, he proposed as a substitute a developmental-ecological model which incorporates the preceding culturally specific recommendations. His model envisioned a shift from the study of clients to the study of systems, i.e., the family, the school, or office, and their development as social processes. Adherents to this model would no longer assess behavioral products, but would instead assess behavioral processes and as a consequence examine the nature of intellectual and social functioning for the individual and describe those functions qualitatively—in short, a movement away from prediction to prescription or from identification and placement in available opportunities to the creation of, and placement in, appropriate situations. In addition, the subscriber would no longer rely upon didactic exhortation, but on discovery and modeling as vehicles for learning and give more attention to the use of natually occurring or contrived environments to provide interactions supportive of learning and development in specified directions. Gordon further suggests that counseling, which he said should be abandoned as a field, should be shifted from interpretation to environmental orientation as its principle focus. Greater emphasis, he imagined, should be given to consultation. Finally, but not inclusive of all his points, he felt there should be a shift from primary concern with socialization to a major concern with politicalization, that is, systems maneuvering skills which would be skills that were not only essential to adequate concept of self but also to future survival.

Third, the Black perspective gave new interpretations of Black behavior and posited new images based upon strengths to supplant the old images based upon weakness. To illustrate, while most counselors subscribe to the notion advanced by Freud that a counselor should be a blank screen or a reflector of the client's problems, it was acknowledged finally that such an approach registered to Black students as indifference, remoteness and superiority (Scheffler, 1969). In lieu of the blank screen idea was the acclamation that a willingness to reveal something personal is a key to reaching Black students (Lefkowitz & Baker, 1971) and can build strong bonds of trust and rapport (Stikes, 1972). In a similar vein, the notion that Black people are somehow innately non-verbal was exposed on a number of fronts. It was found, for example, that they disclosed less than whites to certain target persons (Braithwaite, 1973). More importantly, this reservation to reveal oneself is based upon their minority status

(English, 1957) and the need to maintain a facade in order to survive in a land that metes out rewards and punishments according to skin color (Phillips, 1961). Again, failure to recognize the genesis of observed behavior is not only an indictment of the training of the professional but the institutions which provide such training and the profession which proposes inclusion in such programs. What is suggested, also, is complicity in the scheme where Black people are not viewed in terms of how they are generally mistreated but in terms of their resistance to becoming totally assimilated into American society. In short, the phenomenon is a classic instance of the self-fulfilling prophecy (Rosenthal & Jacobson, 1968) in operation by a profession avowing humanistic principles. This ambiguity, as well as other discrepancies, is clearly seen by adherents of the Black perspective and has served as one of its motivational forces. Another dimly grasped reality, based upon cultural difference, were the fact that Blacks and whites have different ways of communicating and the implication of this lack of recognition by the professional. Dr. Scheffler (1969), for example, reported that her expectation of verbal proficiency was a middle-class bias rooted in her experience in college and psychiatric settings where articulateness was often used as a convenient "hallmark of intelligence or potential" (p. 114). She discovered that ghetto residents were less fluent than middle-class people in vocabulary and form of middle-class English and were inhibited in using street language with those in authority, but only because the precise use of English she was accustomed to was less important to them. More important for communicating was observing gestures, intonations, facial expressions, or a variety of uses for a single word or phrase. From a Black point of view, if professionals such as Dr. Scheffler had been familiar with the life-style of inhabitants of the ghetto, they would know also that ghetto residents, too, give prestige and power to the fast talker, so that non-verbal really translates to "non-verbal in white terms" (Sager, Brayboy & Waxenberg, 1972). It is, therefore, as Scheffler indicated, the expectation of a certain way of being fluent verbally and a lack of cognition of non-verbal messages which result in the label of "uncommunicative," "silent" or "non-verbal" (Barnes, 1972). The real problem, then, from the Black perspective, is that the so-called non-verbal client is the one who usually receives the little help from the counselor who, in turn, often gets frustrated and gives up his attempt to establish contact, especially when the lure of heavy case loads can be used as a rationalization (Patterson, 1973). Another example of the disadvantage of the designation "non-verbal" is the case of the clinical and counseling psychology students who were provided with a practicum experience with Black trainees (Payne & Mills, 1970). The graduate students reported that the subjects were "non-verbal," and as a consequence, they discovered that they had to abandon the traditional interviewing format which depended on high verbal interactions and focus greater attention on the non-verbal cues. Two shortcomings are illustrated by the observations made by students: first, that the subjects were defined as non-verbal as a label when the behavior manifested could merely have been a reflection of the appropriate tact to take under the circumstances and had nothing to do with the subject's verbal proficiency. Second, the assumption by such persons that Black clients enjoy such roles as professional examinee and should be cooperative, energetic and enthusiastic is naive and illustrative of how a well intentioned learning experience can be undermined by a lack of knowledge of the culture and history of Black people.

Beyond the challenges to the old notions held of Black people as indolent, recalcitrant and, in general, without singular distinctions, is a new view of them as initiators, problem-solvers and competent. For instance, in one setting a peer counseling program utilizing disadvantaged high school students found that it bettered classroom skills, improved grades, and raised levels of vocational and educational aspirations among the students (Vriend, 1969). In another case, Black students demonstrated competencies in counseling peers in a variety of settings, initiating guidance programs, and assessing how an educational system operates to the detriment of Black students (Jackson, 1972a). Critical to the point that Black people possess unusual strengths are the reports that Black students have been trained to serve in a counseling capacity where professionally trained counselors were found to be inadequate (Sue, 1973); initiated and conducted programs on drug abuse (Jones, 1970); and conducted programs on career guidance (Amsterdam News, 1972). Finally, a program was developed to convert minority school teachers into qualified school counselors. The program had as one of its premises the fact that skin color, language or inner-city social origin were advantages in counseling minority students (Lindberg & Wrenn, 1972). It was reported also that one of the indirect benefits of the program was the positive reaction of the inner-city community to it and, as a consequence, a greater support for the total counseling program.

In addition to the struggle for positive recognition is the concomitant struggle to gain personnel who will not only have a Black philosophical orientation, but a commitment to the new role carved out of this perspective as well. What follows is a description of the struggle for personnel, followed by a consideration of the roles evolving from the struggles.

STRUGGLE FOR SERVICES

One of the earliest studies on guidance services for Black students which reported some of the problems entailed found that Black high schools in the southeast region of the United States suffered from: 1) inadequately trained personnel, 2) inadequate facilities, and 3) inadequate programs and personnel (Himes, 1948). It was noted further that, in some instances, the community was an additional hindrance. For example, some officials pointed to parental indifference, poor school-community relations, and lack of cooperation from community leaders. Even though the facilities were manned by Black people which suggests that guidance problems may be independent from the factor of race, racial prejudice was blamed in part for the inadequacies cited. In a similar study, poor training of teachers was cited as the number one cause for the problem in guidance and the conclusion drawn from the data that it was probable that the expansion of guidance was making little positive contribution to the success of the total school program (Manley & Himes, 1948). Guidance programs at Black colleges started during the 1940's (Russell, 1949) and a report by Patterson (1947) indicated that Black students were in need of this form of assistance since the close guidance relationship between student and faculty was no longer a significant practice. A study of Black rural high school students found the guidance services were indaequate and the recommendation made that more attention should be devoted to this area (Waters, 1953).

Intregrated Settings

In a study which focused on the relative guidance services given in a segregated surrounding, white schools had greater services (Brazziel, 1958). It has been noted similarly that even in cities where Black students are not segregated on the basis of race, they are still under-serviced (Hypps, 1959). To amplify, in a study conducted in an integrated high school which sought to determine if students felt Black youth were discriminated against in educational counseling (Barney & Hall, 1965), no statistical difference was found. However, a review of individaul cases revealed that counselors tended to be a little less willing to advise Black marginal students to apply for college admission.

Attitudes Toward Services Given

Civil rights organization frequently saw counselors who indirectly encouraged Black students to drop-out or to aspire to low level occupations or to form poor self-images (Record, 1966) as an integral part of the whole apparatus of discrimination. Brazziel (1970) noted that in 1940 ten per cent of Black students went to college in comparison to twenty percent for whites. However, in 1969 twenty per cent of Black students went to college whereas forty per cent of whites did so.

In terms of the Black community, Tolson (1972) observed that Blacks were angry and impatient with the traditional role of the counselor which was seen as maintaining the status quo rather than improving the condition of any individual or group. She noted that they were becoming increasingly suspicious of counselors and counseling bodies, to the point that suspicion often becomes rejection. In her view, a counselor was good for working with the powerless only when he had proven in their eyes his effectiveness in working toward a real change in their behalf. Corroborating her belief, Russell (1970) interviewed Black residents of one community who were unskilled and seasonal workers and found them to be unanimous in their belief that all guidance did for Black children was to put them in special classes, punish them for infractions, and get rid of them as soon as possible. Patterson (1973) noted two extreme and inappropriate practices of many counselors. They either encouraged Black clients to accept, in the name of reality testing, menial "Black" jobs which required little education or, after 1960 and the realization of new opportunities, they encouraged Black clients to aspire to any imaginable goal regardless of apparent qualifications or abilities. This erratic behavior on the part of counselors often stems from their inability to sort out inappropriate behavior on the part of the counselee from the inappropriate behavior on the part of society in engendering such behavior. For example, in a training program for drop-outs in which Southern reared females were transplanted from the South to the North and then released to work in northern urban settings, one white employer complained that he was disappointed that prospective candidates from the program would not look him in the eye. He interpreted such behavior as a lack of confidence. The Black counselor, on the other hand, informed the employer that the students had been conditioned to respond to whites in power in that manner and that it was his responsibility to give the students the security to be themselves. The counselor went a step further, however, and used behavioral rehearsal and role-playing techniques to assist the students in being more assertive in the job interview situation (Jackson, 1972b). In short, he worked on both aspects of the problem and indicated to the students that they did not have to accept the offer of appointment. This counselor also had some of his clients enroll in a local college even though the program was not designed to have its graduates seek further education (Bates College newspaper, 1969).

Failure in Counselor Orientation

The implications of the preceding are apparent. First, the remarkable number and variety of college placement programs that developed outside the schools, with or without federal support, suggest that there is a crisis in guidance services in the school (Kendrick and Thomas, 1970). Second, this crisis or failure, from a Black perspective, can be traced to the application of traditional middle-class pre-college guidance techniques to Black youth which are inappropriate (Kadota & Menacker, 1971).

Another means of delimiting the services given to Black clients is the traditional way in which counselors arrange to be seen and how they structure such interviews. Irvine (1968), for example, asserted that a counselor interested in serving such individuals may have to "permit himself to establish contacts in what appears to be inappropriate places at inappropriate times with the most inappropriate people" (p. 177). This is a point supported by Mitchell's (1970) observation that, "The counselor must also be willing to leave the security of his office in order to deal with some of the situational factors in white institutions which cause problems for Black students. He should be willing to make a personal contact for the student who is overwhelmed by the bureaucracy" (p. 36). Banks (1973) and Gordon (1965) both support this approach to counseling.

In short, the Black perspective castigates counselors for administering services solely from their offices (Washington, 1970) or waiting for Black youth to seek them out first (Kadota & Menacker, 1971; Smith, 1971a; Banks 1973). Specifically, Brown (1973) observed that a counseling center, staffed primarily by whites, is generally perceived as a potentially hostile agency whose structure and office atmosphere projects to the Black student a sense of "going to see the Man." The problem with changing the situation, he indicated, was the tradition in higher education that often blocks the modification of programs and structures even when adult members of ethnic minority groups are involved in establishing the program or designing the structure. In fact, he was struck by his finding that programs set up on college campuses specifically for ethnic minority students have more often than not been structured in almost identical ways to similar programs offered by the institution for the general student body. By traditional he meant being assigned office space, given a desk, and expected to maintain regular posted office hours. As a consequence, he noted: "I have not been surprised that many students will not come for assistance under these conditions even when they are in serious academic or personal difficulty, but I have been bewildered that nonwhite administrators would expect ethnic minority students to feel comfortable and to relate to counselors under these conditions" (p. 169). This point is not difficult to understand, however, if one consideres who trained the administrators and the bulk of their staff, and from what framework the institution operates.

Selection of Staff

Another dilemma encountered, then, in the administration of services is the problem of selecting suitable staff. Russell (1970), for example, suggested that the demand for Black counselors by Black students was the result of the latter's dissatisfaction with the present functioning of guidance which they considered to be "irrelevant" to their needs and an instrument of repression which was controlled by counselors who constituted roadblocks that they had to somehow manage to get around, particularly if their ambitions did not coincide with those which their counselors considered appropriate for them.

Feelings vary, however, on the subject of the significance of the race of the counselor who attempts to counsel Blacks. Taylor (1973) expressed a consensus that it is generally undesirable for whites to be involved in mental health research and treatment with Black people because of the former's racist proclivities; and others have concurred. White counselors have been charged with lacking awareness of the problems, feelings and outlook of Blacks (Hypps, 1959; Brown, 1973), the ability to identify with Black counselees (Rousseve, 1965) and the inability to assist when the decision entails rejecting society (Kincaid, 1969). Moreover, white counselors have been viewed in general as being discouraging and defeatist (Smith, 1967), and young white females, in particular, as anxiety-ridden when attempting to assist Black males of comparable age (Vontress, 1969b). Smith (1971a) saw one of the major problems as that of overcoming a sense of superiority. In terms of student perceptions, Lewis (1969) reported that most Black youth doubted the sincerity of a "helping" white counselor. Similarly, Russell (1970) conveyed that Black students' belief that racial bias existed in interracial counseling thwarted them from believing that a white counselor could regard them as individuals who possessed the same emotions, aspirations and potentials as whites. It was observed that a white skin automatically placed one strike against the counselor (Mitchell, 1970).

On the opposite side of the pendulum, it has been stressed that some Black counselors who were born and bred in the ghetto have negative attitudes toward relating to Black youth (Smith, 1968). In the same vein, one writer speculated that Black militant counselors would reject clients who termed themselves colored (Vontress, 1972). In more specific terms, Hypps (1959) expressed the view that because most Black counselors have been limited traditionally in the United States as a consequence of their race in their vocational, social, and political experiences they would not be able to impart the full evaluation of the business, industrial, and political life in a free society to their counselees. McDaniels (1968) felt that in a Black-Black relationship there was the persistent danger that the counselor will have difficulty with the counselee because he perceives the counselor as being a person who is a member of the establishment and, as a consequence, a threat to his existence. McDaniels noted that he found it easier to work with white clients because the prejudiced ones did not seek his assistance, whereas Black students did and wondered whether or not he had been a traitor. Personally, he found greater success with juniors and seniors in college because they had the opportunity to observe his behavior and had at least come to the tentative conclusion that maybe he was not an Uncle Tom and, therefore was able to relate to them in a meaningful way. Mitchell (1970) saw two distinct problems for the Black counselor. First, if he had not examined himself, Mitchell felt, there would be a tendency to project his attitudes and feelings onto other Blacks and as a consequence he would be just as "uptight" as the white counselor. Second, if he works in a white institution he will have to demonstrate his legitimacy to Black students who need to feel that he is someone who is honestly interested in them and not an "Uncle Tom" or an unqualified showpiece. Finally, Lindberg and Wrenn reported (1972) that one criticism occasionally registered about minority counselors was that they tended to be militant at times and push minority causes. Interestingly enough though, as counselor educators these authors did not see such behavior as a criticism but rather an indication of success because they wanted their counselors to be in the front line of the current ethnic-social struggles and fully involved with students who were experiencing these struggles.

Research studies conducted on the race of the counselor point to the employment of Black counselors to assist Black counselees. To illustrate, a number of reports demonstrate either the efficacy of Black counselors over white ones (Phillips, 1960; Stranges & Riccio, 1970; Heffernon & Bruehl, 1971; Gardner, 1972; Grantham, 1973) or that Black counselees found comparatively less satisfaction with white counselors than white counselees (Burrell & Rayder, 1971; Brown, Frey & Crapo, 1972). In the same vein, trained Black adults were preferred over white professional counselors (Carkhuff, 1970) and white counselors were found to have low linguistic compatibility with Black students (Schumacher, Banikiotes, & Banikiotes, 1972). Other studies on the subject found that race was relatively insignificant (Backner, 1970; Barrett & Perlmutter, 1972; Cimbolic, 1972; Cimbolic, 1973) and in only one instance favored white counselors over Black ones (Bryson & Cody, 1973).

From the Black perspective, the rhetoric on the subject and even the mounting research which favors the employment of Black counselors are embellishments of two central concerns. First, as Barnes (1972) has indicated, if we take seriously what we know about the process of psychological identification, we must inevitably conclude that the white counselor contributes to the identity crisis of the Black student. In his view, identification in this instance was simultaneously denying self and identifying with the symbol of the oppressive system. A Black counselor, on the other hand, who shares a common experience with his counselee and who has not rejected his own personal history, presents an appropriate figure for identification and is most able to inspire a feeling of confidence and a sense of hope in his Black counselees. Second, Banks (1971) argued that in light of the Black man's struggle to establish that Black people can do something for themselves, proving that they can establish an effective helping program for themselves will give them some additional sense of identity and manhood. In a Black context then, the encompassing consideration is the general plight of Black people and not solely the advancement of one individual who happens to be Black.

THE INTERIM

Today, a number of Black students are pleading that skin color be noticed and ask that they not be expected to find their heritage in a counter-part of white society (Siegel, 1970). Black professionals, too, have rejected the notion that a student is a student whether he is black, white, red, or polka dot (Banks, 1970).These developments partially account for why the belief that students are students and that all they need is to be listened to appreciated, guided, given moral and social examples, and given alternatives has not worked (Charnofsky, 1971). What is posed as a substitute for the doctrine of color-blindness is a view which recognizes that skin color has an enormous consequence in the U.S. and that if one is defined as Black, then such a person's condition is significantly different from that of any white immigrant or native (Tucker, 1973). Given this perspective, the traditional role of the counselor is no longer acceptable as an aid to Black people. In fact, one writer (Adams, 1973) went so far as to suggest that if counselors were to be helpful in the struggle for fundamental change requisite to assist minorities, they would have to abandon the following traditional activities: 1) vocational guidance, because it made an unfair and inadequate job market more acceptable and also helped to fill "manpower" needs of an economy based on exploitation; 2) large-scale achievement and intelligence testing, because it performed a stratification function; 3) crisis intervention counseling, because it served to keep the lid on potentially explosive situations; and 4) personal adjustment counseling, because it served to convince clients that the source of their alienation was within the self. As an alternative, counselors would use their skills to help people realize the source of their alienation and organize them to take action. A more general consensus seems to be the abandonment of the individualistic orientation of the profession and movement towards the assumption of responsibility for addressing societal issues which bear upon the effectiveness of counseling. To illustrate, Anderson and Love (1973) advocated that counselors help Black clients to develop a sense of pride and white clients an increased racial understanding. To bolster this goal, they developed a program of exercises to increase racial awareness by enhancing relations for the school. Similar in thrust, Sedlacek and Brooks (1973a) reported how research could be employed to lessen the practice of institutional racism. Similar to Love and Anderson, these writers also reported a model for solving the problem of racism in educational settings (Sedlacek & Brooks 1973b) and viewed as a whole, this model can be interpreted as implying two poorly recognized needs: first, that racism does not only exist in the larger society but the framework of educational settings as well; and second, that it is the responsibility of counselors to not only be cognizant of the phenomena but to actually initiate programs to ameliorate its occurrence. This approach, by the way, is not an autonomous function but is an integral part of the broader role of consultant which Gordon (1970) felt should replace the counseling function. In general the role of consultant includes work with the faculty (Proctor, 1970), administration, staff, and community (Banks, 1973) and, in effect, catapults the counselor from the role of individual ministration to environmental manipulator (Harper, 1973b). It has been further defined as entailing the demonstration to teachers of the power of their expectations (Coffin, Dietz & Thompson, 1971), the translation of the needs of students to teachers (Bolden, 1970), the presentation of culturally oriented programs in school, (Charnofsky, 1971) and curriculum adviser (Washington, 1968). In terms of the community, this new role includes seeking employment opportunities and financial aid for Black students (Trueblood, 1960), introducing the school to the home (Rousseve, 1965), and giving talks at churches, social organizations and schools (Jones, M. C. & Jones, M. H., 1970).

Another role emanating from the Black perspective is that of innovator. Examples of this role would be the work of Toldson and Pasteur (1972) who developed techniques for therapeutic intervention based upon a synthesis of Rogerian principles and Black spirituality, and Stikes's (1972) eclectic use of behavioral and analytical techniques based upon a unified concept of Black culture. An additonal case of an innovative advance is the movement by Black professionals to make the professional association more responsive to the needs of the Black client. Jones and Jones (1970) recommended that Black counselors form their own association so they would have a forum to exchange methods and ideology regarding the "neglected" client. Historically though, at the 1969 national convention in Las Vegas, a minority caucus presented a resolution to establish a salaried National Office of Non-White Concerns within the executive structure of the American Personnel and Guidance Association (APGA). These caucus members, according to Daley (1972), were: "tired of aquiesence; they were tired of an 'acceptable' existence; they were tired of all the rhetoric about warmth, acceptance, and development of each one's maximum potential" (p. 495). Each year until 1972 when a separate division within APGA was formed, caucuses met and presented grievances. At present the separate division has its own journal which projects the Black perspective in counseling, conducts programs related to minority interests both during conventions and throughout the year, and has moved from the smallest division out of eleven to the seventh in size.

Given the historical roots of the Black perspective and the continuation of conditions in the environment which gave rise to this outlook, one may infer that in the ensuing years this perspective will probably grow in substance and acquire a firmer shape. Schools employing counselors and counselor educators who train these counselors will have to adjust their policies and procedures to embrace this expanding point of view. In the absense of such resourses, counseling may transpire outside of traditional institutions and training be relegated to other agents.

BIBLIOGRAPHY

Adams, H. J. The Progressive Heritage of Guidance: A View From the Left. *Personnel and Guidance Journal,* 1973, 50, 531–538.

Amsterdam News (N.Y.), "School Program Studies Local Community Role," December 30, 1972, p. 8.

Anderson, N. J. & Love, B. Psychological Education for Racial Awareness. *Personnel and Guidance Journal,* 1973, 51, 666–670.

Backner, B. L. Counseling Black Students: Any Place for Whitey. *Journal of Higher Education,* 1970, 41, 630–637.

Banks, G.; Berenson, G. G.; & Carkhuff, R. R. The Effects of a Counselor Race and Training Upon Counseling Process With Negro Clients in Initial Interviews. *Journal of Clinical Psychology,* 1967, 23, 70–72.

Banks, G. P. The Effects of Race on One-to-One Helping Interviews. *Social Service Review,* 1971, 45, 137–146.

Banks, W. M. The Changing Attitudes of Black Students. *Personnel and Guidance Journal,* 1970, 48, 739–745.

Banks, W.M. The Black Client and the Helping Professional. In Reginald L. Jones (ed.), *Black Psychology.* New York: Harper & Row, 1972. (a)

Banks, W. M. Militant Counselors: Riffraff or Vanguard? *Personnel and Guidance Journal,* 1972, 50, 575, 581–584. (b)

Banks, W. M. & Martens, K. Counseling: The Reactionary Profession. *Personnel and Guidance Journal,* 1973, 51, 457–462.

Barnes, E. J. Counseling and the Black Student: The Need for a New View. In Reginald L. Jones (ed.) *Black Psychology.* New York: Harper & Row, 1972.

Barney, O. P. & Hall, L. D. A Study in Discrimination. *Personnel and Guidance Journal,* 1965, 43, 707–709.

Barrett, F. T. & Perlmutter, F. Black Clients and White Workers: A Report From the Field. *Child Welfare,* 1972, 51, 19–54.

Bolden, J. A. Black Students and the School Counselor. *The School Counselor,* 1970, 17, 204–207.

Boxley, R. & Wagner, N. Clinical Psychology Training Programs and Minority Groups: A Survey. *Professional Psychology,* 1971, 2, 75–81.

Boxley, R.; Padilla, E.; & Wagner, N. The Desegregation of Clinical Psychology Training. *Professional Psychology,* 1973, 4, 259–264.

Boykins, L. Personality Aspects of Counseling the Negro College Student. *Quarterly Review of Higher Education Among Negroes,* 1959, 27, 64–73.

Braithwaithe, R. A. A Paired Study of Self-Disclosure of Black and White Inmates. *Journal of Non-White Concerns,* 1973, 1, 87–94.

Brazziel, W. F. Meeting the Psychosocial Crisis of Negro Youth Through a Coordinated Guidance Service. *Journal of Negro Education,* 1958, 27, 79–83.

Brazziel, W. F. Getting Black Kids into College. *Personnel and Guidance Journal,* 1970, 48, 747–751.

Brown, R. D.; Frey, D. H.; & Crapo, S. E. Attitudes of Black Junior College Students Towards Counseling Services. *Journal of College Student Personnel,* 1972, 13, 420–424.

Brown, R. A. Counseling Blacks: Abstractions and Reality. In Charles F. Warnath (ed.), *New Directions for College Counselors*. San Francisco: Jossey-Bass, 1973.

Bryson, S. & Cody, J. Relationship of Race and Level of Understanding Between Counselor and Client. *Journal of Counseling Psychology,* 1973, 20, 495–498.

Burrell, L. & Rayder, N. Black and White Students' Attitudes Toward White Counselors. *Journal of Negro Education,* 1971, 40, 48–52.

Carkhuff, R. R. The Development of Effective Courses of Action for Ghetto School Children. *Psychology in the Schools,* 1970, 7, 272–274.

Carkhuff, R. R. Black and White in Helping. *Professional Psychology,* 1972, 3, 18–22.

Charnofsky, S. Counseling for Power. *Personnel and Guidance Journal,* 1971, 49, 351–357.

Cimbolic, P. Counselor Race and Experience Effects on Black Clients. *Journal of Consulting and Clinical Psychology,* 1972, 39, 328–332.

Cimbolic, P. T. Group Effects on Black Clients' Perceptions of Counselors. *Journal of College Student Personnel,* 1973, 14, 296–302.

Coffin, B.; Dietz, S.; & Thompson, C. Academic Achievement in a Poverty Area High School: Implications for Counseling. *Journal of Negro Education,* 1971, 40, 365–368.

Cross, W. The Negro-to-Black Conversion Experience. *Black World.* 1971, 20, 13–27.

Daley, T. T. Life Ain't Been No Crystal Stair. *Personnel and Guidance Journal,* 1972, 50, 491–496.

Denmark, F. & Trachtman, J. The Psychologist as Counselor in College 'High Risk' Programs. *The Counseling Psychologist,* 1973, 4, 87–92.

English, W. H. Minority Group Attitudes of Negroes and Implications for Guidance. *Journal of Negro Education,* 1957, 26, 99–107.

Fibush, E. The White Worker and the Negro Client. *Social Casework,* 1965, 36, 271–277.

Gardner, W. E. The Differential Effects of Race, Education and Experience. *Journal of Clincal Psychology,* 1972, 28, 87–89.

Gordon, J. E. Project Cause, the Federal Anti-Poverty Program and Some Implications of Sub-professional Training. *American Psychologist,* 1965, 20, 334–343.

Gordon, J. E. Counseling the Disadvantaged Boy. In William E. Amos and Jean Dresden Grambs (eds.) *Counseling the Disadvantaged Youth.* New Jersey: Prentice-Hall, 1968.

Gordon, E. W. Perspective on Counseling and Other Approaches to Guided Behavioral Change. *The Counseling Psychologist,* 1970, 2, 105–114. (a)

Gordon E. W. Guidance in an Urban Setting. *ERIC-IRCD Urban Disadvantaged Series,* 1970, 15, 1–14. (b)

Grantham, R. J. Effects of Counselor Sex, Race, and Language Style on Black Students in Initial Interviews. *Journal of Counseling Psychology,* 1973, 20, 553–559.

Gunnings, T. S. & Simpkins, G. A Systemic Approach to Counseling Disadvantaged Youth. *Journal of Non-White Concerns,* 1972, 1, 4–8.

Haettenschwiller, D. L. Counseling College Students in Special Programs. *Personnel and Guidance Journal,* 1971, 50, 29–35.

Hardy, R. E. & Cull, J. G. Verbal Dissimilarity Among Black and White Subjects: A Prime Consideration in Counseling and Communication. *Journal of Negro Education,* 1973, 42, 67–70.

Harper, F. D. What Counselors Must Know About the Social Sciences of Black Americans. *Journal of Negro Education,* 1973, 42, 109–116.(a)

Harper, F. D. Counseling the Poor Child. *Journal of Non-White Concerns,* 1973, 1, 79–84. (b)

Hayes, W. A. & Banks, W. M. The Nigger Box or a Redefinition of the Counselor's Role. In Reginald L. Jones (ed.), *Black Psychology.* New York: Harper & Row, 1972.

Heffernon, A. R. & Bruehl, D. Some Effects of Race of Inexperienced Lay Counselors on Black Junior High School Students. *Journal of School Psychology,* 1971, 9, 35–37.

Himes, J. S. Guidance in Negro Secondary Schools in the Southeastern Region. *Journal of Negro Education,* 1948, 17, 106–113.

Hypps, I. C. The Role of the School in Juvenile Delinquency Prevention (With Especial Reference to Pupil Personnel Services). *Journal of Negro Education,* 1959, 28, 318–328.

Irvine, D. J. Needed for Disadvantaged Youth: An Expanded Concept of Counseling. *School Counselor,* 1968, 15, 176–179.

Island, D. Counseling Students with Special Problems. *Review of Educational Research,* 1969, 39, 239–250.

Jackson, G. G. Black Youth as Peer Counselors. *Personnel and Guidance Journal,* 1972, 51, 280–285. (a)

Jackson, G. G. The Use of Roleplaying in Job Interviews With Job Corps Females. *Journal of Employment Counseling,* 1972, 9, 130–139. (b)

Jackson, G. G. & Kirschner, S. A. Racial Self-Designation and Preference for a Counselor. *Journal of Counseling Psychology,* 1973, 20, 560–564.

Job Corps Comes to Bates; Girls Discover Passivity. *Bates College Newspaper,* Lewiston, Maine, January 15, 1969, 7.

Johnson, S. H. Presidential Memo. (Association for Non-White Concerns). In *Personnel and Guidance,* December 18, 1973, 1.

Jones, M. H. & Jones, M. C. The Neglected Client. *Black Scholar,* 1970, 1, 35–42.

Jones, L. Rap's Her Way Fighting Drugs. *New York Amsterdam News,* June 6, 1970, p. L83.

Kadota, P. & Menacker, J. Community-Based Guidance for the Disadvantaged. *Personnel and Guidance Journal,* 1971, 50, 175–181.

Kendrick, S. A. & Thomas, C. L. Transition from School to College. *Review of Educational Research,* 1970, 40, 151–174.

Kincaid, M. Identity and Therapy in the Black Community. *Personnel and Guidance Journal* 1969, 47, 884–890.

Lefkowitz, D. & Baker, J. Black Youth: A Counseling Experience. *School Counselor,* 1971, 18, 290–293.

Lewis, S. O. Racism Encountered in Counseling. *Counselor Education and Supervision,* 1969, 9, 49–54.

Lewis, M. D. & Lewis J. A. Relevant Training for Relevant Roles: A Model for Educating Inner-city Counselor. *Counselor Education and Supervision,* 1970, 10, 31–38.

Lindberg, R. & Wrenn, C. G. Minority Teachers Become Minority Counselors. *Personnel and Guidance Journal,* 1972, 50, 219–222.

Manley, A. E. & Himes, J. S. Guidance: A Critical Problem in Negro Secondary Education. *School Review,* 1948, 56, 219–222.

McDaniels, R. Counseling the Disadvantaged Negro, Paper presented at American Personnel and Guidance Association Convention, Monday, April 8, 1968, 1–4.

McGrew, J. M. Counseling the Disadvantaged Child: A Practice in Search of a Rationale. *School Counselor,* 1971, 18, 165–176.

Mickelson, D. & Stevic, R. Preparing Counselors to Meet the Needs of Students. *Counselor Education and Supervision,* 1967, 7, 76–77.

Mitchell, H. The Black Experience in Higher Education. *Counseling Psychologist,* 1970, 2, 30–36.

Patterson, F. D. The Place of Guidance in Education. *Quarterly Review of Higher Education Among Negroes,* 1947, 15, 76–81.

Patterson, L. The Strange Verbal World. *Journal of Non-White Concerns,* 1973, 1, 95–101.

Payne, P. A. & Mills, R. B. Practicum Placement in a Counseling Employment Agency for Disadvantaged Youth. *Counselor Education and Supervision,* 1970, 9, 189–193.

Phillips, W. Counseling Negro Pupils: An Educational Dilemma. *Journal of Negro Education,* 1960, 29, 505–508.

Phillips, W. Notes From Readers. *Harvard Educational Review,* 1961, 31, 324–326.

Proctor, S. A. Reversing the Spiral Toward Futility. *Personnel and Guidance Journal,* 1970, 48, 707–712.

Record, W. Counseling and Color: Crisis and Conscience. *Integrated Education,* 1966, 4, 34–41.

Rosenthal, R. & Jacobson, L. F. Teacher Expectations for the Disadvantaged. *Scientific American,* 1968, 19–23.

Rothenberg, L. Relevance is a Many-Splendored Thing. *School Counselor,* 1970, 17, 367–369.

Rousseve, R. J. Counselor Education and the Culturally Isolated: An Alliance for Mutual Benefit. *Journal of Negro Education,* 1965, 4, 395–403.

Rousseve, R. J. Reason and Reality in Counseling the Student-Client Who is Black. *School Counselor,* 1970, 48, 561–567.

Russell, R. D. Guidance Developments in Negro Colleges. *Occupations,* 1949, 27, 25–27.

Russell, R. D. Black Perceptions of Guidance. *Personnel and Guidance Journal,* 1970, 48, 721–728.

Sager, C. J.; Brayboy, T. L.; & Waxenberg, B. R. Black Patient-White Therapist. *American Journal of Orthopsychiatry,* 1972, 42, 415–423.

Sattler, J. M. Racial Experimenter Effects in Experimentation, Testing, Interviewing, and Psychotherapy. *Psychological Bulletin,* 1970, 73, 137–160.

Scheffler, L. M. What 70 SEEK Kids Taught Their Counselor. *New York Times Magazine,* November 16, 1969, 54–55, 109, 110, 112, 114, 116, 119, 120, 122, 126.

Schumacher, L. C.; Banikiotes, P. G.; & Banikiotes, F. G. Language Compatibility and Minority Group Counseling. *Journal of Counseling Psychology,* 1972, 19, 255–256.

Sedlacek, W. E. & Brooks, G. C. Racism and Research: Using Data to Initiate Change. *Personnel and Guidance Journal,* 1973, 52, 184–188. (a)

Sedlacek, W. E. & Brooks, G. C. Racism in the Public Schools: A Model for Change. *Journal of Non-White Concerns,* 1973, 1, 133–143. (b)

Siegel, B. Counseling the Color-Conscious. *School Counselor,* 1970, 17, 168–170.

Simpkins, G.; Gunning, T.; & Kearney, A. The Black Six-Hour Retarded Child. *Journal of Non-White Concerns,* 1973, 2, 29–34.

Smith, D. H. The White Counselor in the Negro Slum School. *School Counselor,* 1967, 14, 268–272.

Smith, P. M. Counselors for Ghetto Youth. *Personnel and Guidance Journal,* 1968, 47, 279–281.

Smith, P. M. Alienation or APGA's Black Image. *Personnel and Guidance Journal,* 1970, 18, 312.

Smith, P.M. The Role of the Guidance Counselor in the Desegration Process. *Journal of Negro Education,* 1971, 11, 347–351. (a)

Smith, P.M. Black Activists for Liberation, Not Guidance. *Personnel and Guidance Journal,* 1971, 49, 721–726. (b)

Smith, P.M. Help: Change the Emphasis. *Journal of Non-White Concerns,* 1973, 2, 42–45.

Stikes, C. S. Culturally Specific Counseling—The Black Client. *Journal of Non-White Concerns,* 1972, 1, 15–23.

Stranges, R. J. & Riccio, A. C. Counselee Preference for Counselors: Some Implications for Counselor Education. *Counselor Education and Supervision,* 1970, 10, 39–45.

Sue, S. Training of "Third-World" Students to Function as Counselors. *Journal of Counseling Psychology,* 1973, 20, 73–78.

Taylor, P. Research for Liberation: Shaping a New Black Identity in America. *Black World,* 1973, 22, 7, 4–14, 65–72.

Thomas, A. Pseudo-Transference Reactions Due to Cultural Stereotyping. *American Journal of Orthopsychiatry,* 1962, 32, 894–900.

Toldson, I. L. The Human Potential Movement and Black Unity: Counseling Blacks in Groups. *Journal of Non-White Concerns,* 1973, 1, 69–76.

Toldson, I. L. & Pasteur, A. B. Soul Music: Techniques for Therapeutic Intervention. *Journal of Non-White Concerns,* 1972, 1, 31–39.

Tolson, N. Counseling the 'Disadvantaged.' *Personnel and Guidance Journal.* 1972, 50, 735–738.

Trueblood, D. L. The Role of the Counselor in the Guidance of Negro Students. *Harvard Educational Review,* 1960, 30, 324–326.

Tucker, S. J. Action Counseling: An Accountability Procedure for Counseling the Oppressed. *Journal of Non-White Concerns,* 1973, 2, 35–41.

Vontress, C. E. Counseling Negro Adolescents. *School Counselor,* 1967, 15, 86–91.

Vontress, C. E. Counseling Negro Students for College. *Journal of Negro Education,* 1968, 37, 37–44.

Vontress, C. E. Cultural Differences: Implications for Counseling. *Journal of Negro Education,* 1969, 37, 266–275. (a)

Vontress, C. E. Cultural Barriers in the Counseling Relationship, *Personnel and Guidance Journal,* 1969, 48, 11–17. (b)

Vontress, C. E. Racial Differences: Impediments to Rapport. *Journal of Counseling Psychology,* 1971, 18, 7–13.

Vontress, C. E. The Black Militant as a Counselor. *Personnel and Guidance Journal,* 1972, 50, 574, 576–580.

Vontress, C. E. Counseling the Racial and Ethnic Minorities. *Focus on Guidance,* 1973, 5, 1–12.

Vriend, T. High-Performing Inner-City Adolescents Assist Low-Performing Peers in Counseling Groups. *Personnel and Guidance Journal,* 1969, 47, 897–904.

Ward, E. J. A Gift from the Ghetto. *Personnel and Guidance Journal,* 1970, 48, 753–756.

Washington, B. Perceptions and Possibilities. *Personnel and Guidance Journal,* 1970, 48, 757–761.

Washington, K. S. What Counselors Must Know About Black Power. *Personnel and Guidance Journal*, 1968, 47, 204–208.

Washington, K. S., & Anderson, N. J. Scarcity of Black Counselors: A Crisis in Urban Education. *Journal of Non-White Concerns*, 1974, 2, 99–105.

Waters, E. W. Problems of Rural Negro High School Seniors on the Eastern Shore of Maryland: A Consideration for Guidance. *Journal of Negro Education*, 1953, 22, 115–125.

Williams, C. T. Special Consideration in Counseling. *Journal of Educational Sociology*, 1949, 22, 608–613.

Williams, R. L., & Kirkland, J. The White Counselor and the Black Client. *Counseling Psychologist*, 1971, 4, 114–116.

14

Stylistic Dimensions
of Counseling Blacks

Johnnie McFadden

There are basically three stylistic dimensions of counseling Blacks: cultural-historical, psycho-social, and scientific-ideological (see Figure 1). For the purposes of this article I have developed one-third of the total model. This portion's descriptors may be seen in Figure 2.

This inclusive model encompasses various cubes within each dimension. Under the cultural-historical dimension there are such cubes as racial discrimination, leaders and heroes, dynamics of slavery, civil rights, and family patterns. Under the psycho-social dimension there are the following cubes: racial identity, self-development, social forces, psychological security, mind building, human dignity, personality formation, and perceptions of others. Under the scientific-ideological dimension there are nine cubes: politics, race relations, media influences, logic-behavioral chains, meaningful alternatives, economic potency, individual goals, institutional goals, and relevant programs.

In order to understand the model, one must observe a correlation among the three primary dimensions and the various segments that exist within each group. For example, within the cultural-historical dimension, I suggest that it is essential for the counselor to understand the covert and overt forms of racial discrimination historically practiced toward Black people and the nature of oppression to which Black people have been systematically subjected. Combining such awareness with racial identity under the psycho-social dimension and race relations under the scientific-ideological dimension, the counselor must be sure that he or she has a very basic knowledge of how and why and when a counselee feels the need to become integrally and racially identified with his or her cultural group. This identity is based on what the helper, having been victimized by discrimination throughout his or her livelihood, feels.

Under the stylistic dimension of cultural-historical, one becomes cognizant of the fact that racial discrimination plays a major part in the

Reprinted with permission from the *Journal of Non-white Concerns*, 1976, *5*, 23–28. Copyright (1976) American Personnel and Guidance Association.

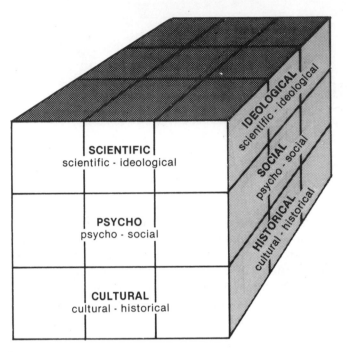

Figure 1. Stylisic dimensions of counseling Blacks.

formation of racial identity under the psycho-social dimension, identity having critical influence on the development of race relations within the scientific-ideological dimension. The person assuming the role of counselor needs to comprehend that Black people do not comfortably, uniformly, or automatically move from a cultural-historical dimension of racial discrimination to a scientific-ideological dimension of race relations. How can a helper, whether he or she is a minister, community leader, teacher, counselor, or parent, expect a Black student to progress from racial discrimination to acceptance of persons of the dominant society without undergoing a transitional period of racial identification? More important, it is necessary for anyone in counselor training or even counselor educators to recognize that Black people, particularly those with a keen perception of self, do in fact recall aspects of their background—discriminatory practices, past and present—and are cognizant of a need to engage in introspection in the formation of a racial identity that fosters improved race relations.

When a Black high school student goes to a counselor, particularly a white counselor, and is reluctant to reveal anything about himself or herself, the student may be having some inner conflicts with racial identity and choose not to participate in cross-racial relations at that time.

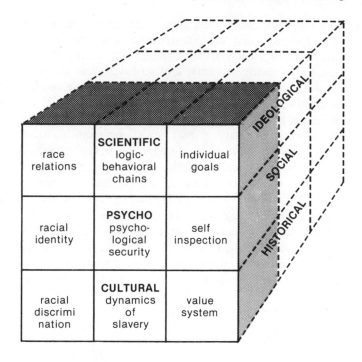

CUBICAL COLUMNS

A...Racial discrimination - Racial identity - Race relations
B...Dynamics of slavery · Psychological security - Logic/behavioral chains
C...Value system - Self inspection - Individual goals

Figure 2. Cubical descriptors.

Therefore, it becomes categorically necessary to realize the significance of having Black counselors in schools in which there are large Black populations; this is vital, because having only white counselors may have a detrimental impact on Black students. It is also important to remain cognizant of the need for Black students to experience a feeling of acceptance and openness as they move into a cross-racial counselor-counselee relationship.

Another category under the cultural-historical dimension is the dynamics-of-slavery cube. The correlating cube to the psycho-social dimension includes psychological security and, under the scientific-ideological dimension, encompasses logic-behavioral chains. In other words, what is logical and what is behavioral in a logic-behavioral chain for Black people is based on the psychological security of that person with himself or herself. Psychological security of a Black person might or might not have been influenced by the dynamics of slavery within the familial institution of that person. For example, a teenager who grew up in a rural section of South Carolina might have been influenced by parents, grandparents, or great-grandparents who previously were and still are influenced by aspects of the institution of slavery: sharecropping, tenant farming, domestic servants, and so forth. But the dynamics of slavery as a dehumanizing aspect of life for Black people could influence the formation of one's image of self. Images that create security or lack of security are often activated by behavior, be it logical or illogical.

Those aspects of slavery that most poignantly affected the psychological security of Black people were numerous: change of name, denial of personhood, separation of families, forced removal from native country, denial of religious beliefs, destruction of language, and references to Africans as "Negroes." In spite of these psychological and physical debasements, slaves on plantations did indeed form communities. Such communities are best described by John Blassingame (1972), who maintains that, in spite of the physical and psychological damage that they suffered, slaves formed a community that acted as a family substitute, a survival mechanism. It taught mores, culture, religion, and history.

Additionally, according to Blassingame, the slave community produced three types of slaves: Nats—the rebellious slaves who would go to any odds to proclaim their freedom. Nats included heroes such as Harriet Tubman, Denmark Vesey, Nat Turner, Gabriel Prosser, Henry "Box" Brown, and Frederick Douglass. Jacks—the slaves who accepted their plight, did their work, did not want to be hostile, but fled if the opportunity availed itself. Sambos—the grinning, shuffling, happy slaves who often used that image as a mask to dupe planters or overseers, to aid their fellow slaves, and to flee.

These psychological dimensions can be extended to contemporary society. The Sambo syndrome, for instance, may be demonstrated by the contemporary domestic servant who performs a role when working for the "master" that is out of character with his or her lifestyle. Such servants cook the food, serve the table, wash the clothes, dust the furniture, and mop the floors. On the surface all seems well; they seem to enjoy their work and those for whom they work when, in actuality, they are attempting to "get over," to obtain minimal resources in order to sustain themselves and their families. The Nat, on the other hand, may be characterized as the Black person who refuses to accept an inferior status in society, the leader who organizes his or her people to rebel against oppression. Finally, the Jack is the relatively disillusioned Black who accepts his or her fate, desires to be left alone, and reacts overtly only if provoked.

It is imperative for the counselor to understand these dimensions that are extensions of the psychological and physical oppression of Blacks from the time of slavery to the present. An awareness of such will not only aid in communication between counselor and counselee but also will guide the counselor in his or her effort to channel the counselee's energies. To cite a case, the most active and progressive Black students are often viewed as disruptive when in essence, they frequently display the much-needed qualities of leadership.

The best example of psychological security rests with those Blassingame calls the Nats: persons who, because of a positive degree of psychological security, are able to act in spite of what might have been viewed as overwhelming odds. The counselor should recognize, however, that action on the part of these persons might be in the form of physical activity, orations, written communications, or covert schemes. Black teenagers often display forms of rebellion to which white counselors are completely oblivious because of their inability to recognize psycho-social or cultural-historical dimensions that are germane to Blacks.

The third cube within the cultural-historical dimension is value systems, which, of course, are related somewhat to the foregoing cube. Value systems constitute how a person identifies and what he or she articulates to be of value to him or her, what he or she believes. A differentiation must be made, however, between Black and white values. Black students' values might be very different from white students' values. For example, examine acceptance or rejection of an individual's speech patterns. A student from the Sea Islands who speaks a Gullah dialect, to whom that form of speech is historically and culturally very important and valuable, must know that a counselor recognizes this. The same student may attend a local high school and encounter a white teacher, student, or counselor who might have a different set of values. The white person may not appreciate the Black student's linguistic heritage. So the Black student begins to form his or her images around the sanctity of those uniquely African values. The student clings to his or her own heritage in order not to be shunned or ridiculed and in order to safeguard this value that is a major part of his or her existence.

As one moves from a projection of values, the next cube is self-inspection. Some social scientists use the term self-concept. For the purposes of this article, self-inspection is used because of the diverse levels of inner activity that make up one's self-image. Do you as counselors or counselor trainees understand how Black students begin to form images of themselves? Do you as counselors support or destroy self-inspections? This question is especially applicable to counselors who are interested in preschool or elementary school counseling. Self-inspection formation for Blacks, especially for Black students, needs to be supported by school counselors, mental health workers, social workers, and psychologists because these are the poeple who might have a major impact on the expansion of self-inspection for Black people. Emerging from this cube is the establishment or setting of individual goals: life goals, short-range goals, goals for learning, goals for teaching, and goals for interacting with other people. So the flow proceeds from the cultural-historical dimension (values systems), into the psycho-social dimension (self-inspection), into the scientific-ideological (individual goals).

Gradual progression among the core characteristics of the cultural-historical, psycho-social, and scientific-ideological dimensions represents areas of knowledge and awareness with which each counselor who wants to work successfully with Black people must be familiar. Mastering such areas is contingent on multicultural training programs and substantive field experiences relevant to and inclusive of Blacks. To what extent does your counselor-training program adequately address the stylistic dimensions discussed in this article?

REFERENCE

Blassingame, J. W. *The slave community: Plantation life in the ante-bellum South*. New York: Oxford University Press, 1972.

15

Dimensions of the Relationship between the Black Client and the White Therapist
A Theoretical Overview

Alison Jones and Arthur A. Seagull

The issue of white therapists treating black clients is complicated by the fact that blacks in this country have been systematically oppressed economically, politically, educationally, and socially for hundreds of years by whites (Frazier, 1965; Kardiner & Ovesey, 1951); that is, racism is deeply embedded in our predominantly white culture (Clark, 1965). Against that background, questions about how and in what capacity whites can help blacks in a counseling situation are extremely relevant, especially since white persons far outnumber black persons in the helping professions, and blacks are going to request their fair share of mental health resources. So, white therapists are going to have black clients to counsel. Given this reality, in this article we examine the conditions under which white counselors can be of most assistance to black clients and make concrete suggestions about ways of understanding and handling areas of difficulty.

WHITE FEELINGS

First, the white therapist working with black clients must examine and understand his or her feelings about blacks. Quite obviously, a white therapist who has blatantly racist attitudes toward blacks should not counsel blacks. (In fact, people with this pathology should be in therapy themselves.) However, for the therapist not in this category, introspection

The authors are indebted to John P. McKinney, Department of Psychology, and Elizabeth A. W. Seagull, Department of Human Development, College of Human Medicine, Michigan State University, for their critical readings of earlier drafts.

regarding his or her own racial attitudes is still essential. Rosen and Frank (1962), two white psychiatrists, state, "Few of us are entirely free from race prejudice; with some, this is overt; with others it may be below the level of conscious awareness" (p. 456). Further, according to Sager, Brayboy, and Waxenberg (1972), "This latent reserve of racism, this submerged sense that the black man is 'different,' not governed by the white's warm, human emotions or worthy motivations, is part of our American heritage" (p. 417.)

The prejudiced, ill-trained, or inexperienced may stereotypically see blacks as nonverbal, concrete, and hence ill-suited for psychotherapy. They may see blacks as a group as untrusting and with character disorders that are unchangeable (Pinderhughes, 1973). But such preconceived notions may elicit these very responses as self-fulfilling prophesies.

Furthermore, white therapists who view all blacks as "culturally deprived," "disadvantaged," "underprivileged," etc., are demonstrating the subtle form of racism inherent in the use of these labels and are simply misinformed. For example, although black culture differs from white culture and has different forms and assumptions, it would be ethnocentric to label it deprived. According to Vontress (1969)

> The problem is not that certain population segments are without culture; rather it seems to be that the powerful dominant cultural group rejects sub-cultural groups in society. By their rejection, they convey the notion that those unlike themselves are inferior, deprived, or disadvantaged. (p. 12)

If the therapist views blacks stereotypically, she or he neither sees nor treats an individual (Kagan, 1964). As Calia (1966) warns, "Such generalizations lead to categorical prescriptions and the attendant loss of the client's uniqueness and worth" (p. 102). Tolson (1972) adds, "Some of these adjectives, such as 'black,' have become so culturally powerful that they control our perceptions and thereby limit our ability to apply what we know to be good counseling techniques" (p. 735). One must accept that such sterotypical attitudes are held by most whites toward blacks, and it is important that these feelings be understood and "owned" so that one does not unknowingly let them interfere in the therapeutic process.

This is not to say, however, that these stereotyped client behaviors may not sometimes be manifested by fearful blacks (or whites) in therapists' offices. But, we insist, "nonverbal," "mumbling," "unsophisticated," "nonconceptualizing" clients may be responding with a 300-year-old method called "shuckin," which was used by field slaves as a defense against their masters (Foster, 1974). It has been successfully utilized by other groups that feel oppressed and powerless, such as adolescents (Foster, 1974), incarcerated prisoners, who call it "dummying up'' (Spewack & Spewack, 1953), and concentration camp inmates (Bettleheim, 1960; Frankl, 1963).

One fights the oppressor with the weapons one has. If weakness is what one has, one uses that. For example, Gandhi forced the British to give up India through nonviolent resistance, the limiting case of powerlessness used as a power maneuver (Gandhi, 1960). Haley (1971) made the same point in his provocative essay "The Power Tactics of Jesus Christ."

The issue in therapy should not be that the client acts as if she or he had no power, but that she or he cannot exhibit other behaviors when she or he wishes, even though the old pattern has proved ineffective, demeaning, and ultimately destructive and leads to a loss of positive self-concept. The task of the therapist is to help the client distinguish when the use of powerlessness is to his or her advantage, and when other forms of interaction seem more efficacious, such as self-disclosure, retreat, confrontation, distraction, or flattery.

As to the alleged "lack of verbal skills" of the black, lower-socioeconomic-level client, the problem may lie in the situation or in the examiner's lack of skill. What are the verbal skills of a black youth who composes the following poetic insult?

> Aw, man, you trying to show you grandma how to milk ducks. Best you can do is to confidence some kitchen-mechanic out of a dime or two. Me, I knocks de pad with them cack-broads up on Sugar Hill and fills 'em full of melody. Man, I'm quick death and easy judgement. Youse just a home-byoy [sic], Jelly, don't try to follow me. (Foster, 1974, p. 220)

Now imagine how this same black person would speak if sent to a white therapist by his parole officer!

It is interesting to note that therapists who would reject a client's complaints that he can "do nothing" about an inability to argue with a friend or maintain an erection, tend to accept without further investigation a client's seeming inability to verbalize feelings. Yet the differences between a black client and a white therapist can be enormous. They may differ in color, sex, socioeconomic level, vocabulary, accent, syntax, mores, religion, and attitude toward time. They meet, perhaps, in the therapist's well-appointed business suite, within a posh office building, in an unfamiliar part of town for an appointment exactly 50 minutes long! And the therapist then wonders why the client doesn't express his deepest feelings.

Clients may also seem "nonverbal" because one does not speak their language (Bernstein, 1958; Foster, 1974), one fears their rage (Grier & Cobbs, 1969), one exhibits countertransference (Vontress, 1971), one lacks knowledge and skill (Foster, 1974), or because of a subtly racist assumption that blacks are inherently less intelligent (Jensen, 1969). So there may be reluctance to challenge the client's use of lack of verbal clarity as a defense (Foster, 1974).

COUNTERTRANSFERENCE

Countertransference occurs when a therapist does not fully understand and acknowledge his or her own feelings and it influences the therapy. Stereotypic reactions toward blacks are also countertransference. According to Vontress (1971), "Countertransference refers to the counselor's reacting to the counselee as he has reacted to someone else in his past. It means that the white counselor unconsiously perceives the black counselee as he always has perceived other blacks" (p. 9). Since many white counselors have middle-class values and mores, they may well bring with them certain feelings about and attitudes toward blacks, which may influence the process of therapy negatively. Because therapy is ambiguous and unstructured, it is possible for the therapist to influence its process by the emotional reactions she or he has toward the client.

Bloch (1968), in "The White Worker and the Negro Client in Psychotherapy," discussed the symbolic value of black persons for whites in America and its influence on the course of therapy. She observed that whites have projected their own unacceptable drives and impulses on to blacks, who are then seen as being supersexual or more aggressive than the white norm. An uninsightful white therapist may feel threatened by his or her own repressions in treating a black client and may thus tend to protect his or her own comfort in the setting at the expense of the client (see Pinderhughes, 1973).

The white therapist must understand his or her own motivation for working with black clients if he or she seeks them out. According to Vontress (1971),

> Productive counseling depends on the ability of the counselor to permit himself to become a part of the total counseling situation. . . . The counselor must know what he is doing and why, and this is not possible unless he understands to some degree his own psychodynamics and his cultural conditioning. (p. 12)

Therapists must understand their own feelings to deal effectively with minority clients or those differing from them on other powerful dimensions such as age, sex, religion, politics, sexual mores or preferences, wealth, or education.

GUILT AND THE WHITE CONSCIENCE

Guilt about their own racism motivates some whites who want to counsel blacks and seek them as clients. Such a therapist is likely to be quite *inef-*

fective. First, according to Heine (1950), a person acting from feelings of guilt is likely to identify with the client and to be too sympathetic to be of much assistance. This type of counselor is likely to fear a realistic confrontation and try to be ingratiating, so that the chance to use the therapy relationship as a springboard for reality testing is lost.

Second, feelings of guilt on the part of the therapist are likely to communicate to the client that the therapist is anxious, which will cause the client to strengthen his or her defenses and cease to explore certain areas either in deference to or from compassion for the therapist, or because the client correctly senses that the therapist will not be helpful for that problem.

Third, guilt feelings on the therapist's part can cause the therapist to become overzealous in helping the black client. "Trying too hard" can defeat therapy. If the therapist is working very hard to help, and the client chooses not to respond to the therapist's efforts to help him or her, the therapist can become angry with the client and, through lack of self-awareness, thwart the client's progress.

Fourth, the guilt-ridden therapist may tend to react defensively or to misperceive the black client's rage (Grier & Cobbs, 1969) and hence, rather than encouraging the expression of anger, discourage it. Or the therapist may waste time trying to prove to the client that he or she is different from other whites.

Fifth, the therapist who is motivated by a sense of guilt may easily become unrealistic about the client's real-life problems. He or she will not be respected by the client, and hence will be of little value to the black person.

Any of the above could make therapy ineffective, since the dishonest relationship on which the therapy would be based would make the interaction essentially "duplicitous," in Kaiser's phrase (Fierman, 1965). That is, the therapist would be saying through his or her behavior, "I will appear empathic, but I am motivated by my own sense of guilt rather than by true concern for the client."

THE NEED TO BE POWERFUL

Some whites counseling blacks exhibit a need to be powerful and to be in a dominating role. According to Pinderhughes (1973)

> One problem area for many patients lies in the unconscious needs of many psychotherapists to be in helping, knowledgeable, or controlling roles. Unwittingly they wish to be initiators and have patients accommodate to them or to their style or approach. More Black patients than White perceive in this kind of relationship the basic ingredients of a master-slave pattern. (p. 104)

The therapist trying to meet this need is likely to behave in a paternalistic, patronizing fashion toward the client. For example, the therapist might see all of the client's problems as stemming from his or her blackness rather than being able to see him or her as a human being who has racial concerns. Needing to help the black client for one's own power needs constitutes "the great white father syndrome" (Vontress, 1971) and is condescending, paternalistic, and ultimately enraging.

> The counselor must communicate to the black client that he is not only somewhat omnipotent (probably because he is white) but that he literally guarantees the black counselee that he can "deliver," if he will only put himself in his hands. Simultaneously, he communicates, albeit unconsciously, the implication that if the black client does not depend on him, he will be doomed to catastrophe. (Vontress, 1971, p. 9)

The dangers stemming from the "great white father syndrome" are apparent. If the counselor assumes an omnipotent, all-knowing role, the chances of the client feeling helpless and at his or her mercy are increased. This role parallels the client's problem vis-à-vis society and hence is counterproductive.

Those who counsel blacks should be familiar with and understand black culture, life-styles, and heritage. The counselor should have some feel for what the client's environment and experiences are like if he or she is going to be of help. According to Sager et al. (1972)

> It is essential that the therapist know and, more importantly, want to know and to understand the living conditions, cultural patterns, and value systems of the people he seeks to help. Without this appreciation it may be difficult for persons removed from the ghetto to accept the style of life of those who are part of it and to refrain from attempting to impose a Puritan-ethic-tinged morality upon it. (p. 417)

THE ROLE OF CLIENT-THERAPIST SIMILARITY

Real awareness of interpersonal similarity between client and therapist is essential. It increases the ability of the counselor to accept, understand, and empathize with clients and permits unconditional positive regard, genuineness, and empathy, which are emotional ingredients required for effective, growth-promoting relationships (Rogers, 1962). Accordingly to Calia (1966), the qualities of unconditional positive regard and empathy correlate positively with perceived similarity between counselor and counselee. Although a white person can never become black, certainly his or her familiarity with blacks and black culture will help to decrease the interpersonal differences between them.

The issue is even more complex. Hollingshead and Redlich (1958) found that counselors had better feelings toward clients of their own social class, a finding that supports the importance of perceived similarity for acceptance by a therapist. When therapists have an understanding of themselves and their clients, they will try to be open and honest, which means taking the risk of not being accepted by their clients. If therapists present therapeutic facades or personae, they will most likely be seen as insincere and will have trouble establishing relationships.

The establishment of trust, which is essential for self-disclosure in therapy, also increases as the similarities between the therapist and client increase (Jourard, 1964). According to Vontress (1971), "People disclose themselves when they are fairly sure that the target person (the person to whom they are disclosing) will evaluate their disclosures and react to them as they themselves, do" (p. 10). (See also, for example, Bienenfeld and Seagull [Note 1], for a case study illustrating the resolution of culturally determined misunderstandings between a middle-class, white therapist and a tough, black, welfare, client.) Thus, a therapist with a knowledge of a client's culture and background will be perceived as being more similar to the client and hence will be better able to establish an effective, productive relationship.

There is experimental support for the position that prejudice is a function of perceived differences in belief systems (Rokeach, 1960; Stein, Hardyck, & Smith, 1965). "The prejudiced person does not reject a person of another race, religion, or nationality because of his ethnic membership per se, but rather because he perceives that the other differs from him in important beliefs and values" (Stein et al., 1965, p. 281). Having the white counselor learn about the black perspective can help dispel his or her stereotypes. In doing so, he or she will gain a better understanding of black society and help bridge the gap between himself or herself and the client. She or he will become realistic about the problems presented.

UNDERSTANDING OUR SOCIAL SYSTEM

Understanding our social system and the ways in which blacks in this country have been oppressed, discriminated against, and systematically denied equal opportunity is essential for a white therapist working with black clients. It is no service simply to fit black people back into the society that has trapped them. According to Gladwin (1968), "The clinic does the walking wounded of the Negro community no favor by patching them up and sending them back into battle against a system everyone knows they cannot beat" (p. 479). Psychotherapy can be oppressive rather than constructive, according to Pinderhughes (1973)

> Many psychotherapists have value systems which encourage them to help patients to adjust to oppressive conditions rather than to seek changes in the conditions. . . . This is one reason why psychotherapy has sometimes been labeled as an opiate or instrument of oppression. (p. 99)

Instead of merely helping the black client adjust to a destructive social system, goals for therapy should include helping the client work for change in that system if the client so desires. Further, Kincaid (1969) emphasizes that the counselor who is truly working in the black client's best interests will encourage him or her in making choices that may be alien to the values of mainstream, middle-class America. She says,

> If the counselor is committed to his client's freedom, then he must see his task as one of helping black clients understand the discrepancy between their values and those of the larger society and make choices based on their own values, free of the threat of external evaluation and condemnation by the counselor for "wrong choices." (p. 887)

And finally, the white therapist working with black clients should be sensitive to the clients' needs, rather than working within his or her own rigid framework and imposing his or her own goals. The counselor should discover the clients' needs and wants. For example, the therapist does a grave disservice to any client by insisting on approaching the client in a traditional manner when the client comes in with questions about how to live in the slums with rats and roaches, how to make ends meet on a welfare budget, where to take the children when both parents go to work, etc. The therapist owes it to the client to deal with these more immediate real-life problems, either directly or through referral, before dealing with intrapsychic issues. In the statement, "I'll talk about my father if you want me to, but you have to know that there's no food to feed my kids tonight," lies a real dilemma. However, it can also be destructive for a therapist, white or black, to insist that the black client become more politically aware and fight for racial or social betterment if this is not what the *client* perceives as his or her problem. (See Foster, 1974, especially p. 245.) This is not to say that the aims of the therapist may not be moral or valid, but only that the client must set the goal with the therapist. There is a contradiction inherent in having the client blindly follow the dictates, however well-meaning, of the therapist, and that is that the client must be completely dependent in order to learn autonomy! (See Seagull and Johnson [1968] for a discussion of this issue, which we termed "the problem of form and function.")

If the therapist is to help the client meet his or her own needs and grow, it is essential that the therapist understand what the client is saying or asking for before working for change. For example, the counselor who interprets the black client's expression of anger toward whites as displacement, transference, or a defense against dealing with other issues, as does Adams (1950) in his article "The Negro Patient in Psychiatric Treatment," both undermines the client's trust and interferes with his or her reality testing. According to Gochros (1966), "In denying the validity of just complaints or by seeing the mere voicing of anger as an end in itself

. . . workers may appear to the client as either insincere or ineffectual''
(p. 34). Further, Sager et al. (1972) state

> It can be disastrous for the therapist either to deny the suspicion and hostility
> of the black patient or to feel guilty that these negative sentiments exist. The
> therapist works with these powerful negative feelings as distortion and
> resistance when they are unfounded, and, conversely, accepts them when
> they are accurate. (p. 417)

It is essential for the therapist to understand the client and to work toward
having black clients gain pride in themselves, their culture, and their identity just as he or she would for any other clients. Wilson (1971) sums up
the direction in which we feel therapy should move when he says

> Counselors should relate to clients with cultural differences in ways that will
> enhance the cultural identities of their clients. Counselors should relate to
> clients in ways which will permit the cultural identities of their clients to
> become positive sources of pride and major motivators of behavior. To do
> less is to denigrate a client's identity. To do less is to ask a client to give up his
> values in order to participate in the dominant culture. To do less is to con-
> tribute to the destruction of life; and our mission is not to destroy life but to
> enhance life. (p. 424)

THE WHITE THERAPIST—ALTERNATIVES

So what can be done by white therapists who want to help those who come
to them yet who feel that they lack the requisite skills or harbor some
racist feelings of which they are not proud but which are real none the
less? Clearly the first step is self-knowledge, just as it would be for any
therapist who found that she or he harbored irrational or potentially
destructive feelings. Talking to colleagues, white and black, about it,
playing tapes for colleagues, or organizing discussion groups and arrang-
ing speakers on the topic through professional groups would be useful.

Second, the issue of color difference should be brought up early in
the relationship, certainly not later than the second session, preferably in
the first. "I wonder if the fact that I'm white and you are black is affecting our working together?" "How do you feel about that?" The therapist
must be willing to explore the issues in depth, including being willing to
verbalize nonverbal cues indicating that the client is telling the therapist
what she or he feels the therapist wants to hear. The white therapist
should model such openness by examining his or her own feelings if they
are relevant to the relationship.

Third, books can be read that give one a view of black culture,
aspirations, and mores. And fourth, a willingness to accept one's own
fallibility with some humor and wry grace is helpful. Therapists are not

perfect, but their openness to change is the one attribute they possess that allows them to try to help others.

Foster (1974, pp. 243–245) writes of the traits necessary for the "natural inner-city teacher" to teach black children successfully. We think the concepts are relevant to the white therapist who genuinely wants to help black clients. The assumptions underlying these traits are honesty, interpersonal/personal integrity, and a respect for others as human beings, which includes the belief that people can learn to change. In a larger sense, these issues of black-white interaction are really the most salient example of the constant, basic issue in therapy—namely, How do we treat with dignity and positive regard those who differ from us on some major dimension such as age, color, wealth, sex, politics, religion, sexual mores, or personal beliefs? This is the task of the "helping professions" and a task, basically, for the whole country.

REFERENCE NOTE

1. Bienenfeld, S. & Seagull, A. A. *Treating a difficult black client: Some observations by a white therapist in supervision.* Manuscript submitted for publication, 1977.

REFERENCES

Adams W. A. The Negro patient in psychiatric treatment. *American Journal of Orthopsychiatry,* 1950, *20,* 305–310.

Bernstein, B. A. Some sociological determinants of perception—An inquiry into subculture differences. *The British Journal of Sociology,* 1958, *9,* 159–174.

Bettelheim, B. *The informed heart; Autonomy in a mass age.* Glencoe, Ill.: Free Press, 1960.

Bloch, J. B. The white worker and the Negro client in psychotherapy. *Social Work,* 1968, *13*(2), 36–42.

Calia, V. F. The culturally deprived client: A re-formulation of the counselor's role. *Journal of Counseling Psychology,* 1966, *13,* 100–105.

Clark, K. *Dark ghetto.* New York: Harper & Row, 1965.

Fierman, L. B. (Ed.) *Effective psychotherapy: The countribution of Hellmuth Kaiser.* New York: Free Press, 1965.

Foster, H. L. *Ribbin', jivin', and playin' the dozens: The unrecognized dilemma of inner city schools.* Cambridge, Mass.: Ballinger, 1974.

Frankl, V. E. *Man's search for meaning; An introduction to logotherapy.* Boston: Beacon Press, 1963.

Frazier, E. F. *Black bourgeoisie.* New York: Free Press, 1965.

Gandhi, M. K. [*An autobiography; The story of my experiments with truth*] (M. Desai, Trans.). Boston: Beacon Press, 1960.

Gladwin, T. The mental health service as conspirator. *Community Mental Health Journal,* 1968, *4,* 475–481.

Gochros, J. S. Recognition and use of anger in Negro clients. *Jounal of Social Work, 1966, 11,* 28–34.

Grier, W. H., & Cobbs, P. M. *Black rage*. New York: Bantam Books, 1969.

Haley, J. *The power tactics of Jesus Christ, and other essays*. New York: Avon, 1971.

Heine, R. W. The Negro patient in psychotherapy. *Journal of Clinical Psychology*, 1950, *6*, 373–376.

Hollingshead, A. B., & Redlich, F. C. *Social class and mental illness*. New York: Wiley, 1958.

Jensen, A. R. How much can we boost IQ and scholastic achievement? *Harvard Educational Review*, 1969, *39*, 1–123.

Jourard, S. M. *The transparent self*. Princeton, N J.: Van Nostrand, 1964.

Kagan, N. Three dimensions of counselor encapsultation *Journal of Counseling Psychology*, 1964, *11*, 361–365.

Kardiner, A., & Ovesey, L. *The mark of oppression*. New York: Norton, 1951.

Kincaid, M. Identity and therapy in the black community. *Personnel and Guidance Journal*, 1969, *47*, 884–890.

Pinderhughes, C. A. Racism and psychotherapy. In C. Willie, B. Kramer, & B. Brown (Eds.), *Racism and mental health*. Pittsburgh: University of Pittsburgh Press, 1973.

Rogers, C. R. The interpersonal relationship. The core of guidance. *Harvard Educational Review*, 1962, *32*, 416–429.

Rokeach, M (Ed.). *The open and closed mind*. New York: Basic Books, 1960.

Rosen, H., & Frank, J. D. Negroes in psychotherapy. *American Journal of Psychiatry*, 1962, *119*, 456–460.

Sager, C. J., Brayboy, T. L., & Waxenberg, B. R. Black patient-white therapist. *American Journal of Orthopsychiatry*, 1972, *42*, 415–423.

Seagull, A. A., & Johnson, J. H. ". . . But do as I preach": Form and function in the affective training of teachers. *Phi Delta Kappan*, 1968, *50*, 166–170.

Spewack, S., & Spewack, B. *My three angels*. New York: Random House, 1953.

Stein, D. D., Hardyck, J. A., & Smith, M. B. Race and belief: An open and shut case. *Journal of Personality and Social Psychology*, 1965, *1*, 281–289.

Tolson, H. Counseling the "disadvantaged." *Personnel and Guidance Journal*, 1972, *50*, 735–738.

Vontress, C. E. Cultural differences: Implications for counseling. *Journal of Negro Education*, 1969, *38*, 266–275.

Vontress, C. E. Racial differences: Impediments to rapport. *Journal of Counseling Psychology*, 1971, *18*, 7–13.

Wilson, M. E. The significance of communication in counseling the culturally disadvantaged. In R. Wilcox (Ed.), *The psychological consequences of being a black American*. New York: Wiley, 1971.

16

A Course on
Counseling Ethnic Minorities
A Model

Roderick J. McDavis and Max Parker

There is a need for content courses and practicum experiences in the area of counseling ethnic minorities in counselor education departments across the country. Generally, the only preparation that counselor trainees and others receive in this important area is provided through workshops and conferences, since few such formal courses exist today.

The paucity of formal courses on counseling ethnic minorities may be accountable to the different points of view held by counselor educators regarding this subject. In discussions with counselor educators at national and state professional conventions one group expresses the view that existing counseling techniques and strategies are sufficient and effective for all people regardless of race, sex, or background. On the other hand, another group states that existing counseling models are developed around the culture of middle-class white Americans and generally are not effective with ethnic minority clients. The latter group tends to be supported by working counselors who feel that their work effectiveness would be vastly improved if they had previous course work or practicum experiences in counseling ethnic minorities. Many ethnic minority clients receive ineffective counseling due to the inadequate preparation of counselors. It is the purpose of this paper to describe an existing course on counseling ethnic minorities which aids counselor trainees in becoming more effective when counseling ethnic minority clients.

PLANNING THE COURSE

The first step in planning the course was to seek information from various sources to assist in the selection of texts and readings, objectives, requirements, grading procedures, and content for the course. Faculty members at other universities who taught such a course were asked to send copies of their course syllabi. Most of these syllabi proved useful as

Reprinted with permission from *Counselor Education and Supervision*, 1977, *17*(2), 146–149. Copyright (1977) American Personnel and Guidance Association.

models in structuring the course. In addition, discussions were held with faculty and students in counselor education departments to determine what they considered essential elements for the course. Finally, counselors in the field who work with minorities were consulted for their ideas for the course.

Second, a reference list was developed containing more than 100 books and articles dealing with counseling Asian-Americans, Blacks, Cuban-Americans, Mexican-Americans, Native-Americans, and Puerto Rican-Americans. Most were published since 1970. Both the theoretical and research literature on counseling ethnic minorities were included in the reference list. These references formed the nucleus of the readings for the course.

GOALS OF THE COURSE

The goals of the course are as follows:

1. To help students become aware of their attitudes toward ethnic minorities and the attitudes of others toward ethnic minorities.
2. To help students learn approaches and techniques to facilitate inter-racial group experiences.
3. To help students become aware of the perceptions and attitudes of ethnic minorities toward counseling and counselors.
4. To help students learn approaches and techniques to establish rapport with ethnic minority clients.
5. To help students learn approaches and techniques to effectively counsel ethnic minority clients in one-to-one relationships.

CONTENT OF THE COURSE

The four-hour course is offered during the fall and spring quarters of each academic year. The course consists of 20 two-hour class sessions and includes the following topics and experiences.

Awareness Group Experience (AGE)

The AGE is four two-hour group experiences aimed at helping the students enrolled become aware of their and others' attitudes toward ethnic minorities. During the first session the purpose of the AGE is explained and then the students are asked to divide into dyads and discuss what previous experiences they have had with ethnic minorities. Then, the dyads combine to make groups of fours, eights, etc. until the whole group comes back together to discuss these experiences. In the second session students continue to discuss their past experiences with ethnic minorities in small groups and their present attitudes and feelings toward them. In the third session an activity is provided. A card on which a stereotypic role is written is attached to the back of each student. Each student, unaware of the attached label, is asked to interact with other students according to the role attached to their backs. Examples of some of the roles written on the cards are "welfare mother," "black militant," "hippie," and "migrant worker." Then, the activity is processed by students stating how they felt when other people interacted with them based on the assigned role. During the fourth session students are divided into small groups and asked to develop a list of action-oriented behaviors that can help them to initiate or improve relationships with ethnic minorities. In the fifth session students are taken to lunch in a local Black owned and operated restaurant and then on a tour of the local Black community.

Facilitating Interracial Groups (FIG)

The purpose of FIG is to teach the students how to organize and facilitate an interracial group experience. Counselors need to be able to assist students, minorities and whites, to form better interpersonal relationships. During the sixth session some of the literature on organizing and facilitating interracial group experiences is discussed. This literature includes articles by Kaneshige (1973), Ruiz (1975), Toldson (1973), Walker and Hamilton (1973), and Woods (1977). Each of these articles presents ideas on organizing and facilitating group experiences with various minorities. In the seventh session students view a videotape of the instructors facilitating an interracial group experience with a group of college students utilizing some of the techniques described in the AGE section above. Then, the class members critique this session. Also, students who participated in the group provide feedback on their feelings regarding the experience. In the eighth and ninth sessions students in the class practice some of the techniques of facilitating an interracial group experience by role playing with other class members in small groups.

Minority Student Panels

In the 10th session students view a videotape of 10 Black college students discussing their perceptions and attitudes toward counseling and counselors and then the students discuss implications for counselors. Then, in the 11th session students view a videotape of 10 Cuban-American college students expressing their perceptions and attitudes toward these same areas and then the students discuss implications for counselors. In both sessions, students in the videotaped discussions come to class and share their thoughts and feelings.

Counseling Ethnic Minorities Individually (CEMI)

The purpose of CEMI is to teach students the counseling approaches and techniques that are effective with ethnic minority clients. During the 12th session some of the approaches and techniques that are thought to be more effective with ethnic minority clients are discussed. These approaches and techniques include the systemic approach (Gunnings & Simpkins 1972), the action-oriented approach (Tucker 1973), an assertive training program for Asian-Americans (Sue 1977), and techniques for counseling Latinos (Ruiz & Padilla 1977). In the 13th and 14th sessions students view videotapes of the instructors demonstrating how to counsel ethnic minority clients. Then, class members critique the instructor's techniques. During the 15th, 16th and 17th sessions students role play a counseling interview with an ethnic minority client. These clients are college students who volunteer to role play in the class. At the end of each session the instructors provide feedback on the students' counseling skills.

Class Projects

As a part of their class requirements, students conduct a research study on some area of counseling ethnic minorities, develop resource materials that can be used by counselors in their work with same, or write an article on counseling ethnic minorities for publication. Students begin to work on their projects early in the quarter and present oral reports on them during the 18th and 19th class sessions.

Ethnic Dinner

An ethnic dinner is held at the home of one of the instructors during the 20th and last class session. Students are asked to bring a dish that is representative of their ethnic group. The purpose of the dinner is to bring students together in a social setting and discuss attitudinal and behavioral changes they have experienced as a result of the course.

RESULTANT STUDENT BEHAVIOR AND FEEDBACK

Student behavior and feedback following the course have been gratifying. One student developed a slide tape presentation concerning Black role models in various professions and has used it with vocational groups in the university counseling center, with practicum and intern students in case conferences, and with ethnic minority students in career day programs. Another former student is currently developing a test to determine the amount of vocational information held by ethnic minority students on the campus. Also, former students have been making special attempts to better acquaint themselves with ethnic minority people and their respective cultures. The attitude changes toward ethnic minorities that occur as a result of taking the course which are salient for counseling ethnic minorities are difficult to measure by standard instruments.

The following are sample comments about the class which were made by students in evaluation reports submitted at the end of one course: a) I found that exposure to Black and minority attitudes and opinions did much to open the channels of communications between me as a white and another person as a Black. b) The class has had specific relevance to my job because I now feel more comfortable counseling Black female clients. And c) One of the things I really appreciated about the class was the informal structure that allowed for student input.

CONCLUSIONS

The value of a course on counseling ethnic minorities is that it affords counselor trainees opportunity to expand their knowledge of the cultures and lifestyles of minority group members. Students become aware of their own attitudes toward minority group members, as well as the attitudes of others toward them. They also become aware of the perceptions and attitudes of minorities toward counseling and counselors. Furthermore, students learn approaches and techniques which help them to establish rapport with minority clients, to counsel them in one-to-one relationships, and to facilitate interracial group experiences.

While those involved with the course feel a great sense of success, there is certainly room for growth and improvement. The success of the course in the future will depend on a continued evaluation process and a sincere attempt to meet student needs. Hopefully, counselor trainees who are enrolled in such a course are better prepared to understand and communicate with ethnic minority clients.

REFERENCES

Gunnings, T., & Simpkins, G. A systemic approach to counseling disadvantaged youth. *Journal of Non-White Concerns*, 1972, 1, 4–8.

Kaneshige, E. Cultural factors in group counseling and interaction. *Personnel and Guidance Journal*, 1973, 51, 407–412.

Ruiz, A. Chicano group catalysts. *Personnel and Guidance Journal*, 1975, 53, 462–466.

Ruiz, R., & Padilla, A. Counseling Latinos. *Personnel and Guidance Journal*, 1977, 55, 401–408.

Sue, S. Psychological theory and implications for Asian Americans. *Personnel and Guidance Journal*, 1977, 55, 381–389.

Toldson, I. The human potential movement and Black unity: Counseling Blacks in groups. *Journal of Non-White Concerns*, 1973, 1, 69–76.

Tucker, S. Action counseling: An accountability procedure for counseling the oppressed. *Journal of Non-White Concerns*, 1973, 2, 35–41.

Walker, J., & Hamilton, L. A Chicano/Black/White encounter. *Personnel and Guidance Journal*, 1973, 51, 471–477.

Woods, E. Counseling minority students: A program model. *Personnel and Guidance Journal*, 1977, 55, 416–418.

17

The Interpersonal Orientation in Mental Health Consultation
Toward a Model of Ethnic Variations in Consultation

Jewelle Taylor Gibbs

In an extensive review of the consultation literature by Mannino, Mac-Lennan, and Shore (1975), there were few references which directly addressed the issue of ethnic differences in the use of consultation. While several authors have commented on the problems of establishing rapport and the difficulties of cross-cultural communication in implementing consultation services to nonwhite minority groups, there have been no systematic attempts to analyze these issues in a conceptual framework which would enable mental health professionals to serve these groups more effectively.

This paper is an initial effort to analyze the differences between Blacks and Whites in establishing a consultation relationship, viewing this relationship as a paradigm for all professional interpersonal transactions, e.g., psychotherapy, counseling, and supervision. The analysis is based on clinical, experimental, and sociological data on Black-White differences in counseling and psychotherapy, interactional processes, language and communication patterns, expressive styles, and values influencing interpersonal relationships.

From this synthesis of social science findings the author has formulated the following three propositions: a) there are ethnic (e.g., Black-White) differences in the initial orientation to the consultant-consultee relationship; b) these differences are along the dimension of interpersonal versus instrumental competence; and c) these differences have significant

This is a revised version of a paper presented at the Western Psychological Association, San Francisco, California, March 1978. The author gratefully acknowledges the helpful comments of Rhona Weinstein and other participants in the school consultation practicum of the Psychology Clinic, University of California at Berkeley.

Reprinted with permission from *Journal of Community Psychology*, 1980, *8*, 195–207.

implications for the implementation of the consultation process and its outcome.

A model of these ethnic variations in the entry phase of consultation is proposed, delineating the stages, the behaviors and the themes which differentially characterize the orientation of Black consultees to the consultation relationship. In order to illustrate the application of this conceptual framework, the author provides examples from an inner-city school mental health consultation project in the San Francisco Bay area. The implications of this model for developing more effective consultation services to Black groups are discussed, as well as its potential generalizability to consultation relationships between mental health professionals and other ethnic minority groups.

REVIEW OF LITERATURE

Existing models for consultation, such as those developed by Caplan (1970), Altrocchi (1972) and Glidewell (1959), do not deal with the issue of ethnic variations among consultees in their attitudes toward consultation, their use of consultation or their relationship with the consultant. Both Caplan (1970) and Altrocchi (1972) share certain basic assumptions about the importance of building a solid base and establishing good communication in the initial phase of consultation. These assumptions are derived from a mono-cultural perspective about human communication, human values, and human behavior, e.g., that consultant and consultee can easily develop effective channels of communication, that they can develop a common verbal and nonverbal language, that mutual trust will be shared, and that distortions of perception and expectations can be easily clarified. However, when a traditionally trained consultant is involved in a predominantly non-White setting, the limitations of these models become immediately apparent.

Glidewell (1959) emphasized the importance of congruence, or goodness of fit, between the consultant and consultee in terms of values, role expectations, resource and reward allocation, and feelings about the control of dependency. These are some of the central issues that arise in the entry phase of consultation to a predominantly Black staff in an agency serving low-income clients or in an inner-city school where the consultant and the consultees may share very different perceptions about all of these areas.

In a series of papers describing consultation services to agencies and neighborhood organizations in an impoverished urban area, Scheidlinger and colleagues (1970, 1971) emphasized the difficulties of establishing a common frame of reference and a "common language" with the minority staff members of grassroots agencies. In order to develop mutual rapport and trust between the consultants and the indigenous leaders, these authors noted the importance of initially allaying the consultees' feelings of suspicion and fears of being patronized or manipulated.

Morrison (1970) also raised the issue of communication barriers between White consultants and Black poverty workers, pointing out that certain techniques may be more effective with indigenous workers than with middle-class groups, e.g., sharing more personal information and maintaining a more flexible and a warmer relationship. Reports of consultation to teaching staffs of inner-city schools (Brody & Schneider, 1973; Broskowski, 1973) further underscore the need to clarify communication processes, values, and expectations between consultant and consultees.

Similar issues were broached in reports of consultation to the staffs of Head Start programs by Bonkowski (1968) and Goldberg (1968). In pointing out the lack of trust, the frequent "irrational" responses and the feelings of inferiority and powerlessness of minority paraprofessional staff members vis à vis White consultants, Bonkowski (1968) advocated the need to develop a "...comprehensive theory of the social environment and its effects on behavior... as a model for community consultation" (p. 770).

These studies all suggest that consultants experience greater difficulties in establishing relationships with Black and other minority consultees, particularly in the entry phase. Some factors that may contribute to these difficulties are briefly summarized below.

BLACK-WHITE RELATIONSHIPS

The history of Black-White relationships and the subordinate position of Black people in American society has important implications for interactions between Black and White persons (or those representing white institutions) in the consultation relationship, as well as in interpersonal transactions. Sociological investigations of Black family and peer relationships have described culturally patterned behaviors which are characterized by openness, frankness, expressiveness, playfulness, and intense verbal interaction (Clark, 1965; Drake, 1967; Frazier, 1960). Conversely, in their interpersonal transactions with White people, Black persons tend to be more guarded, more inhibited, more formal, and less verbal (Coles, 1965; Hannerz, 1970; Kochman, 1970).

Moreover, there are social class differences among Black people in the degree of their conformity to these culturally patterned behaviors, as well as in the degree to which they are familiar with and assimilated to the behaviors and expectations which are normative in middle-class white social interactions (Billingsley, 1968; Frazier, 1960; Thompson, 1974).

Knowledge of these general cultural differences, as well as the social class variations, are essential to the effective functioning of the consultant in the entry phase of consultation.

According to Hall and Whyte (1960) there are a number of tangible and intangible factors which influence intercultural communication: the use of language (including meanings, voice tones, and emotions), the attitudes toward physical contact (patterns of personal space, touching, expressing affection), the orientation to time, the significance of place, and the social class hierarchy. Pinderhughes (1979) views the power differential between White and Black people as one of the most powerful influences on an interracial helping relationship, shaping differences in perceptions and attitudes toward responsibility and autonomy. These aspects of ethnic differences in communication and in perceived power and authority have significant effects on all professional interpersonal relationships between Black and White persons.

Clinical investigations of Black patients in psychotherapy have consistently documented initial feelings of suspiciousness, hostility, and paranoia toward their therapists, both Black and White, suggesting the effects of social class differences as well (Grier & Cobbs, 1968; Rosen & Frank, 1962; Sager, Brayboy, & Waxenberg, 1972). Conversely, both Black and White therapists often experience countertransference in treating Black patients due to cultural stereotyping, liberal ideology, or overidentification (Calnek, 1970; Jones, 1974; Schacter & Butts, 1968; Thomas, 1962). While Black college students were found to exhibit similar feelings of initial distrust and distorted perceptions of the therapeutic process (Davis & Swartz, 1972; Hammond, 1970), Gibbs (1975) found that they tended to stay in treatment longer with Black therapists than with Whites, perhaps reflecting a perceived sense of similarity and empathy.

When patients and therapists share similar ethnic and social class backgrounds, Carkhuff and Pierce (1967) found that both Black and White patients experienced greater depth of self-exploration in therapy than those patients who were not as similar. Banks (1972) also replicated these findings in his study of Black and White high school students who rated initial rapport and depth of self-exploration higher in their first interview with counselors of their own race.

When the results of these sociological and clinical studies on Black-White differences are combined with reports of difficulties in establishing interracial consultation relationships, the common source of conflict appears to derive from different sets of expectations concerning professional interaction processes. It is the author's contention that Blacks typically evaluate professional interactions in terms of the *interpersonal* skills demonstrated in initial encounters, while Whites typically evaluate similar interactions in terms of the *instrumental* skills demonstrated. An elaboration of these concepts and their relevance to the consultation process are discussed in the following section.

INTERPERSONAL COMPETENCE

Although both Sarason (1966) and Berlin (1962) acknowledged the importance of interpersonal skills in facilitating the relationship building between the consultant and consultee, they did not distinguish between interpersonal skills and instrumental skills as two different sets of skills that might serve different functions at different stages of the consultation process. In categorizing interpersonal skills as an important complement to professional knowledge and skills, Hinkle and Silverstein (1977) stated that "...the consultant who displays these interpersonal skills will be at an advantage in establishing rapport with consultees" (p. 264). I am proposing that, in settings where the consultee agency or staff is predominantly Black, it is helpful to conceptualize these two sets of competencies as distinct but overlapping skills, related to two different phases of consultation, e.g., the entry phase and the task-oriented phase (which are often difficult to demarcate in precise terms).

Weinstein (1969), in his review paper on *The Development of Interpersonal Competence*, defined it as "...the ability to accomplish interpersonal tasks...interpersonal competence boils down to the ability to manipulate others' responses" (p. 755). While he noted that very little research had been done on the development of this ability and the context in which it is socialized, he identified three aspects of the ability: a) socialization for empathic behavior, b) acquiring a repertoire of tactics, and c) variations in personal orientations. I would add a fourth aspect, which was not considered at all by Weinstein, i.e., variations in value orientations among different ethnic groups with respect to this ability.

Just as there is very little research in general on this ability, there is almost no research which is directly relevant to Black people, except for the studies which are relevant to various aspects of the three areas outlined by Weinstein. To summarize these studies in terms of the above dimensions: a) Black lower-class groups appear to be more sensitive to some types of nonverbal and communicational cues, while Black students appear to be more skillful at enacting and judging emotions (Gitter, Black & Mostofsky, 1972); b) lower-class Black people and inner-city ghetto youth have developed distinctive culturally patterned styles of language (Kochman, 1970; Valentine & Valentine, 1970), social interactions, and strategies for the maintenance of status and self-esteem (Hannerz, 1965; Rainwater, 1965; Schulz, 1969): these strategies and defensive styles may be appropriate in segregated situations, but may be counterproductive and threatening in interracial situations (Allport, 1954; Clark, 1965; Pettigrew, 1964) and c) there are variations in these expressive styles and strategies among lower-class and middle-class Blacks (Billingsley, 1968; Staples, 1971). Finally, Baumrind (Note 1), in a paper on subcultural variations in social competence, proposed that expressiveness, metacommunication skills and role-playing skills are areas in which Black people generally demonstrate more competence than Whites. Most of the studies deal with lower-class Black persons and inner-city ghetto communities, so the results have limited applicability to these groups. However, to the extent that the majority of American Black persons have had some contact with a homogeneous Black, lower-income community, they will share some of these behavioral traits and interaction patterns, or they will at least be able to relate to and to communicate with other Black people who do exhibit these culturally distinctive expressive styles and strategies.

While Weinstein provided a theoretical framework in which to view the study of interpersonal competence, a team of researchers at the University of Oregon has been investigating the techniques of the assessment and development of interpersonal competence (Sundberg, Fehnel, McQueen, Moursound & Muñoz, Note 2). They proposed that the development of interpersonal skills is influenced by family and cultural factors, and that culturally specific behaviors which are effective in a specific setting may be inappropriate in other settings. However, they also pointed out that there are no clearly established criteria for defining or evaluating interpersonal competence, nor is there a framework for matching specific skills with specific settings where they are most appropriate and most effective.

Interpersonal orientation is defined in this study as the value of a group or individual which focuses on the process rather than the content of the interactions, both verbal and nonverbal, between two people. *Interpersonal competence* is a measure of the ability of the individual to evoke attitudes and to obtain favorable responses to his actions. *Instrumental orientation* is the value of a group or individual which focuses on the goal- or task-related aspects in the relationship between two people; thus, *instrumental competence* is a measure of the degree of effectiveness with which that goal or task is accomplished by the individual. A tentative model of the interpersonal orientation which may characterize the behavior of Black consultees in the entry phase of consultation is presented below.

MODEL OF INTERPERSONAL ORIENTATION TO CONSULTATION

The proposed model, developed from a synthesis of the social science findings and consultation studies previously summarized, identifies stages, behaviors, and themes in the relationship between the consultant and Black consultees. The stages and themes reflect the *interpersonal orientation* of Black consultees to the consultation relationship, which is contrasted to the *instrumental orientation* of White consultees. The corollary to these differing orientations is the effect on the initial evaluation of the consultant, i.e., Black consultees tend to focus on the *interpersonal competence* of the consultant, while Whites tend to focus on his/her *instrumental competence.*

It is further suggested that the stages will follow a predictable sequence in the majority of interactions between consultants and Black consultees, but this sequence will be modified by the perceived degree of ethnic and social class similarity between the consultant and the consultees. However, this current model does not specifically account for such shared perceptions of similarities or differences.

Stage I: Appraisal Stage

This is the initial stage of contact between consultant and consultee, during which the Black consultee "sizes up" the consultant, has minimal interactions with him/her, and behaves in an aloof, reserved, or superficially pleasant manner. The consultee does not show any overt interest or curiosity about the consultant, but observes him/her in a rather surreptitious, "cool" manner. Underlying this reserved stance may be feelings of distrust and hostility toward the consultant. While the Black consultees are "playing it cool," the White consultees are evaluating the overall consultation project and the professional skills of the consultant entering the system.

Stage II: Investigation Stage

This is the second stage of contact, which is characterized by the consultee "checking out" the consultant. In this stage, the Black consultee may inquire about the consultant's personal life, background, opinions, and values. This is an attempt to place the consultant in a social status hierarchy, along an ideological spectrum, or to evaluate the consultant's previous professional experiences. The White consultee will inquire about the details of the consultant project, not about the consultant's personal life.

Stage III: Involvement Stage

This stage may only follow the two previous stages if the consultee feels that the consultant has "checked out" favorably; otherwise, the consultant may find further efforts to gain cooperation and to perform his/her professional task will be doomed to failure or mediocrity. The Black consultee may make overtures to the consultant to establish a personal relationship, characterized by the exchange of personal information, personal favors, mutual obligations, and quasi-social interactions (lunch, coffee breaks, etc.). The response of the consultant to these overtures is crucial, if the Black consultee is to accept the consultant's expertise. White consultees will maintain the relationship on a formal professional level.

Stage IV: Commitment Stage

This stage will witness the translation of personal support into program support, i.e., the consultee will express greater interest in the consultation tasks and less interest in the consultant's personality. However, initial commitment to the task will be expressed in terms of loyalty and personal regard for the consultant by the Black consultees, while the White consultees will express their commitment in terms of the goals to be accomplished.

Stage V: Engagement Stage

This stage overlaps with the task-oriented phase of the consultation process. In this stage, both Black and White consultees have made the final commitment to participate fully in the consultation process. While Black persons will make this commitment as a result of their evaluation of the consultant's *interpersonal competence* in the first four stages, White persons will make this commitment in terms of the *instrumental competence* shown by the consultant up to this time.

I have referred several times to the evaluation of the consultant's interpersonal competence by the consultee, but have not yet delineated what the criteria are that I believe the consultee is to apply. I am proposing that the criteria by which the consultee evaluates the interpersonal competence of the consultant are closely related to the dimensions which were previously identified as major cultural patterns among Black people in terms of expressive behavior and social interactions. While these dimensions can be identified rather easily, it is more difficult to define the criteria without empirical evidence from questionnaires and rating instruments. However, I suggest that the following dimensions are used as indicators of interpersonal competence by Black consultees. Each dimension is stage-related in that it is the most relevant to the consultee's evaluation of the consultant's behavior at that particular period of the entry phase of consultation.

Dimension 1: Personal Authenticity

This dimension is most salient in the Appraisal Stage, where the consultee is evaluating the consultant for his/her perceived "genuineness" and the degree to which s/he projects the qualities of being "real," "down-to-earth," and "not uppity."

Dimension 2: Egalitarianism

This dimension is most salient in the Investigation Stage, where the consultee is judging the manner in which the consultant relates to people of similar and different educational, social, and cultural backgrounds. The degree to which the consultant is able to equalize the differences between himself and the consultees in any of these areas will determine his acceptance as a democratic and nonauthoritarian person. His/her ability to use nontechnical language and to communicate the program to all levels of the consultee institution is a major factor in a positive evaluation on this dimension.

Dimension 3: Identification

This dimension is most salient in the Involvement Stage, where the consultee is evaluating the consultant's degree of identification with his/her ethnic background and with the sociocultural milieu of the institution. If the consultant is a middle-class Black person, s/he may be judged on his/her attitude toward his/her ethnicity and general level of identification with the Black subculture; but, if s/he is White, s/he would probably be judged on his/her familiarity with Black culture and his/her tolerance for and comprehension of certain symbolic Black behaviors, attitudes, and values.

Dimension 4: Acceptance

This dimension is most salient in the Commitment Stage, where the consultee evaluates the empathic skills of the consultant, the degree to which the consultant demonstrates his/her comprehension of the problems of the consultee institution and recognizes the complexities of the system, as well as offering support and nonjudgmental attitudes toward the consultees when they express their personal conflicts or professional frustrations.

Dimension 5: Performance

This dimension becomes most salient in the Engagement Stage, when the consultees have made their commitment to cooperate with the consultant to identify and modify or resolve the current dysfunctions in the consultee organization. This is the beginning of the evaluation of the consultant's instrumental competence as the consultees shift their dominant orientation from the interpersonal sphere to the instrumental sphere.

The model of interpersonal orientation to consultation can be graphically outlined in Table 1 below:

CASE ILLUSTRATION

The case example described below is based on the author's experiences as a clinical-community psychology intern for one academic year in a school mental health consultation project in the San Francisco Bay area. The project was an attempt to develop a collaborative school prevention and intervention program through weekly group meetings with the faculty, administration, and special services personnel at the school.

As the female member of a two-person team of Black intern-consultants from the Psychology Clinic at the University of California at Berkeley, I worked in a predominantly Black inner-city elementary school with a racially integrated faculty for one day a week throughout the school year.

The school consultation literature (Berkowitz, 1973; Berlin, 1962; Newman, 1967), while generally preparing us for the technical aspects of consultation, did not adequately deal with the process aspects of consultation in this particular type of institution, i.e., where racial and cultural factors were influencing the intrainstitutional relationships with the consultants.

In order to illustrate the stages and dimensions of the model, seven examples of interpersonal transactions between the Black female consultant (the author) and various teachers and staff members of the school are discussed. These critical incidents have been selected as characteristic of the differential orientation of the Black and White consultees to the entry phase of consultation.

Table 1.   A model of interpersonal orientation to consultation.

Consultee Evaluation Stages (Themes of Evaluation)		Consultant Behavior Responses (Dimensions of Competence)	
I.	Appraisal Stage ("Sizing Up")	I.	Personal Authenticity ("Genuineness")
II.	Investigation Stage ("Checking Out")	II.	Egalitarianism (Status Equalization)
III.	Involvement Stage (Social Interactions)	III.	Identification (Positive Identity)
IV.	Commitment (Personal Loyalty)	IV.	Acceptance (Empathy, Support)
V.	Engagement (Task Involvement)	V.	Performance (Task Performance)

Incident 1

At the first meeting of our consultation team with the school faculty, the principal, a middle-aged Black woman, gave us a cursory introduction and did not provide the group with an adequate explanation of our reason for attending the meeting. During the presentation by the White leader of the group, the White faculty members seemed more attentive than the Blacks, who seemed restless or detached. During the question period, there was a clear difference in the responses of the White and Black teachers to the presentation: the White teachers tended to ask questions relating to the theory, the methods and goals of the project, while the Black teachers tended to ask questions or make comments about the motivations of the team and the impact of the project on the welfare of the school pupils.

The major concern expressed by Black teachers dealt with *the potential harmful effects of the project on the Black children*, whom they wanted to protect from exploitation and manipulation, while the major concern of the White teachers dealt with *the issue of clarifying the details of the project and the criteria for participation.*

Incident 2

A week after this first meeting with the faculty, I requested an appointment with the principal, Mrs. B., in order to obtain faculty reactions to our proposed consultation project. She greeted me warmly and frankly told me that the Black faculty members had reacted very negatively to the presentation, primarily because they suspected that we, as a Berkeley research group, had ulterior motivations to use the Black children as guinea pigs. After prolonged discussion to negotiate a mutually satisfactory arrangement with the faculty, through Mrs. B., she agreed to support the project if we would drop the research component. After this agreement was reached, she abruptly changed the subject, asked me some personal questions, and then offered me some personal data about her teaching career and her relationships with several teachers in the school. The meeting ended on a cordial note, with Mrs. B. promising to support the project *because she "liked" me and my male colleague and thought it would be "fun" to work with us.* (We learned several weeks later that this was a unilateral decision and was never referred to the full faculty for discussion or action again.)

Incident 3

Mrs. R., a Black resource teacher who had been initially critical of the project, was reserved and aloof with us during the first two weeks of our work in the school. On the third week, she joined me for lunch in the faculty lunch room and we had a conversation with a sixth grade teacher about dealing with the social and emotional problems of preadolescent girls. She seemed interested in my previous experiences with this age group, and was subsequently friendlier to me. When I asked her input on a program I was developing for the sixth grade girls, she was very constructive and enthusiastic. At the end of the discussion, she asked me if I were a member of a national Black women's service organization; when I replied affirmatively, she exclaimed, "Well, I'll bet we have a lot in common. We must have lunch together more often and get to know each other." Subsequently, she also asked me a number of personal questions and shared similar information with me. Although she never requested any direct services from me, she attended the first group meeting and was an active participant throughout the duration of the group. After the first meeting of the group, she called me aside and asked how I thought the meeting had turned out. I gave a noncommittal response, but asked her opinion and she said, "I think it went very well and *I was so pleased for you and Bob* (my colleague). I really want this group to go well *because I really like you and Bob and I want you to be successful with your project*." She did not discuss any of the substantive issues raised in the group's meeting.

Incident 4

Mr. D., a youthful Black resource teacher, was polite and reserved whenever I saw him at the school. In conjunction with my assessment of a sixth grade girl who had been referred to me for acting-out behavior, I asked Mr. D. if I could observe her in his class and on the playground, and later asked him for his evaluation of her behavior in these settings. He seemed very pleased to be consulted and was very cooperative. The next week he spontaneously commented to me that he had really enjoyed our "little talk" and he had decided to join the group. He then said that he had initially felt reservations about our project and about our motivations, but he had been observing me and Bob and felt that we really had *"our heads in the right place"* and that we were "OK folks."

The previous four illustrations all occurred between Black consultees and the Black consultant; the following three incidents represent interactions with White teachers and are intended to serve as a contrast to the interactions with Black teachers and staff.

Incident 5

Miss J., another resource teacher, had shown great interest in the project from our first meeting with the faculty. On my first visit to the school, she set up appointments for me to observe teachers who were participating in the school's voluntary precision teaching program. After the first meeting of the group, she commented that she was really looking forward to the next meeting, *because she was interested in psychology and felt that she could learn something with a new perspective on children.* She resigned her position shortly after our group meetings began due to pregnancy, but she said she would be sorry to miss future meetings of the group *because the two sessions had whetted her appetite to learn more about preventive techniques in dealing with emotionally troubled children.*

Incident 6

Mrs. P., one of the resource specialists in the school, was one of the oldest and most experienced teachers there. She had been one of the most responsive teachers in our initial visits to the school, orienting us to the history, faculty divisions, and leadership issues in the school. She felt that this information would be helpful to us as we formed the new group and pledged her support of the project. When she missed one meeting of the group, she apologized to us and said she "hated to miss these group meetings because I'm enjoying them so much and *I'm learning how to look at old problems in a new way.*" She also commented that she wished that our group could talk about the interpersonal tensions among the faculty because "an outsider would probably *help them with their morale problems and get the school moving in the right direction again.*"

Incident 7

Miss R., the White sixth-grade teacher, had expressed only a lukewarm interest in the group, but was always quite friendly and open to me when we met in the lunchroom. She was one of two sixth grade teachers who initally helped to develop a program with a group discussion format for the sixth grade girls. Although Miss R. did not attend the group meeting regularly, she was an effective co-leader with the girls' group which met weekly during lunch hour. In her later comments on this experience, she said that *she had really learned a lot about how to elicit responses from the girls* and how to encourage them to talk about issues which really concerned them. At the end of the group, she said that the experience had been very valuable to her because *she had some new ideas about programming for sixth graders* and thought that she now understood some of the girls much better and was more aware of some of their family and community problems, *which would make her more effective in dealing with them in the classroom.*

CONSULTANT-CONSULTEE INTERACTIONS

The above "critical incidents" were selected to illustrate major differences in the orientation of the Black and White teachers and staff members to the consultation process. However, I do want to emphasize that Black teachers and staff also commented on the content and goals of the consultation, on their professional reactions to the project, and on their professional and personal gains from the project. Specifically, it is a matter of timing and degree, i.e., Black teachers tended to respond to us in a very personal, non-task-oriented way in the initial phase of the consultation, and became task-oriented much later in the project; while White teachers tended to be very task-oriented initially, and developed personal relationships with us much later in the project, if at all.

Since both members of the team were Black, the question may be raised about generalizing these interactional patterns to White consultants and Black or White consultees. However, similar experiences were reported by an interracial team of consultants working in another school in the area.

IMPLICATIONS OF THE PROPOSED MODEL

This approach, in which interpersonal competence must initially be evaluated before instrumental competence is demonstrated, has been noted in many analogous relationships of Black people. The interpersonal orientation has been exhibited by Black students dealing with white educational institutions and their administrators (Haettenschwiller, 1971; Mackey, 1972); by low-income Blacks in their orientation to organizational bureaucracy (cf. Moguloff, 1974; Moynihan, 1969); in their orientation to the political system (cf. Wilson, 1967); and in their orientation to religion (cf. Mitchell, 1970).

The scheme I have outlined, along with the model I have tentatively proposed, has a number of significant implications both in terms of its explanatory power and its application to a more sophisticated understanding of Black communication and interaction patterns, as well as its application to the analysis of professional relationships between Black people and other ethnic groups. Some of these implications will be briefly discussed.

First, the concept of an interpersonal orientation among Black persons in professional relationships has heuristic value in explaining the observed differences in the ways Black and White people respond to the entry phase of consultation, the beginning phase of therapy, and the initial adjustment to educational and organizational bureaucracies. The interpersonal orientation derives from attempts to personalize relationships which are usually considered impersonal in the dominant culture, i.e., to treat a universalistic situation in a particularistic way. Naturally, this creates communication problems and often leads to prematurely terminated or permanently impaired relationships because of mutual misunderstanding on the part of the Black person and the other person involved in the transaction.

Second, the conceptualization of interpersonal competence as a distinct set of skills which can be differentiated from instrumental skills is useful in analyzing the requirements of different consultation requests. If these skills are important in order to establish communication and mutual trust in predominantly Black institutions or organizations, the consultant can be in a better position to evaluate his/her own resources and effectiveness for such a job. Much time and energy could probably be saved if consultant and consultee were more congruent in terms of this important factor; this issue was particularly crucial during the peak of the poverty program and was probably at the root of much of the dissension between poverty agencies and their consultants (cf. Moynihan, 1969).

Third, a stage-related model of interpersonal orientation and the dimensions of interpersonal competence offer the consultant a framework in which to judge his/her relative progress through the entry phase into the actual task performance phase. If conflicts or problems arise at any of these stages in the entry phase, the consultant might be better able to identify the sources of the problems and deal with them before s/he loses ground and alienates the consultee.

Fourth, the entire model can be useful in training professionals in the helping professions, educators, business managers, and politicians who will be better equipped to understand the perspectives of Black persons who have this interpersonal orientation, and will thus be better able to deliver services to them. At the same time, educators and mental health professionals can point out the inappropriateness of the interpersonal orientation in some situations, so that students and clients can learn to be more effective in their dealings with the dominant culture.

Fifth, an understanding of this interpersonal orientation-interpersonal competence model is useful for cross-cultural purposes, particularly for training programs (cf. Lynch & Lombardi, 1976; Mannino et al., 1975). As Sundberg et al. (1975) have pointed out, some skills which are appropriate for some situations are inappropriate for others. It seems that other ethnic groups might benefit from paying more attention to the interpersonal dimension of all human interactions, particularly in bureaucratic settings and in work-related encounters. Conversely, Black persons can benefit from learning how to accept the instrumental knowledge and skills of those who are not skilled in interpersonal strategies. I agree with Baumrind (1976) that the future world will demand greater interpersonal skills, and I feel that Black persons and other minority groups need to learn how to manipulate the political and economic systems and to negotiate educational bureaucracies with the optimal combination of interpersonal and instrumental competencies (Gibbs, 1973).

Finally, the concept of an interpersonal orientation in the use of consultation may be generalizable to other ethnic minority groups, particularly those who share with Black people a relatively disadvantaged position in American society and have developed adaptive strategies to cope with their lower status. For example, studies of preventive mental health programs and consultation to Latino groups focus on the importance of professionals understanding the distinctive cultural attitudes, values, and linguistic variations among different Spanish-speaking groups (Abad, Ramos, & Boyce, 1974; Cohen, 1972; Martinez, 1973). In enumerating the cultural characteristics common to Puerto Ricans, Abad et al. (1974) described a very similar value as follows: *"Personalismo* refers to the inclination of Latin people, in general, to relate to and trust persons, rather than institutions, and their dislike for formal, impersonal structures and organizations" (p. 588).

This is a very tentative model based on theoretical, clinical, and sociological data from several disciplinary perspectives. Research designs are needed to test the validity of the model and to test its applicability to other situations involving Blacks in interpersonal transactions. Studies of the consultation process should be conducted in natural settings, using interracial teams of consultants to deliver services to interracial consultee staffs in order to compare intraethnic and interethnic effects in consultation. Other characteristics of the consultant to be manipulated for their effects on interracial consultation are the status of the consultant (student versus professional), his/her age, and sex. In addition, the model should be investigated for its applicability to other ethnic groups, particularly those which are low-status and disadvantaged, for they also have developed unique expressive styles and behavioral strategies to survive and adapt in American society.

REFERENCE NOTES

1. Baumrind, D. *Subcultural variations in values defining social competence.* Paper presented at the meeting of The Society for Research in Child Development, Western Regional Conference, April 1976.
2. Sundberg, N., Fehnel, R., McQueen, L., Moursound, J., & Muñoz, R. *Assessing and assisting development of interpersonal competence for the human services.* Paper presented at the meeting of the American Psychological Association, Chicago, September 1975.

REFERENCES

Abad, V., Ramos, J., & Boyce, E. A model for delivery of mental health services to Spanish-speaking minorities. *American Journal of Orthopsychiatry*, 1974, *44,* 584–595.

Allport, G. *The nature of prejudice*. Cambridge, Mass.: Addison-Wesley, 1954.

Altrocchi, J. Mental health consultation. In S. Golann and C. Eisdorfer (Eds.), *Handbook of community mental health*. New York: Appleton-Century-Crofts, 1972.

Banks, W. The differential effects of race and social class in helping. *Journal of Clinical Psychology*, 1972, *28,* 90–92.

Berkowitz, H. A collaborative approach to mental health consultation in school settings. In W. Claiborn and R. Cohen (Eds.), *School intervention*. New York: Behavioral Publications, 1973.

Berlin, I. Mental health consultation as a means of communicating mental health principles. *Journal of the American Academy of Child Psychiatry*, 1962, *1,* 671–679.

Billingsley, A. *Black families in white America*. Englewood Cliffs, N.J.: Prentice-Hall, 1968.

Bonkowski, R. Mental health consultation and Operation Head Start. *American Psychologist*, 1968, *23,* 769–772.

Brody, M., & Schneider, I. The psychiatrist as classroom teacher: School consultation in the inner city. *Hospital and Community Psychiatry*, 1973, *24,* 248–251.

Broskowski, A. Teacher-centered consultation in an inner-city junior high school. In W. Claiborn and R. Cohen (Eds.), *School intervention*. New York: Behavioral Publications, 1973.

Calnek, M. Racial factors in countertransference: The Black therapist and the Black client. *American Journal of Orthopsychiatry*, 1970, *40,* 39–46.

Caplan, G. *The theory and practice of mental health consultaion*. New York: Basic Books, 1970.

Carkhuff, R., & Pierce, R. Differential effects of therapist race and social class upon patient depth of self-exploration in the initial clinical interview. *Journal of Consulting Psychology*, 1967, *31,* 632–634.

Clark, K. *Dark ghetto*. New York: Harper & Row, 1965.

Cohen, R. Principles of preventive mental health programs for ethnic minority populations: The acculturation of Puerto Ricans to the United States. *American Journal of Psychiatry*, 1972, *128,* 1529–1533.

Coles, R. Observation or participation: The problem of psychiatric research on social issues. *Journal of Nervous and Mental Disease*, 1965, *141,* 274–284.

Davis, K., & Swartz, J. Increasing Black students' utilization of mental health services. *American Journal of Orthopsychiatry*, 1972, *42,* 771–776.

Drake, St. C. The social and economic status of the Negro in the United States. In T. Parsons and K. Clark (Eds.), *The Negro American*. Boston: Beacon Press, 1967.

Frazier, E. *The Negro family in the United States*. Chicago: University of Chicago Press, 1960.

Gibbs, J. Black students/white university: Different expectations. *Personnel and Guidance Journal*, 1973, *51,* 463–469.

Gibbs, J. Use of mental health services by black students at a predominantly white university: A three-year study. *American Journal of Orthopsychiatry*, 1975, *45,* 430–445.

Gitter, A., Black, H., & Mostofsky, D. Race and sex in the perception of emotion. *Journal of Social Issues*, 1972, *28,* 63–78.

Glidewell, J. The entry problem in consultation. *Journal of Social Issues*, 1959, *15,* 51–59.

Goldberg, H. The psychologist in Head Start: New aspects of the role. *American*

Psychologist, 1968, *23*, 773–774.

Grier, W., & Cobbs, P. *Black rage*. New York: Basic Books, 1968.

Haettenschwiller, D. Counseling black students in special programs. *Personnel and Guidance Journal*, 1971, *50*, 29–37.

Hall, E., & Whyte, W. Intercultural communication: A guide to men of action. *Human Organization*, 1960, *19*, 5–12.

Hammond, C. Paranoia and prejudice: Recognition and management of the student from a deprived background. *International Psychiatry Clinics*, 1970, *7*, 35–48.

Hannerz, U. What ghetto males are like: Another look. In N. Whitten and J. Szwed (Eds.), *Afro-American anthropology: Contemporary perspectives*. New York: Free Press, 1970.

Hinkle, A., & Silverstein, B. A method for the evaluation of mental health consultation to the public schools. *Journal of Community Psychology*, 1977, *5*, 262–265.

Jones, E. Social class and psychotherapy: A critical review of research. *Psychiatry*, 1974, *37*, 307–320.

Kochman, T. Toward an ethnography of black American speech behavior. In N. Whitten and J. Szwed (Eds.), *Afro-American anthropology: Contemporary perspectives*. New York: Free Press, 1970.

Lynch, A., & Lombardi, J. An experientially based course on consultation. *Professional Psychology*, 1976, *7*, 323–330.

Mackey, E. Some observations on coping styles of black students on white campuses. *Journal of the American College Health Association*, 1972, *21*, 126–130.

Mannino, F., MacLennan, B., & Shore, M. *The practice of mental health consultation*, (DHEW Pub. No. (ADM) 74-112). Washington, D.C.: U.S. Government Printing Office, 1975.

Martinez, C. Community mental health and the Chicano movement. *American Journal of Orthopsychiatry*, 1973, *43*, 595–601.

Mitchell, H. *Black preaching*. Philadelphia: Lippincott, 1970.

Moguloff, M. Advocates for themselves: Citizen participation in federally supported community organizations. *Community Mental Health Journal*, 1974, *10*, 66–76.

Morrison, A. Consultation and group process with indigenous neighborhood workers. *Community Mental Health Journal*, 1970, *6*, 3–12.

Moynihan, D. *Maximum feasible misunderstanding*. New York: Free Press, 1969.

Newman, R. *Psychological consultation in the schools: A catalyst for learning*. New York: Basic Books, 1967.

Pettigrew, T. *A profile of the Negro American*. Princeton: Van Nostrand, 1964.

Pinderhughes, E. Teaching empathy in cross-cultural social work. *Social Work*, 1979, *24*, 312–316.

Rainwater, L. Crucible of identity: The lower-class Negro family. *Daedalus*, 1965, *95*, 258–264.

Rosen, H., & Frank, J. Negroes in psychotherapy. *American Journal of Psychiatry*, 1962, *119*, 456–460.

Sager, C., Brayboy, T., & Waxenberg, B. Black patient-white therapist. *American Journal of Orthopsychiatry*, 1972, *42*, 415–423.

Sarason, S., Levine, M., Goldenberg, I., Cherlin, D., & Bennett, E. *Psychology in community settings*. New York: Wiley, 1966.

Schacter, J., & Butts, H. Transference and countertransference in inter-racial analyses. *Journal of the American Psychoanalytic Association*, 1968, *16*, 792–808.

Scheidlinger, S., Struening, E., & Rabkin, J. Evaluation of a mental health consultation service in a ghetto area. *American Journal of Psychotherapy*, 1970, *24*, 485–493.

Scheidlinger, S., Sarcka, A., & Mendes, H. A mental health consultation service to neighborhood organizations in an inner city area. *Community Mental Health Journal*, 1971, *7*, 264–271.

Schulz, D. *Coming up black*. Englewood Cliffs, N.J.: Prentice-Hall, 1969.

Staples, R. (Ed.) *The black family*. Belmont, Ca.: Wadsworth Publishing Company, 1971.

Thomas, A. Pseudo-transference reactions due to cultural stereotyping. *American Journal of Orthopsychiatry*, 1962, *32*, 894–900.

Thompson, D. *Sociology of the black experience*. Westport, Connecticut: Greenwood Press, 1974.

Valentine, C., & Valentine, B. Making the scene, digging the action, and telling it like it is: Anthropologists at work in a dark ghetto. In N. Whitten and J. Szwed (Eds.), *Afro-American anthropology: Contemporary perspectives*. New York: Free Press, 1970.

Weinstein, E. The development of interpersonal competence. In D. Goslin (Ed.), *Handbook of socialization theory and research*. Chicago: Rand McNally, 1969.

Wilson, J. The negro in politics. In T. Parsons and K. Clark (Eds.). *The Negro American*. Boston: Beacon Press, 1967.

Section III

HISPANIC AMERICANS

18

Editorial Introduction

Hispanic Americans, or Latinos, are the most urban of minority populations, and regional in their residences, with Chicanos in the Southwest, Puerto Ricans in Connecticut, New Jersey, and New York, and Cubans in Florida. In spite of diverse origins, however, their culture is homogeneous, as Rene Ruiz and Amado Padilla document in the first selection. They present general information on Latino distinctiveness, including demography, language, religion, family and kinship relations, and sources of psychological stress. Cultural reasons for underutilization of available human services are summarized, and two illustrative case histories are included.

The next two selections orient the reader to culturally indigenous therapists, or folk healers. Melvin Delgado emphasizes the similarity of their healing roles in spiritism (Puerto Rico), curanderismo (Mexico), and santeria (Cuba). A five-point continuum for describing the extent to which healers are affiliated with human service delivery systems is described. Training, consultation, referral variations, and cotherapy represent increasing involvement and participation. Pedro Ruiz and John Langrod explore the legitimate service domains of folk healers. They see a good fit between the services provided and the needs of a Hispanic population. For example, folk healers use nonverbal communication, honor the existing cultural perceptions of how the distress was caused, and practice in the same environment, thereby sharing the ghetto frustrations with their clients. Folk healers also are on the home ground in crisis, make use of the extended family for social support, and accept talking with God, spirit communication, and emotionally-charged, trancelike states, or *ataques*, as reasonable phenomena.

The next three selections present treatment for specific problems within a culturally knowledgeable framework. Herbert Freudenberger describes the treatment of young drug abusers within a Puerto Rican milieu. The potentially damaging effects of imposing Anglo identities and an Anglo-oriented value system are offset by use of a case conference encounter approach in an outpatient, therapeutic community setting. Wayne Maes and John Rinaldi provide a family case history with focus on the children in order to illustrate the interface of culture and school-related difficulties. Counselor personal characteristics, bilingualism, cultural awareness, and special skills are described as necessary ingredients for helping relationships. Melvin Delgado presents a foster family program that uses culturally sophisticated, bilingual staff in order to recruit and train prospective foster parents in child care and problem management.

The selection by Melvin Delgado and John Scott shows the manner in which the foster parents program fits in a complete community service program that emphasizes "strategic intervention." "Strategic intervention" is planful, flexible, and originates in service needs as defined within the community. The training of indigenous leaders and service specialists as well as provision of consultation are central features. Primary prevention and service delivery in nonstigmatic settings are stressed.

Samuel Roll, Leverett Millen, and Ricardo Martinez present reasons for underutilization and ineffective utilization of human services by Hispanic clients. Since ethnicity is not responded to as part of personality, clients are pathologized and medication is the treatment option that is often preferred to psychotherapy. Nonetheless, Latino culture has an affective emphasis including *personalismo* and a history of *curanderos* as service providers that argues for psychotherapy as a legitimate treatment. However, therapists should be bicultural, bilingual, and understand their own reactions to Hispanics. Therapists who do not understand Latino culture often fail to be sufficiently flexible in the separation of a formal style of professional self-presentation from a necessary personalization of the process by "small talk." Similarly, the predominantly passive coping style of Hispanics is often equated with passivity. As a result there is failure to appreciate a world view that has a reality-based recognition of the limitations of personal power. One cannot make pejorative judgments about persons who are less competitive and achievement-oriented and more cooperative than middle-class Americans of Anglo-Saxon and Protestant origins. Finally, *machismo* is misconstrued to be limited to a willingness to fight or be sexually assertive although the concept includes freedom to express feeling and to be tender and protective. Therapists should also be aware that culturally distinctive personality traits coexist with Spanish as the primary language.

19

Counseling Latinos

Rene A. Ruiz and Amado M. Padilla

Our purpose here is to provide background information and techniques that will enable counselors to communicate more effectively and to counsel more successfully with Latino clients. To achieve this, we have summarized information that communicates the many ways in which Latino clients are similar and dissimilar to other non-Latino clients. Deliberate effort is made to identify resource documentation to provide interested counselors an opportunity to explore contact areas in greater depth, if desired. This summary material, which is designed to facilitate understanding of typical and unique problems faced by Latinos, is organized around the following topical outlines: a) Demographic characteristics of the target population, b) Ethnohistory and culture, c) Sources of psychological stress, d) Utilization of services, and e) Factors reducing self-referral.

Following presentation of this introductory material, case histories of two Latino clients appear. These were deliberately selected to illustrate points made in preceding sections; but, in addition, they serve to facilitate the presentation of specific recommendations for the counseling of Latino clients. The case histories are followed by a concluding section presenting general recommendations for counselors and the settings in which they function.

DEMOGRAPHIC CHARACTERISTICS OF THE TARGET POPULATION

The term "Latino" is used in this article as a generic label including all people of Spanish origin and descent. United States Bureau of the Census reports (1971a, 1971b) indicate the existence of at least 9,000,000 Latino residents in the United States. While this figure almost certainly underestimates the current size of the Latino group, it appears adequate for our purposes. Analyzing the Latino group by geographic area of origin, and rounding by millions, population estimates as of 1972 are as follows: Central and South America (0.5), Cuba (0.6), Mexico (5.0), Puerto Rico (1.5), and other (1.5).

The census data further indicate that an absolute and relative majority of Latinos are urban-dwellers; 82.5 percent compared with 67.8 percent for the total population and 76 percent for Blacks. Furthermore, locus of residence and Latino subgroup membership are related. More specifically, Chicanos are heavily represented in the Southwest United States; 87 percent reside in Arizona, California, Colorado, New Mexico, and Texas. Most Puerto Ricans reside in either Connecticut, New Jersey, or New York (76%); while most immigrants from Cuba are situated in Florida.

In addition to being urban dwellers, disproportionately large numbers of Latinos are members of the lower income groups. The 1971 census reports that 2.4 million Latinos or 26.7 percent were classified as living "in poverty." Closer examination of census data on personal and family income support the inference that the standard of living among Latinos is relatively lower than the general population. In 1970, for example, the median income for Latino males was $6,220 compared with $8,220 for non-Latino males. Examination of family income confirms the general trend; overrepresentation for Latinos in the lower income groups and underrepresentation in the higher income groups. More specifically, 23 percent of the families reported income of less than $5,000 a year compared with 14.7 percent of the general population; while only 18.4 percent had incomes greater than $15,000 compared with 35.5 percent of the general population. There is no reason to believe that this situation has improved from 1970 to 1976.

Difference in patterns of employment and unemployment between Latinos and the non-Latino population exist, and these are interpreted as representing additional stress for Latinos. With regard to status of employment, Latinos are overrepresented in occupations that are menial and low paying; for example, 76 percent are blue-collar workers. With regard to unemployment, a 1975 Bureau of Labor Statistics report indicates that during the third quarter of 1974 the unemployment rate among Latinos was 8 percent, which is intermediate between the national level (5%) and that among Blacks (10.5%). These data are somewhat deceptive, however, unless one considers the increase in unemployment during the preceding year was 29 percent among Latinos, compared with 22 percent among the general population and 8 percent among Blacks.

With respect to education the U.S. census reports the following for Anglos, Black, and Latino males aged 25 years and older; median years of education: 12.2, 9.6, and 9.3 years; fewer than five years of schooling: 5.0, 13.5, and 19.5 percent; and, graduation from high school: 56.4, 34.7, and 32.6 percent. Thus, regardless of which of three educational criteria is examined, the inference remains unchanged. Latinos are provided the least education, compared with either the general population or to American Blacks.

In conclusion, Latinos are, on the *average*, urban dwellers, poor and low paid, menially employed and fearful of layoffs, and undereducated relative to age peers who are not Latino. Factors such as these are unquestionably significant sources of stress in U.S. society. It also follows that we would expect, because of increased stress, a relatively higher frequency of self-referrals for counseling and psychotherapy among Latinos. Keep this syllogism in mind while examining subsequent sections of this article.

ETHNOHISTORY AND CULTURE

Above, we presented demographic data that demonstrates how Latinos differ from the general population. Here we describe the Latino experience from a historical perspective as a means of documenting three major points. First, we maintain that Latinos may be thought of as members of a single cultural group in the sense they share historically similarities in language, values, and tradition. Second, we simultaneously maintain that this Latino culture group is highly heterogeneous, and that for some purposes, *should* be conceptualized as an aggregate of distinct subcultures, each possessing a recognizable pattern of unique traits. Third, we believe that information on ethnohistory and culture is important for non-Latino counselors who need to be able to differentiate between members of different Latino subcultures.

In terms of a commonsense example of relevance to our topic, we are arguing that a particular counseling program designed to deal with a specific type of problem might be highly successful with Chicanos, moderately successful with Cubans, and of only limited success with Puerto Ricans because of subcultural differences across groups.

The preceding argument is complex and subtle. What is involved is the identification of patterns of similarity among *individual* members of different subcultural groups, who are by definition unique in many aspects. The next step, of course, is to create "culturally relevant" programs of counseling and psychotherapy based on intragroup subculture similarities that achieve maximum success rates in constructive behavior change and personal growth. The interested reader is referred to Padilla and Ruiz (1973) and Padilla, Ruiz, and Alvarez (1975) for an analysis of culturally relevant counseling programs for Latinos.

Our ethnohistorical account begins with the Spanish explorers who arrived in the New World in the early 16th century, bringing with them a relatively homogeneous culture similar in language, values, tradition, and costume. In Mexico, they overthrew the Aztec empire, intermarried with the natives, and soon thereafter began to migrate north. The Rio Grande, or "Big River," current border between the United States and Mexico, was crossed in 1528. By the mid-16th century, settlements had been created in what today is Northern New Mexico. These original immigrants included Spaniards from Europe, native Americans from Mexico, and the *mestizo* or "mixed blood" progeny of these two groups.

These events contribute to our thesis in three ways. First, genetic merger resulted in the gradual creation of a new Indo-Hispanic culture. Second, Spaniards as well as the *mestizo* offspring sought new lands to explore and colonize. Third, the settlers who reached Northern New Mexico remained relatively isolated from Mexico and Spain, because of geographic distance and dilatory transportation. Later, they were outgrouped by the immigrants who came to call themselves the "Americans" of the United States. These Latinos came to refer to themselves as "Spanish-Americans," or Hispanos, and coincidentally were the first people of European or European-Indian stock to settle in what is present day United States.

This process of Spanish-Indian intermarriage and cultural fusion was occurring simultaneously in other parts of the New World. In some areas, native inhabitants were slain or driven off their land, and their cultures destroyed. Slaves from Africa were sometimes imported (Puerto Rico is a prime example) and the process of intermarriage and culture fusion continued for several hundred years. The net result, of course, was that a number of subculture groups were formed. The subgroups are commonly referred to as Latinos, or "the Latino culture," which blurs significant differences across groups. As our ethnohistorical analysis reveals, Latinos differ in genetic heritage as indicated by observable physical characteristics, and in cultural tradition (the relative extent to which a given subculture is based on influences from Europe, and the New World, or Africa). Let's examine some of these differences more closely to learn how they can determine need for, and response to, counseling intervention.

Skin color is one obvious physical characteristic with a genetic link that differentiates Latino subgroups. The range in skin coloration is from "white," through *mestizo* and mulatto "brown," to African "black." Considering the long-standing prejudice in this country to people of color, it seems certain that darker Latinos experienced greater discrimination than lighter ones.

The types of subcultures formed were also influenced by original motivations for leaving their country of birth and migrating to a new country. Some Spaniards migrated for immediate personal gain with no thought of creating a new home. These people came to explore, colonize, exploit, and return. Others built new homes; they sought economic opportunity and personal liberty. Still others came because of interactions between complex social, political, economic, and personal factors. Today, Latinos have migrated to the United States in waves, to seek employment or to escape periods of civil strife in their country of origin.

Thus we can see that a large group of Latinos can be identified on the basis of shared characteristics: primarily, language, values, and tradition. Further, this large group includes a number of distinct subcultures that share these characteristics, but to varying degrees. This variation is attributable to the degree of acculturation among Latinos to the majority culture of the United States that is basically WASP and monolingual English. Here we will turn to an examination of acculturation because it bears directly upon the kinds of social stresses experienced by Latinos in the United States, which in turn is one factor that determines need for counseling.

One characteristic that determines rate of acculturation is fluency in English, yet the commitment to Spanish among Latinos is so strong that 50 percent report it as their "native language," and as their preferred "home language." What this means in effect is that unlike many other ethnic groups, Latinos overall have tenaciously held on to their Spanish language, despite the fact that English is the language of the school, work, and play.

Latinos also differ from mainstream Americans with regard to values (e.g., religious preference). The vast majority of Latinos profess Roman Catholicism, with only a relatively small percentage professing Protestant faiths. In contrast, the dominant religious preference of the majority culture is reversed; that is, more professed Protestants than Roman Catholics.

The characteristic of Latino tradition is extremely complex, and therefore more difficult to describe succinctly in terms of variation from the majority culture. The most prominent features, and those of greater significance for the counselor formulating programs based on cultural and subcultural differences, appear in the areas of family structure and attendant sex roles. The extended family structure is most common by far, but characteristically includes: a) respect for the authority of a dominant father who rules the household; b) unwavering love for the mother who serves a unifying function within the family; c) formalized kinship relations such as the *compadrazgo* "godfather" system; and d) loyalty to the family that takes precedence over other social institutions. In addition, sex roles are traditionally more rigid and demarcated more clearly, males are granted greater independence and at an earlier age than females, and there are greater expectations for achievement outside the home for males. Again, the reader is reminded these are summary statements; a more detailed analysis of family structure and sex-role behavior appears in Ruiz and Padilla (unpublished manuscript).

There exists an additional pattern of behavior, which seems to stem from family structure and sex role, which differentiates Latinos from non-Latinos. Latinos typically manifest *personalismo*, a term denoting a preference for personal contact and individualized attention in dealing with power structures, such as social institutions. Anglos, in contrast, seem to favor an organizational approach that follows impersonal regulations (the "chain of command"). Consistent with a preference for more personalized interaction is the observation of relatively more frequent physical contact among Latinos. For example, handshakes between acquaintances and *abrazos* (embraces) among friends are the norm upon meeting and leaving. The influence of *personalismo* appears early and is reflected in play. Mexican children are the most cooperative, Anglos the most competitive, and Mexican-American children are intermediate (Madsen & Shapira, 1970). Of more immediate relevance to our thesis is the finding that Latino clients prefer to use first names rather than formal titles in centers dispensing counseling and psychotherapy services (Kline, 1969).

Counselors interested in increasing their counseling skills by learning more about Latino culture will probably explore the social science literature. This may prove to be hazardous, however, because this literature contains a certain degree of misinformation concerning the "true nature" of the Latino character. Unsupported "findings" based on single-study research, or subjective opinions presented in the context of unsubstantiated essays, seem to have been accepted by a segment of the scientific community. What may have occurred is that a certain degree of spurious "validity" has been created through constant repetition rather than through the gradual accumulation of validating research. Without casting aspersions on the motivation of persons creating or perpetuating such myths, it does seem as if the most widely disseminated and firmly held are pejorative in nature.

It has been alleged often, for example, that Latinos are fatalists (Heller, 1967). The belief that Latinos adhere to predestination has been supported by a few studies showing, to use more technical language, higher "external reinforcement" scores on tests of "locus of control" (Lefcourt, 1966; Rotter, 1954, 1966). This finding disappears, however, when socioeconomic status is controlled (Stone & Ruiz, 1974). Related to the myth of fatalism and belief in predestination is the idea that Latinos possess distorted attitudes toward time. Specifically, Latinos are presumably present time oriented, unduly emphasizing immediate gratification, and displaying underdeveloped skills in future planning. This tendency to enjoy the moment and to defer unpleasant responsibilities to some vague, indeterminate point in the future, seems widely accepted despite a dearth of supportive evidence. What may be occurring is that some non-Latinos translate common Latino responses such as *mañana* ("Tomorrow"), or *Lo que Dios desea* ("Whatever God wills"), into literal English equivalents. Any translation that ignores cultural and subcultural *values* runs the risk, of course, of communicating *meaning* inaccurately. It is at least conceivable that a Latino youngster who expends minimal effort in the pursuit of scholastic or academic goals is responding realistically to societal constraints based on discrimination and prejudice, rather than displaying any deficiency in "achievement motivation."

The last concept we explore to better acquaint counselors with the unique aspects of Latino clients is acculturation. Each Latino client, in addition to being a member of the greater Latino culture and some smaller Latino subculture, is simultaneously a member of the majority, Anglo culture to some degree. Degree of acculturation can be inferred from degree of commitment of cultural variables; that is, language values, tradition, diet, and costume. Thus, a Latino client who is monolingual Spanish or bilingual Spanish-English, with Spanish dominant; Roman Catholic; a member of an extended family; and who prefers ethnic food and dress is probably much less acculturated to the majority, Anglo culture of the United States than some other Latino client who is monolingual English, non-Catholic, from or in a nuclear family, and without preferences for the diet or clothing characteristic of his ethnic group. As we hope to show later, these variables of cultural preference and acculturation interact with the variable of *source of stress* to determine what type of counseling approach will be maximally successful with a given Latino client. It now seems appropriate to examine sources of stress for Latino clients.

SOURCES OF STRESS

In this section, we differentiate between *intrapsychic* and *extrapsychic* sources of stress. We use the former term (intrapsychic) to identify problems of a personal or individual nature that arise independent of ethnic minority group membership. We propose—although empirical evidence corroborating this supposition has not yet been collected—that Latino clients experiencing intrapsychic stress will respond similarly, if not exactly, as will non-Latino clients experiencing the same stress. For example, if a young person is graduating from high school, uncertain as to whether to attend college or which major to pursue, it probably makes relatively little difference whether this student is Latino or not. Regardless of ethnicity, a young person in such a dilemma would probably complain about feelings of uncertainty, indecision, insecurity, personal inadequacy, and general apprehension concerning his or her own, and familial expectations. Finally, ethnicity would probably have relatively little influence upon the type of counseling approach designed to help such a client formulate and achieve more compatible life goals with less personal discomfort.

We have reserved the term *extrapsychic* to refer to sources of stress that stem from outside the person and that are basically societal or environmental rather than personal. Our interest, of course, lies with extrapsychic stress associated with ethnic minority group membership. Thus, we focus upon prejudices against Latinos and the effect of discriminatory practices upon character formation, personality function, and coping. We have already documented earlier, for example, that Latinos are victims of the "poverty cycle": depressed personal and family incomes, fewer years of education, overrepresentation in menial occupations, and elevated rates of unemployment. This cycle is self-perpetuating because the victims are less able to subsidize their own education, those of their children, or to qualify for better, higher paying employment. Furthermore, in comparison with other ethnic groups, Latino students possess fewer "role models" to imitate who have achieved success through continued education or training. Other stressful consequences of poverty include decreased social status, inadequate health care and nutrition, and a generally reduced quality of life.

This discussion suggests that the counselor may anticipate three "types" of Latino clients with regard to the sources of stress that motivate self-referral for counseling. Some will complain of intrapsychic stress and present problems similar to those of non-Latino clients. Others will be experiencing extrapsychic stress and will appear similar to other clients who are victims of prejudice and discrimination. But most Latino clients will probably seek counseling for problems stemming from both sources of stress. In any event, this analysis suggests that rates of self-referral for counseling and psychotherapy are expected to be elevated relative to the general population. Now let's examine relevant data to determine the accuracy of this prediction.

UTILIZATION OF SERVICES

Available utilization data of public mental health service facilities indicates that Latinos, contrary to expectations, and despite *greater* stress, refer themselves *less* often for counseling and psychotherapy, relative to the general population (for review see Padilla & Ruiz, 1973; Padilla et al., 1975; Ruiz, Padilla & Alvarez, in press). The most recent survey of utilization of state and county mental hospitals across the nation (Bachrach,

1975) reveals the following: a) the age-adjusted rate of admission for Latinos is 155 per 100,000 population, compared with 181 for other white and 334 for non-whites, b) age-adjusted rate of admission rates are approximately double for Latino males compared with Latino females (212 to 103 per 100,000 population), and c) adjusting for relative differences in the sizes of ethnic groups, Latino admissions are highest among the youngest (ages 14-25 years), and oldest (age 65 years and older).

Moving from the national scene and turning to geographic areas impacted with Mexican Americans, underutilization of counseling and psychotherapy continues. It has been estimated by Karno and Edgerton (1969) that Mexican Americans made up between 9 to 10 percent of California's population from 1962 to 1968. During this period, the percentages of Mexican Americans admitted for treatment in California facilities were as follows: 2.2 percent to the state hospital system, 3.4 percent to state mental hygiene clinics, 10.9 percent to the neuropsychiatric institute, and 2.3 percent to state and local facilities. The resident in-patient population was 3.8 percent. A similar pattern of underutilization of private and public mental hospitals by Mexican Americans has been found in Texas (Jaco, 1960). Of even greater direct relevance are findings reported in an unpublished manuscript by Perez (1975) of significant underutilization of university counseling services by Chicano students.

FACTORS REDUCING SELF-REFERRAL

Discouraging institutional policies may be largely responsible for the underutilization of counseling and psychotherapeutic services by Latinos. A sufficiently large body of literature describes counseling services as "inappropriate" or "irrelevant" in meeting the needs of the Latino community. All too frequently, services are provided in agencies or centers situated at unrealistic geographic distances from the residences of the target population. Further, it is obvious that monolingual Spanish, or bilingual Spanish-English clients, cannot be served adequately by monolingual English speaking professionals. Yet, this is precisely the situation at a number of treatment centers as described by Torrey (1972), Edgerton and Karno (1971), and Karno and Edgerton (1969). Other authors (Abad et al., 1974; Kline, 1969; Torrey, 1972; Yamamoto et al., 1968) have theorized that the process of counseling will be retarded when clients and counselors are members of different socioeconomic class groups or possess different sets of cultural values.

Elsewhere (Padilla & Ruiz, 1973; Padilla et al., 1975; Ruiz et al., in press), we have summarized arguments by others suggesting that Latinos refer themselves less often because of factors such as "pride" or some hypothetical characteristic of Latino culture that somehow functions to reduce the destructive effects of stress. Typical "stress resistant" factors have included the extended family, religious belief, and recourse to *curanderos* or "faith healers." In general, we have rejected these unsupported speculations, and have argued instead that Latinos have rejected traditional counseling services because of discouraging institutional practices, linguistic problems, and culture differences that retard communication. It now seems appropriate to review case histories—and to share our recommendations—as a means of showing how the sensitive counselor can create culturally relevant counseling programs that are specific to his Latino clients and that are more valid.

CASE HISTORIES

Here, we present case histories from Latino clients seeking counseling. We exercise our ethical responsibility to preserve confidentiality by minimizing identifying information. Nevertheless, these are "real," albeit disguised cases. Furthermore, we have fictionalized certain elements, as you shall see, to communicate theoretical points more lucidly. Even though both clients are "alike" because they are Latinos, we strongly advise the counselor to remain alert to individual differences based upon subculture group membership (such as Chicano versus Cuban), sources of stress (intrapsychic versus extrapsychic), and degree of acculturation (that is, relative degree of commitment to the majority group versus the subculture group). We propose that these are the variables of major significance in designing valid counseling programs for culturally different clients.

Case 1: Maria

This client identifies herself as "Spanish-American." Her ancestors have resided in Northern New Mexico under conditions of relative sociocultural isolation for generations. She is fluent in both Spanish and English, but her Spanish retains regional archaisms unfamiliar to other Latinos and her English is slightly accented. Her politics are conservative, she was educated in a Roman Catholic school system, is committed to the dicta of her faith, and was reared in the large extended family structure that is traditional in that region.

Maria's life adjustment was uneventful until she left home for the first time and enrolled in a California college. There she was shocked by her encounters with Chicanos and Chicanas who were personally assertive, less inhibited in personal decorum, and more liberal politically. She could not deal with the rejection and disdain she experienced when she identified herself as "Spanish," rather than Chicana. This is her opening statement when she sought counseling.

Moving away from home had a great psychological impact on me and my ideals. I had some difficulty adjusting myself to a completely new and independent form of life. Being Spanish-American, I was always closely bound to the family. When I tried to deviate from the norm, I was reprimanded and reminded of the obligation I had to the family. Living away from home taught me to appreciate them (family) and their conservative values more than I had before...but we sure are different from the people in California!

The brief history and presenting complaint identify Maria as a Latina whose subcultural identification is Hispano. Our comments on Latino ethnohistory, as well as the client's own opening comments, confirm the contention of differences across Latino subculture groups. Maria voices awareness that she is "different from the people (Chicanos) in California!" and we agree. Furthermore, we argue that Maria would become aware of other subculture group differences if her encounter had been with Puerto Ricans (or Cubans, or other Latinos), rather than California Chicanos.

With regard to degree of acculturation, Maria seems basically bicultural. Available history indicates she is a bilingual who is equally familiar with the values and traditions of both the majority culture and the Latino culture. Examining her personal value system stemming from identification with her Hispano subculture, she seems less assimilated into the Chicano subculture attending California colleges, than to the majority culture in some ways! This is an important point, expanded further in our discussion of sources of stress and recommendations for counseling.

Examining intrapsychic sources of stress first, Maria's major problem seems to be she is a college freshman away from home for the first time. Like other young people in a similar situation (regardless of ethnicity), Maria is almost certainly homesick and lonely. She probably misses friends, relatives, and familiar places. Her opening statement refers to problems in "adjusting." Her ability to tolerate and lessen distress is lowered because of her absence from familiar support systems (home, family, and church), while in a new, taxing, demanding, different, and frightening environment. At a less obvious level of analysis, there are hints that Maria is experiencing an identity crisis. She is clearly uncertain of subculture group identification as reflected by questions such as, "Am I Spanish as we call ourselves within the family, or Chicana as my new friends insist?" Maria has noted that fellow students are more assertive, striving, and goal-oriented; now she is beginning to wonder if perhaps she would get more of what she wanted out of life if she were less passive. For example, feminism and the Chicano movement intrigue Maria, but the people involved seem "pushy" to her in many ways. And at a more personal and intimate level, Maria is beginning to question her traditional conservatism and her decorous sexual mores.

With regard to extrapsychic sources of stress, Maria denies any major hassles with the dominant culture. While she is subjected to the same general level of prejudice and discrimination that other Latinos are, it seems neither personal or excessive at this time. Note, however, the anomalous situation with regard to her treatment by Chicanos and Chicanas. The Chicano student community rejects Maria because her self-designated "Spanishness" is misperceived as an attempt to deny her "Mexicanness."

How does the counselor respond to this complex of problems, and in what priority? We shall outline a culturally relevant treatment program but encourage the reader to anticipate our recommendations and to amplify upon them as he or she goes along. First, it seems to us the problem of priority is Maria's sense of personal isolation. We would recommend a supportive approach to minimize this intrapsychic source of stress. Although unstated, Maria is almost certainly experiencing dysphoric affect, probably depression ranging somewhere between mild to moderate degrees of severity. An initial approach that works well with problems of this sort is to minimize any tendencies toward apathy and social withdrawal by encouraging interpersonal interaction. Specifically, Maria, like any young person with depressive tendencies, should be encouraged to date, to go to parties, to mix with people her own age and so on. Simultaneously, Maria's major assets should be identified and reflected back to her, repeatedly if necessary, to enhance self-esteem. For example, if she is doing well academically she should be reminded of her intellectual assets: her bright mind, her good study habits, her perseverance, and so on. This supportive approach of confronting Maria with positive aspects of her life adjustment will tend to retard movement in the direction of increased depression.

A problem of second-order priority for Maria is her estrangement from the local Chicano student community. This is particularly lamentable for Maria because this group represents a "natural" but underutilized resource to combat what has been termed Maria's "first problem": her combined sense of low self-esteem, loneliness, mild depression, and isolation. Maria is a Chicana in more ways than she is not; and mutual realization of this aspect of her identity will facilitate Maria's admission into the Chicano group; in turn, it can provide her with much needed emotional support.

One reason Maria and the Chicano group have failed to achieve harmonious rapprochement may be a mutual misjudgment of how each perceives the other. It is conceivable that Maria is unaware that Chicanos perceive Mexican Americans who call themselves "Spanish" as denying their heritage; and some of the Chicanos may not know that Mexican Americans from Northern New Mexico refer to themselves in that manner with no connotation of deliberate efforts to "pass" from one ethnic group to another. Reconciliation may be achieved if both parties become more familiar with their own ethnohistory. While this goal could be attained by the counselor bringing this issue to the attention of the ethnic studies department, if one exists, and having them plan a course or lecture on ethnohistory, we propose an alternative course. We recommend Maria be informed of the possible source of the mutual misunderstanding discussed here, and that she be encouraged to confront those Chicanos who have been scornful. This approach has several advantages; Maria will be required to become more assertive; her approach behavior toward others will counteract her withdrawal tendencies; and everyone involved examines the problem from a fresh perspective.

The third problem for Maria is her blurred, changing, and developing sense of personal identity. She seems to be going through a psychological growth phase that involves questioning life values, but this process is evaluated by us as "normal" or "healthy" (Wrenn & Ruiz, 1970). She is not exactly certain "who she is" as yet, but continued self-exploration should be encouraged by her counselor because enhanced self-awareness will minimize subjective discomfort and expediate self-actualization. The counselor maintains the responsibility, of course, for determining whether this third general recommendation is appropriate for Maria; and if so, of selecting the techniques and methods thought to be maximally growth-inducing for this client.

Case 2: Antonio

Like Maria, Antonio is bicultural and bilingual. Unlike Maria, however, he is a native Californian Chicano, he only attends college part-time, and he is a committed activist politically. In fact, Antonio attends so many Chicano meetings that his grades are suffering and his employers have chided him for his absenteeism and tardiness. Let's examine part of his opening statement during an initial interview to get a stronger sense of what he is like as a person.

> Because of Mexican American descent my parents wish to see their son attend a college or university and further the Chicano cause. We speak Spanish frequently at home and maintain the Mexican heritage. We are a proud family— of our home, community, and heritage...I wish to become something proud, an example to my thousands of little brothers and sisters in the barrios across the nation.

In a subsequent session, Antonio complained of oppression by local police due to their alleged prejudice against La Raza. When pressed for details, Antonio reported this pattern: he would visit one of the elementary school playgrounds in the neighborhood, introduce himself to small groups of children at play, and begin to instruct his "little brothers and sisters" in Chicano culture. Parents or school officials would contact the police, who would come to investigate "loitering" by a grown man in his late twenties. Antonio also complained of snide remarks made by various officers to the effect that he should shorten his hair length and stop wearing a decorated leather headband ("He looks like a damned Indian in a John Wayne movie.").

Here we present the same type of analysis as with Maria, but we can be more succinct because our theoretical approach is familiar by now. In terms of cultural group membership, Antonio is self-identified as "Chicano," and we concur with his opinion. He fails to recognize, however, the degree to which he is acculturated into the majority culture. Despite his Chicanismo, for example, his unaccented English is fluent and he is already far beyond the average Chicano in terms of number of years of education and potential employment and earning power.

The discrimination between intrapsychic and extrapsychic sources of stress becomes especially difficult when the two are conmingled, as with Antonio. Regardless of source of stress we can be fairly certain he is uncomfortable since he referred himself for counseling. His complaint that "people just don't understand" (elicited in a later part of the first meeting), can be interpreted in at least two ways. He may feel he may try harder to communicate more effectively. That is, he may believe major change must come from within. This is a classic example, of course, of motivation for personal change based on intrapsychic stress. On the other hand, Antonio may believe "he's O.K.," but that society is "not O.K." (Harris, 1973). In such a case, he would experience stress as extrapsychic; that is, he would identify the source of his discomfort as environmental, rather than personal.

The first step in formulating a counseling program for Antonio is to render an opinion concerning the accuracy of his reporting and the quality of his judgment. To state the proposition as bluntly as possible, we are recommending that the counselor deal immediately with the question of whether or not Antonio is distorting reality. One needs to know, to use Antonio's polemic rhetoric, whether he is a hapless victim of "police oppression" as he claims, or, which is equally possible given the sparse information provided here, whether his relations with figures of authority are essentially "paranoid."

The answer to this question is important, because it tells us whether stress is mainly internal or external. This information can be used to create treatment programs of maximum relevance and efficacy. If it turns out that Antonio is psychotic and is imagining or exaggerating police intervention, then the counselor may respond with immediate support, seek psychiatric consultation concerning the need for ataractic medication or institutionalization, and begin preparing for whatever intervention model has the greatest probability for change in the direction of less inappropriate behavior. With regard to this latter point, we are referring to preferred modes of therapeutic theory and technique, such as, nondirective counseling versus psychoanalytic psychotherapy, reflection versus free association, and so on. If on the other hand, Antonio is not psychotic and is reporting accurately, then a much different approach is called for. Before describing a counseling program for Antonio based upon the opinion he is neither psychotic nor paranoid, but is reporting discrimination accurately, we discuss how such an opinion might be reached.

At the risk of appearing melodramatic, we ask the reader to examine his or her own biases concerning relations between ethnic minority group people and organized power structures such as civic agencies, government bureaucracies, or the police. This exercise in introspection bears upon points that follow and may be illuminating, particularly if the reader has given relatively little thought to the issue.

Our first point concerning this issue is that preconceptions and prejudices are dangerous since they obscure critical judgment. The skilled and responsible counselor responds to the needs of the client, not to idiosyncratic prejudgments. Regardless of whether your exercise in introspection revealed a "conservative" or "liberal" perception of relations between police and ethnics, it is a fact that some police, in some locales, at some times, do harass ethnics. It is equally true that some ethnics develop paranoid reactions of psychotic proportions and that imaginary police harassment is sometimes incorporated into a delusional system. Thus when ethnic clients report harassment, it is especially crucial that counselors avoid prejudgment and evaluate each report on its own merits.

In cases such as Antonio's, the accuracy of reporting of interaction with the police can be evaluated in several ways. If Antonio presents additional material for discussion that is unbelievable; for example, religious delusions, then it is more likely (but not absolutely certain) that his description of interactions with the police are equally distorted. His veracity can also be evaluated through the use of informants; for example, contacts with family members, friends, fellow employees, and so on. It goes without saying, of course, that evidence of previous delusional periods—whether reported by informants or documented by official records—tends to discredit current reporting. Psychological assessment devices, including tests and interviews, can help determine current personality functioning, but they may be of questionable validity when used by professionals with only superficial understanding of the client's culture (Padilla & Ruiz, 1975).

The issue of Antonio's questionable judgment permeates the area of interpersonal relations. He appears relatively insensitive to the impact of certain aspects of his behavior and appearance upon others. Specifically, almost any stranger approaching unknown children on a playground will arouse suspicion. This seems especially true if the stranger is dressed in a manner that a more conservative school administrator or police would perceive as unusual or exotic. We are not recommending that counselors assume the function of sartorial consultants; but from what we know of Antonio, it appears he would benefit from some dispassionate and disinterested feedback concerning how he affects other people.

Little is known of Antonio's social life outside of his involvement with the Chicano movement. Regardless of ethnicity of client, many counselors would explore with a client his age-related peer interactions, his marital status, marriage plans, dating behavior, and heterosexual interest. Because Antonio is a member of a cultural group with a tradition of close family ties, and because he verbalizes the importance of family life, he would also recommend exploration of relevant experiences. Where does Antonio reside? Who does he live with? What is the extent of his interactions with related family members? Answers to questions about social and family life will help counselors determine whether or not Antonio experiences problems in these areas.

One final comment about Antonio. He states he wants a college degree, and even works part-time to subsidize his education, but his performance at school and on the job is marginal. We are *not* arguing that everyone must adhere to the so-called "Protestant ethic" by formulating life goals and by striving arduously to achieve them. Antonio has formulated life goals all right; he wants a college degree to further the cause of the Chicano movement. His goal-oriented behavior is so inefficient, however, that both goals are in jeopardy. Most people, Antonio included, would experience anxiety and frustration in such a life situation. Our recommendation for Antonio is that these aspects of his life be explored more closely with him. He may elect to reorder the priorities of his life, he may choose to modify his life schedule, or he may do both. But he must change something in order to reduce frustration, to achieve a more satisfying life adjustment, and to become more efficient in getting what he wants out of life.

CONCLUSION

Here we present general principles that can be applied in formulating more culturally relevant counseling programs for Latinos. For instance, the counselor knowledgeable of the importance of *personalismo* among Latinos may wish to greet Latino clients as soon as they arrive at the agency, even if it requires brief interruption of an ongoing session. A counselor sensitive to the Latino culture will immediately extend his hand and introduce himself, including first name rather than formal title. So-called small talk at this initial meeting, and at the beginning of subsequent sessions, is believed to be very important with Latino clients to establish and maintain rapport. Because of possible differences in the perception of time, we urge counselors to make an appointment to meet with the prospective client immediately, and to schedule that meeting as soon as possible, preferably that same morning, afternoon, or evening. As we have indicated earlier, cultural differences in temporal perspective are not perceived by us as pathological procrastination. We have argued elsewhere (Padilla et al., 1975) that Latinos *tend* to perceive psychological problems as more similar to physical problems than do non-Latinos. Thus nondirective approaches, requests for reviews of childhood history, or instructions to introspect should be used judiciously. In general, many Latino clients may have preconceptions of counseling interviews and sessions based on an analogue of a medical examination. Thus, they may anticipate a more active approach from the counselor; for example, inquiry that is goal-oriented and leading to concrete solutions for identified problems.

The higher frequency of extended family structure and the greater importance of family interaction in the daily lives of most Latinos indicate that family and other group approaches should be used more often. Family-oriented therapies would probably yield higher success rates among Latinos than among non-Latinos regardless of whether the problem is intrapsychic or extrapsychic. It is important to keep in mind, however, that sex roles are more rigidly defined, sons have more and earlier independence, fathers have more prestige and authority, and the aged receive more respect. Such knowledge can be exploited to shape more valid counseling intervention. Thus the culturally sensitive counselor will not impute unconscious incestuous desire to a Latino father who expresses sharp interest in his daughter's suitors; nor would such a counselor misperceive the Latino daughter who tolerated such supervision as immature, unduly submissive, or pathologically compliant. Therapeutic responses based on an understanding, rather than a misinterpretation, of the meaning of certain behaviors within a given cultural context will obviously be more effective. Furthermore, familial interdependence, for example, married sons visiting their parents frequently, does not carry the connotation of pathological dependency such behavior might imply in other cultures.

These recommendations for culturally relevant counseling programs are meaningless unless Latinos can be motivated to refer themselves with greater fequency. To achieve this end, the centers and agencies that offer counseling services will have to be modified. Again, we summarize here recommendations presented in greater detail elsewhere (Padilla & Ruiz, 1973; Padilla et al., 1975; Ruiz et al., in press).

First, we advocate that counseling centers emphasize a "business model" approach, and aggressively pursue clientele for their services. For example, one might begin with a local needs assessment program, simultaneously contacting and involving community people in planning, training, administration, and delivery of services. Once community needs have been identified and the relevant service programs established, it is time to advertise the availability of services. A multimedia approach in both English and Spanish would probably reach the largest number of Latinos. Second, new services are needed to deal with the Latino pattern of extrapsychic problems that make Latino clients different from non-Latino clients. Counseling centers could and should offer innovative services for Latinos such as these: written and oral translation contact with government agencies, building skill in obtaining employment and securing promotions, remedial education, and some type of course work teaching rights, responsibilities and privileges of a politico-legal nature. One example of the course work indicated in the final recommendation would be an educational experience teaching the structure of government, the effectiveness of political coalition, voting, and the impact of legislation on equal opportunity and affirmative action.

The third general recommendation for agency change concerns staffing. Our interpretation of the literature is that Latino clients will obtain maximum benefit from counselors knowledgeable with Latino ethnohistory and culture. To be effective, the counselors must "speak the language" of the client, both literally and figuratively. The number of Latino professionals already available is infinitesimally small (Ruiz, 1971), and the disproportionately small number of Latinos enrolled in baccalaureate or doctoral programs (El-Khawas & Kinzer, 1974) indicates underrepresentation of Latinos in the professions is going to continue in the forseeable future. The short-range solution to this problem is two-fold; teach Spanish and Latino culture to non-Latino counselors, and teach counseling skills to Latinos at the paraprofessional level.

The fourth recommendation has been implied but is now made explicit. To become successful in delivering counseling services to the Latino community, agencies offering services must first gain the confidence and support of prospective clients. To accomplish this end, members of the community must infiltrate the agency at all levels of administration, be active in policy change and decision making, and be involved as teachers or students in the educational programs described earlier. To convince community people the agency is truly theirs, and therefore for their benefit, it would probably be wise to encourage the use of agency facilities for community events. In this context, the agency might celebrate Latino holidays in some appropriate way in addition to occasionally offering programs in the arts and humanities that would interest and attract potential users of available services. Consistent with our statements on the "business model," programs attracting participants represent excellent opportunities to inform people of agency activities. Latinos come to participate in a cultural program sponsored by the centers but simultaneously receive information via a brochure or brief announcement of the services offered by the agency.

REFERENCES

Abad, V.; Ramos, J.; & Boyce, E. A model for delivery of mental health services to Spanish-speaking minorities. *American Journal of Orthopsychiatry*, 1974, *44*, 584–595.

Bachrach, L. L. *Utilization of state and county mental hospitals by Spanish Americans in 1972*. Statistical Note 116. DHEW Publication No. (ADM), 1975, 75–158.

Edgerton, R. B., & Karno, M. Mexican American bilingualism and the perception of mental illness. *Archives of General Psychiatry*, 1971, *24*, 286–290.

El-Khawas, E. H., & Kinzer, J. L. Enrollment of minority graduate students at PhD granting institutions. *Higher Education Panel Reports*, Number 19, August, 1974.

Harris, T. A. *I'm OK—You're OK*. New York: Avon, 1973.

Heller, C. *Mexican-American youth*. New York: Random House, 1967.

Jaco, E. G. *The social epidemiology of mental disorders: A psychiatric survey of Texas*. New York: Russell Sage Foundation, 1960.

Karno, M., & Edgerton, R. B. Perception of mental illness in a Mexican-American community. *Archives of General Psychiatry*, 1969, *20*, 233–238.

Kline, L. Y. Some factors in the psychiatric treatment of Spanish Americans. *American Journal of Psychiatry*, 1969, *125*, 1674–1681.

Lefcourt, H. M. Internal versus external control of reinforcement. *Psychological Bulletin*, 1966, *65*, 206–220.

Madsen, M. C., & Shapira, A. Cooperative and competitive behavior of urban Afro-American, Anglo-American, Mexican-American, and Mexican village children. *Developmental Psychology*, 1970, *3*, 16–20.

Padilla, A. M., & Ruiz, R. A. *Latino Mental Health*. Washington, D.C.: U.S. Superintendent of Documents, 1973.

Padilla, A. M., & Ruiz, R. A. Personality assessment and test interpretation of Mexican Americans: A critique. *Journal of Personality Assessment*, 1975, *39*, 103–109.

Padilla, A. M.; Ruiz, R. A.; & Alvarez, R. Community mental health services for the Spanish-speaking/surnamed population. *American Psychologist*, 1975, *30*, 892–905.

Perez, M. S. Counseling services at UCSC: Attitudes and perspectives of Chicano students. Unpublished manuscript, 1975.

Rotter, J. B. *Social learning and clinical psychology*. Englewood Cliffs, N.J.: Prentice-Hall, 1954.

Rotter, J. B. Generalized expectancies for internal versus external control of reinforcement. *Psychological Monographs*, 1966, *80*, 1–28.

Ruiz, R. A. Relative frequency of Americans with Spanish surnames in associations of psychology, psychiatry, and sociology. *American Psychologist*, 1971, *26*, 1022–1024.

Ruiz, R. A., & Padilla, A. M. Chicano psychology: The family and the *macho*. Unpublished manuscript, 1973.

Ruiz, R. A.; Padilla, A. M.; & Alvarez, R. Issues in the counseling of Spanish-speaking/surnamed clients: Recommendations for therapeutic services. In L. Benjamin (Ed.), *Counseling Minority Students*, in press.

Stone, P. C., & Ruiz, R. A. Race and class as differential determinants of under-achievement and underaspiration among Mexican Americans. *Journal of Educational Research*, 1974, *68*, 99–101.

Torrey, E. F. *The mind game: Witchdoctors and psychiatrists*. New York: Emerson Hall, 1972.

U.S. Bureau of the Census. Persons of Spanish origin in the United States: November 1969. In *Current population reports* (Series P-20, No. 213). Washington, D.C.: U.S. Government Printing Office, 1971 (a).

U.S. Bureau of the Census. Selected characteristics of persons and families of Mexican, Puerto Rican, and other Spanish origin: March 1971. In *Current population reports* (Series P-20, No. 224). Washington, D.C.: U.S. Government Printing Office, 1971 (b).

Wrenn, R. L., & Ruiz, R. A. *The normal personality: Issues to insight*. Monterey, Calif.: Brooks/Cole, 1970.

Yamamoto, J.; James, Q. C.; & Palley, N. Cultural problems in psychiatric therapy. *Archives of General Psychiatry*, 1968, *19*, 45–49.

20

Therapy Latino Style
Implications for Psychiatric Care

Melvin Delgado

As mental health practitioners, we can no longer ignore the existence of alternative theories of disease etiology and methods of treatment. If we attempt to understand different approaches, and modify our practices and delivery systems when feasible to accommodate these differences, we can improve the quality of mental health services offered to minority groups, and promote the use of existing services by ethnic minorities.

Until recently, mental health professionals with rare exceptions have viewed folk healers as charlatans or, to put it more charitably, as individuals who are misguided despite the best intentions. However, folk healers are a force to be reckoned with within their own cultures, especially in the Hispanic community where they have achieved the status of charismatic folk heroes. The reverence with which they are regarded can be attributed to important functions they perform, functions which may prove beneficial to the mental health field.

Although the movement to view mental health from a cultural perspective has existed for well over fifty years (Favazza and Oman, 1977), recent evidence suggests a noticeable increase in its momentum (Kiev, 1972; Crapanzano and Garrison, 1976; Malpass, 1977; Favazza and Oman, 1978). Folk therapists, especially in the Hispanic community, have within the past decade been the object of heightened interest fueled by growing awareness of similarities between folk therapy and psychotherapy.

The prospect that the folk therapist could become a major new force in the field of mental health is especially attractive because delivery of services to ethnic minority groups has been seriously limited, particularly for the non-English speaking. Folk healers represent a vast untapped resource in a field that is understaffed, and requires large operating budgets and lengthy training periods to overcome language and cultural barriers.

The need to deliver mental health services to all persons, regardless of their cultural background and ability to pay (Scherl, 1970), emerged during the community mental health movement in the 1960s. However,

Reprinted with permission from *Perspectives in Psychiatric Care,* 1979, *17,* 107–113.

despite this mandate, it is well documented that Hispanics as a group remain sorely in need of mental health services (Philippus, 1971; Padilla and Ruiz, 1973; Abad, Ramos, and Boyce, 1974; Padilla, Ruiz, and Alvarez, 1975). But those mental health professionals who attempt to deliver services to Hispanic populations often encounter folk healers. Why do these therapists traditionally assume such a prominent role within their respective communities?

Although the literature delineates the healers' role within the Hispanic cultures, presents case studies, and compares healers with their Western counterparts, relatively few references are made to efforts to incorporate folk healers into mental health services.

This article will provide an overview of folk healing within Hispanic cultures; describe possible ways to make use of folk healers within mental health settings; and recommend methods to improve the training of mental health professionals and the planning of mental health services for ethnic minority groups.

OVERVIEW OF FOLK HEALERS

Anthropological literature is rich with descriptive accounts of healers in Africa, Latin America, and Asia (Foster and Anderson, 1978), accounts that provide first-hand evidence that similar systems of healing exist among all cultures. Some differences are apparent, however. In food gathering societies, there is limited medical leadership with few privileges accorded the healer, and virtually no systemized set of medical ideas. In contrast, folk healers operating in hunting and fishing societies are likely to enjoy greater prestige and economic rewards as well as to exercise more social influence and authority. In agricultural societies, the ability to heal is based on the mastery of specific knowledge and skills. Accordingly, the most intelligent children are chosen for elaborate training programs leading to specialized healing roles (Kiev, 1962).

Regardless of the economic and technological base of society, however, there appears to be a consistent attempt to integrate medical roles into the conceptual framework of everyday life, so that all members can share the same theories of disease causation and treatment (Kiev, 1962; Delgado, 1977a). Literally hundreds of case studies exist which describe various healing methods employed by folk therapists, explain theories of causation and treatment, and examine the capability of achieving therapeutic results.

Even though folk therapy is based on supernatural beliefs and practices as means of channeling aggression and relieving tension (Malinowski, 1948; Joy, 1976), there are striking similarities between folk therapy and psychotherapy. They both utilize a diagnostic process, prognosis, disease description, theory of etiology, and treatment plans. Treatment plans, in turn, may entail use of medication and various modalities (individual, family, group). Consequently, with the exception of the basic premise, spirits versus intrapsychic, the similarities far outnumber the differences.

Folk healing in its various manifestations takes place throughout the Caribbean and Latin America. However, for the purpose of this analysis, only the three major Hispanic groups in the United States will be highlighted: Puerto Rican, Mexican, and Cuban. An overview of each group will focus on the conceptual framework, treatment orientation, and therapeutic factors operative in achieving symptom relief.

PUERTO RICAN CULTURE

Spiritism is a belief system found among Puerto Ricans in Puerto Rico as well as in the United States. Spiritism holds that the world is inhabited by both good and evil spirits: the former are responsible for health and good luck; the latter are associated with illness and misfortune (Harwood, 1977; Garrison, 1977; Delgado, 1977b).

Evil influence may be the result of envy or sorcery; or may occur if the afflicted person is a medium who must develop spiritual powers. Other kinds of evil are viewed as a punishment, trial, or test from God; or emanate from the spirit of a deceased relative (Harwood, 1977). The medium alone has the power to diagnose the source of the presenting problem and to prescribe an appropriate plan of treatment.

With the exception of evil that is attributed to punishment by God, all other causes have a good prognosis because the therapeutic arsenal at the medium's disposal is extensive and formidable. A typical treatment plan will require ritualistic behavior on the part of the patient, such as the preparation of herbal concoctions or the use of such magical paraphernalia as candles and prayers. The process usually requires active involvement of the patient in his or her treatment plan over an extended period of time.

In my article analyzing key factors operative in spiritism (Delgado, 1978), I noted that some are universal and can be found in virtually all forms of therapy, while others are characteristic of the Puerto Rican culture. In spiritism, both healer and patron share similar treatment expectations, and folk therapists have unquestioned authority and power. The power of suggestion and hypnotic techniques are important tools of the spiritist or medium. Also, a common language facilitates communication between client and healer. In spiritism, the naming process serves to relieve anxiety in the patient by providing an understanding of the cause of his/her presenting problems. Invariably, the healer attributes the presenting problem to some outside source, which in turn assures patients that they did not cause the problem, and therefore, are not at fault. In essence, a family dispute may be perceived as being caused by some evil influence instead of the emotional problems of a family member. The former interpretation is less threatening to the patient and family and makes it easier to seek assistance.

Folk therapy is action-oriented, with active involvement of the patient and significant others, and serves to re-establish in the patient a sense of control over the environment (Delgado, 1978:51–52).

As a result of their study in Puerto Rico, Rogler and Hollingshead (1961) concluded that mediums serve a vital function by structuring, defining, and rendering aberrant behavior institutionally meaningful. In this way, the afflicted are able to avoid the stigma often associated with modern psychiatric care.

A recent study of attitudes toward mental illness exhibited by mediums revealed that although they did not use the same phraseology, their mode of thinking was comparable to that of the psychotherapist (Lubchansky, Egri, and Stokes, 1970). Moreover, mediums displayed a broader view of mental illness than did community leaders and a cross-section of residents of the community.

MEXICAN CULTURE

The *curandero* is the Mexican folk healer (Kiev, 1962), and religion is the central focus of curanderismo. The theme of Christ permeates much of the curandero's thinking about illness and misfortune, which are caused by weakened ties with the Catholic church, family, and culture (Martinez, 1977; Tamez, 1978).

As a result, the curandero will seek to reestablish an equilibrium in the afflicted person's life that is more in harmony with church, family, and culture. In common with the Puerto Rican spiritist, curanderos preach authoritarianism and faith, and rely upon action-oriented treatment plans which involve significant other persons to aid the patient's recovery.

Treatment may involve various acts or stages, in which the individual is required to promise (*promese*) that he or she is willing to undergo great sacrifice to achieve a cure. For example, the sacrifice may entail undertaking a pilgrimage on foot, dressing in white over a long period of time, or promising to help others. In the event that a cure is achieved but the promise is not kept, the individual may be subject to further illness or misfortune.

In one of the few existing studies of curanderos, Hamburger notes that the average curandero has characteristics that are typical of the profession, and is aware of community resources available to him.

The average curandero is 56 years of age and married and has five and one-half years of schooling.... His conception of illness is based on the germ theory and other organic causes, but he does not dismiss the possibility of illness as God's punishment for sins.... He consults with others (this includes family and friends of the patient) and refers to clinics and doctors. He offers services to anyone seeking them and considers his service area to extend beyond that of his immediate neighborhood. (Hamburger, 1978:21)

Like the Puerto Rican medium, the curandero has social-demographic characteristics similar to the persons he serves, which means that healing need not be restricted by presenting problems, geographic catchement areas, or eligibility criteria. The lack of barriers helps encourage the population to use the curandero's services.

CUBAN CULTURE

Santeria is the Cuban version of folk healing, however, this form of folk therapy is also prevalent within Puerto Rican culture (Gleason, 1975).

As in Puerto Rican spiritism and Mexican curanderismo, Cuban santerismo has been influenced by Catholicism. However, santeria is a mixture of African (Yoruba) religious beliefs and Catholicism. This synchronism is manifested through the representation of Yoruba gods in the form of Catholic saints. As noted by Harwood:

This incorporation is based on a view of history in which Africans are the chosen people and have experienced a prueba (trial) from God through generations of slavery and European domination. During this Gran Prueba (Great Trial), orichas (African Spirits) are said to have become incarnate in the bodies of Whites. (1977:45–46)

Santeria followers believe that illness is the result of object intrusion, imitative or contagious magic, loss of one's soul, spirit intrusion, or anger of gods (Sandoval, 1977).

Santeria employs a much more ceremonial and ritualistic orientation to healing than do spiritism and curanderism.

Sessions are conducted in front of an alter colorfully decorated with objects pertaining to a particular deity and offerings from the congregation. Ceremonies utilize African songs and music and may entail the sacrifice of animals. (Delgado, 1978:53)

Ceremonies may last for several days with active participation by as many as thirty individuals. Santeros, like their Puerto Rican and Mexican counterparts, are sociologically similar to those who seek their services. Furthermore, fees are generally based upon ability to pay, and sometimes may take the form of donations of nonmonetary items, such as food.

It is the ritualistic and ceremonial base of folk therapy that creates the greatest obstacles to its acceptance by mental health practitioners in the United States. It should be recognized that there are other legitimate interpretations of emotional illness than those encompassed by scientific medicine (King, 1962).

UTILIZATION OF FOLK HEALERS

Because of the prevailing attitude of skepticism, it is not surprising that there are few documented instances of folk healers functioning in official roles within mental health settings. This does not necessarily mean that no formal attempts have been undertaken; rather, that efforts may have been undertaken which were not published. However, this examination of the use of folk healers will be restricted to formal efforts. Unlike informal endeavors which can occur privately without widespread publicity, formal attempts imply an administrative decision, that is, an official policy set in motion to meet agency requirements.

The literature notes only three attempts at formally incorporating healers into mental health treatment. Two of these instances occurred in New York City, in the South Bronx, an area with a heavy concentration of Puerto Ricans. They took place at Lincoln Community Mental Health Center and the Tremont Crisis Center (Fields, 1976; Ruiz and Langrod, 1976b). The third instance involved the Navajo Indians of Arizona (Bergman, 1973).

In all these examples, folk healers were used in a training capacity. In New York City, psychiatric residents were exposed to Puerto Rican spiritists in an effort to sensitize the residents as well as to develop knowledge and skills related to the practice of folk healing. In Arizona, Navajo medicine men, with the aid of a grant from the National Institute of Mental Health, developed a program to train a cadre of Navajo medicine men.

Attempts at integrating folk healers within mental health programs can be classified according to various roles and responsibilities. For the purposes of analysis, the five types of affiliation with folk therapists can be plotted on a continuum representing increased involvement of the folk healer in established mental health settings. Type I at one end of the continuum represents a minimal degree of involvement in co-therapeutic tasks, and Type V at the other end indicates the highest degree of involvement.

Type I represents the involvement of the folk healer in a training capacity, in which the healer makes presentations to the mental health staff. These presentations can be merely periodic, or can represent a long-term commitment on a regular basis. Training sessions can be held at the mental health setting, at the healer's residence, or, a combination of both.

Training for the mental health staff is still the main objective of Type II, but the format is consultee-centered consultation by the healer to the psychotherapist.

Type III limits the healer to the role of referral agent. Through a formalized agreement, the healer is provided with a contact person within the mental health setting. Procedures are modified to accommodate the special nature of the working relationship between healer and staff member. For instance, the healer may be present throughout the diagnostic phase, and without a waiting period, or the intake worker may be required to conduct the initial intake session in the healer's home. In essence, the folk healer maintains certain rights and privileges in this type of relationship.

Type IV represents a variation on Type III, in which a reciprocal arrangement for referrals is established whereby both the healer and practitioners in the mental health setting exchange referrals for treatment.

Type V sets up a co-therapeutic relationship, which requires the physical presence of the healer at the mental health setting, or the psychotherapist at the healer's setting for the purposes of therapeutic counseling. This form of affiliation thrusts the folk healer into a relationship of equality with the psychotherapist.

Needless to say, the various types of affiliation are not mutually exclusive. Rather, each one can build upon the other. Psychological/mental health practitioners who are seriously considering formal affiliation with folk healers would be wise to implement the type of affiliation most conducive to accomplishing their objectives. As a rule, however, it is advisable to start with a minimal involvement and eventually expand the role of the folk healer to encompass additional activities.

RECOMMENDATIONS FOR IMPROVED
MENTAL HEALTH SERVICES TO ETHNIC MINORITIES

The most obvious way to improve mental health services now provided to ethnic minorities is to enlist the aid of the folk healer. Before any formal affiliation with folk healers can take place, however, some fundamental changes in attitude and methodology are needed. Although these changes do not require a major reshaping of current training programs and systems of service delivery they can have far-reaching implications for patterns of mental health utilization in Hispanic communities. Moreover, they can provide a solid foundation on which to base the possibility of future affiliation between mental health settings and healers.

To begin, it is important for psychological/mental health practitioners to develop a basic knowledge of mental health attitudes normally found within Hispanic communities to aid in the diagnostic assessment of emotional problems. Furthermore, practitioners should recognize the significance of commonly held attitudes and the value of folk healing techniques for Hispanic peoples.

The interview technique should help establish whether or not the patient believes the presenting problems are the result of supernatural forces. The most effective interviews are the result of an active approach that symbolizes caring instead of merely listening to what the patient has to say, which could be construed as indifference. Moreover, an appreciation of a patient's language and vocabulary is likely to increase the prospect of developing a positive relationship.

There is a high probability that folk healers may have played an influential role throughout the help-seeking process. An attempt should be made to judge the degree of involvement of the folk therapist, as well as to determine whether he was used for consultation or on a long-term basis. If the patient is still using the healer's services, contact should be established with the healer in an effort to understand the goals of folk therapy for the patient. In turn, the psychotherapist can share treatment objectives with the healer. Even though it generally requires a considerable length of time before a patient or healer feels comfortable in sharing with the therapist, it is a goal that is worth pursuing. Further, in devising treatment plans the therapist should adopt an action (task) orientation whenever possible.

If at all possible, the psychotherapist should make it a point to visit the patient's community as a means of determining what community resources are available to assist with treatment. Visits to the community also help in identifying individuals who are knowledgeable about folk healers, so that healers can be contacted to serve as consultants and trainers. Although they are not healers themselves, the contact persons may serve as a connecting link that can eventually lead to the inclusion of folk healers within the program.

It is time to recognize that emotional illness does not occur in a social vacuum, but rather takes place within an existing context that has specific frames of reference. Culture is one such frame of reference, and it is an important one to consider.

REFERENCES

Abad, V., J. Ramos, and E. Boyce, "A Model for Delivery of Mental Health Services to Spanish-Speaking Minorities," *American Journal of Orthopsychiatry*, 1974, Vol. 44, pp. 584–595.

Bergman, R. L., "A School for Medicine Men," *Mental Health Digest*, Vol. 5, 1973, pp. 28–32.

Crapanzano, V. and V. Garrison, *Case Studies in Spirit Possession*, New York: John Wiley & Sons, 1976.

Delgado, M., "A Study of Mental Health Workers' Perceptions of Mental Illness in the Puerto Rican Community," Simmons School of Social Work, Boston (May) 1977(a).

Delgado, M., "Puerto Rican Spiritualism and the Social Work Profession," *Social Casework*, Vol. 58, 1977(b), pp. 451–458.

Delgado, M., "Folk Medicine in the Puerto Rican Culture," *International Social Work*, Vol. 21, 1978, pp. 46–54.

Delgado, M., "Herbal Medicine and the Puerto Rican Community," *Health & Social Work*, (May) 1979.

Favazza, A., and A. Oman, *Anthropological and Cross-Cultural Themes in Mental Health*, Columbia: University of Missouri Press, 1977.

Favazza, A., and A. Oman, "Overview: Foundations of Cultural Psychiatry," *American Journal of Psychiatry*, Vol. 133, 1978, pp. 293–303.

Fields, S., "Storefront Psychotherapy Through Seance," *Innovations*, Vol. 3, 1976, pp. 3–11.

Foster, G., and B. G. Anderson, *Medical Anthropology*, New York: John Wiley & Sons, 1978.

Garrison, V., "Doctor, Espiritista or Psychiatrist? Health-Seeking Behavior in a Puerto Rican Neighborhood in New York City," *Medical Anthropology* (Spring) 1977, pp. 65–180.

Gleason, J., *Santeria, Bronx*, New York: Atheneum Press, 1975.

Hamburger, S., "Profile of Curanderismo: A Study of Mexican Folk Practitioners," *International Journal of Social Psychiatry*, Vol. 24, 1978, pp. 19–25.

Harwood, A., *Rx Spiritist As Needed*, New York: John Wiley & Sons, 1977.

Joy, G., *Spiritualism: A Critical Survey*, Great Britain: Aquarian Press, 1976.

Kiev, A., "The Psychotherapeutic Aspects of Primitive Medicine," *Human Organization*, Vol. 21, 1962, pp. 25–29.

Kiev, A., *Transcultural Psychiatry*, New York: The Free Press, 1972.

King, S. H., *Perceptions of Illness and Medical Practice*, New York: Russel Sage Foundation, 1962.

Lubchansky, I., G. Egri, and J. Stokes, "Puerto Rican Spiritualist Views Mental Illness: The Faith Healer as a Paraprofessional," *American Journal of Psychiatry*, 1970, Vol. 127, pp. 88–97.

Malinowski, B., *Magic, Science and Religion*, Garden City: Anchor Books, 1948.

Malpass, R. S., "Theory and Method in Cross-Cultural Psychology," *American Psychologist*, 1977, pp. 1069–1079.

Martinez, C. Group process and the Chicano: Clinical issues. *International Journal of Group Psychotherapy*, Vol. 27, 1977, pp. 225–231.

Padilla, A. M., and R. A. Ruiz, *Latino Mental Health*, Rockville, Md.: National Institute of Mental Health, 1973.

Padilla, A. M., R. A. Ruiz, and R. Alvarez, "Community Mental Health Services to Spanish-Speaking/Surnamed Population," *American Psychologist*, Vol. 30, 1975, pp. 892–905.

Philippus, M. J., "Successful and Unsuccessful Approaches to Mental Health Services for an Urban Hispano American Population," *American Journal of Public Health*, Vol. 61, 1971, pp. 820–830.

Rogler, L. and A. B. Hollingshead, "The Puerto Rican Spiritualist as a Psychiatrist," *American Journal of Sociology*, Vol. 67, 1961, pp. 17–21.

Ruiz, P., and J. Langrod, "The Role of Folk Healers in Community Mental Health Services," *Community Mental Health Journal*, Vol. 12, 1976(a), pp.

392–398.

Ruiz, P., and J. Langrod, "Psychiatric and Folk Healing: A Dichotomy?" *American Journal of Psychiatry*, Vol. 133, 1976(b), pp. 95–97.

Sandoval, M. C., "Santeria: Afrocuban Concepts of Disease and Its Treatment in Miami," *Journal of Operational Psychiatry*, Vol. 8, 1977, pp. 52–63.

Scherl, D. J., "The Community Mental Health Center and Mental Health Services for the Poor," in *The Practice of Community Mental Health*, H. Grunebaum, ed., Boston: Little, Brown & Co., 1970, pp. 171–196.

Steward, G. H. *Psychotherapy and Culture Conflict in Community Mental Health*, New York: Roland Press, 1972.

Tamez, E. G. Curanderismo: Folk Mexican-American health care system. *Journal of Psychiatric Nursing*, Vol. 16, no. 12, 1978, pp. 34–39.

21

The Role of Folk Healers in Community Mental Health Services

Pedro Ruiz and John Langrod

In the field of psychiatry, during recent years, considerable emphasis has been placed on social action. One consequence of this is the increasing attention paid in the medical literature to poverty stricken areas of the nation and therefore to minority groups. As a result of this, important changes in program structure, such as decentralization, and planning of services are being considered. Experiments with innovative ideas are being conducted, particularly into the utilization of nonprofessional personnel. This emphasis has brought about better and more effective service delivery. Unfortunately other aspects related to mental illness, which should be receiving greater attention, have been relegated to a secondary level.

CULTURAL BACKGROUND OF PATIENTS

One of these aspects relates to the cultural background of mental patients. We believe that difference in cultural background is one of the most important problems confronted by contemporary mental health practitioners. The development of industrialization, especially in transportation and communications, has contributed to the rapid migration of certain ethnic groups and persons of lower socioeconomic levels toward zones of greater economic progress. An important consequence of this migration is the diffusion of cultural characteristics as a group moves from one area to another. This type of sociocultural migration has outpaced the accommodations that must be made in mental health programs dealing with these populations. As a result of this phenomenon it is easy to find severe cultural shock in those metropolitan areas that are most economically developed. Mental health programs have not kept pace with or adapted to these needs.

Reprinted with permission from *Community Mental Health Journal*, 1976, *12*(4), 392–398.

The Hispanic Ethnic Group

Our study will call attention to the type of mental health needs produced by this social upheaval and will deal primarily with some cultural problems faced by the Hispanic ethnic group. We believe that this group deserves special attention because it consists of close to 15 million persons in the United States. For close to 6 years, the authors have worked in an area in which 60% of the population consists of first- and second-generation Hispanics, primarily Puerto Ricans. This ethnic group has certain cultural characteristics that are generally forgotten by or are unknown to mental health specialists who have received classical training. We are referring primarily to the religious beliefs of these groups. Generally speaking, the Hispanic citizen is Roman Catholic, and this fact is accepted without question by therapists who are not fully familiar with the Spanish culture. The experience of the authors indicates that Catholicism is only one aspect of religious belief. The majority of the Hispanic population, although professing the Catholic religion, also makes use of other religious resources such as spiritualism, witchcraft, and black magic.

This fact, we believe, is extremely relevant to the field of mental health. We assume that the relationship between religion and psychiatry is obvious to most mental health specialists. Since we view religion as a cultural manifestation, we share Kiev's (1972) view that:

> Culture determines the specific ways in which individuals perceive and conceive of the environment and strongly influences the forms of conflict, behavior, and psychopathology that occur in members of the culture. Social and cultural phenomena influence disorders which in turn have a significant effect on the social system. (p. xi)

The above concept makes it easier to understand the importance of cultural factors in relation to psychopathology, principally among ethnic minorities who are subjected to migratory processes involving cross-cultural confrontations. In our 6 years experience in the South Bronx, we have had the opportunity of observing therapists of Anglo-American origin or trained in the United States diagnosing numerous clients as being schizophrenic, solely on the basis of their belief in generally nonaccepted supernatural phenomenology. This diagnosis often results in state hospitalizations. In addition to the consequences of hospitalization, the patient will have to face for the rest of his life the stigma of having been diagnosed as psychotic.

Catholicism and a Second Religion

Psychiatrists tend to reject the possibility of belonging to two religions at the same time, mainly because of their concepts of ambivalence and confusion. Spiritualists do accept this, however, thus offering greater understanding to their clients. Supernatural beliefs such as voodoo and spiritualism are considered by western therapists generally as being part of a psychotic process rather than part of the Hispanic's cultural background. Also based on our experience, we have observed that those patients who do not trust their American therapists and who limit themselves to informing them superficially about their Catholic belief are more likely to be considered subjects for outpatient treatment, even though the basis for their distrust may be due to paranoid processes of great severity.

DIFFERENT MODES OF COMMUNICATION

Folk healers communicate in the same terminology that their clients use; psychiatrists do not, thus jeopardizing identification and development of a therapeutic alliance. By the same token, folk healers accept nonverbal communication, a common means of communicating among Hispanic migrants. Psychiatrists tend to place greater value on verbal expressions, thus causing serious identification problems, as well as limiting the therapeutic approaches used. For instance, these patients are not considered suitable for psychotherapy but rather for somatic therapies such as electroshock or chemotherapy.

Communication problems also create serious difficulties in developing empathy toward the patients. Along these lines, psychiatrists try to cure phenomena believed to be supernatural by natural means and approaches, whereas folk healers use methods more closely related to the patient's perception of causative factors, thus winning greater acceptance from their clients. Also, psychiatrists, being bound to their own culture, must look with fear and suspicion on what they consider to be unethical and unscientific practices. Folk healers do not have this kind of constraint, and relate to their clients in their own natural milieu. They see clients in their own homes, listen to so-called unscientific material, and permit some forms of acting out. All this provides the folk healer with a better understanding of the clients' problems, thus offering them a better opportunity for arriving at a correct diagnosis and treatment strategy. In addition, folk healers often understand their clients' frustrations better than psychiatrists do because the folk healers live in the same neighborhood and know it well. They share the day-to-day frustrations of ghetto living: unemployment; lack of adequate sanitation, housing, and medical care; and estrangement from the outside world of which the psychiatrist is a part. Western-trained psychiatrists adhere to a different ethnocentric culture and often ignore or are unaware of the way of life of communities that do not fit the mold with which they are familiar. They will, for instance, often diagnose unrest and rebellion as indications of personal immaturity, and fail to see that such behavior may be connected with social and cultural change, poverty, urbanization, and other social stresses experienced by the patient.

Modus Operandi of Folk Healers

The modus operandi of folk healers in the South Bronx is very effective because they take into account and utilize cultural concepts that are vital in the Hispanic community, such as the extended family network of ahijados (Godchildren) and padrinos (Godparents). Folk healers also reach more patients in a state of crisis than psychiatrists do, that is, at a time when they are more amenable to change. Many cultural manifestations that are rejected forthwith by psychiatrists, such as ataques (highly emotional trancelike states) and talking to God, are accepted and worked with by folk healers, who have been especially trained in handling them.

Again, an advantage of the availability of folk healers is that they offer professional manpower in ghetto areas where resources may be scarce; in fact, there are no private psychiatrists in the South Bronx. Also, the services of the folk healers are considerably cheaper than those of psychiatrists. This, without any doubt, is an important consideration in areas where financial resources are severely limited.

As a result of our experience in the South Bronx ghetto, we firmly believe that treatment personnel must be familiar with the cultural characteristics of their patients. This is not only essential in relation to treatment, but must also be an integral part of the planning and development of all types of mental health programs. Along these lines, we have noted at the Lincoln Community Mental Health Center program on numerous occasions, that nonprofessional employees can render more effective treatment because they belong to the same ethnic groups as their patients. This has also been observed in part by Sidel (1973) who stated that one of the principles we might learn from indigenous neighborhood health workers is the

> Minimization of the social distance between primary care health workers and those they serve, one form of which has been called deprofessionalization; while there may be some negative aspects—for example, problems of inadequate technical quality of care—what we actually observed was mostly positive; apparent ease of access and of communication between health workers and patients. (p. 742)

This factor is of special relevance because it is known that in the United States, when planning programs for migrants and minority groups, very few members of the group being serviced are employed during the planning phase. Further, no legislation exists in relation to the utilization or recognition of community folk healers; this hampers any approach to them with the aim of offering training or receiving training from them.

In our experience with folk healers we have noted that the techniques they utilize, such as suggestion, persuasion, and manipulation, are similar to those used by psychiatrists employed at the Lincoln program. Nevertheless, services offered by folk healers are rejected by most mental health authorities, whereas those offered by psychiatrists are accepted. In this respect we are in agreement with Torrey (1972), who stated,

> The techniques used by western therapists (in the field of psychiatry) are on exactly the same scientific plane as those used by witch doctors.... The reasons we have failed to see this in the past is that we have confused our technology with our techniques, in other words, whatever goes on in a modern office must be science, whereas what goes on in a grass hut must be magic. (p. 74)

In some aspects, the spiritualists can do even better than psychiatrists. For instance, they can provide possibilities for acting out of wishes not normally accepted by society; they can favor abreaction through the practice of spiritual rituals; and, finally, they can bring about an increase in their clients' self-esteem by making them part of a group—that is, the spiritual community.

An additional point of interest which we observed in our work was that classical therapists and folk healers both tend to impose their own moral values on their clients, often doing more harm than good. This has been noted by other workers. Guthrie (1973), for example, has stated that

> In some groups it is expected that one will hear God's voice in moments of spiritual exaltation, while in other groups, especially those that profess no religious commitments, hearing God's voice is strongly suggestive of a schizophrenic disorder. (pp. 39–40)

In the South Bronx, we have seen psychiatrists arguing with Hispanic patients about their communication with supernatural beings and trying to convince them of its impossibility. At the same time we have observed spiritualists stressing to their clients the importance of being able to communicate with the spirit world.

Our comparison of folk healers and classical therapists takes on added importance in the light of Nelson and Torrey's (1973) statement that "Many of the functions previously carried out by organized religions in the United States have been and are being assumed by psychiatry" (p. 363). This fact further underlines the need for special training for those in the mental health field; if this training is neglected, serious iatrogenic conflicts could result when these specialists attempt to take over religious functions that they themselves do not fully understand.

THE PATIENT'S SYMPTOMATOLOGY

We wish to pay special attention to the manner in which spiritualists and psychiatrists relate to the patient's symptomatology. We have found that the great majority of psychiatrists tend to view patients' symptoms primarily in negative terms. This leads to an emphasis on the need for symptom eradication as the first step in curing the patient. Thus patients are often simply given medication until their symptoms disappear. The folk healers on the other hand tend to use the patient's symptomatology in a positive way. They do not consider symptom removal as an indispensable precondition for healing the patient; on the contrary, they view the client's symptoms as a gift or a quality. The client is viewed as someone who can control or reduce his symptomatology by relying primarily on his inner strength; this offers him hope of achieving greater autonomy in life. This quality is generally known as mediumship. In our opinion, folk healers have a better understanding of patients' symptomatology than western psychiatrists. Lubchansky, Egri, and Stokes (1970) bear out our opinion stating,

> It appears that spiritualists have highly idiosyncratic conceptions of mental illness, showing a tendency to describe it in terms of the less visible behaviors— primarily disorganized thought processes—in contrast to other groups. Moreover, spiritualists are consistently oriented toward the possibility of change in the illness over time and consequently to the possibility of intervention and the avoidance of chronicity. (pp. 316–317)

CAUSATIVE FACTORS FOR THE USE OF FOLK HEALING

Having analyzed the diverse sociocultural aspects of the Hispanic population in relation to religious beliefs and practices, we shall now examine hypotheses related to causative factors. First, the practice of spiritualism has been ascribed only to primitive cultures and underdeveloped countries. Other authors feel that this type of belief is related rather to behavioral adaptation to societal demands. For instance, Karush and Ovesey (1961) have stated that

> Unlike the physiological needs, the social needs are not innate. They develop only after the person's exposure to the society into which he has been born, and their nature is determined by the demands of the society. (p. 56)

We do not share either interpretation. Others may argue that spiritualism is used only in areas where medical facilities are not available. Our experience clearly rejects this interpretation, since the existence of our mental healh program did not deter our clients from visiting the botanicas (pharmacy selling herbs, statues, and so on) and spiritualist centers located in our catchment area while at the same time coming to our clinics, in most instances for the same types of problems. In analyzing causative factors, we must also take into account the fact that Hispanic groups in general resist medical approaches for the treatment of mental illness.

CONCLUSION

Finally, we would like to offer an interpretation that relates the existence of supernatural beliefs to the achievement of socioeconomic success. We feel that this hypothesis is the most acceptable one in explaining the causative factors of this behavior. Wintrob (1972) agrees with this hypothesis when he states that

> The greater the uncertainty of people about their chances of achieving socially valued goals, the greater the tendency to seek and accept alternative paths to these goals, magic among them. (p. 61)

We would like to describe briefly some meaures that have been implemented during the past 3 years at the Lincoln Community Mental Health Center in an attempt to shorten the gap between folk healers and classical mental health therapists. To date we have a) identified mediums in our program, b) visited spiritual centers and observed their modus operandi, c) exchanged views with mediums, d) accepted referrals from and referred cases to them, and e) carried out research and produced a film that is used for training of non-Hispanic staff. Further, we are in the process of developing share-training workshops among mediums, folk healers, community leaders, and the staff of the center. These steps have been taken in recognition of the fact that the unique aspects of a culture must be identified and dealt with in any mental health program.

In conclusion we have called attention to psychiatry's neglect of sociocultural problems among Hispanic groups and pointed out differences in cultural and technical orientation between classically trained mental health workers and folk healers in an urban metropolis, pointing up the need for the implementation of appropriate training curricula for classically trained professionals who work with Hispanic patients. We also recommend a closer link between professional mental health workers and folk healers, with the expectation that such interaction will provide a mutual alliance toward better understanding of cultural phenomena in the Hispanic community resulting in more relevant and rewarding therapy for the patient.

REFERENCES

Guthrie, G. M. Culture and mental disorder. In *Addison-Wesley Module Anthropology* (Module 39). Reading, Mass.: Addison Wesley, 1973.
Karush, A., & Ovesey, L. Unconscious mechanisms of magical repair. *Archives of*

General Psychiatry, 1961, *5*, 55–69.

Kiev, A. *Transcultural psychiatry*. New York: Free Press, 1972.

Lubchansky, I., Egri, G., & Stokes, J. Puerto Rican spiritualists view mental illness: The faith healer as a paraprofessional. *American Journal of Psychiatry*, 1970, *127*, 312–321.

Nelson, S. H., & Torrey, E. F. The religious functions of psychiatry. *American Journal of Orthopsychiatry*, 1973, *43*, 362–367.

Sidel, V. W. The health workers of the Fengsheng neighborhood of Peking. *American Journal of Orthopsychiatry*, 1973, *43*, 737–743.

Torrey, E. F. What Western psychotherapists can learn from witch doctors. *American Journal of Orthopsychiatry*, 1972, *42*, 69–76.

Wintrob, R. Hexes, roots, snake eggs? MD vs. occult. *Medical Opinion*, November 1972, 54–61.

22

The Dynamics and Treatment of the Young Drug Abuser in an Hispanic Therapeutic Community

Herbert J. Freudenberger

All too frequently young Hispanic drug abusers are placed into a therapeutic community environment with young black and white abusers and eventually drop out of these treatment programs. The cultural, familial and value heritage differences of Hispanic youths require that we take a look at how these young adults may differ from other young polydrug abusers and what can be done to increase their stay in treatment programs.

This paper covers some of the personality dynamics and familial relationships of young Hispanic drug abusers seen in SERA (an Hispanic therapeutic community) and in other New York City outreach programs.

Most of the treatment population are between 12 and 18 years, come from broken homes and have spent a portion of their lives in institutions. They are usually referred by the courts, probation officers, schools or neighborhood social service departments, and often come into treatment under pressure. Few come in voluntarily or are brought in by members of their family. If they are accompanied by a member of the family, it is usually a mother who no longer knows how to cope with the child and is looking to the program for some solutions. Obviously the "pressured treatment" approach will have implications from the very start as to the young adults' motivations for their staying in treatment.

At the outset, a major aspect of treatment is to hold the kids in the program. We do this by making them feel at home as much as possible. They are shown around the facility and introduced to other young people already in the program. This helps alleviate their negative attitudes, as well as begin the treatment process. The approach is to individualize the treatment and meet the client's specific needs within the structure of the

Presented at the North American Congress on Alcohol and Drug Problems, San Francisco, California. December 14, 1974.

Reprinted with permission from the *Journal of Psychedelic Drugs,* 1975, 7(3), 273–280.

program. Many of the youngsters come from the surrounding neighbor-hoods and know each other. A friend or an admired street hero in the facility can act as a "bridge" between the inductee and the program. It is more difficult for a Latino youngster to identify with a successful black or white addict role model than it is to identify with another Puerto Rican. The importance of each minority group having a sense of appropriate identification is often crucial for treatment success. As staff members of minority programs it is incumbent on us to keep in mind that if there are Latino residents, then we need Latino staff; the same applies for Asian Americans, native Americans and Mexican Americans. This does not mean that there need be exclusivity, but the majority of the treatment staff in a dominant minority group neighborhood ought to be from the same ethnic background.

As the inductee moves along, s/he is seen by a case worker or social worker who conducts an initial case summary interview. Some of the material elicited in the interview deals with family constellation, drug abuse history, physical description, educational background, medical history, institutionalizations, foster home placement, court cases pending and the case worker's impressions. Most of our social workers are either bilingual or Puerto Rican which aids in communication.

A composite picture of the typical young polydrug abuser found in the therapeutic community is that of a person who is the product of a bro-ken home where the father is either physically or psychically absent. It ap-pears that the father's role reverses as the family moves from Puerto Rico to the mainland. The father is the authority figure and the mother plays a subordinate role in the traditional Puerto Rican family structure. How-ever, once the family moves to the mainland as a unit, or the father comes alone initially, or the mother comes with the children and lives with an-other family member, the economic break up and separation of the family structure tends to create cultural shock within the family—a shock often traumatic to its young members and very difficult to reverse once started.

Economic realities immediately confront the family on their arrival. Either the father has taken up with another woman and his ability to pro-vide for the family is lessened in the U.S. Or if the family arrives as a whole unit, a roleshift reversal occurs wherein the mother becomes more capable of earning a salary than the father. This has serious consequences in terms of who retains authority within the family. The father may react to the shock by becoming brutal, punishing and sexually acting out in order to assert his felt loss of strength, power and machismo. The mother, on the other hand, is realistically economically stronger, but is still bat-tling with her self concept of old, that of the subordinate and passive mother-wife-woman-little girl. The mother in her conflicts becomes a more dependent, child-like, hysterical person but also becomes more economically self-sufficient. The family's previous cohesiveness is threatened further and more confusion ensues from the youngster's behavior.

The all too usual picture is clearly portrayed in Piri Thomas's novel *Down These Mean Streets* (1967). The young adult, once s/he gets onto the streets of New York, more and more identifies with the peer group. The peer group of New York is much less respecting, more aggressive and competitive, and more self-assertive than in Puerto Rico. Some families react to this beginning generation conflict by sending their children back to Puerto Rico and others begin the never ceasing battle for control and dominance. It is sad to hear how many of the children have been on continued shuttle flights between members of the family in Puerto Rico and members on the mainland. All these movements further the alienation, the loneliness and the lack of cohesive on-going identification for mature and stable growth to occur. Their identification is often a composite of many people, e.g., an older sister, an aunt, a grandmother, a step-father, an uncle or older brother. Furthermore, too many of these people have not been in the children's lives long enough to bring about any real sense of substance and solid bases of personality formation.

When these young people first enter treatment programs, they come in from the streets. They are, as one staff member described them, "street-wise and street-strong, but seriously suffering from ego weaknesses." Many of them are "tough" and have learned that in order to live, they have had to do so through an imposed image. For many, acquiring an image has necessitated their closing off any exchange of intimate or trusting feelings toward others. They can't afford to recognize or admit to human feelings. To do so might appear as being weak, ineffectual and inadequate. Their survival image is further expressed in their attire, their language, and the roles they play out for us, both manifest and fantasized. One often finds that they have great difficulty communicating verbally. They appear all locked up within themselves, suffer from serious emotional deprivation, a sense of emptiness and loss. This personality picture may be a function, as previously indicated (Freudenberger, 1971), of educational as well as interpersonal lacks.

Therefore, they come into the program undisciplined, unstructured, directionless, and for the most part, lost. As indicated in a previous paper, they are the true nomads of the 70s (Freudenberger & Overby, 1969). They have learned to roam the streets so well that no place is truly their home.

Many do not have an address that has lasted for more than a few months. They have been shifted about so often from relative to relative from one location to another and from institution to institution that they have acquired an institutional survival syndrome. This in turn adds to their character "toughness," and contributes to their lack of sensing that there really is a place for them anywhere on this earth.

In time, their "world" becomes a limited one, circumscribed by the neighborhood or institution. This often results in an extreme narrowing of their perspective on the total world. The writer has the impression that their emotional and environmental deprivations have led to a perceptual deprivation. They are poor readers and manifest a poor reasoning facility. In their need to blunt themselves from the brutality of their environment they have stunted their psychic and cognitive development. Their emotional deprivation has led to an impoverishment of conceptual abilities. They view life in a very narrow almost "tunnel-vision" manner. They do not see more than one solution to a problem; their problem-solving approach is often simplistic and very concrete. It is as if they could not allow themselves the luxury of entertaining more than one solution. Street brutality survival requires simplistic solutions.

Initially, we sought to bring more creative aspects into the program, such as working in art, theater, music and crafts. At the beginning, they will only accept the familiar and will reject the introduction of new projects or materials. A combination of the Latino background and lack of exposure leads to the immediate turning away and disparaging comments about the novel activities. Time, effort and persistence permits some to open up sufficiently and look at something different.

Further perceptual problems which may in part be a consequence of their past, includes a poor time sense as well as difficulties keeping appointments. If we do not take into account that some of this is the Hispanic culture but seek to arbitrarily impose an Anglo-oriented value system, then once again we are capable of losing the young people during treatment. The helper needs to *not* impose Anglo identities on Latino children.

As a group, they are not open or flexible. In their rigidities, they hold on tightly to themselves so that to open up would mean their loose ego structure would break. Their ego structure appears so diffuse and their infantile, unresolved needs seem to be so dependent that they will follow anyone who appears strong. Others who cannot accept any dependency needs within must remain tough and inflexible, and are very difficult to work with therapeutically. Regardless of what kind of teenager we are working with, we need to recognize that the presenting symptoms are only covers for deeper and more underlying disturbances. The Latino adolescent often uses drugs to cover more significant pathology, such as life problems, marital and family discords, depression and feelings of loneliness. Programs should be cognizant that once the character defenses and psychosomatic symptoms are removed and the drug abuse is stopped then a more intensive therapeutic process needs to be introduced.

Further major presenting symptoms are in the nature of depressions. Many youngsters are also given to lying, stealing, violence and brutality. They have suffered all sorts of sexual abuse in their past, either from members of their immediate family, or from strangers. This is especially true of the girl residents, many of whom have harrowing tales of rape and incest. For some, this may have done much to further their acting out and asserting themselves in the sexual arena, consequently, frequent abortions and pregnancies are a part of their histories.

Discipline, as most of us know it in the traditional sense just has not been present for the young population. They left school at an early age, or if they attended bodily, they did not get much out of the experience except further derisiveness regarding authority.

Another dynamic is the amount of discipline they can initially tolerate. This is evident in their inability to adjust to the youth component and to the school structure within the facility. To keep their interest in school, a great deal of teaching flexibility is required. A lot of individualized instruction, bi-lingual education, careful selection and diversity of materials are needed. Since discipline has often broken down in the home, their frustration tolerance is low; therefore, the role of structure in the therapeutic community becomes crucial. The typical Hispanic youngsters who enter the program are paranoid—a paranoia realistically based insofar as their street and neighborhood world is concerned. Confronting them with their reality as it is at the moment is crucial. The first reality we seek to convey is that they are in big trouble; that they are not able to make it in the way they have been living, that they may be suffering from hepatitis, venereal diseases, vitamin and nutritional deficiencies, no money, poor education, no work skills and that their survival ability is becoming increasingly less, from day to day, and as they grow older (Freudenberger, 1973).

The true value of a therapeutic community or out-patient environment for Latino youngsters is that it will provide a structured, consistent and human surrounding where a regrowing can take place. The youngsters must feel a sense of protection and need to feel that they are offered a high support system. In this regrowing process the staff of the facility must be constant, trustworthy, caring and flexible. They need to do good re-parenting. The regrowing, through daily demonstration, requires developing new role models. This happens through simple job skills, activities, sports, in school or in the kitchen. All of these activities are so structured that they will teach the importance of having a personal routine of life, including a system of personal values. The restructuring process requires therapeutic treatment, a kind of treatment that is *not* the hard line encounter. Young people have not lived long enough or solidified enough within themselves that their defenses are impregnable. They require confrontation for their lies, their con, their manipulations and their perceptual distortions, but this can be done within rap groups, individual counseling, family therapy sessions and the on-going consistent structure of the program.

Initially, we at SERA leaned heavily on the encounter as our tool of treatment intervention. Our staff was familiar with this technique as a consequence of their own treatment experiences, and we believed it would be a viable means of reaching these teenagers. We found in time that we were in error. We were not reaching them; they were fooling us and were really using the program in a street-wise manipulative sense without being touched.

As a result we now have introduced a case conference approach. Each young adult is presented to the social worker and then to the whole staff, from the director to the house manager; the nurse, the teacher and the clinicians participate. We discuss our own observations of the youngster and we share in the development of an overall treatment plan. This approach has reduced the manipulations, the rivalries and distortions among the staff, as well as between the staff and the kids. It has decreased the residents' ability to go from one staff member to another with different stories. The social worker refers the more disturbed youngsters to the psychologist or psychiatrist for further evaluation.

Youth training was introduced to the staff since they have had minimal experience with young polydrug abusers. Although most of the staff is Puerto Rican, they tend to be older addicts and are not as aware, or as understanding in treating and dealing with young people as we initially assumed. The old therapeutic treatment approaches just do not work with this population, and the older staff members' education must be upgraded.

Our family therapy sessions up to this time have not been successful. We have sent workers into the homes and have met with a great deal of opposition. Although the therapists are fluent in Spanish (some even come from the neighborhood), gaining access to the home has been difficult. If we find someone home we are met with all sorts of promises, but the mother or father does not show up for the appointment. We have sought to have meetings in the home, as well as in our facility, but with a minimum of success. We seem to be dealing with men and women who are having a difficult time just coping with the realities of their daily existence. They are glad that we are working with their children, but in some ways seem to have given over *their* responsibility of raising their children, to us. Many are tired, overworked, not satisfied with their lives, troubled and conflicted and involved with basic survival struggles. But we will keep on trying to see if a more fruitful family treatment contact is feasible in the future.

Hispanic adolescent drug abusers are visually oriented in terms of learning. They have spent a great deal of their childhood in front of the television and in the movies. This has furthered a sense of passivity, a need to be done for and not to initiate. The acquisition of knowledge appears to have been largely through the visual and auditory areas. They do not read much, but do retain what they have seen or heard. Consequently, our teachers use an approach to learning that involves giving simple directions, repeating them if necessary, and beginning learning stimulation through the seeing and hearing senses, rather than insisting primarily on increasing reading skills. Initially, reading bores them and "turns them off." Therefore, we seek to reach them where they are at, and not impose our expected rules of Anglo learning and behavior.

Their creativity and self-creative reliance have suffered much because of their life orientation. This, in turn, requires of us an awakening of some potential for their accomplishing in a more imaginative manner. Many of the Hispanic adolescents channel a large amount of their creativity and self-expression into the areas of attire, dance, music, language, sex and violence. They do not seem to know that there are additional avenues of self-expression. A Latino youth treatment program needs to recognize this.

A deadening and dulling seems to have occurred with their sensory awareness. They appear to have been so flooded by the loud sounds, the high playing music, the shrieking, the bellowing voices of their neighborhoods that they have learned to shut down parts of themselves, maybe to gain some inner private space. There appears to be a real preoccupation with physical space. Their gangs are very much concerned with not having their street, their "turf" (space), invaded. Their home conditions are usually extremely crowded and completely lacking in living, eating, studying and sleeping space. A place where one can be private and alone is offered only at night in some dark corner, on a roof, in a cellar, under a bed cover, in an abandoned building—or within the private darkness of alcohol and drugs.

Personal privacy, a private time for oneself is not known, nor is it even conceived. Yet the constant bombardment of their senses, their bodies, their thoughts, and their very lives leads to a further hardening of their psyches, an increasing of their character armor. We observe this holding in ("stuffing"), and repressing of feeling in their rap groups wherein tremendous rages and emotional outbursts occur. They dump their furies and frustrations on each other without any sensitivity or mercy. It is as if compassion would only lead to self destruction. We seek to make the encounters a rap session where talking, as well as confrontation may take place. This approach provides an opportunity for the expression of dignity (dignidad) for the adolescent, dignidad without assault. The *ability to be* is critical for development of the Latino. This non-assaultive approach may be reinforced by teaching them how to really listen to each other without being critical, and to accept the uniqueness of themselves and of people. We use sensitivity and gestalt group techniques to permit the expression of warmth and compassion without the threat of laughter, ridicule or criticism. We try to provide an atmosphere of good supportive sharing. Further, we need to teach them how to be sensitive to each other. We need to help them to learn, often for the first time, what it means to be close to a person and aware of their feelings.

A way that we at SERA accomplish this sense of privacy is to permit them to bring in personal belongings, to have Teddy bears and dolls on the beds and dressers, to give time off for themselves without bombarding them with therapeutic explanations. All these approaches help the youngsters experience the beginnings of private space if they wish or need it, and teach them a further sensitivity to themselves.

For Theresa, a 14-year-old, to be able to place some dolls on her bed, without "an older brother" tearing them up in her absence, was truly a sight to behold. At first, she could not believe that once she left the room she would come back and still find the dolls—and in one piece. Personal property is a very big issue. For some, like Adolfo, a shirt of his own was a first. He always wore the shirts of an older brother, and when he had his own polo shirt, he became very possessive of it. The day that another kid ripped it up, Adolfo ran away from the program. It was fortunate for us that we knew his neighborhood hiding places and were able to send a teacher out to find him, talk to him and have him return. The degree of impoverishment of the Latino kids is startling.

The writer has also found that to feel hurt, to feel sad, to feel disappointed—these are often unacceptable and non-demonstrated emotions. They are hidden and denied because they are feelings that have usually been dealt with in the environment by means of derision, disparagement, ridicule, avoidance and contempt, but rarely, if at all, by means of acceptance, understanding and sympathy. Latino parents, because of their own problems, can be very tough on their children.

For some, anger is difficult to express because of fear of reprisals, or because of felt homosexuality, or effeminacy, or because of insecurity. The anger is then often turned inward, with suicide or suicidal attempts often quite common. This holding in is often demonstrated in self-criticism, in their low self-esteem, and in the ease with which they can be hurt or made to feel inferior by others.

Their fears of the dark, of being alone and their sexual insecurities often make them organize and stay within cliques formed around sexual acting out, sports interests or a common culture. They often try to bring the gang structure into a treatment facility. This is because the gang is the only sense of belonging and security that many have known. Therefore, they seek to bring into the facility the same clique control and behavior within which they have lived. As indicated in an earlier section of this paper, the youngsters who know each other can become a "bridge" between new residents and those who have been in the program for a period of time. The clique phenomenon may be a reasonably successful one as an initial means of holding on to the acting out, tough and non-communicative youngster.

Most of the young adults, when they first enter the program, suffer from severe vitamin deficiencies and malnutrition. They have accumulated a number of very poor eating habits and as a rule do not know how to care for their bodily needs. Part of regrowing and parenting ought to deal with teaching them how to eat properly, to incorporate culturally meaningful food, not to anglicize the diet, but to eat in a healthful manner. This is part of the value building process that we use. To eat better and take better care of oneself has within it an implicit structure of personal and economic self-caring.

Further initial bodily symptoms and diseases range from neglected venereal infections to bad teeth, pimples, filthy hair and rashes. These are all signs of neglect and emotional deprivation. Teaching cleanliness and body care is in order. We do that through thorough medical and dental examinations. The in-house staff as well as neighborhood hospitals are utilized.

The young adults suffer from serious value distortions when they enter the program. Honesty, loyalty, trust, caring and affection are either distorted, confused or missing. The program seeks to lay the foundations for value building through close attention to and steady insistence on some very basic house chores, such as putting cigarette ash in an ashtray, making a bed, changing shirts, socks and underwear, and getting up on time. These are very simple functions, yet without them no real personality reorganization can occur and no foundation may be laid for future personality restructuring.

A program that works with deprived Hispanic young people needs to be aware of the desperate, non-caring, non-educating conditions from which many have come, as well as the very basic life structure changes that must occur in order for growth to take place. Merely to do therapy, to go through encounters with or to "head-trip" a resident, often leads to a very poor outcome. By themselves, these measures do not stand up under the test of time, because they do not adequately prepare the adolescent for re-entry into the stream of society. That therapeutic programs ultimately face a high recidivism rate is due to the many youngsters who are able to con their way through a program, learn the argot of treatment community survival, but are never really touched in the process.

It must be remembered that a significant number of those entering the program do not realize the depth of their inner disturbances and have a lack of awareness about all areas of their lives—educational, lingual, sexual, economic—as well as emotional. Many are suffering from disturbances that border on the psychotic, which requires of us an awareness of the limited goals for improvement that we ought to set initially.

Looking further at the Hispanic drug abuser's family, the father is often either a tyrant to be feared or an unpredictable man. He can be drunk or happy, cruel or disinterested. The relationship of the Puerto Rican son to his father often starts out as the son being submissive to the father, but later a real acting out of dominance over the father, either at home or on the streets, takes place.

The Puerto Rican father is often an immature man who appears to be overwhelmed by his role and responsibilities. He tends to regress to infantile behavior, has real difficulty facing adversities and tends to run away from troubles, either through alcohol, gambling or women. The Puerto Rican father who has been transplanted from Puerto Rico to a New York barrio must cope with a changing material vs. spiritual value system, a dichotomy of authority roles, based on wage earnings between his wife and himself; a having to deal with a sense of fatalism and passivity as opposed to an energetic and active coping with life. Further, he must try to overcome the peer role models of all the other men on the streets surrounding him who have given up and no longer much care. This is the concept of a man that the young Puerto Rican boy must seek to live up to or negatively measure himself against.

The Puerto Rican mother is often a defeated woman who strives to maintain some control over her son, either through bribed, guilt-producing tactics, excessive indulgent affections or seductive behavior. In time she tends to lose control over her sons and may seek help from an institutional authority, be it the schools, the law or a treatment facility. Her relationship with her daughters, on the other hand, is usually one of making excessive demands, being over-protective and over-disciplinary. The sad facts are that too often the male Puerto Rican child takes to the streets, joins youth gangs, and tends to gravitate to and adopt male role models that are often antisocial in nature. The girl, on the other hand, tends to become inadequate, has a poor sexual model to emulate and finds herself in a value conflict between attempting to remain the sexual virgin that is often expected by her mother, or the sexually experiencing young woman that her peer culture imposes on her.

Sexism is very rampant in the Puerto Rican community as well as in the treatment programs. Women are still relegated to subordinate and secondary roles in the family. Too many young drug-abusing girls merely find a semblance of femininity through early sex or tend to evolve life patterns dependent on and masochistically involved with men who are often economically supported through the girls' work or prostitution. In spite of this, the girls once they become young women or mothers are viewed as hopeless, weak, dependent and helpless.

In Puerto Rico there is, for so many, more of an identity, a sense of pride, of community, an extended family and a culture than in New York City. Once they come to New York, disintegration sets in. Their initial family structure is Spanish, but once here, such a mixture of roles occurs, such difficulties of adjustment in terms of first generation and second generation clashes arise, that the Puerto Rican family is ill prepared economically, vocationally, linguistically, educationally and psychically to cope with the consequent urban pressures. Further adjustment difficulties are heightened through their continued viewing of television wherein they see that so many people "out there" appear to have much more than they. Jealousies, rage, competition and wants are further aroused through this visual awakening and bombardment.

Additionally, frustration is heightened in the school system that too often does not relate to Hispanic children. The teacher's inability to speak Spanish, often not understanding the subtleties, innuendos, images, associations and special meanings of gestures and body language, further serves to enlarge the barrier between the children and the anglicized environment. The Hispanic setting, where most of the staff speaks Spanish, is their first contact with staff that really understands them. So many talk of wanting and enjoying some of their therapy and counseling sessions when conducted in Spanish. At SERA at least half the treatment is in Spanish. A religious conflict exists for many Hispanic youths. It is a conflict between the large and impersonal catholic church that many have known, and the more intimate and personal pentecostal church that their mothers attend. Many turn to herbs, magic and amulets for answers because it is part of a cultural heritage. A treatment environment needs to be aware of the importance of these religious practices in Latino youngsters. It may be another means for assisting communication, reaching youngsters and encouraging personal Latino identity.

Our initial inability to relate to young Hispanic adults may be a consequence of their severe turn off from their parents and authority. There is a lack of trust. Their fear is a cover for tremendous anger and rage, tending to express itself in homicide and suicide. Along with this rage there is a shaky sexual identification, which may be a consequence of the immature regressed (father) man and the often seductive, hopeless (mother) woman.

The first thing in treatment the youngsters require is basic structure that we seek to heighten through individual counseling. They need to be allowed to establish trust, affection and real friendship. The reparenting is necessary because so many essentially raised themselves, and had to be their own parents. Since they lack the ability to be consistent for any length of time, we must teach them the concepts of consistency and constancy.

Yet, in spite of the need to show consistency, there is also the need to show flexibility. Room for some degree of acting out and regression must be allowed within the safety of treatment.

The importance of basic structure with flexibility for the Hispanic youth cannot be over-emphasized. The value of this structure requires that the *staff be consistent* but not militant. A staff cannot operate with dissention, personal anxieties and conflicts and in turn expect a youth to respond constructively.

One of the main elements that a treatment environment offers to young people is a *new model of living*, a model they did not find in their home environment, a model within which they can begin to find a sense of themselves. This may be accomplished through the *routines*, the *schedules*, the *time*, and the *vocational* and *educational expectations* that are set. For some youngsters, those who are more in touch with what they want and who they are, it is also important to convey to them a sense of personal and vocational alternatives. Not all need to or should go by the middle-class value route. Some may be much happier if they are shown alternatives. A staff ought to be flexible enough to encourage alternative life styles. This author has observed however, that because the Latino and Chicano are just beginning to reach for some of the life style values of the Anglos, that it is difficult to change their course. It might be necessary to raise the consciousness of the Latino staff so they may be aware of alternatives. An apartment, a car, new furniture may not be of the same importance for all, if they are given the opportunity to reflect.

The staff serves as a *role model* for identification for these young people. We find it essential to also have young staff people working in our program.

It is important to point out that initially drug abusers form a strong attachment to people who care about them. They tend to become attached to strong people, but in doing so, they often cannot differentiate between *strong* and *good*. This is, of course, a result of what they learned on the street, and requires clarification.

In the therapeutic community, the young quickly tend to form strong attachments. For some, this is a first expression of dependency and affection. The staff, therefore, needs to be aware of its own countertransference feelings, in order to avoid encouraging dependency. Correctly used, these first feelings of dependency and affection, in those who have never before allowed themselves to open up to anyone, can be a huge force in regrowth. These feelings can also be used to illuminate the fact that *tough* does not have to mean *unfeeling* and that affection for someone does not have to mean losing oneself. These feelings can also be used to get over the idea that *consistency* does not have to mean *severity* and that *strong* people can be *good* people, that *good* does not mean *weak*. From that point on therapy can progress.

In conclusion, the observations made in this paper concerning the unique dynamics and treatment approaches of young drug abusers in a *Hispanic* setting will serve to point to the need for careful individual study of all the *other* different ethnic groups requiring therapy. Each group has its own personality dynamics and familial relationship.

Each ethnic group has its own cultural, linguistic, ethnic, educational and adjustment particularities to be considered. We cannot lump all "ethnics" together and expect to be able to reach them. The young Latino drug abuser is a very different individual from the young Black, White, native American or Chicano drug abuser. The emerging young Asian American drug abuser is very different from all of these. The sooner we attempt to discover, familiarize ourselves with, respect, and work within the differences between individuals, the sooner will we arrive at more successful treatment methods useful for all. We need to incorporate in the treatment programs a sense of cultural identification, history, customs and personal natures for all ethnic groups. Each has something to say to us; it is up to us to listen.

ACKNOWLEDGMENTS

The author is indebted to Mathew Thompson, a social worker and Josef Carbone, a teacher at SERA for their time and counsel in helping to prepare this paper.

REFERENCES

Freudenberger, H. J. Spring 1971. New Psychotherapy Approaches with Teenagers in a New World. *Psychotherapy* Vol. 8(1): 38–44.

Freudenberger, H. J. 1973. A Patient in Need of Mothering. *The Psychoanalytic Review* Vol. 60(1): 7–14.

Freudenberger, H. J. & Overby, A. 1969. Patients from an Emotionally Deprived Environment. *The Psychoanalytic Review* Vol. 56(2): 299–314.

Thomas, P. 1967. *Down These Mean Streets*. New York: Alfred Knopf.

23

Counseling the Chicano Child

Wayne R. Maes and John R. Rinaldi

Comenzémos con una descripcion breve de la familia Romero y de los ninos Carmen y Jesús. Let's begin with a description of the Romero family and of the children, Carmen and Jesús.

The family is the place to begin because it is the center of Chicano culture. *Chicano,* a word commonly used only recently, denotes a resident of the United States who is of Mexican descent and often also of Spanish descent. Such people are sometimes referred to as Spanish-Americans or Mexican-Americans.

The Romeros are in every sense of the word a family. They spend a great deal of time together working, playing, worshiping, and just plain talking. Mr. Juan Romero is a plasterer, as were his father and grandfather. He is a fine craftsman and makes a livable wage. Jesús, who is seven, already is dirtying himself in sand and cement at his father's work site at every chance he gets on weekends or when there is no school. He really prefers the slap and scrape of the trowel and the clean, damp, sweet smell of the plaster to the classroom. School is a hassle. Jesús reads just well enough to make it in his second grade class, and his math isn't much better. The teacher prods and pushes a lot, and Jesús doesn't openly resist, but inside he resents it. "What's school got to do with plastering anyway," he thinks. Worse yet is social studies. There are all of those embarrassing questions with hard-to-understand words. Besides, the teacher says he must learn to pronounce words correctly. She doesn't make much allowance for the fact that he heard and spoke mostly Spanish for the first five years of his life.

Carmen is twelve, the oldest child, and she likes boys. She gets by in school and is a good help to her mother around the house and with her baby sister. But she thinks of boys. Like her mother before her, and generations before that she will marry, keep house, and raise children.

Mrs. Maria Romero is an affable sort. She is kind but firm with her children, keeps a neat house, and prepares tasty, nourishing food. She is accustomed to having neighbors in and out of the house, and her parents and Juan's parents, along with uncles, aunts, cousins, nephews, and nieces, come by frequently. It's nice to have friends and relatives near at hand. There's a warm, comforting feeling about it, even though there are occasional spats.

Juan, Maria, the children, and their relatives find it a bit easier to deal with the prejudicial behavior in the larger culture when they have each other. Nevertheless, it galls them to be prevented full access to social and economic resources because of what are thought to be quirks of speech or because of skin color. It can make one very bitter.

Whatever unfairness Jesús feels at school, he responds to in the typical way he usually handles his fear and embarrassment. He becomes combative with his male classmates or does things that are risky. He has been acting this way more often lately, and he resists his mother's embraces whereas he once liked to cuddle. These are the beginnings of what is often referred to in Chicano culture as "machismo." Its counterpart in Anglo culture is described in Adler's concept of the "masculine protest."

This is the Romero family. While there is obviously wide diversity among Chicano families, the Romeros are fairly representative. They provide a picture of a warm, cooperative, interdependent family. They are a family to some extent caught between what they know and value—the Chicano culture—and the broader American culture. Jesús and Carmen face, even more than their parents ever have or will, the challenge of guarding the values of their heritage while learning to gain greater access to the social and economic advantages available.

THE WORK OF THE COUNSELOR

Even our rather superficial acquaintance with the Romero family and with Jesús and Carmen helps us identify some priorities for providing assistance as counselors. The four most important are (a) language and cognitive skill development, (b) expansion of career choice options, (c) personal respect and pride in the Chicano culture, and (d) personal value exploration.

Language and Cognitive Skill Development

Underprivileged Chicanos do not score as well on standardized intelligence tests as do the test norm groups. This is due primarily to lower verbal scores (Mercer, 1971). What can be done to help? Some promising breakthroughs are occurring in teaching cognitive skills to young minority children (Blank & Solomon, 1968). Dramatic gains—an average of 14.5 IQ points—for a group of preschoolers after three months of tutoring were highly encouraging. The counselor's role in this regard may include design and implementation of programs that teach cognitive skill development. The counselor can use this opportunity to build cooperative relations with the principal and teachers. While team teaching and tutorial work should be limited so as to allow time for numerous other counselor activities, they can be excellent ways of becoming better acquainted and assisting children and teachers.

An excellent preschool program (Right-to-Read) utilizing parents as tutors has been used in the La Luz Elementary School in Albuquerque. Parents are trained as tutors to assist the child in reading and reading readiness activities. An interesting by-product of this program is the sense of satisfaction and self-fulfillment of the tutors and the more positive attitude toward the school on the part of the parents whose children were tutored. The initiation of such a program provides an excellent entrée for the counselor to be involved along with the principal and/or curriculum specialists in the community by training and supervising the work of the parent tutors.

Upper elementary grade children can serve as tutors for their peers and for the lower grade children. Such a program can be of direct benefit to the student-tutors in a program designed to improve their ability to help. Selective attention skills, listening skills, and questioning strategies may be taught, and the children may be provided supervision in their tutoring (Gumaer, 1973).

There are also numerous small group activities that the counselor can employ to facilitate language and cognitive development. Dora Macias and Dorothy Crouch, who counsel Chicano children in the El Paso Public Schools, have found the following procedures to be effective:

1. Use newspaper cartoons or magazine pictures that illustrate sharing, good manners, etc. The students paste them on tag board or paper and discuss the situations with the counselor facilitating the discussion.
2. Using the magazine pictures displaying various emotions and moods in people, have the students discuss the pictures and situations which they have experienced which prompted similar emotions.

Expansion of Career Choice Options

Jesús' and Carmen's career choices were restricted to plastering and being a housewife. The counselor can design programs to make the child aware of careers with which he or she has had very little experience. Community workers might be invited to the school, and visits to work sites might be arranged. Activities can be planned which expose children to many options for women beyond being housewives and options for men in the sciences and other professions. Chicano role models in these new career option areas are essential.

Self-Respect and Pride in Chicano Culture

This is as often achieved in subtle ways as it is in direct ways. Respected, effective Chicano teachers and counselors in their daily work can convey a sense of pride in self and culture. This can have a positive impact on the children. Assisting children in language and cognitive development has its payoff in more successful achievement, a strong influence on self-acceptance. Chicano community leaders can be invited to the school (for example, in relation to career exploration) and share with the children their success and achievement. The integration of Chicano culture into social studies units can help give children a sense of pride in their food, music, and customs and an opportunity to share these with those less familiar with the Chicano culture.

Exploration and Clarification of Personal Values

Dora Macias and Dorothy Crouch have found unfinished stories depicting home or school situations to be useful in stimulating discussion among Chicano children. These stories may be read to the children, and the children may be directed to the question, "What should he do now?" Or, paper sacks can be used to make puppets representing different members of the family. These can be used to dramatize the roles and feelings of family members. Such techniques surface important values and attitudes. For example, the almost unquestioning obedience to parents and authority is commonly brought up. The counselor can skillfully assist the children to examine courses of action that are based on overly selfish desires by the child as well as those based on arbitrary or overly stringent demands by parents and others. This conflict between what "I want " and parents or the church demand is frequent. The objective is to help the child be aware of and employ intelligent solutions which represent enlightened self-interest and a concern for others. Such discussions may be quite sensitive and should be handled carefully. For example, certain courses of action may be contrary to what children learn at home (questioning authority and making a rational decision), and the task will be to help the children be aware of these new alternatives without undermining affection and respect for parents.

CHARACTERISTICS OF THE COUNSELOR

Who can do the work of the counselor with Chicano children? Not every counselor! Children like Jesús and Carmen require some unique attributes on the part of the helper.

Bilingualism

In working with Chicano children, particularly during early elementary school, the ability to speak Spanish and English fluently is at least highly desirable and probably necessary. Parent contacts are often impossible without fluency in Spanish or a translator (a second best option of questionable value). Spanish is necessary to have full range of discussion with the children, not to mention its rapport-building benefits.

Cultural Awareness

In order to better understand the values, goals, and behavior of the Chicano child, the counselor should have extensive first-hand experience with and an understanding of Chicano religion, history, art, music, dance, and literature. Experiencing and understanding the cultural script of the Chicano is as important as individual life scripts are in the counseling process.

Counseling Repertoire

The counselor needs more than traditional individual and group counseling relationship skills in his repertoire. Language is often not the most expedient vehicle for change. Behavior modification and Adlerian techniques which influence the environment so as to change it and to face the child with the consequences of his behavior are often more effective. Influencing the environment extends to the family. Since the family is of utmost importance to the child, the counselor must work with the family in effecting change. Finally, the counselor must function as a consultant to teachers and principals to influence the educational setting to be more responsive to the child's language, culture, and psychosocial needs.

The Person of the Counselor

The counselor should possess helping characteristics such as empathy, warmth, positive regard, congruence, and authenticity. The question is often raised, "Must the counselor be Chicano?" The answer has to be "No." Unique people can defy all conventional standards. However, the above mentioned characteristics are usually essential to highly effective work and are not often possessed by persons other than Chicanos.

The counselor of Chicano children such as Jesús and Carmen is first and foremost a counselor of children whose motivation, learning styles, and basic satisfiers are like those of the children of the world. But the counselor of Chicanitos (Chicano children) is more. Standing at the interface of two cultures, the counselor must assist the Chicanito to partake fully of the social and economic resources of the larger culture without sacrificing what is unique and valued in the Chicano culture. The sensitive counselor knows the economic and social necessity of assimilation in the larger culture, while at the same time realizing the danger of loss of personal identity in "selling out" one's heritage and folkways in order to gain the fruits of participation. The counselor's task is to open up more options in the life of the Chicanito as the child grows toward adulthood. These expanded options usually require impacting the people and institutions surrounding the child as well as enhancing the child's skills and attitudes so he can take advantage of opportunities. Both are formidable tasks for the counselor, whose day-to-day efforts sometimes seem to pale into insignificance. But, a stone thrown into a pool does cause ever expanding concentric ripples which go on and on.

REFERENCES

Blank, M., & Solomon, F. A. A tutorial language program to develop abstract thinking in socially disadvantaged pre-school children. *Child Development,* 1968, *39,* 379–389.

Gumaer, J. Peer-facilitated groups. *Elementary School Guidance and Counseling,* 1973, *8,* 4–11.

Mercer, J. R. Institutionalized Anglocentrism: Labeling mental retardates in the public schools. In P. Orleans and W. Ellis (Eds.), *Race, Change and Urban Society. Volume 5. Urban Affairs Annual Reviews.* Beverly Hills, Calif.: Sage Publications, 1971. Pp. 311–338.

24

A Hispanic Foster Parents Program

Melvin Delgado

The continuing increase in the Hispanic population in the United States has pressed social agencies to carry out programs focused on the needs of this population. The need to recruit and train foster families in the Hispanic community has received only slight attention in the professional literature. This need, combined with an ever-increasing demand for temporary placement of Hispanic children, has been of great concern to child caring agencies and professionals. This article describes a foster family program to provide this type of child care in a Hispanic community. The Hispanic Foster Parents Program is a direct result of a collaborative effort between two child welfare agencies in Worcester, Massachusetts.

Worcester is in the central part of the state and has a population of almost 200,000, of whom about 10,000 are of Hispanic origin, predominantly Puerto Rican. The Hispanic population has quadrupled in the last 5 years and has had a corresponding impact on social service agencies. Worcester Youth Guidance Center's (WYGC) Hispanic Program is multidisciplinary and multifaceted, providing a wide range of primary and secondary intervention services to the Hispanic community of Worcester.

Youth Opportunities Upheld's (YOU) Hispanic Program is also multifaceted. In addition to the Hispanic Foster Parents Project, an ongoing mothers' group deals with the difficulties of having children involved in the juvenile court system. Staff also provides counseling to Hispanic children and families.

The Hispanic Foster Parents Program provides child care services on a short-term basis. It consists of several components, under the aegis of a multidisciplinary staff, using the services of four bilingual and bicultural staff members. YOU's Hispanic staff recruits potential foster homes, assists in training, places the foster child, and provides the services of two mental health professionals, who assess potential foster homes, structure and lead training sessions, and consult with foster parents once a child is placed in a home.

Reprinted with permission from *Child Welfare,* 1978, *7,* 427–431.

RECRUITMENT OF FOSTER HOMES

Research studies have noted that foster families usually do not differ significantly from the general population [11:295-304]. Parker [10:69-70] found that similarity of socioeconomic characteristics between foster homes and foster children is positively correlated with degree of success in placement. These findings have been substantiated by the Hispanic program experiences.

Successful recruitment of Hispanic foster homes requires a varied approach. The Hispanic program uses Spanish radio announcements and agency and community contacts. The latter are the most successful; Hispanic people usually react more favorably to personal rather than impersonal contacts, such as posters and letters.

When as many as 10 to 12 prospective applicants have expressed interest in becoming foster parents, a general meeting is held, and questions about foster care are answered. After this meeting, program staff begin the evaluation of potential homes. The program's experience is that about one-third of the participants in the meeting do not follow through to the evaluation phase.

ASSESSMENT AND EVALUATION

In home studies of Hispanic applicants, it is imperative to have either a Hispanic staff member or someone who is bilingual, with an excellent grasp of the culture. Consideration must be given to the nature and extent of the extended family [9:76-83], psychocultural adaptation [1:413-421; 6:459-468], roles of significant family members [5:167-181], religious beliefs and superstitions [3:451-458; 7], and cultural values [8:53-67]. This approach, together with a comparable approach to foster children and their natural families, is crucial in ensuring a proper placement and effective support services.

TRAINING

The Hispanic Foster Parents training component consists of preservice and inservice phases and involves significant members of the foster family whenever possible [2:100-108]. The training combines an overview of the foster care system and roles of significant members of the team, with development of foster parenting abilities. Training goals include: 1) participation in a team; 2) self-awareness and handling one's feelings and reactions in the foster parenting role; 3) recognizing, understanding and dealing with the needs of foster children; 4) identifying one's own learning needs in foster parenting, and seeking one's own growth and development in response to these needs; and 5) promoting successful foster parenting experiences [4:591].

The training consists of 26 hours of instruction scheduled into 13 2-hour sessions twice a week, over a 6½-week period. Sessions alternate between agency setting and the homes of the participating foster parents. Transportation is arranged for participants who need it, ensuring maximum participation. The availability of transportation is particularly important, since many of the potential foster families do not have a car.

Training sessions are conducted in Spanish and have a multimodality format. In addition to didactic presentations, role playing and written exercises stress potentially difficult situations. Weekly assignments require applicants to discuss with significant members of their families such issues as initial reactions to a new member of the family, sibling rivalry, acting-out behavior of a foster child, etc. Some sessions focus on rudimentary behavior modification techniques and how to use the services of a consultant.

Participants are required to attend three-fourths of the sessions to complete the training program successfully. At the end of the training phase, participants fill out forms evaluating instructors and the curriculum, and recommending changes. They are also asked to provide the names of families they think would be interested in becoming foster families.

The final training session, in addition to review and evaluation of material, is devoted to graduation ceremonies and an agency-funded party, usually held in the home of one of the graduates, and including the preparation of ethnic food by all of the graduates. Diplomas are handed out by the executive director of one of the two agencies collaborating in the program, giving the participants tangible evidence of successful completion of a long and difficult process; many of the foster parents frame their diplomas and display them prominently in their homes.

In monthly inservice training sessions foster care experiences are shared and intervention strategies are developed. Various topics suggested by group members, ranging from disciplinary issues to how to handle termination feelings, are discussed in detail.

SUPPORT SERVICES

The removal of a child from his parents should be the last alternative in a treatment plan; the return of the child to his home as soon as therapeutically possible should be the primary objective of a foster care program. These principles also apply, of course, to Hispanic children and families.

To achieve the objective of a united family, a foster care program should provide a variety of services. Youth Opportunities Upheld, with clinical support from Worcester Youth Guidance Center staff, provides counseling to the foster child. Worcester Youth Guidance staff, in turn, attempts to involve the natural family in some form of therapy (individual, marital, family). Foster parents are also helped to facilitate the transition of the foster child to and from the foster home [12:82–90].

Continuing consultation with the foster parents is provided by a Hispanic staff member of WYGC.

During consultation, which can occur as frequently as once or twice a week, depending upon the severity of the situation, the foster parents and the consultant assess the progress of the child. Either the foster parents or the consultant determine the agenda. This support, combined with 24-hour emergency coverage, allows foster families to handle extremely difficult children.

CONCLUSION

The collaborative foster care program described in this article attempts to meet an increasing need for child care services in one Hispanic community. This need is no doubt present in countless numbers of communities throughout the United States. The Hispanic Foster Parents Program's success is due in large part to the dedicated work of foster families and agency staff.

For one agency to develop a Hispanic foster care program is difficult, in light of the time and resources necessary. However, through collaborative efforts such as the one carried out by Youth Opportunities Upheld and Worcester Youth Guidance Center, similar and more ambitious comprehensive services to underserved communities can become a reality.

REFERENCES

1. Cohen, Lucy M., and Fernandez, Carmen L. "Ethnic Identity and Psychocultural Adaptation of Spanish-Speaking Families," Child Welfare, LIII, 7 (July 1974).
2. Davids, Leo. "Foster Fatherhood: The Untapped Resource," Child Welfare, LII, 2 (February 1973).
3. Delgado, Melvin. "Puerto Rican Spiritualism and the Social Work Profession," Social Casework, LVIII, 8 (1977).
4. Dorgan, Marsha P. "Initiating a Program of Foster Parent Education," Child Welfare, LIII, 9 (November 1974).
5. Fernandez-Marina, R., Maldonado-Sierra, E. D., and Trent, R. D. "Three Basic Themes in Mexican and Puerto Rican Family Values," Journal of Social Psychology, XLVIII, 2 (November 1958).
6. Ghali, Sonia Badillo. "Culture Sensitivity and the Puerto Rican Client," Social Casework, LVIII, 8 (1977).

7. Harwood, Alan. Puerto Rican Spiritism as a Community Mental Health Resource. New York: Basic Books, 1976.
8. Lauria, A. J. "Respecto, Relajo and Interpersonal Relations in Puerto Rico," Anthropological Quarterly, XXXVII, 2 (April 1964).
9. Mizio, E. "Impact of External System on the Puerto Rican Family," Social Casework, LV, 2 (1974).
10. Parker, R. A. Decisioning in Child Care, London: Allen and Unwin, 1966.
11. Peterson, James C., and Pierce, A. Dean. "Socioeconomic Characteristics of Foster Parents," Child Welfare, LIII, 5 (May 1974).
12. Simonds, John F. "A Foster Home for Crisis Placements," Child Welfare, LII, 2 (February 1973).

25

Strategic Intervention
A Mental Health Program for the Hispanic Community

Melvin Delgado and John F. Scott

Over the past three years the Worcester Youth Guidance Center has developed a series of mental health programs directed to the Hispanic community of Worcester, Massachusetts. The model for these programs has been strategic intervention. It was recognized that the traditional delivery of child mental health services to the Hispanic subcommunity had been ineffective in the past and that relevant and innovative treatment techniques were required. Such an approach, identified as strategic intervention, was developed on the basis of knowledge gained from the literature on Hispanic lifestyles and extensive exploratory contacts with key leaders in the Hispanic community.

The Worcester Youth Guidance Center's Hispanic Program consists of five basic components: 1) community education and training, 2) clinical consultation, 3) program consultation, 4) research, and 5) clinical intervention and case management (Delgado & Scott, Note 1).

The Setting

The Worcester Youth Guidance Center is a joint undertaking of the Child Guidance Association of Worcester and the Department of Mental Health of the Commonwealth of Massachusetts. The Center is a multidisciplinary agency that has been in existence since 1922. It is a member of the American Association of Psychiatric Clinics for Children. In addition to providing a wide range of psychiatric services to children and families, the Center also serves as a training facility for social workers, psychologists, and psychiatric residents.

The City of Worcester is located in the central part of Massachusetts, approximately 40 miles west of Boston. The city has a population of almost 200,000, of which over 10,000 are of Hispanic origin, predomi-

Reprinted with permission from the *Journal of Community Psychology,* 1979, 7 187–197.

nantly Puerto Rican (92%). Worcester has seen a rapid expansion in the number of Hispanic residents during the past few years, from close to 2500 in 1971 to over 10,000 in 1978.

Overview of Puerto Rican Migration Patterns

Puerto Ricans have resided in the United States since 1830 (U.S. Commission on Civil Rights, 1976, p. 19). However, full-scale migration can be traced to the post-World-War-II period. During this period the United States increased steadily from 300,000 in 1950 to 887,000 in 1960 and over 1.7 million as of 1975 (U.S. Commission on Civil Rights, 1976, p. 19).

During the past decade, Puerto Rican dispersal within the United States has, with few exceptions, gone unnoticed by social scientists. Jaffe and Carreras-Carleton (Note 2) studied dispersal of Puerto Ricans within the United States and noted a prodigious increase within the past decade. Recent estimates show Puerto Ricans have settled in all 50 states, an increase from 38 states in 1960 (Hernandez-Alvarez, 1968). Approximately 30 cities have Puerto Rican populations of 5,000 or more (Delgado, Note 3; U.S. Commission on Civil Rights, 1976, p. 21).

As a result of return migration to Puerto Rico (Nordheimer, 1978), and dispersal within the United States, New York City's percentage of the Puerto Rican population in the United States has decreased over the past two decades from 82% in 1950 to 59% in 1970 (U.S. Commission on Civil Rights, 1976, p. 21).

As these statistics indicate, the rapid increase in the Puerto Rican population of Worcester is not atypical. Similar patterns have been detected throughout the state of Massachusetts and other northeastern states. Such a dispersal pattern will have far-reaching implications for human service programs. This mass influx of culturally different people is of concern for many social and mental health agencies. Services which were monolingual (English) in the past must now contend with delivery of bilingual services. The paucity of data regarding these new communities will make rational planning and delivery of services arduous.

Overview of the Literature

Both the need for mental health services and the low utilization of these services by Puerto Ricans and other Hispanics have been well documented (Fitzpatrick, 1971, pp. 161–169; Padilla & Ruiz, 1974; Phillipus, 1971; Puerto Rican Task Force Report, Note 4). One of the most recent studies on utilization rates of mental health services among Puerto Ricans residing in the United States noted that, when compared with other ethnic groups from the same catchment area, Puerto Ricans had a much lower rate of utilization (Abad, Ramos, & Boyce, 1974).

In response to this discrepancy between need and service utilization in the Hispanic community, treatment and service delivery models have been developed to address this important issue (Padilla, Ruiz, & Alvarez, 1975; Philippus, 1971; Szapocznik, Scopetta, & King, 1978). Following a review of treatment and service delivery models for Hispanics, Padilla, et al. (1975) delineated three basic models: 1) professional adaptation, 2) family adaptation, and 3) the "barrio" service center model.

In brief, the professional model concentrates on preparing staff to "adapt" themselves to the client population by noting and implementing changes that are congruent with sociocultural concepts of Hispanic communities. The family model requires clinics to utilize primary social relationships in their treatment. The "barrio" model, in turn, focuses on delivery of "social broker" services along with counseling in the community.

These mental health service delivery models emphasize various approaches to treatment. However, each of these must take into account the following factors during the planning process if the mental health program is not to be undermined: 1) awareness of environmental factors and the influence they play on intrapsychic conflicts (Clifford et al., 1970, p. 128; Cohen & Fernandez, 1974); 2) appreciation and sensitivity regarding Hispanic culture (Bruhn & Fuentes, 1977; Ghali, 1977; Kline, 1969); 3) provision of services by bilingual, and preferably, by bicultural staff (Arce, 1975; Cagel, 1977; Freedman, 1977; Glen, 1975); 4) neighborhood-based services with community input into program planning (Kline, 1969, p. 1680; Meyer, 1977, pp. 606–607; Scott & Delgado, Note 5); 5) cognizance of the importance of the family within the Hispanic culture (Fernandez-Marina et al., 1958; Mizio, 1974; Szapocznik, Scopetta, & King, 1978); 6) appreciation of the valuable function of the folk therapist within the culture (Delgado, 1977, 1978a, 1979b; Hamburger, 1978; Harwood, 1977; Kiev, 1968; Koss, 1975, 1978; Martinez, 1977; Rogler & Hollingshead, 1965; Ruiz & Langrod, 1976a, 1976b, Sandoval, 1977); and lastly, 7) flexibility in program design for provision of a wide range of services (Bryant, 1975; Delgado & Montalvo, 1979; Lefley, 1975; Sue, 1977).

WORCESTER YOUTH GUIDANCE CENTER AND THE HISPANIC PROGRAM

The Hispanic Program of the Worcester Youth Guidance Center is staffed by a team of five mental health professionals who are bilingual and bicultural, with varying degrees of experience with children. Staff members represent the disciplines of education, counseling, psychology, and social work. The program addresses the needs of the Hispanic community through five distinct, yet related, programmatic components. Each staff member is called upon to provide any of the services the program has to offer. Through formal training, each staff member has specialized in children of a particular age group, and receives assignments related to this expertise.

The Hispanic Program staff maintains offices at the Center and fulfills training and administrative responsibilities within this setting, However, the Center is located on the outskirts of Worcester and, as a result, is difficult to reach. Thus, the Hispanic staff carried out most of their functions within community-based sites (Scott & Delgado, Note 5).

The Hispanic Program receives funding from the Massachusetts Department of Mental Health, United Way of Central Massachusetts, and fees from consultation and training activities. The latter source of funds represents approximately 8% of the total operating costs of the program. Fees are based on ability to pay for services.

The Hispanic Program utilizes many of the concepts delineated by Padilla et al. (1975). Through the implementation of micro-orientated programs (focus on individuals rather than institutions), a series of mental health programs have been implemented which seek to sensitize non-Hispanic professionals to Hispanic lifestyles and values (professional adaptation). In addition, attempts have been made to utilize culturally based informal systems of help in the provision of services (family adaptation). These attempts have ranged from consultation with folk healers concerning cases, to training and consulting with extended family members of children with emotional problems to take on foster parenting roles. In the provision of counseling services, social broker ("barrio") tasks have been provided, e.g., advocacy.

However, unlike other models of service delivery, in which emphasis is usually placed upon individual treatment in various forms, the Hispanic Program has sought to bring institutional changes within other human service settings (macro-approach). This systems-oriented approach to mental health has been accomplished through a series of consultation and education programs. Further, the Hispanic Program has undertaken several of these projects with an interagency focus. Through the combination of two or more agencies, limited resources can be concentrated on a given goal, e.g., training Hispanic foster parents.

The aims of the macro-oriented approach have been to identify and train indigenous leaders and service providers, as well as to develop Hispanic services within non-Hispanic human service agencies. The philosophy of the Hispanic Program calls for assisting other agencies and individuals in developing programs rather than attempting to address all mental health needs itself. The program thus takes a macro-view in looking for the most important and efficient points for intervention in the community; in this sense, it may be referred to as a model of "strategic intervention."

In addition to the principle of interagency collaboration, the following five principles form the philosophical foundation of the Hispanic Program: 1) flexibility in program design to accomodate changing needs; 2) primary prevention programs as an integral part of service delivery; 3) multifaceted programming stressing micro- and macro-approaches; 4) community-based services accessible to all geographical areas and segments of the population; and 5) counseling in generic settings, if possible, to avoid the stigma associated with mental health services.

Community Education and Training Component

The community education and training component has sought to have an impact on all levels of human services in Worcester. This component has focused on four different populations: 1) Hispanic human services staff, 2) non-Hispanic staff, 3) community leaders, and 4) Hispanic parents. Training programs have focused on upgrading skills and knowledge of Hispanic staff about mental health principles, sensitizing non-Hispanic staff to the Hispanic culture, training community leaders for participation on agency boards, and, through a series of parent-focused programs, better preparing Hispanic parents for foster parenting roles.

The programs targeted at Hispanic human service staff have sought to accomplish four major goals: 1) development of interviewing and behavior management skills, 2) facilitation of the identification and referral of Hispanic children who displayed severe emotional problems, 3) improvement of intrastaff relations, and 4) development of advocacy techniques (Delgado, Notes 6 & 7). Hispanic staff from various agencies have participated in the training program.

The Worcester public school system, for example, is one of several major human service systems which has benefited from this training program. Over the past few years the Hispanic Program has been actively involved in training bilingual personnel in the school system. The first year of involvement, 1976, focused exclusively on training teacher aides to better prepare them for their classroom role. A total of 25 aides participated in a training program which encompassed a total of 24 hours of instruction over the academic year, and sought to develop tutoring, behavior management, and relationship skills.

In the second year, the training continued to focus on aides but also involved classroom teachers. The primary goal of this training was to improve the working relationship of aides and teachers; this was accomplished through various small and large group exercises which developed listening and communication skills. In addition, a teacher aide manual was developed aimed at increasing knowledge and skills related to: 1) role and responsibilities of aides and teachers, 2) effective aide-teacher relations, 3) community resources, 4) job benefits and other concerns, and 5) meaning of the Federal and state bilingual education law.

The training program oriented towards non-Hispanic human service providers sought to: 1) better prepare them to understand the richness of the Hispanic culture, 2) facilitate the development of rapport between social agencies and the community, 3) provide a conceptual framework for appreciation of the assimilation issues confronting the Hispanic community, and 4) facilitate the identification and referral of Hispanic children with emotional problems.

Over a period of two years approximately 200 non-Hispanic human service staff have participated in this training, representing over 50 agencies in Worcester. The training focused on six major content areas: 1) Puerto Rican history, 2) cultural patterns, 3) socioeconomic status of Puerto Ricans in the United States, 4) migration trends, 5) mental and physical health issues within the Worcester community, and 6) data on the sociodemographic characteristics of the Puerto Rican population in Worcester (Delgado, 1979a).

The Hispanic Program, in collaboration with ALPA, an Hispanic community agency, received a grant to train a cadre of community leaders for potential membership on social agency boards of directors (Delgado, 1978c). This program attempted to identify and train members of the community to play influential roles in the human service field.

The training consisted of 36 hours of instruction covering organizational bylaws, parliamentary procedures, program-planning principles, budgets, staff evaluations, fund raising, and principles of community organization. Through an arrangement with Quinsigamond, a local community college, participants received three college credits. A total of 19 members enrolled and completed the training. It is hoped that these trained members of the community will serve a vital role in drawing further attention and resources to the needs of children and families.

A recently completed program identified and trained a select group of Hispanic mothers and fathers for the role of foster parents for children referred from juvenile court. The training developed the foster-parenting abilities of the participants through pursuit of the following five goals: 1) participation in a team, 2) self-awareness and handling one's feelings and reactions in the foster parenting role, 3) recognizing, understanding and dealing with the needs of foster children, 4) identifying one's own growth and development in response to these needs, and 5) promoting successful foster-parenting experiences (Dorgan, 1974, p. 591).

The training consisted of 26 hours of instruction. Sessions alternated between agency setting and the homes of the participants. Transportation was arranged for those who needed it, insuring maximum participation.

Sessions were conducted in Spanish, since the majority of the participants had limited English language skills. Course content was presented through didactic presentations, role play situations, and written exercises. The training curriculum stressed material and situations dealing with the potential impact of a foster child on family equilibrium (Delgado, 1978b).

Clinical Consultation Component

The high demand for mental health services, represented in various forms in social agencies throughout Worcester, combined with limited bilingual mental health resources, served as an impetus to develop a clinical consultation component (Delgado, Note 8). Clinical consultation was defined as the provision of outside intervention in developing/upgrading clinical skills of staff as they relate to clients (consultee-centered), or in understanding how to deal with particular clients (client-centered), for the purposes of evaluation (Caplan, 1970).

Consultation was provided to staff in drug (Delgado, Note 6), youth, recreational, health, and day care settings, (Delgado & Montalvo, 1979). With the exception of one agency, consultation was provided to Hispanic staff in predominantly non-Hispanic agencies.

Human service settings have been finding it increasingly necessary to provide bilingual services to Hispanic communities. However, the propensity of many settings to hire just one Hispanic worker, usually a paraprofessional, has undermined any serious effort to deliver high quality services to the Hispanic community. Being the "Lone Ranger" has often resulted in low staff morale and high turnover rates (Delgado, Note 9).

As Abad, Ramos, and Boyce (1977, p. 31) have noted, abuses of paraprofessionals diminish their capabilities:

> The issue of the use of paraprofessionals has become one that almost implicitly enters into any discussion on mental health and minorities. For Puerto Ricans, the indigenous paraprofessional has opened doors to service otherwise denied them by virtue of language and cultural barriers. Our concern is that paraprofessionals receive training and ongoing supervision for their assignments and they be complemented by bilingual and bicultural, professional staff. We are aware that the scarcity of professional staff qualified to work with Spanish speaking patients can easily result in the abuse of paraprofessionals through assignment of them to excessive clinical responsibilities.

Complaints by agency administrators of high turnover rates among their Hispanic staff have been common. However, few administrators have been willing to scrutinize their practices, but instead shift the focus of attention to the Hispanic staff member. Hispanic staff have often refused to work in what were perceived to be hostile surroundings.

Hispanic consultees in predominantly non-Hispanic settings in Worcester have found consultation beneficial for both their clients and themselves. Consultation has been an effective means of providing support and advocacy for Hispanic staff since the consultant, both a professional and outsider to the agency, could apply pressure on agency administrators when injustices were perpetrated. In addition, consultation has insured the provision of culturally relevant suggestions which ultimately may benefit Hispanic clients.

Program Consultation Component.

This component represents an added dimension to the clinical program. Although program consultation in the past had been limited to Hispanic agencies, it has slowly expanded to include non-Hispanic agencies providing key services to the Hispanic community. These agencies are faced with the need to expand services and have required technical assistance in developing their Hispanic programs.

Program consultation has provided Hispanic agencies with technical assistance in developing and strengthening their programs. Assistance has ranged from short-term assignments focused on budget development, proposal writing, and program development, to long-term intervention centered on bi-weekly meetings dealing with administrative concerns (Delgado, Note 6).

The Hispanic Program, as noted, has been in the process of expanding program consultation to non-Hispanic agencies. An example of this service was a collaborative agreement with a local court and youth-related agency (Delgado, 1978b). Through a formalized agreement, this agency was responsible for recruiting potential foster parents and assisting in home evaluations. The Hispanic Program, in turn, provided technical assistance in program development, training of participants, and consultation services to foster parents once children were placed in their homes. Similar types of arrangements have been made with recreational, day care, and social service agencies.

The Hispanic Program has developed comprehensive consultation services to facilitate agency entry into non-Hispanic settings. This "consultation package" has consisted of assistance in developing proposals, hiring of staff, in-service training, and consultation to the staff members. Thus, consultation has been provided throughout the process of program development and implementation (Delgado, Note 9).

Research Component.

Research focused on Puerto Rican mental health needs, migratory patterns, and programs are of crucial importance if mental health programs are to be effectively planned and implemented. Although the needs assessment model used by the Hispanic Program was developed for use in a predominantly Puerto Rican geographic area, its use is not restricted to this community. Nevertheless, it is particularly well suited for Hispanic communities. In addition, this model is of particular importance to grassroots organizations since it does not require major outside funding (Delgado, Note 10).

The need to identify sociodemographic characteristics and needs of the target population is self-evident. However, such endeavors have often resulted in high costs and formidable administrative issues. In addition, surveys in Hispanic communities must have bilingual, and preferably bicultural, interviewers who are also known and respected by the community. In essence, surveys, if they are to be successful, must be community based.

These factors were taken into consideration in developing the Worcester model. Through collaboration among three key agencies, each of which provided valuable expertise and resources, three surveys were completed.

The Neighborhood Youth Corps (Comprehensive Employment and Training Act), made available bilingual and bicultural teenagers (ages 13–19) to be interviewers as part of their summer employment. In 1975 and 1976, Primera Parada, an Hispanic agency, provided supervision of interviewers and represented this agency when asked about the survey. In 1977, Prospect House, another community-based agency, fulfilled this role in another sector of the city.

The Hispanic Program provided technical assistance in developing the methodology and instrument, training of interviewers, analysis of data, and report writing and dissemination. The training covered a period of three days with intensive focus on interviewing techniques.

In 1975, the research site was a large public housing project, situated on the outskirts of Worcester, approximately six miles from the center of the city. In 1976, the survey concentrated on a 25-block grouping with a high concentration of Hispanic families, close to the center of the city and formerly designated a Model Cities area. In 1977, the third major study was undertaken in an area mid-way between the center and the outskirts of the city, which has the third highest concentration of Hispanic families. The first survey involved 100 families; the second survey, 130; and the third survey, 45 families.

The surveys have provided valuable data which have had an impact on program delivery throughout Worcester, and have allowed for comparison of the Hispanic populations residing in various sectors of the city, with regard to variables such as the average number and ages of children. For example, the finding that all of the areas are primarily composed of young children has brought increased pressure on human service agencies to specifically address the needs of Hispanic children. As a result, the Hispanic Program has concentrated a significant portion of its staff resources on programs for preschool and elementary-school-aged children.

The Hispanic Program has on an infrequent basis been requested to perform program evaluation assignments. However, this is a service which, although available, has not been widely utilized. It is hoped that once more non-Hispanic settings develop Hispanic programs, a need will result for program evaluation on a periodic basis in order to insure relevant and efficient services.

Clinical Intervention and Case Management Component

A mental health program, if it is to be relevant and have an impact on the population it seeks to serve, must provide direct as well as indirect services. The Hispanic Program has allocated approximately 50% of each staff member's time to direct clinical intervention and case management. It should be noted that although the Hispanic staff have received formal training in a variety of therapies (psychodynamic, reality, behavior modification), an attempt is made to provide short-term intervention (less than 12 sessions) whenever possible.

Clinical intervention modalities have ranged from individual counseling to family therapy. Whenever possible, an attempt has been made to include significant family members in the therapeutic process (Borras, Note 11). In cases involving children of preschool age, the clinician may have visited the home to observe mother-child interactions and assist mothers, through modeling, to understand and handle problems as they arise (Delgado & Montalvo, 1979). In situations where the child was older, the clinician may have provided individual therapy for the child, or attempted family therapy, if appropriate.

In situations where the client was in need of multiple services, i.e., counseling, housing, financial assistance, etc., the Hispanic Program staff may have initiated a case management approach to facilitate service delivery. This approach has been particularly useful in situations in which the child was developmentally disabled, requiring the services of multiple agencies. Since Hispanic families with developmentally disabled children face tremendous demands and stresses upon their limited resources, it has been suggested that such an approach should be especially beneficial (Budner, Goodman, & Aponte, 1969).

The Hispanic Program has attempted to deliver clinical services in the community while taking into consideration various factors. Staff were assigned to each of the city's three major Hispanic neighborhoods for clinical cases. Clinical time was allocated according to the percentage of the child population falling within particular age groups. Preschool children represent the highest concentration of children and thus had the highest allocation of clinical time; elementary-school-aged children represent the second highest concentration; and junior- and senior-high-school-aged children, the third highest. The latter category had a part-time staff member with the former two having full-time clinicians.

While it is imperative to provide clinical services within the community itself, preferably in sites that are generic in nature and are not associated with "mental illness," this has often been difficult. The start-up costs and operating demands make it arduous to provide services in several geographical locations. Also, a considerable amount of time and effort are required to establish a reputation and develop a demand for services in the Hispanic community.

The Hispanic Program has been able to circumvent many of these issues in service delivery through collaborative agreements with two health and social service centers in the two sections of Worcester with the highest concentration of Hispanics. The Center maintains an office in the third site (a housing project), and the Hispanic Program may use space as it is needed.

Three staff members were assigned to each of these sites on a part-time basis. Their integration into the two non-Center sites was facilitated through extensive negotiations and periodic meetings with agency administrators to insure a positive relationship. This model of service integration required no expenditure of funds for outreach centers and used the "positive" image of the host agencies to destigmatize mental health services. In addition, staff members provided many services in the home and did not adhere to a policy whereby Hispanics must come to them for services.

CONCLUSION

The limited availability of bilingual and bicultural mental health professionals in the United States (Olmedo & Lopez, 1977) has required the development of innovative treatment modalities and service delivery models which maximize resource utilization (Glenn, 1975). In addressing mental health needs, Hispanic mental health programs must not only address their community directly, but must also work with Hispanic and non-Hispanic settings on organizational levels.

The Worcester Youth Guidance Center's Hispanic Program has incorporated many of the principles developed by other Hispanic programs throughout the United States and developed several of its own. Hispanic mental health programs must endeavor to be dynamic in nature and attempt innovative programs which seek to reach a population which is widely regarded as "difficult" to reach.

Last, Hispanic mental health professionals must attempt to disseminate the results of their efforts at innovative programming. Many innovative and successful programs can be found throughout the country. However, unless an attempt is made to inform other communities and professionals of these programs, we are doomed at best to "reinvent the wheel."

REFERENCE NOTES

1. Delgado, M., & Scott, J. F. *Strategic Intervention: A multi-disciplinary and multi-faceted mental health program for the Hispanic community.* Paper presented at the meeting of the American Association of Psychiatric Services for Children, Washington, D.C., November 1977.
2. Jaffe, A. J. & Carreras-Carleton, Z. *Some demographic and economic characteristics of the Puerto Rican population living on the mainland, U.S.A.* New York: Columbia University, Applied Research Center, 1974.
3. Delgado, M. *Puerto Rican dispersal within the United States: A case study of Worcester, Massachusetts.* Unpublished manuscript, 1978. (Available from the author).
4. *Puerto Rican task force report,* January 1979. (Available from the Family Service Association of America, 44 East 23rd Street, New York, New York, 10010).
5. Scott, J. F., & Delgado, M. *Adminstrative issues in planning mental health programs in Hispanic communities: A case study.* Manuscript submitted for publication, 1978.
6. Delgado, M. *A consultation program for a Puerto Rican drug abuse agency.* Paper presented at the meeting of the National Drug Abuse Conference, Seattle, April 1978.
7. Delgado, M. *A Multi-faceted mental health program for Hispanic children in an urban public school system.* Paper submitted for publication, 1978.
8. Delgado, M. *The cultural consultant: Implications for Latino mental health.* Paper presented at the meeting of the National Council of Community Mental Health Centers, Washington, D.C., February 1979.
9. Delgado, M. *The lone ranger: Issues and strategies for providing consultation to Hispanic staff in non-Hispanic settings.* Paper presented at the meeting of the American Association of Psychiatric Services for Children, Atlanta, November 1978.
10. Delgado, M. *A grass-roots model for needs assessment in Hispanic communities.* Manuscript submitted for publication, 1978.
11. Borras, V. *Child discipline modes among mothers in fatherless migrant Puerto Rican families: From tradition to inconsistency.* Paper presented at the meeting of the American Association of Psychiatric Services for Children, Atlanta, November 1978.

REFERENCES

Abad, V., Ramos, J., & Boyce, E. A model for delivery of mental health services to Spanish-speaking minorities. *American Journal of Orthopsychiatry,* 1974, *44,* 584–585.

Abad, V., Ramos, J., & Boyce, E. Cultural issues in the psychiatric treatment of Puerto Ricans. In E. Padilla and A. Padilla (Eds.), *Transcultural Psychiatry: An Hispanic Perspective.* Los Angeles: University of California, 1977.

Arce, A. A. Ethnicity, Hispanic community, and issues in mental health, In D. J. Curren, J. J. Rivera, and R. B. Sanchez (Eds.), *Proceedings of Puerto Rican conferences on human services.* Washington, D.C.: National Coalition of

Spanish-Speaking Mental Health Organizations, 1975.

Bruhn, J. G., & Fuentes, R. G. Cultural factors affecting utilization of services by Mexican-Americans. *Psychiatric Annals,* 1977, *7,* 20–32.

Bryant, C. A. The Puerto Rican mental health unit. *Psychiatric Annals,* 1975, *5,* 66–75.

Budner, S., Goodman, L., & Aponte, R. The minority retardate: A paradox and a problem in definition. *Social Service Review,* 1969, *43,* 174–183.

Cagel, W. P. The use of community workers in a Spanish-speaking community. In E. Padilla and A. Padilla (Eds.), *Transcultural psychiatry: An Hispanic perspective.* Los Angeles: University of California, 1977.

Caplan, G. D. *The theory and practice of mental health consultation.* New York: Basic Books, 1970.

Clifford, S., Brayboy, T. L., & Waxenberg, B. R. *Black ghetto family in therapy.* New York: Grove Press, 1970.

Cohen, L. M., & Fernandez, C. L. Ethnic identity and psychocultural adaptation of Spanish-speaking families. *Child Welfare,* 1974, *53,* 413–421.

Delgado, M. Puerto Rican spiritualism and the social work profession. *Social Casework,* 1977, *58,* 451–458.

Delgado, M. Folk medicine in the Puerto Rican culture. *International Social Work,* 1978, *21,* 46–54. (a)

Delgado M. A. Hispanic foster parents program. *Child Welfare,* 1978, *57,* 427–431. (b)

Delgado M. Hispanic leaders share their board skills. *Voluntary Action Leadership,* 1978, Winter, 12. (c)

Delgado, M. An educational program on Puerto Rican culture for non-Hispanic staff. *Hospital & Community Psychiatry,* 1979, *30*(3), 162–163. (a)

Delgado, M. Herbal medicine in the Puerto Rican community. *Health & Social Work,* 1979, *4*(2), 24–40. (b)

Delgado, M., & Montalvo, S. Preventive mental health services for Hispanic preschool children. *Children Today,* 1979, *8*(1), 6–8, 34.

Dorgan, M. P. Initiating a program of foster parent education. *Child Welfare,* 1974, *53,* 588–593.

Fernandez-Marina, R., Maldonado-Sierra, E. D., & Trent, R. D. Three basic themes in Mexican and Puerto Rican family values. *Journal of Social Psychiatry,* 1958, *48,* 167–181.

Fitzpatrick, J. P. Puerto Rican Americans: *The meaning of migration to the mainland.* Englewood Cliffs, N. J.: Prentice-Hall, 1971.

Freedman,A. The community mental health center in the central city: Issues for administrators. In E. Padilla and A. Padilla (Eds.), *Transcultural psychiatry: An Hispanic perspective.* Los Angeles: University of California, 1977.

Ghali, S. B. Culture sensitivity and the Puerto Rican client. *Social Casework,* 1977, *58,* 459–468.

Glen, E. Expanding the service role of community mental health centers. In D. J. Curran, J. J. Rivera, and R. B. Sanchez (Eds.), *Proceedings of Puerto Rican conferences on human services.* Washington, D.C.: National Coalition of Spanish-speaking Mental Health Organizations, 1975.

Hamburger, S. Profile of curanderos: A study of Mexican folk practitioners. *International Journal of Social Psychiatry,* 1978, *24,* 19–25.

Harwood, A. *Rx: Spiritist as needed.* New York: Wiley, 1977.

Hernandez-Alvarez, I. The Movement and settlement of Puerto Rican Migrants within the United States, 1950–1960. *International Migration Review, 1968, 2,* 40–55.

Kiev, A. *Curanderismo.* New York: Free Press, 1968.

Kline, L. Y. Some factors in the psychiatric treatment of Spanish-Americans. *American Journal of Psychiatry,* 1969, *125,* 88–95.

Koss, J. D. Therapeutic aspects of Puerto Rican cult practices. *Psychiatry,* 1975, *38,* 160–171.

Koss, J. D. Religion and science divinely related: A case history of spiritism in Puerto Rico. *Caribbean Studies,* 1978, *16,* 22–43.

Lefley, H. P. Approaches to community mental health: The Miami model. *Psychiatric Annals,* 1975, *5,* 76–83.

Martinez, C. Curanderos: Clinical aspects. *Journal of Operational Psychiatry,* 1977, *8,* 35–38.

Meyer, G. G. The professional in the Chicano community. *Psychiatric Annals,* 1977, *7,* 9–19.

Mizio, E. Impact of external system on the Puerto Rican family. *Social Casework,* 1974, *55,* 76–83.

Nordheimer, J. Puerto Ricans return to crowd homeland accelerating. *New York Times,* 10 May 1978, 1.

Olmedo, E. L., & Lopez, S. (Eds.). *Hispanic mental health professionals.* Los Angeles: University of California, 1977.

Padilla, A. M., & Ruiz, R. A. *Latino mental health: A review of literature.* (Stock number 1724-00317). Washington, D.C.: U.S. Government Printing Office, 1974.

Padilla, A. M., Ruiz, R. A., & Alvarez, R. Community mental health services for the Spanish-Speaking/surnamed population. *American Psychologist,* 1975, *30,* 892–905.

Philippus, M. J. Successful and unsuccessful approaches to mental health services for an urban Hispano American population. *American Journal of Public Health,* 1971, *61,* 820–830.

Rogler, L., & Hollingshead, A. B. *Trapped: Families and schizophrenia.* New York: Wiley, 1965.

Ruiz, P., & Langrod, J. Psychiatry and folk healing: A dichotomy? *American Journal of Psychiatry,* 1976, *133,* 95–97. (a)

Ruiz, P., & Langrod, J. The role of folk healers in community mental health services. *Community Mental Health Journal,* 1976, *12,* 392–398. (b)

Sandoval, M. C. Santeria: Afrocuban concepts of disease and its treatment in Miami. *Journal of Operational Psychiatry,* 1977, *8,* 52–63.

Sue, S. Community mental health services to minority groups: Some optimism, some pessimism. *American Psychologist,* 1977, *32,* 616–624.

Szapocznik, J., Scopetta, M. A., & King, O. E. Theory and practice in matching treatment to the special characteristics and problems of Cuban immigrants. *Journal of Community Psychology.* 1978, *6,* 112–122.

U.S. Commission on Civil Rights. *Puerto Ricans in the continental U.S.: An uncertain future.* Washington, D.C.: U.S. Government Printing Office, 1976.

26

Common Errors in Psychotherapy with Chicanos[1]
Extrapolations from Research and Clinical Experience

Samuel Roll, Leverett Millen, and Ricardo Martinez

The statement that culture and ethnic membership must be taken into account in the treatment of patients has been repeated often enough and authoritatively enough so that it has become a truism. It is also a truism that therapists have an obligation to alert themselves to the ramifications of the ethnic membership of their patients and further that the profession has a responsibility to offer its services to people who are not members of the dominant culture.

As is the case with truisms, it is not difficult to find broad affirmation of these statements within the therapeutic professions. The reality of the situation, however, is that therapists have few ways in which to make themselves more responsive to minority ethnic group patients. The purpose of this article is to help the therapist who works or who might work with Chicano patients by providing a review of the common errors made in working with Chicanos and putting these errors in the context of the existing research and clinical literature. We propose to focus on two major types of errors—errors leading to the exclusion of Chicanos from treatment and errors in treatment when Chicanos do come for services—and possible corrections.

---

[1]Throughout the paper the word "Chicano" will be used. This is done with the recognition that some of the people about whom we are writing would prefer to be called Mexican-Americans, others would prefer to be called Mexicans, others Latinos and yet others would prefer to be called Spanish-Americans. Editors might prefer that they be referred to as "Spanish-Speaking/Spanish Surnamed." Our choice of the word Chicano is a matter of simplicity and not an attempt to minimize the importance of by what names people prefer to be known.

Reprinted with permission from *Psychotherapy: Theory, Research, and Practice*, 1980, *17*(2), 158–168.

MAJOR ERRORS

A. Sins of Omission

The first major error made in working with Chicanos is that services are not offered. The underutilization of psychotherapy by Chicanos has already been thoroughly documented (see especially Cresson et al., 1969; Heiman et al., 1975; Karno, 1966; Karno & Edgerton, 1969; Kline, 1969; Padilla et al., 1975). The degree of underutilization of mental health services by Chicanos is best highlighted by Karno & Edgerton (1969). They estimated that Chicanos made up about 10 per cent of California's population in 1962–63 but accounted for only 2.2 percent of the admissions to State hospitals, 3.4 percent to State mental hygiene clinics, 0.9 percent of use of the Neuropsychiatric Institute and 2.3 percent of State-local facilities. The underrepresentation in mental health institutions is even more severe than were we to judge on the basis of percentages alone, because as Karno & Edgerton (1969) and Torrey (1969) point out, Chicanos are subject to a number of stress inducing factors including difficulties in acculturation, poor communication skills in the dominant language and being stuck in the cycle of poverty and resultant further powerlessness. The major conclusion of these studies is that delivery of services to Chicanos will be ineffective until the profession learns to understand and respond to ethnicity as an integral part of personality. Meanwhile many practitioners continue to explain away the underutilization through two errors which we have labeled "externalization of responsibility" and "the patient as the major difficulty."

1. Externalization of Responsibility   The most common error is concluding that "those kinds of people" are not suitable for psychotherapy and need "something else" instead. The something else usually means a heavier use of medication (Karno, 1966; Yamamoto et al., 1968). While the statements about nonsuitability of Chicanos for treatment might sound like a reasonable recognition of the limitations of our techniques, there is little in the clinical literature or the cross-cultural research literature to support the "nonsuitability" of Chicanos for psychotherapy.

On the contrary, the Mexican and Chicano cultures have a variety of characteristics which would argue for psychotherapy as the treatment of choice in helping Chicanos to cope with stress and difficulties in personality development.

First and most importantly, perhaps, has been the work of Holtzman et al. (1975) which has pointed to the relatively heavy emphasis in the Mexican culture placed on affective rather than cognitive aspects of life. Using interviews, projective techniques, and perceptual-cognitive measures, these authors indicated that Mexicans, in contrast to Anglos, tend to value affective rather than cognitive approaches to life. Further evidence for the relatively high interpersonal orientation of Mexican culture is found in the work of Roll & Brenneis (1976). In their cross-cultural investigation of dreams, these authors noted that Chicanos in comparison to Anglos reported a greater number of people in their dreams and concluded that "the greater number of characters in the dreams of Chicanos is in keeping with the greater number of people whom Chicanos are likely to think of as important in their lives." A related study by Roll & Millen (1976) demonstrated that Chicanos not only reported more friends than did Anglos in their dreams but also that Chicanos perceived their friendships in more cooperative and less egocentric ways than did Anglos. Taken together these studies suggest that Chicanos would respond favorably to psychotherapeutic orientations such as psychoanalytically oriented or client-centered therapy which emphasized affective and interpersonal aspects of the relationship. These findings question the need for the overreliance on medication noted above (Karno, 1966).

A second aspect of the culture of Spanish-Americans which would heighten the appreciation of psychotherapy is the tradition of *curandismo,* the folk system of mental healing in which a patient reveals intimate fears to an understanding and caring person, often a neighbor or friend (Kline, 1969). To be sure, several writers have noted that *curanderas* and their methods appear to vary greatly in quality and that the impact of these folk healers may be less than was previously thought (Edgerton et al., 1970; Kline, 1969; Torrey, 1969), nevertheless this tradition of sharing intimate fears and secrets with another person with the expectation that such sharing will lessen fears and anxieties increases the likelihood that Chicanos would be able to benefit from an interpersonally oriented psychotherapy.

A third trait of the Latin culture which would tend to augment the relevance of psychotherapy for Chicanos is the tradition of *personalismo,* the inclination of Latin people, in general, to relate to and trust persons rather than institutions and to dislike formal, impersonal structures and organizations. Psychotherapy is one of the most individualized forms of helping interactions available and could conform to the Chicano need for *personalismo.*

Proposed Corrections   Attempts to minimize this externalization of responsibility for Chicano underutilization of therapy must be focused in two directions—programmatic and educational. Programmatically, mental health programs must be designed to respond to the interpersonal orientation of Chicanos. Abad et al. (1974) and Heiman et al. (1975) have shown that psychotherapy programs which are structured to intensify the experience of *personalismo* and to encourage cooperation of *curanderas* have been effective. Heiman et al. (1975) reported that Mexican-Americans accounted for 61% of the active cases at a mental health center designed to meet the special needs of Mexican Americans.

Educationally, graduate training programs must emphasize the importance of students and faculty alike familiarizing themselves with the literature on Chicanos—both clinical and cross-cultural — as well as the literature on other ethnic minority groups. The recruitment and training of Chicanos in the helping professions is probably the most effective correction possible.

2. The Patient as the Major Difficulty   Even in the writing about the underutilization of psychotherapy services by Chicanos which recognizes that there is no incompatibility between the Chicano culture and the use of psychotherapy, there is an implicit assumption that we should begin trying to offer services to Chicanos by focusing on the variables related to the Chicano *patient*. For example, Abad et al. (1974) have proposed a mental health program for Spanish-speaking minorities which includes a bilingual staff, walk-in clinic, and educational and preventive programs, while also emphasizing collaboration with faith healers as well as benefits of gaining cooperation and participation of local political leaders. Boulette (1975) described an innovative approach to group therapy with Chicanos which involved the use of bicultural and bilingual therapists; and Heiman et al. (1975) outlined a treatment program for Chicanos which included a bilingual and bicultural staff and had an informal atmosphere with a minimum number of bureaucratic procedures.

Now it is clear that these have been successful. In the case of Heiman et al. (1975) and Boulette (1975) Chicanos did come in for treatment and did have successful outcomes. However, there is a point which might be overlooked. The first step in making therapy available to Chicanos has not to do as much with the patient variable as it has to do with the *therapist* variable. While some authors like Boulette (1975), Edgerton & Karno (1971), Heiman et al. (1975), Helms (1974), Karno & Morales (1971) and Maes & Rinaldi (1974) point out the importance of the therapist understanding Spanish or even being bilingual and the importance of understanding the Chicano culture, it is surprising that so few workers in the area point out the need for the therapist to understand herself and especially her[2] own reactions to treating people from the Chicano culture.

While there is no direct evidence about the need for Spanish or knowledge about Chicano culture for the successful treatment of Chicanos, it is reasonable to accept that these are potent factors. However, there is evidence which compels that we attend to the ethnocentrism of the therapist as a potent and even crucial factor in treating Chicano patients. Yamamoto et al. (1967) reported in a study of 594 consecutive admissions to an outpatient clinic, that patients were being treated differently depending upon the factor of the therapist's ethnocentricity as

---

[2]Throughout the article the authors have used the words "she" and "her" as generic terms for both sexes.

measured by the Boagardus Social Distance Scale. The Boagardus is a scale used to study prejudicial feelings. The individual is asked to place various ethnic groups such as Armenians, Americans, Canadians, Chinese in one of seven categories with regard to the degree of physical social distance that the individual is willing to permit—such as marry into the group, would have as close friends, would have as next door neighbor, etc. Each therapist was asked to check one item for each of 30 ethnic groups. These responses were then tabulated as scores from one to seven with one indicating the least feeling of prejudice and seven, feelings of greatest prejudice. The results showed the impact of the factor of therapist's ethnocentricity on the course of treatment with minority patients. Therapists with low ethnocentricity scores treated more ethnic-minority patients than those therapists with high ethnocentricity scores.

The degree of ethnic blindness and avoidance of ethnicity by otherwise experienced, competent therapists is illustrated by Karno (1966) who noted that many Chicano patients in a mental health center were not ethnically identified in the charts or had only a single reference made to culture. Karno states, "In only 4 of the 28 Mexican-American case records is there evidence of even a moderate degree of awareness of, or exploration into the patient's ethnicity as a fundamental aspect of life in a dominant 'Anglo' socio-cultural system'' (1966, p. 519).

Proposed Correction   Perhaps it is predictable that with the built-in propensity for self-delusion and for the externalization of responsibility away from the self, the therapist would look to the Chicano for reasons for underutilization of therapy by Chicanos. The harder first step is to look to the therapist. Supervision with a supervisor who is alert to ethnocentrism and ethnic blindness is the best training vehicle but this might be combined with didactic experiences about culture.

In addition to supervisors sensitized to ethnocentrism, a second proposal to minimize the impact of ethnocentrism on treatment would include more attention to the variable of the therapist as a factor in the course of all psychotherapy. A third factor would be the increased recruitment efforts to attract minorities to the psychological professions.

B. Sins of Commission

Just as there are erroneous ideas and interfering ethnocentricity which result in the therapeutic professions' avoidance of the Chicano, there are errors which are likely to result when the Chicano patient is in treatment or is being evaluated for treatment.

1. Errors in Diagnosis   There may be a tendency to ascribe all good evaluations and judgments to whatever is most like us and to see as negative whatever is not like us. This tendency is obvious, at least, in the attempts to evaluate Chicanos. Marcos et al. (1973) demonstrated that

Spanish-American patients are consistently rated as showing more pathology when they are interviewed by English speakers than when they are interviewed by Spanish speakers. The authors averred that the Spanish-speaking raters appear to have a more culturally relative attitude and seem better able to evaluate these patients' statements within the context of the Spanish-American cultural background.

This tendency to overdiagnose or to see the Chicano as perhaps more pathological than she is, is compounded by the reliance on instruments like the MMPI which are heavily culture-bound and which cannot be changed to take cultural factors into account. On the MMPI, for example, many of the spiritual and religious beliefs of Chicanos are scored in the direction of pathology. Karno (1966) described an instance of misdiagnosis in the case of a Mexican-American woman who in the course of treatment had proven to be a moderately depressed person with strong motivation for help, but no signs of psychosis. She had originally answered "true" to MMPI items like those about being possessed by evil spirits and as a result had been given the diagnosis of "early schizophrenic reaction."

Proposed Correction   It would be essential for those using an evaluative frame of reference in treatment or in diagnosis to take into account this tendency to misdiagnosis and the other factors which are summarized in this article. Also, those involved in diagnosing Chicanos should be alert to attempts of others to approach the dilemmas of cross-cultural testing. Especially notable are Theodora Abel's *Psychological Testing in Cultural Contexts* (1973) and Samuda's *Testing of American Minorities* (1975). Ideally either a Chicano or someone who is knowledgeable about the culture and experienced in the treatment of Chicanos should be available as a consultant in elaborating a diagnosis and treatment plan. Further, tests like the MMPI which have no way to program cultural factors should be avoided.

2. Balance Between Formality and Personalized Attention   For most Anglo patients, the view of psychotherapy is of a highly formalized and even ritualized activity. The sessions last for a certain amount of time and the relationship is a highly "professionalized" one in which distance is maintained. Some members of the dominant culture in the United States find the formalized aspect of therapy, adopted from European innovators, distasteful and somewhat less than democratic. Also every therapist has dealt with patients who have invited themselves to call the therapist by her first name and who expected to exchange Christmas cards and other indications of familiarity. Some therapists even have responded to this and have reduced or attempted to reduce the level of formality of the therapy sessions. The most common ways of doing this are through highly informal dress, office procedures, posture, and forms of address.

It is obvious from reading what therapists write or from observing their practice that there is disagreement about the degree of formality which should be maintained in the session. The debate is carried on at the level of posture, dress and decor.

In relating the ongoing debate between formality and informality in style of therapy to work with the Chicano patient, it becomes clear that issues relevant to treatment of Chicanos have been missed by both the more "conservative," formal therapist and the more "with it," informal therapist. On the one hand, the conservative therapist is not only likely to be conservative, but frequently (certainly not always) somewhat less than personal; that is, to be professionalized rather than professional. The "with it" therapist, on the other hand, presents to the traditional Chicano a lack of respect for her own (*i.e.,* the therapist) status by dress and manners and forms of address which do not match the therapist's station in life as viewed by the Chicano. To the Chicano who adheres to traditional values it is important that a therapist, indeed, that any person in position of authority maintain the correct level of formality and that at the same time there be a highly personalized touch and flavor to the interactions. It is characteristic of the Anglo culture that personalization and informality are synonymous. For the Chicano there is an articulation of both concepts in such a way that they are orthogonal.

Beginning therapists who are trying to be "humanistic" by avoiding middle class dress feel that they are made more approachable by dressing "down to earth" and being just one of the "plain old folks." In our training of therapists it has often taken many sessions before a student was convinced by the material the patients bring that Chicano patients expect a therapist or doctor to dress "appropriately." In many cases Chicano patients were able to tell the therapist that they (the patients) felt they were given a therapist who did not bother to dress well because the better dressed therapists were reserved for the Anglos or that the patients thought that the therapist's not dressing professionally meant they were not treating the patient seriously.

At the same time, and irrespective of dress, Chicano patients find that the highly impersonalized (by Chicano standards) form of working with patients is insulting or at least alienating. For most therapists, the small talk at the beginning of sessions and especially at the beginning of the early sessions is something to be sat through patiently and some even feel that they should prod patients on to the issues at hand. At times therapists might even "interpret" to the patient that she is avoiding the issue or is having a hard time getting down to business. While such an interpretation might be correct and even very useful to an Anglo patient, to a Chicano patient the desire to get down to work at the expense of the social lubrication which accompanies small talk is not only an indication of rudeness but a manifestation of selfish aggressivity. Within the Chicano culture, it is important to take time to say a few personal words to everyone with whom one interacts, even to the very busy cashier in a checkout counter in a supermarket. To treat the cashier as if she were a person with only a business function would be to treat her as if she were a machine. Never mind the length of the line, for the correct Chicano there is always time for a personal word. Never mind the enormity of the presenting problem or the scarce time of the therapist, there is always time for a personal word. The Chicano patient who feels the impatience of the therapist around the "small talk" will most likely recognize that she is not going to be able to be understood, or worse, takes the lack of interest in establishing a personal relationship as a rejection or a desire to avoid personal contact on the part of the therapist.

The common error along these dimensions, then, is the reduction of formality to the point of making a tradition-respecting patient uncomfortable and confused and the maintenance of an "impersonalized" atmosphere which is inconsistent with the Chicano standards of good manners and rules of conduct.

Proposed Correction   Short of supervision with a Chicano supervisor or a supervisor sensitive to these issues, the therapist who would work with Chicano patients can alert herself to the differences in approach to interpersonal interactions within the Anglo and Chicano cultures. The Anglo therapist might also alert herself to confusion in the dominant culture between level of formality and level of personalized attention. Ideally, though, supervision should be available to the therapist who would devote time to working with Chicano patients.

Of course it is possible to use any aspect of either one's personality, character structure or ethnic identity as a resistance to therapy or as a manifestation of distress. The therapist who works with Chicanos is derelict in her duty if she vows never to interpret small talk and never to prod on patients who are using social lubrication as a way to keep from working or to keep from recognizing that the patient feels incapable of anything but small talk. What we are talking about is a difference in degree and focus and not a difference in the essential process of therapy. The supportive interpretation of transference and resistance and the use of the session to discover and practice modes of interpersonal interaction remain at the core of therapy whether it be with Chicanos or Anglos.

3. Coping with Passive Coping Styles   Psychologists have been able to differentiate coping styles in terms of the relative activity or passivity which the coping styles reflect in cross-cultural psychology. These ideas are best summarized in the works of Diaz-Guerrero (1975) and Holtzman *et al.* (1975). While a full understanding of these ideas and research can be best derived from reading the original sources, a general notion of what is meant by activity in coping style is found in the definition of Etzioni. According to Etzioni, "The active orientation had three major components: a self-conscious knowing actor, one or more goals he is committed to realize and access to levers (for power) that allow resetting of the social code" (1968, p. 4). It is possible to characterize both individuals and cultures on the basis of the extent to which they subscribe to an active orientation.

The work of Diaz-Guerrero (1975) and Holtzman *et al.* (1975) concur in ascribing to the Mexican a relatively greater passive coping style when compared with Anglo counterparts. Diaz-Guerrero has worked primarily through surveys about life values and Holtzman *et al.* have arrived at their position from analysis of a cross-cultural longitudinal and developmental study which relied on psychological tests and interviews. Roll *et al.* (1976) tested the degree of passivity and activity in Chicanos in this country through dream research. Roll *et al.* (1976) hypothesized that a passive approach toward coping with stress would be reflected in the tendency to describe in dream reports a world in which responsibility is deflected to someone or something other than the dreamer. This removes the self-conscious actor required in an active coping style. In the dream this can be done in various ways. For example, the dreamer could change identities and thus the acts which followed were deflected to someone else (*e.g.,* I then became my brother) or a part of the body acting of its own accord could be ascribed responsibility (*e.g.,* my mouth moved by itself and words came out) or an object could take on responsibility for the dreamer's activities (*e.g.,* "suddenly my pants came off by themselves"). Roll *et al.* (1976) found support for the hypothesis that Chicanos have more disclaimed activity in their dreams, and that the passivity reflected in disclaimed activity is found equally in Chicano men and Chicano women.

There are a number of errors which therapists are likely to make which are related to the Chicanos' relatively more passive coping style. One of them has to do with the fact that the dominant culture highly endorses the concept of an active coping style as the only acceptable one. It is difficult in this context to use the word "passive" in any but a pejorative fashion. For members of the U.S. dominant culture and that includes the great majority of therapists, passivity is bad and activity is good. Further, a passive coping style is likely to be confused with inertness or deadness. In therapy *per se* the errors are likely to be seen when a therapist who is highly identified with activity as health and passivity as maladjustment will fail to see the benefits of a passive coping style and the dangers of an active one. It is clear that an active style results in getting things done (the efficiency-as-the-measure-of-all-things factor); it is also clear that it results in social friction, continuous striving for upward mobility and the sense of having to assume too much responsibility for one's world. Just as the therapist is tempted to view passivity as maladjustment, she is likely to be tempted to convert the patient to a more active coping style and to make interpretations and confrontations which might be appropriate, correct, and constructive for an Anglo patient, but are not so for a Chicano patient. One of our supervisees recently discovered that it was useful to think of therapeutic progress in terms of greater and greater autonomy for the patient. However, in moving this discovery into her work with Chicanos she tended to ignore their recognition that many things are not in one's own power to change or modify. Her Chicano patients began to see her as demanding and rejecting and terribly naive about the way in which the world works.

Proposed Correction   It is important to emphasize that a passive coping style is not to be confused with passivity in the sense of inertness or inactivity. It is possible to use a passive coping style and be extremely active (as were the Chicanos in the Roll *et al.* [1976] study). A passive coping style has more to do with the way in which the world is perceived than it has to do with literal activity. The image of the Chicano resting beside a cactus is not only insulting it is incorrect.

Secondly, therapists working with Chicanos should be alerted, through workshops and supervision, to the differences in activity and passivity in coping style, and to explore both the benefits and disadvantages which are involved in either the active or passive style.

Further, it would be important to discover the degree to which a particular patient's coping style is congruent or incongruent with her social context and to see if any difficulties in dealing with the dominant culture might be clarified for the patient by attending to the issues of activity and passivity.

4. Machismo As a Pejorative   Perhaps the first concept which most students of cross-cultural psychology learn about Chicanos is that of *machismo. Machismo,* which might be weakly interpreted as "maleness," refers to the felt necessity of Chicano males to be clear and confident about their sense of masculinity. The clearer aspects of the concept or at least the most well known and most frequently noted relate to sex and aggression. It is deemed appropriate that men are ready to aggress and to be concerned with aggression. One of the demands of *machismo* is that one be ready or at least willing to fight. Another frequently explored aspect of the *machismo* is that a man be ready to be sexually assertive. Men in Latin cultures are directed toward sexual experimentation and exploration. The women, on the contrary, are seen as needing protection, not from their own impulses but from those of the men.

But such a description of *machismo* is so incomplete as to be incorrect. There are other aspects of the *machismo* which cannot be separated from the factors of sex and aggression. *Machismo* also involves a tender and benevolent concern for those who cannot protect themselves against the dangers of the world. Unlike the Anglo concept of supermaleness which is sometimes confused with *machismo,* the Chicano concept of maleness or *machismo* allows and even demands that respect, tenderness and concern be shown for the aged. (In this context it is interesting to note that compared with Anglo patients and taking the general underutilization of psychiatric services into account, older Chicanos seem to need less psychiatric care than their Anglo counterparts or than younger Chicanos [Wignall & Koppin, 1967]). The true macho is not the Chicano who is violent, drunk, or chronically sexually involved, but rather the one who is also devoted to family traditions and values and who is involved in the protection of the young and care of the aged.

Another misunderstood aspect of *machismo* relates to the quality of affective expression. In dream reports of Chicanos and Anglos (Roll & Brenneis, in press), the one area where the Anglo sex difference was more pronounced than the Chicano sex difference was in the amount of affective expression. While it has been typical in the dominant American culture to teach men to stifle their expression of feelings, the same is not true in Latin cultures. The expression of feelings by men and between men is more open in Latin cultures and is frequently embarrassing to Anglo men. For the Chicano man there are a number of ways to express his maleness or *machismo*. There is no demand that the *macho* put aside the expression of feeling.

Therapists who know only the more superficial and incorrect concept of *machismo* will make the mistake of treating this special sense of maleness in their Chicano patients as a form of hypermasculinity or (in the case of all too many therapists) as an expression of homosexuality.

Proposed Corrections Knowledge about *machismo* in its more complete sense is crucial. It should be made clear through didactic presentation and through supervision that the more thorough concept of *machismo* includes a maternal as well as a paternal aspect.

Therapists also make errors in the opposite direction; they sometimes are unable to see rampant sexuality, drunkenness and impulsiveness as part of a person's plea for help because they write it off incorrectly as *"machismo."* One experienced therapist who was beginning to work with Chicanos remarked about an acting out patient, "But isn't that how they are supposed to be."

5. Chicanos As a Monolithic Entity The first times that the senior author worked with a black patient he became so obviously engrossed and involved in trying to understand the experience of being black that he ignored the patient's distress which was not directly related to the black experience. After suffering this for a number of months the patient finally exploded and insisted, "I'm black, man, but that's not all I am—I'm in a bunch of trouble and I need some help." Likewise the therapist just beginning to work with Chicanos may attend so much to the "Chicanismo" of the patient that she will tend to ignore the complexity and variety of the Chicano experience. Chicanos do not constitute a monolithic entity. They are rather a minority cultural group with a great diversity in terms of age, location, socioeconomic status, language skills, levels of adaptation and amount of intrapsychic conflict (Garcia, 1973; Grebler *et al.*, 1970; Ruiz, 1976).

There is, of course, enough uniformity, even in highly acculturated Chicanos, which allows for the usefulness of generalizations about the Chicano experience. At the individual level, though, the therapist is derelict unless she considers differences within the Chicano experience and the highly individualized way in which any individual experiences her culture and organizes its impact into her personality structure. There are some ways in which any particular Chicano is like *all* other Chicanos and there are ways in which a particular Chicano is like *some* other Chicanos and there are some ways in which a particular Chicano is like *no* other Chicano.

Research projects which have attempted to take into account the rich complexity of the Chicano experience include the work of Brenneis & Roll (1975) which relied on the use of Spanish in the home to identify adherence to cultural norms and Edgerton & Karno (1970) which investigated differences between Chicanos who speak mainly Spanish and those who do not speak Spanish. Their findings indicated that "the more commonly described cultural traits of Mexican-American—*e.g.*, fatalism, familism, strong attachment to formal religious values, patriarchal authoritarianism, and conservative morality regarding deviant behavior—are applicable (and even here with many exceptions and qualifications) only to those persons who speak mainly or only Spanish" (1970, p. 290).

Proposed Corrections Supervision and didactic material is a must to help the therapist in being able to respect and understand the cultural aspects of a Chicano's experience without at the same time relating primarily to that experience instead of to the Chicano as an individual. The therapist should also be alert to the degree to which the particular patient can be described as adhering to traditional Chicano values. An assessment of the use of Spanish by the patient would be helpful in this regard.

And again we must alert the profession and the research funding agencies to the need to investigate differences due to the degree of bilingualism, degree of acculturation, and length of residence in the U.S. Courses in ethno-history would also be productive in producing a sensitive awareness of the richness of the Chicano experience.

6. Uncomfortable Themes—For Therapists There are a set of themes which are likely to come up in psychotherapy with Chicano patients which, because of cultural differences between Anglos and Chicanos, may give the Anglo therapist special difficulty. The difficulty in most cases will arise because Chicanos are relatively comfortable with a number of situations and life-adjustments which make the Anglo either anxious or envious.

a. Reduced Need for Competition and Individual Achievement   One characteristic of Anglo culture which is congruent with its focus on an active mode of coping with stress, is a relatively high need for competition and a heavy emphasis on individual achievement. Even in dream reports (Brenneis & Roll, 1976) Anglos are much more likely to organize their experiences so that they are the central figures much more so than Chicanos. In contrast the Chicano culture has placed a higher value on cooperation and collaboration. A series of investigations culminating in a summary article by Nelson & Kagan (1972) have dealt with differences in competition and cooperation in Anglo and Mexican children and conclude that there is consistent difference in the direction of Anglos being more rivalrous and Chicanos being more cooperative. In the Chicano culture when an individual succeeds, it is expected that she will help her extended family to also succeed. In the Anglo culture this level of cooperation is known disdainfully as nepotism. The error which a therapist is likely to make is to directly or indirectly try to guide the patient toward more individual achievement and competition and to either ignore or underestimate the adaptive and enriching aspects of the less competitive and egocentric orientation.

Proposed Correction   In addition to acquainting therapists with these cultural differences, it is important to direct attention at the supervisor's level and at the level of research projects to the therapist and her psychonoxious potential. Involvement in psychotherapy as a patient would help the therapist come to grips with her own ways of coping with stress and her own inclination to avoid areas in her patients which cause the therapist anxiety. The therapist who has been alerted through her own treatment to her conflicts and anxiety about competition will be more open to accepting her patient's development of coping strategies which are different from the therapist's and some of which will cause the therapist discomfort.

We should note that especially psychiatric residents and psychology interns, who are at the end of involved training experiences which are, by design, highly competitive, are likely to have many conflicting feelings about competition and are likely candidates for distorting issues of competition and cooperation. It is for them that the relatively less competitive style of the Chicano will most probably give rise to anxiety and envy.

b. The family that stays together   An important aspect of Hispanic culture is the emphasis on one's own locale and family as a meaningful part of one's identity. In dream research (Brenneis & Roll, 1976) this is reflected in the greater number of familiar characters included in Chicano dreams. The psychological world of members of Latin cultures is heavily populated. The family as a focus of identity is sometimes misinterpreted by Anglo therapists and observers as a form of dependency or even as a symbiosis. In Chicano families, for example, it is not unusual for the child who marries to move to a mobile home on the parent's land and live right on the same property. In more traditional rural homes in New Mexico, for example, the marriage of a son or daughter sometimes means adding on an addition to the adobe home and moving the new extension of the family right in. Leaving home in the Anglo culture is often taken as an indication of independence and psychological health. (At a faculty meeting one of the authors was party to a serious discussion in which a potential candidate for a job was passed over because he still lived with his mother.) While we can question the glib view of attachment to family as dependency or pathology even within the Anglo culture, when we deal with Chicanos we must be especially alert to the realization that staying close to home has an entirely different meaning than it would for the Anglo. The motivations may well be positive (wanting to maintain contact with various generations, accepting responsibility for older people, desiring to guide and protect younger brothers and sisters) and not necessarily maladaptive for the individual or for the culture.

There is a great temptation on the part of young Anglo therapists who for many reasons must accept the injunction, "You Can't Go Home Again" (Wolfe, 1940) to be envious or anxious when young Chicano adults are perfectly comfortable staying home or returning home after college. One graduate student who was in therapy precisely because of unresolved feelings of dependence had to be asked to stop seeing Chicano patients for awhile because he frequently became hostile when he saw the comfort with which they could plan to stay at home or near home for the rest of their lives.

Proposed Correction   Didactic presentations, supervision, recruitment of Chicano therapists and continued research will provide the long-term prophylaxis against an assault on the Chicano's comfort with her home and family.

c. More powerfully held sexual dichotomy   In a series of research reports about cultural differences as revealed in dream patterns Brenneis & Roll (1975, 1976) and Roll & Brenneis (1976) conclude that the most telling manifestation of cultural differences in dreams is the consistently found greater sex differences for Chicanos than for Anglos. (As noted earlier the one exception is in the area of affect expression where Anglos display greater sex differences.) This finding is supported by Ruiz's essay on research priorities in Latino mental health in which he asserts that, "Latinos' sex roles appear more clearly defined, more rigid and more distinct than those one finds in Anglo or Black families" (1976, p. 2).

The therapeutic errors related to the more distinct sex roles adhered to by Chicanos are most often in the direction of the therapist relating negatively or judgmentally to adherence to sexual roles. Anglo therapists are tempted to view any differences in sex roles and division of labor in terms of the dominant culture's current struggle with its own sexism. Ethnocentrism is not a trap for only the politically and socially conservative and even young therapists who are eager to aid in the "liberation" movements are tempted to taint the scope and quality of liberation by the cultural ideals and limitations which are a part of their unconscious heritage.

Proposed Corrections   The basic attack on this type of error lies in the training and supervision of therapists so that they avoid the omnipotent role of judge and arbitrator. Negative and judgmental reactions to patients is psychonoxious for all patients in almost all circumstances. However, a review of the research literature (Bergin, 1971) and a review of our supervisory sessions with student therapists reveal that the development of a nonjudgmental attitude toward patients remains an ideal rather than a reality in our professions. Involvement of Chicanos in training and in research in psychology and a general expansion of the interest paid to cultural factors would be helpful for all of psychology.

SUMMARY

A caution is in order. It has become clear from even the limited amount of research and clinical work with Chicanos that cultural differences exist across a broad range of phenomena. What has also become clear to us is that there has been a serious neglect of the psychology of the Chicano. This is obvious not only in this summary which focuses on issues relevant to therapy but also in the broad review of Latino mental health (Padilla & Ruiz, 1973). It is the expectation of the authors that with greater attention to the Chicano population both in terms of psychological services and psychological research, our pitifully meager collection of knowledge about the Chicano will begin to expand. With that expectation comes the hope that in the future the interpretations made about the Chicano culture in this article will seem woefully incomplete and alarmingly uncomplex.

Further caution is imperative. The literature in the various behavioral disciplines has depreciated the Hispanic culture and the Chicano by stereotyping both as emotional, passive, and noncompetitive. On the surface this article might inadvertently appear to support this pejorative view. However, the opposite is true. These labels are premised on suppositions which separate affect as distinct from cognition, passive coping styles as distinct from active ones, and cooperation as incompatible with competition. The reader is advised to recognize these terms exist for convenience in organization and communication and that reality is not segmented quite as neatly and as simplistically. For example, to assert a cognitive approach *versus* an affective approach implies that cognition is separate and distinct from emotion, and this, of course, does not depict reality. A speculation may serve to illustrate a more useful approach to the Hispano culture. Perhaps the factor of greatest interest is that the nature of significant interpersonal relations for Chicanos has influence across the affective-cognitive, passive-active, competitive-cooperative dimensions such that Chicanos tend to: incorporate more affect in cognition, be less anxious about controlling the environment, be more cooperative in their competition.

It is also important to point out that the majority of Chicanos are poverty stricken and are discriminated against due to racial, economic, and ethnic factors and that the consequential frustrating milieu might have direct motivational implications upon these same dimensions of affect cognition, passive-active, competition-cooperation.

Throughout this review the focus has been on psychotherapy directed primarily to the assistance of patients with intrapsychic conflict or major difficulties in mastering developmental issues and interpersonal situations. There is no suggestion that these types of problems form the core or even the majority of the problems and stress of the Chicano. Instead we concur with Martinez (1973) and Padilla et al. (1975) who point out that such problems represent only a small portion of the social and survival problems of the Chicano.

Authors' note: The quality of friendship as represented in dreams of Anglo and Chicano college students. Unpublished manuscript. Available from the senior author.

REFERENCES

Abad, V., Ramos, J. & Boyce, E. A model for delivery of mental health services to Spanish-speaking minorities. *American Journal of Orthopsychiatry*, **44**, 584–595, 1974.
Abel, T. M. *Psychological testing in cultural contexts*. New Haven: College & Universities Press, 1973.
Bergin, A. E. The evaluation of therapeutic outcomes. *In* A. E. Bergin and S. L. Garfield (Eds.), *Handbook of psychotherapy and behavior change*. New York: Wiley, 1971, pp. 217–270.
Boulette, T. R. Group therapy with low-income Mexican Americans. *Social Work*, **20**, 403–404, 1975.
Brenneis, B. & Roll, S. Ego modalities in the manifest dreams of male and female Chicanos. *Psychiatry*, **38**, 172–185, 1975.
Brenneis, B. & Roll, S. Dream patterns in Anglo and Chicano young adults. *Psychiatry*, 1976, *39*(3), 280–290.
Cresson, D. L., McKinley, C. & Evans, R. Folk medicine in Mexican-American subculture. *Diseases of the Nervous System*, **30**, 264–266, 1969.

Diaz-Guerrero, R. *The psychology of the Mexican.* Austin: University of Texas Press, 1975.

Edgerton, R. B., Karno, M. & Fernandez, I. Curandismo in the metropolis: The diminishing role of folk psychiatry among Los Angeles Mexican-Americans. *American Journal of Psychotherapy,* **24,** 124–134, 1970.

Etzioni, A. *The active society.* New York: Free Press, 1968.

Garcia, F. C. *The political socialization of Chicano children: A comparison with Anglos in California.* Praeger, 1973.

Grebler, L., Moore, J. W. & Guzman, R. C. *The Mexican-American people, the nation's second largest minority.* New York: Free Press, 1970.

Heiman, E. M., Burruel, G. & Chavez, N. Factors determining effective psychiatric outpatient treatment for Mexican-Americans. *Hospital and Community Psychiatry,* **26,** 515–517, 1975.

Helms, L. Mexican-Americans. *Journal of the American College Health Association,* **22,** 269–271, 1974.

Holtzman, W. H., Diaz-Guerrero, R. & Swartz, J. D. *Personality development in two cultures.* Austin: University of Texas Press, 1975.

Karno, M. The enigma of ethnicity in a psychiatric clinic. *Archives of General Psychiatry,* **14,** 516–520, 1966.

Karno, M. & Edgerton, R. B. Perception of mental illness in a Mexican-American community. *Archives of General Psychiatry,* **20,** 233–238, 1969.

Karno, M. & Morales, A. A community mental health service for Mexican-Americans in a metropolis. *Comprehensive Psychiatry,* **12,** 115–121, 1971.

Kline, L. Some factors in the psychiatric treatment of Spanish-Americans. *American Journal of Psychiatry,* **125,** 1674–1681, 1969.

Kreisman, J. J. The curandero's apprentice: A therapeutic integration of folk and medical healing. *American Journal of Psychiatry,* **132,** 81–83, 1975.

Lubchansky, I., Ergi, G. & Stokes, J. Puerto Rican spiritualists' view of mental illness: The faith healer as paraprofessional. *American Journal of Psychiatry,* **127,** 312–321, 1970.

Maes, W. & Rinaldi, J. Counseling the Chicano child. *Elementary School Guidance and Counseling,* **9,** 279–284, 1974.

Marcos, L. R., Alpert, M., Urcuoy, L. & Kesselman, M. The effect of interview language on the evaluation of psychopathology in Spanish-American schizophrenic patients. *American Journal of Psychiatry,* **130,** 549–553, 1973.

Martinez, C. Community mental health and the Chicano movement. *American Journal of Orthopsychiatry,* **43,** 595–601, 1973.

Nelson, L. L. & Kagan, S. Competition: The star-spangled scramble. *Psychology Today,* **6,** 53–54, 56, 90–91, 1972.

Padilla, A. M. & Ruiz, R. A. *Latino mental health: A review of the literature.* Washington, D.C.: U.S. Government Printing Office, 1973.

Padilla, A. M., Ruiz, R. A. & Alverez, R. Community health services for the Spanish-speaking/Spanish-surnamed population. *American Psychologist,* **30,** 892–905, 1975.

Roll, S. & Brenneis, B. Chicano dreams: Investigations in cross-cultural research. *In* J. M. Herrera and M. S. Sam Vargas (Eds.), *The Chicano community: Psychological theory and practice.* New Haven: Yale University Press, in press.

Roll, S., Rabold, K. & McArdle, L. Disclaimed activity in dreams of Chicanos and Anglos. *Journal of Cross-Cultural Psychology,* 1976, *7*(3), 335–345.

Ruiz, R. A. Research priorities in Latino mental health. *Interamerican Psycholo-*

gist, **45,** 1–3, 1976.

Samuda, R. J. *Testing of American minorities.* New York: Dodd-Mead, 1975.

Torrey, E. F. The case for the indigenous therapist. *Archives of General Psychiatry*, **20,** 365–373, 1969.

Wignall, C. F. & Koppin, L. L. Mexican-American usage of State mental hospital facilities. *Community Mental Health Journal*, **3,** 137–148, 1967.

Wolfe, T. *You can't go home again.* New York: Harper & Row, 1940.

Yamamoto, J., James, Q. C., Bloombaum, M. & HaHem, J. Racial factors in patient selection. *American Journal of Psychiatry*, **124,** 630–636, 1967.

Yamamoto, J., James, Q. C. & Palley, N. Cultural problems in psychiatric therapy. *Archives of General Psychiatry*, **19,** 45–49, 1968.

Section IV

ASIAN AMERICANS

27

Editorial Introduction

The first two selections present historical and descriptive information about Asian Americans. Stanley, Derald, and David Sue describe some inconsistent policies, attitudes, and data regarding Asian Americans. These Americans have been relatively successful financially and educationally in spite of stress from racism and oppression. Their mental illness rates are also low. These authors suggest that these statistics are deceptive due to a paucity of available knowledge on the attitudes that Asian Americans have toward psychological concepts and human services.

Elizabeth Toupin provides historical perspective on the 2½ million Asian Americans. Asian Americans come from cultures that stress different values, especially in regard to interpersonal relationships and reliance upon nonverbal behaviors to clarify the discrepancy between thought and action. As a consequence white counselors may be unable to provide treatment without special training. Man Kueng Ho details some cultural values of Asian Americans that are relevant to the delivery of human services. These values include filial piety, paternalism, self-control, shame, middle position or social norm virtue, subordination to social group, fatalism, and inconspicuousness. Some of the consequences of these values for human services are explored with examples suggesting how to respond to individual clients. A modified group approach includes the nuclear family as well as the extended family and illustrates an incorporation of existing cultural practices into therapy procedures. Interventions that make use of the existing power structures in the community are recommended.

In the next selection Amy Iwasaki Mass specifically explores the discrepancy between stereotypes of Japanese Americans and reality. Japanese character is related to generational group. Issei are first generation pioneers, now aged, who lack English fluency and have retained a relatively intact cultural identity. Nisei have also maintained a Japanese identity but were damaged by concentration camp experience during World War II that left survival characteristics of docility, patience, and industriousness. Sansei, children of Nisei parents, have been driven to achieve but have often discovered despair and drugs as an aftermath.

Joe Yamamoto further documents underutilization of services among Asian Americans and provides an exposition of therapies that are relevant, especially for Japanese Americans. Bicultural therapists are needed who can focus upon specific kinds of symptom relief within a service delivery model that includes the patient and the family. Examples of Morita and Naikan therapies are cited as culturally appropriate for Japanese patients. The model therapist is a Sensei, or learned teacher, who can lead toward problem-solving and improved functioning of the entire family.

Vita Sommers presents psychotherapy cases of Japanese and Chinese origins to illustrate the impact of culture upon identity conflicts and psychoneurosis. Both individual and group therapy are used to foster a unique and balanced identity that contains ingredients of Asian and American culture.

In the last selection Derald Sue presents a working theory of how race and culture combine to produce characteristic psychological orientations that affect utilization of human service interventions. Locus of control (LC) refers to the relative impact of one's own actions or chance-luck in determining life outcomes. Locus of responsibility (LR) refers to attribution of blame to either person or society for life problems. Four combinations accrue from interactions of these two dimensions and fit the psychological orientations of all clients. White, middle-class persons value responsibility and achievement (Internal LC and Internal LR). Some minority persons accept the dominant cultural demand for self-responsibility while experiencing minimal control over their own lives (External LC and Internal LR). Others, however, feel neither personal power nor personal responsibility over their own lives (External LC and External LR). Finally, some minority persons, especially Asian Americans, feel that control of their own lives is feasible in spite of external impediments of discrimination, prejudice, and exploitation (Internal LC and External LR).

28

Asian Americans as a Minority Group

Stanley Sue, Derald Wing Sue, and David W. Sue

We usually think of an oppressed minority group as one that has experienced prejudice and discrimination. In the case of blacks, Chicanos, and native Americans, oppression is unquestionably a reality, as indicated by measures of income, education, employment opportunities, housing patterns, and life expectancy. However, in the minds of many individuals, considerable doubt exists concerning the Asian American minority (Chinese, Filipinos, Japanese, Koreans, etc.) as an *oppressed* group. This doubt is reflected in the kinds of inconsistent policies that we see. At some institutions, Asian Americans are not considered for affirmative action or other special programs for minority groups; yet, when these institutions are required to submit information on the number of minorities present, Asians are always included. One Japanese American student applying to graduate school was told that in order to qualify for consideration as a minority group member, he would have to show that he came from a disadvantaged background. If he could prove that he was poor or raised in a ghetto, he would then qualify. Members of more "recognized" minority groups were not asked for such information. Their disadvantaged status was assumed.

Those of us who have worked with Asian Americans have been frustrated by these inconsistent policies, by the myths regarding the status of this minority, and by the general lack of attention given to Asian Americans. With respect to the latter, for example, few individuals are aware of the fact that there is an Association of Asian American Psychologists with nearly 150 members. Many more persons are familiar with organizations such as the Association of Black Psychologists, Chicano Psychologists in La Raza, and the Committee on Women in Psychology.

The purpose of this article is not to attack the neglect of Asian Americans. Rather, we are arguing for a more realistic appraisal of their status.

An earlier version of this article was presented in a symposium at the meeting of the American Psychological Association, New Orleans, September 1974. It was supported in part by Research Grant MH22009-01 from the National Institute of Mental Health.

Reprinted with permission from *American Psychologist*, 1975, *30*, 906–910.

In order to do so, we have examined the 1970 statistics concerning income, education, interracial marriage, and mental health among the 435,000 Chinese, 343,000 Filipinos, and 591,000 Japanese in the United States. Other minority groups are mentioned only for comparative purposes, without any conclusions about their status.

THE DILEMMA

During May 1974, at a national convention sponsored by an organization of Chinese Americans, there was a great deal of debate over who we (Chinese) are. Some participants argued that Chinese are successful and well-respected Americans; others heatedly asserted that Chinese are an oppressed and neglected minority group. These two views of Chinese in particular, and of Asian Americans in general, have only recently received some degree of scrutiny. It seems vital to present the rationale for the two viewpoints and, using the analysis made of the 1970 Census by Urban Associates (1974), to critically examine them.

The Success Image

One could easily build a case for the success of Asian Americans in economic, educational, social, and mental health areas. Indeed, as indicated in Table 1, the 1970 U.S. Census revealed that Chinese and Japanese in this country have exceeded the national median family income. Even Filipino Americans, who were far below others in 1960, now have an income level similar to the rest of the nation. The same is true for educational attainment: Chinese, Filipinos, and Japanese showed a higher median number of grades completed than the national median. In these areas, then, Asian Americans, unlike blacks, Chicanos, and native Americans, are quite successful.

But even more striking evidence of success is indicated by the reduction of social distance between Asians and whites. The Social Distance Scale (Bogardus, 1925) has traditionally been used as a measure of prejudice and/or discrimination against minority groups. Presumably, if a

Table 1.   Median income and education

Group	Family income	Education for ages 16 and over
U.S. total	$9,590	12.1 years
Chinese	$10,610	12.5 years
Filipinos	$9,318	12.2 years
Japanese	$12,515	12.5 years

Note: Data are based on Urban Associates (1974).

minority group is allowed to intermarry and to form intimate relationships with the dominant group, then there is a reduction in social distance; hence, the minority group is accepted by the dominant one. In the case of Japanese Americans, Kikumura and Kitano (1973) and Tinker (1973) estimated that the incidence of intermarriage (predominantly Japanese to whites) in 1970 was nearly 50% in areas such as Los Angeles, San Francisco, and Fresno, California. Because the children of these marriages appeared to be marrying members of the dominant group, there is the possibility that in the future, Japanese may be assimilated and physically disappear as a significant minority in this country. Statistics are also available on the prevalence of intermarriages among Chinese, Filipinos, and Japanese in 1970. As shown in Table 2, the rates of "outmarriage" are relatively high for Filipinos and Japanese and those for Chinese are relatively low. When consideration is made of marriages among younger Asian Americans, which presumably are more recent marriages, we find an even higher prevalence rate for outmarriage. Table 3 indicates which groups were involved in the outmarriages. It is clear that Asian-white marriages accounted for the major bulk. Interestingly, the prevalence of black-white marriages for all married blacks in 1970 is well under 2% and never exceeds 8%, regardless of whether consideration is made of urban-nonurban rates, male-female rates, or rates for different sections of the country (Heer, 1974).

In addition to these economic and social measures of well-being, one must consider psychological indicators. It has been argued that stress on minority groups derived from racism and oppression often results in self-hatred, anger and rage, and mental disorders in general (Clark, 1965; Grier & Cobbs, 1968; Kardiner & Ovesey, 1951; Lerner, 1972). If Asian Americans face oppression as a minority group, we would expect to find

Table 2.   Percentage of outmarriage

Group	Age 16–24	25–44	45 and over	Total
Chinese				
Males	41	16	10	13
Females	28	13	7	12
Filipino				
Males	49	28	37	33
Females	50	28	12	28
Japanese				
Males	38	16	7	12
Females	46	43	16	33

Note: Data are based on Urban Associates (1974).

Table 3.   Asian Americans marrying outside own group by origin of spouse

Group	Origin of spouse (in %)				
	Other Asian	White	Spanish speaking	Black	Other
Chinese husband	25	49	12	3	11
Filipino husband	12	42	30	3	12
Japanese husband	14	65	8	1	12
Chinese wife	18	59	8	3	13
Filipino wife	7	54	22	7	9
Japanese wife	8	81	4	3	4

Note: Data are based on Urban Associates (1974).

some expression of this, perhaps in the form of high rates of psychopathology. But this is not the case. The rates of mental illness among Asian Americans are quite low according to their admissions to psychiatric institutions (Brown, Stein, Huang, & Harris, 1973; Kitano, 1969; Sue & Sue, 1974; State of Hawaii, Note 2). For example, Sue and McKinney (1975) found that Chinese, Filipinos, and Japanese represented only 0.6% of the patients in 17 community mental health centers, while these Asian groups comprised 2.38% of the population served by these centers. On the other hand, blacks were overrepresented in these facilities by twice the expected proportion. Although rates of utilization are not perfect correlates of the actual rates of psychopathology in the population, they nevertheless constitute a widely used research definition of mental illness (Scott, 1958). Finally, the low rates of divorce and juvenile delinquency (Sue & Kitano, 1973) also support the notion that Asian Americans experience little stress. These findings have resulted in an extremely positive public image of Asian-American adjustment.

The Oppressed Image

If Asian Americans are successful, why do we see increased alliances between Asians and other groups such as blacks, Chicanos, and native Americans? Why are there angry demands for equality? Is this merely a fad, with Asian Americans being caught up in an ethnic movement? Our belief is that the alliance with other minorities is not a fad. If it were, it probably would not have lasted so long.

We can easily document the kinds of problems seen in most Chinatowns and Manilatowns: poverty, unemployment, ill health, suicides, youth gangs, crimes, sweatshops, and immigrant survival (Charnofsky, 1971; Jacobs, Landau, & Pell, 1971; Lyman, 1970). True, not all Asian Americans live in ethnic ghettos; and indeed, some Chinatown residents are wealthy. However, these ghetto problems are significant and have not received adequate examination.

Another area that needs closer attention is the inferences drawn from 1970 statistics on income and education. For example, references made to the high median family income of Asian Americans are not tempered by findings that in such families, there is a higher proportion of incomes derived from more than one earner. The national percentage of families with more than one earner is 51%. This figure is 60% or more for Chinese, Filipinos, and Japanese. Three other points merit consideration. First, despite a good median family income, the incidence of poverty (as defined by the U.S. Bureau of Census) is 10% for Chinese and 12% for Filipino families, which is quite similar to the 11% rate for the nation. Thus, a significant proportion of Chinese and Filipinos is poverty stricken. Only Japanese show a low 6% incidence. Further, perhaps because of cultural factors, misinformation, immigrant status, or even discriminatory practices, Chinese and Japanese are behind the rest of the country in obtaining much-needed public assistance. While a United States average of 0.48 families in poverty receive public assistance or welfare, this figure is 0.36 for Chinese, 0.45 for Japanese, and 0.48 for Filipinos. Second, Daniels and Kitano (1970) reported that despite high levels of education, Asian Americans tended to receive lower incomes. Data from the 1970 U.S. Census also indicate discrepancies between education and income. The ratio of persons anually earning $10,000 or more to persons with a college education is 1.4 for the country and only 0.7 for Chinese, 0.4 for Filipinos, and 1.2 for Japanese. Third, there is evidence that Asian Americans do experience educational difficulties. A recent study reported by Watanabe (1973) revealed that over 50% of Asian students at the University of California, Berkeley, failed to pass an entrance examination in basic English compared to the 25% failure rate by the general campus population. This problem may be further exacerbated by the continuing influx of immigrants whose bilingual needs necessitate attention. The number of immigrants is quite high. During 1973, approximately 21,700 Chinese, 30,800 Filipinos, and 5,500 Japanese immigrants arrived. All of these facts illustrate how misleading gross statistics can be about the success of Asian Americans.

Even in the area of mental health, we find evidence that the success image is inappropriate. In examining the adjustment of Chinese and Japanese American students at the University of California, Berkeley, Sue and Kirk (1973) found that these students expressed greater feelings of loneliness, isolation, and anxiety than others in the general student body. Other studies (Brown et al., 1973; Sue & McKinney, 1975; Sue & Sue, 1974) suggest that the low utilization of mental health facilities gives a misleading impression that Asian Americans have low rates of psychopathology. They show that the small numbers of Asians who use psychiatric facilities are more disturbed than other patients. The implication is that Asian Americans with milder problems merely avoid the use of such services. Avoidance probably occurs not only because cultural values inhibit self-referral but also because these services are often unresponsive. In support of the latter theory, Sue and McKinney (1975) found that in 17 community mental health centers over 50% of the Asian American patients dropped out of therapy after a single session, whereas the termination rate for white patients was 29%. Our conclusion thus is that mental health services are not responding to the needs of Asian Americans; hence, many fail to use these services or prematurely terminate after one session.

Finally, the personal experiences of prejudice and discrimination, though hard to document, are nevertheless a reality. Many Asian Americans readily report that they have been the victims of racism in housing, employment, and interpersonal relationships. An Asian American Advisory Council to the Washington State Governor recently held public meetings to investigate testimonies given by Asian Americans on their personal experiences of discrimination. This investigation, one of the first of its kind in the United States, resulted in a 1973 document entitled "Discrimination Against Asians" that clearly showed the various forms of discrimination reported by Asians.

FINAL COMMENTS

The issue at stake is not which view of Asian Americans is correct. As in any ethnic group, we can always find some Asian Americans who are wealthy, highly educated, and influential and those who are poverty stricken and powerless. The real issue is the extent to which we are willing to put aside blanket stereotypes, to begin the task of accurately assessing their experiences and needs, and to eliminate direct or subtle forms of racism aimed at this minority group. Only then can psychological tools and services be meaningfully applied for the welfare of Asian Americans, and then the currently inconsistent social policies can be based upon realistic considerations rather than upon myths, political whims, or mere convenience. There is much work to be done in these areas.

Current stereotypes of Chinese and Japanese are exceedingly favorable (Sue & Kitano, 1973), which makes it all the more necessary to document the forms of discrimination encountered by them. Furthermore, little is actually known about the personal attitudes Asian Americans have regarding psychological concepts or services. Such information would be useful in directing our mental health services. In an interesting exploratory survey, Lum (Note 1) found that Chinese in Chinatown, San Francisco, believed that mental health resulted from a) will power and b) the avoidance of morbid thoughts. These provocative findings, if valid, will raise additional questions. How does the concept of will power fit into traditional Chinese culture? What does the lack of will power imply in terms of the individual's self-worth? What is the relationship, if any, between the avoidance of morbid thoughts and self-disclosure or psycho-dynamic notions of suppression and repression? How can we use these findings in the delivery of more adequate mental health services?

Finally, there is an increasing tendency for various Asian groups to unify and be considered as one group. Various organizations, such as the Japanese American Citizens League and the Organization of Chinese Americans, have discussed the issue of merging with other Asian American groups. Yet, we know that significant differences within Asians exist. How can we explain these differences? For example, why are rates of interracial marriage much lower for Chinese than for Filipinos and Japanese? By merging into one group and advocating an Asian American identity, will structural assimilation be avoided? How valid are our impressions that Asian American youths are now developing a strong ethnic pride? The list of such questions could obviously be much longer and clearly demonstrates the extent of our knowledge. We have only scratched the surface of these issues.

REFERENCE NOTES

1. Lum, R. *Issues in the study of Asian American communities.* Paper presented at the meeting of the Western Psychological Association, San Francisco, April 1974.
2. State of Hawaii. *Statistical report.* Honolulu: Department of Health, 1970.

REFERENCES

Bogardus, E. Measuring social distance. *Journal of Applied Sociology*, 1925, *9*, 299–308.
Brown, T. R., Stein, K., Huang, K., & Harris, D. Mental illness and the role of mental health facilities in Chinatown. In S. Sue & N. Wagner (Eds.), *Asian Americans: Psychological perspectives.* Ben Lomond, Calif.: Science and Behavior Books, 1973.
Charnofsky, S. Counseling for power. *Personnel and Guidance Journal*, 1971, *49*, 351–357.
Clark, K. B. *Dark ghetto: Dilemmas of social power.* New York: Harper & Row, 1965.
Daniels, R., & Kitano, H. H. *American racism: Exploration of the nature of prejudice.* Englewood Cliffs, N.J.: Prentice-Hall, 1970.
Grier, W., & Cobbs, P. M. *Black rage.* New York: Basic Books, 1968.
Heer, D. M. The prevalence of black-white marriage in the United States, 1960 and 1970. *Journal of Marriage and the Family*, 1974, *36*, 246–258.
Jacobs, P., Landau, S., & Pell, E. *To serve the devil: Colonials and sojourners.* New York: Vintage Books, 1971.

Kardiner, A., & Ovesey, L. *The mark of oppression.* New York: Norton, 1951.

Kikumura, A., & Kitano, H. H. Interracial marriage: A picture of the Japanese Americans. *Journal of Social Issues*, 1973, *29*(2), 67–81.

Kitano, H. H. Japanese-American mental illness. In S. Plog & R. Edgerton (Eds.), *Changing perspectives in mental illness.* San Francisco: Holt, Rinehart & Winston, 1969.

Lerner, B. *Therapy in the ghetto: Political impotence and personal disintegration.* Baltimore, Md.: Johns Hopkins University Press, 1972.

Lyman, S. M. *The Asian in the west.* Reno, Nev.: Western Studies Center, Desert Research Institute, 1970.

Scott, W. Research definitions of mental health and mental illness. *Psychological Bulletin*, 1958, *55*, 29–45.

Sue, D. W., & Kirk, B. A. Differential characteristics of Japanese American and Chinese American college students. *Journal of Counseling Psychology*, 1973, *20*, 142–146.

Sue, S., & Kitano, H. H. Stereotypes as a measure of success. *Journal of Social Issues*, 1973, *29*(2), 83–98.

Sue, S., & McKinney, H. Asian Americans in the community mental health care system. *American Journal of Orthopsychiatry*, 1975, *45*, 111–118.

Sue, S., & Sue, D. W. MMPI comparisons between Asian-American and non-Asian students utilizing a student health psychiatric clinic. *Journal of Counseling Psychology*, 1974, *21*, 423–427.

Tinker, J. N. Intermarriage and ethnic boundaries: The Japanese American case. *Journal of Social Issues*, 1973, *29*(2), 49–66.

Urban Associates. *A study of selected socioeconomic characteristics based on the 1970 census. Vol. 2: Asian Americans.* Washington, D.C.: U.S. Government Printing Office, 1974.

Watanabe, C. Self-expression and the Asian American experience. *Personnel and Guidance Journal*, 1973, *51*, 390–396.

29

Counseling Asians
Psychotherapy in the Context of
Racism and Asian-American History

Elizabeth Sook Wha Ahn Toupin

For Asian-Americans, America is a rapidly changing scene reflecting as much the dramatic shifts of global power and politics as the moods in the United States.

Since the end of World War II, the United States has been directly involved in two unpopular wars in Asia. The fight on behalf of some Asians to ensure the right to self-determination has been a difficult task for this country—for America has barely begun to come to terms with its own racism against Asians. Are Manzanar, the first Japanese relocation center of World War II and a symbol as powerful to Asian-Americans as Dachau is to the Jews, and Hiroshima true reflections of the more oppressive side of American attitudes toward Asians? Manzanar was 1941; Hiroshima, 1945. Was the intervention in Korea in 1950 and in Vietnam in 1958 possible to American minds because of the earlier unquestioning acceptance of Manzanar and Hiroshima?

Three years after the 1970 census, the number of Asians in the United States has increased significantly: the Chinese population rose 14% to 496,000; Filipinos increased by 26% to 43,000; Koreans by 80% to 126,000. At the end of World War II, the Asians in the United States numbered slightly over one half million, and the majority were U.S. citizens. Today the number is over 2½ million, and half are now foreign born. Unlike their predecessors, the new immigrants include middle-class entrepeneurs and professionals as well as laborers.

In 1969, sociologist Harry Kitano[4] noted the gradual breakdown of ethnic structures and the successful social assimilation of Asians into the mainstream of American life. A 1970 study[2] revealed that structural assimilation was no longer taking place, that

> ...Japanese Americans are still a structurally separate group...it is questionable whether they prefer to remain as such.

Reprinted with permission from *The American Journal of Orthopsychiatry*, 1980, *50* (1) 76–86. Copyright © 1980 by the American Orthopsychiatric Association, Inc.

The recent immigrants have diffused the picture. Some 1976 data on the Koreans might shed light on the important changes that have taken place. Koreans are admitted to the U.S. at the rate of 30,000 a year. At the present rate of growth, they may reach the half million mark in 1980. Today, of 290,000 Koreans in this country, 215,000 are in households where Korean is spoken as a first or second language. Also, there are more female immigrants than male—68 males for every 100 females, compared with the turn of the century when 80% of the Korean immigrants were male.[8]

What are some of the dominant features of Asians settling on American soil? To what extent do Asian cultural values conflict with American values? How are such cultural conflicts resolved, individually and in the group?

I will discuss three areas that play a major role in the development of the Asian personality. While there are differences among the Chinese, Japanese, and Koreans, they do share, broadly speaking, a common cultural heritage. Also, the receptivity of the various states to the Asian immigrants did not differentiate among Chinese, Japanese, and Koreans. Most of the following material is drawn from the experiences of the Japanese, who constitute one of the largest Asian groups and on whom there is a considerable amount of data.

First, it is important to know when and why Asians migrated to the United States and where they settled; a brief review of Asian-American history will reveal some important historical differences in the way different states responded to Asian immigrants.

Second, while the impact of public education on the second generation of Asian immigrants was similar to that on other immigrants, the roots of their languages, religions, and values are from Eastern tradition. Hence, behavior patterns are more strenuously challenged, modified, or in need of replacement in the resocialization process in the new American homeland.

Third, cultural factors, both Asian and American, will be explored for their relevance to individual behavior and interpersonal relations. New rules for public and private roles characterize the shift from immigrant to acculturated American.

RECEPTIVITY TO ASIANS

The policies governing Asian migration to the United States were distinctly different from those affecting other migrations. Asian immigrants were recruited as a source of cheap, temporary labor for Hawaii, as well as the continental U.S. For 50 years, 1857 to 1907, bachelors were the prime target for recruitment into the United States. The intention of the recruiters, the bachelor-laborers, and the U.S. government was that the immigrants from Asia would ultimately return to their homeland. To the Asian immigrant, the major motivation in coming to the United States (nicknamed "Mountain of Gold" by the Chinese) was to make a fortune. They were called sojourners.

The contract labor system bore a close resemblance to the slave trade: workers were recruited on a credit-ticket system whereby passage money was advanced by a broker. The immigrant was expected to buy his way out of debt with future earnings.

As problems grew with controlling and containing the Chinese workers, (the first Asian immigrants) in menial jobs and within specific geographical pockets, recruiters of labor moved to Korea, Japan, and then to the Philippines for a cheaper and, hopefully, less troublesome workforce. Language and cultural differences and centuries of historical animosity separated these Asian minorities from each other as well as from the American core culture. The fact that the Japanese were historically enemies of the Chinese, Koreans, and the Filipinos, led to separate ethnic societies that were reinforced geographically by vocation as well as by avocation. There were strict taboos against dating outside the ethnic group, indeed outside of one's caste within each group. Among the Chinese, a *punti* did not date a *hakkas;* nor, within the Japanese group, were *Etas* considered suitable mates.

The demand for labor by sugar and pineapple plantations in Hawaii closely paralleled the increase in Asian immigration to the continental United States. However, as organized labor in California continued to agitate and attack Japanese immigrants, President Theodore Roosevelt, to avoid confrontation with Japan over treatment of its citizens in the U.S., signed the "Gentleman's Agreement" with Japan, which cut down Japanese immigration to the U.S. By executive order, he further barred immigration of Japanese from Mexico and Canada and migration from Hawaii to the mainland to prevent a further increase of Japanese immigrants to the West Coast. This executive order extended to citizens of Asian ancestry. Hence, even migration from Hawaii to the West Coast or to any part of the United States required a passport. The executive order would probably have been declared unconstitutional if it had been tested. It was revoked by President Harry Truman in 1948.

By 1924, Congress passed the Exclusion Act, which effectively barred all migration from Asia. There were considerable differences in the attitudes of communities in Hawaii and on the West Coast toward the new immigrants. These reflect the different histories of Hawaii and of the West Coast.

The monarchy of Hawaii was forcefully overthrown and annexed as a territory of the United States in 1898. Its largest source of income was from sugar and pineapple. Its economic system—based on sugar, pine, and shipping—as well as its political system, were dominated by a small, highly organized group, tightly held together by intermarriage and a complex of interlocking directorates of five major corporations. This group, known as the "Big Five," included a large number of sons of missionaries. They were extremely exploitative—plantation wages in Hawaii in 1909 were a minimum of $9/month, compared to wages of $4/day on the West Coast. While housing and food were also provided, the costs for these were arbitrarily estimated by the plantation companies, which then deducted these cost from future earnings.

Total control over the livelihood of the Asian plantation workers led to abusive treatment. However, the Hawaii planters, who were white, were actually a racial minority in a multiracial community, physically isolated and far removed from the protection of the U.S. government. Ironically, a bit of the Christian spirit plus a commitment to *laissez faire* economics and the spirit of *aloha* or the total acceptance of each new immigrant group by native Hawaiians, led to the establishment of the myth of racial harmony. The myth of racial harmony based on racial equality was crucial, for it provided the framework for the development of the islands. Hence, while immigration laws affected the quota of Asians, there were no laws prohibiting Asians in Hawaii from owning land or intermarrying; and public education was available to all.

The result was the development and movement of Asian immigrants into the mainstream of American life. By pooling their meager resources through *kaes, tanomoshi, huis,** Asians slowly made their way out of the plantation system into small business and property ownership. The process was hampered but not deterred by language barriers and cultural traditions rooted in oriental philosophy. Even with the absence of any Asians, who constituted the majority of the population in Hawaii, in managerial or administrative jobs in these basic industries controlled by the white minority—the "Big Five"—the myth of racial harmony persisted and racial tokenism was an established way of life by 1940. All ethnic groups are honored at island celebrations. Not one but seven beauty queens are selected, one from each ethnic group. The interracial marriage rate rose to close to 40% by 1941.

Hence, island-born Asians or recent immigrants who have settled there have different orientations, perspectives, and options available to them than do West Coast Asians.

---

*Korean, Japanese and Chinese terms for a banking-loan system based on honor. Example: A person wanting $1000 would ask ten friends with $1000 each to join his *kae*. The first month he would bid 20% interest for a loan of $100 from each member of the *kae*. Three months later, another member would bid 15% interest for $1000; three months later it would be another member's turn. For those with notes due or cash-flow problems, it was a most useful money scheme. For those with no immediate need for $1000, the interest rates made it a highly profitable investment.

The reception accorded Asians on the West Coast was hostile. If we use the law as a reflection of the attitudes of mainland society, we find several pieces of anti-Asian legislation that were enacted primarily to keep Asians from coming to and settling in the United States. The laws included the Foreign Miner's tax passed in 1850, which levied a tax of $20 a month on nonnative born miners. This tax on miners of foreign nationalities was the major source of funding the California State Government for 20 years, 1850 to 1870.[1] A tax requiring each laundry business to pay $15 per month was passed in 1873; a head tax of $50 was charged to the owners of vessels for each passenger not eligible for citizenship (passed in 1855); another tax was a federal law limiting ships to carrying 15 Chinese passengers (1879). Statutes also excluded them from serving as witnesses in trials involving white men. (This led to the idiom, "You haven't got a Chinaman's chance!") Finally, the Chinese Exclusion Act of 1882 barred Chinese laborers from entering the U.S. The Scott Act of 1888 prevented Chinese laborers returning home from reentering the U.S. (20,000 workers were involved). A Gentleman's Agreement Act, the Alien Land Act of 1913, prohibited aliens who were ineligible for citizenship in California from owning or leasing property.

These laws, in effect until 1965, not only ended Chinese migration to the United States but prevented spouses from joining their husbands, thereby frustrating attempts to establish natural families. It was not until 1946 that the U. S. Supreme Court reversed the California Supreme Court on the right of American-born children of these same immigrants to own land. This was also the year that a final attempt was made to add discriminatory alien land laws of 1920 to the State Constitution. Clearly, forces still exist to push forward *and* backward. In 1979, the California legislature is considering a bill to limit the amount of land owned by an alien.

In part, the hatred toward Asian immigrants, whose cheap labor western states actually needed for economic development, fed on the obvious physical and cultural differences of the Asian people *vis-à-vis* mainlanders. But the animosity was intensified because the Asian laborers were primarily bachelors. Asian laborers were potential competitors, since women were a distinct and valued minority in the west.

In spite of all the discriminatory laws, Asians on the West Coast— where over one quarter of a million lived by 1940—were assimilated slowly and painfully into American society. Discrimination in housing, employment, and schools was common. To venture out of certain areas was to risk being refused service at restaurants, barbers, hotels, etc. Interracial marriages were prohibited by law.

But the most glaring act of racism against Asian-Americans is without parallel in American history. All persons of Japanese ancestry—

one-third aliens and two-thirds U.S. citizens—were uprooted from their homes during World War II and put into internment camps without due process of law and without any evidence of sabotage or of any "clear and present danger." According to Ten Broeck, Barnharf and Matson,[7] this episode "embodied one of the most sweeping and complete deprivations of constitutional principle."

After World War II, 35% of the Japanese did not return to their homes on the West Coast. They had no homes to which they could return. As early as 1942, selected internees were given one-way tickets out of the internment camp. There was a shortage of labor in agricultural areas as well as the cities. Internees were sent to Chicago, Detroit, St. Louis, etc.—midwestern cities that accepted these displaced persons.

It is one of the great ironies of history that the internment camp experience, itself an oppressive and essentially un-American act, served as a catalyst for the Americanization and geographic dispersement of the Japanese community. In spite of their "concentration camp surroundings" (barbed wire fences, guards), the destruction of their means of livelihood, loss of homes, disruption of families, exploitation of their labor (they were now paid $16 a month), and loss of dignity, a process confirming the status of Japanese as Americans took place as the government dispersed members of the families into the interior of the country, and as contacts within the camps between inmates and the whites in the administration developed. In the camps, public schools as well as a form of community self-government were established. People voted for representatives, established rules, and developed community services. One could be a fireman, policeman, teacher, administrator, president of the student government, captain of the football team, cheerleader, or go to college with some hope that one's educational goals might be achieved. The sometime-rules of American parliamentary democracy were not only being taught but experienced by the inmates.

At the end of the war, the Japanese were freed and encouraged to leave the West Coast. And many did. Chicago and New York gained Japanese-American populations in 1945.

Many questions have been raised about the acculturation of Asians. Why did the Japanese, the majority of whom were under 20 years old and American citizens, not resist the evacuation? What Asian cultural values actually conflicted with American values? In this group of pre-World War II pioneers, why was there such a low rate for crime, delinquency, mental illness, and suicide? Were there any indications of deviant social behavior?

The lack of resistance to evacuation can be attributed to several cultural factors: 1) The Asian cultural value of obedience and conformity. 2) Given Japanese experience, there was a low expectation among the Japanese immigrants and citizens that they would be treated humanely.

Shigata ga nai ("it can't be helped") expressed their stoic acceptance of the inevitable. As among Jews, there was among the Japanese a denial of reality: "It's not happening to us." 3) Moreover, the rounding up and removal of old, respected community leaders by the U.S. government had serious repercussions on the morale and the ability of the community to respond collectively.

Kitano[4] noted that socially acceptable means of psychological release were, in fact, utilized by the Japanese. Psychosomatic complaints, such as an obsession with stomach problems and high blood pressure went with rigid rules for social interaction, and with occupations that minimized both social interactions (*e.g.,* gardening) and the opportunity for behavioral acting-out among the Japanese-Americans. By the 1960s, however, the highly Americanized third generation had joined the "me" generation. The larger "instant gratification" ideology of a segment of that generation challenged the Asian philosophy of the family, rather than the individual, as the central focal point.

Two factors, however, made complete assimilation difficult: the physical differences of the Asians and the racial prejudice harbored against them by the dominant white group. One could replace language, religion, values, and behavior pattern, but the physical differences and racism were outside any individual's control. Some of the ramifications of these frustrations led to greater militancy, the continuation of structurally separate groups, and an identity conflict fed by racial and cultural factors.

CULTURAL NORMS

At this point, it may be useful to focus on some cultural norms that affect the hypothetically model Asian personality. The most noticeable characteristics (based on historical and anthropological observations) of an Asian are a deference to others and verbal devaluation of self and family. The absence of verbal aggression and direct expression of ones's feelings, and the avoidance of confrontation, are personal qualities that are highly esteemed virtues in Asian society. They complicate the life of an acculturated Asian who tries to join the mainstream of competitive, individualistic American life. One's livelihood, in the American economy, if it is to be more than marginally successful, is based on assertive if not aggressive behavior and on "packaging" oneself into a valued commodity.

The Asian lack of assertiveness fits within its culture and is related to the Asian concept of shame. "Shame" in the Asian sense is guilt collectively shared by the family, as well as feelings of inferiority for not reaching ideals and goals as defined by them. Therefore, shame is a trait with many ethnocultural implications.

In Asia, the family is more important than the individual. All of the Asian's attributes derive from his affiliations: family, institution (the university is more important than the degree), village, etc. A person's rank within a group structure defines roles, governs behavior, even determines speech and general countenance. Where one sits, to whom one bows, who one may marry, whether one's name is changed in marriage are predetermined. Each relationship carries different responsibilities and requires different responses. For example, in the work world, if one differs with a senior colleague, one is required to first summarize the person's work, then humbly depreciate oneself, and *then only* raise the question. Concurrent with this code of behavior is an entire system of acts: nonphysical movements and gestures, rituals that are part of an Asian's implicit nonverbal language.[5]

SHAME

In developing nonverbal dialogue, the Asians discipline their children through the ruthless use of shame. According to Pye,[6] the

> ...child is made hypersensitive to the judgment of ethics, to look to social situations for cues to guide his own actions and to be cautious about initiatives and innovations.

Asian parents have taught their children: "Don't pull the tail of the tiger while he's asleep," meant to convey to a child the consequence of shame for lack of sensitivity to timing. "Have you no eyes?", ask parents of children, meaning, "Can't you see and meet the needs of others without being asked?" Thus, children are taught to be ashamed of their lack of insight and aware that they have exposed themselves to the possible experience of shame, of failure or criticism of any kind. It is also an expression of empathy for the situation. Another term, *ha zu ka ski,* Japanese for "others will laugh at you," is meant to emphasize how "others" will react and bring shame to oneself. However, exposing oneself to shame also places the "others" in the uncomfortable position of causing the embarrassment. One result is a pattern of behavior whereby the Japanese nods in agreement so as not to risk any embarrassment to the "other" by disagreeing.[4]

Weglyn[8] described the circumstances of one of two *Isseis* (first generation Japanese) who chose suicide over being evacuated because he felt that in a camp his trembling would be exposed, and the response would bring shame and disgrace to his daughter and ruin her chances for marriage.

For an acculturated Asian, it is shameful to be showy. A father who brags about his son's grades is expressing a lack of dignity and brings shame to the family. Within the family, the parents *assume* a child will perform well and thereby enhance the family name. Implicit in the concept of "shame to the family" is the need to repress one's own feelings in the service of the whole. An alcoholic father brings shame to the entire family, thus to children; a mother will caution, "Don't do any more to further shame the family name."

To reinforce the use of shame as part of the developmental process are words of warning and wisdom. *Cha ma* and *enryo* are the Korean and Japanese words, respectively, for asking one to enter a state of "being patient, being hesitant, holding back." Such an ability is a highly valued cultural trait. Another Japanese value, *Gaman,* is stressed. This means perseverance, to carry on without complaint, and is an expression of dignity. The Chinese word *Han* encompasses more than checking one's emotions. Not only should anger not be shown, but talent, riches—anything that disrupts group harmony or places one above others—should also not be expressed.

The family name or honor is further reinforced by the rule of not discussing personal problems outside the family and discussing only certain topics within the family. One of Maxine Hong Kingston's mythical Woman Warriors, Fai My Lan, carries on her back a carved list of family grievances:

> We are going to carve revenge on your back...wherever you go, whatever happens to you, people will know our sacrifice...and you'll never forget either.[8]

This internal dialogue, which an Asian child learns early to develop in each social situation, leads to the acceptance of the discrepancy between thought and action. It is this trait that sometimes hampers an Asian interpersonal relationship with Westerners, or even with other Asians of different orientation or generation.

The difficulty in articulating, or in seeing the *need* to articulate this internal dialogue under stressful conditions can have dire personal consequences. Here is an internal dialogue that interfered with the therapeutic process of an Asian student at a critical stage:

> A student in therapy three times a week left for the month during Christmas break. At his last session before the holidays, the therapist said, "Call me if you need to see me." The patient thought, first, it's her (the therapist's) holiday too, and I shouldn't impose myself on her at this time; secondly, she didn't insist (a requirement in his value system for a sincere offer). He felt ashamed to ask for time, for it exposed his vulnerability. Four weeks at home without anyone with whom he felt he could discuss his feelings increased his anxieties to such an extent that, within two weeks of his return, he was hospitalized.

The Asian family may be well in touch with its feelings, but the immediate expressing of feelings does not necessarily bring gratification; indeed it may reflect, negatively, on the family, and thus complicate the family's situation.

The different perceptions of Asians and Westerners are contrasted in Table 1, suggested by the experience of four Asian women recently interview and denied places in a graduate school. The Asian students were clearly at a disadvantage. They were denied entry to graduate school in part for their lack of understanding of Western body language and lack of Western-style assertiveness in self-presentation.

There are clear conflicts between Asian norms and psychotherapy norms. Therapy is based on *verbal assertiveness*. If the ideal client is indeed YAWVIS (young, articulate, white, verbal, intelligent, sensitive), then one would have to assume that therapy may not be an effective learning experience for Asians. Asian clients may be young and intelligent and sensitive, but they are not white, verbal or articulate.

However, a successful therapist is one who has the capacity to start where the client is. As the individual is clearly a product of his environment, a broad range of new factors have to be considered in understanding the dynamics of an Asian client: his nationality (Chinese, Japanese, Korean, Filipino, Vietnamese); where the family settled (rural, suburban, urban); social class and generation; and the family's interaction with other Asians in the community. One must understand that the values of counseling are antithetic to Asian philosophy, namely, that all problems can be solved *only* within the group, the family. In fact, mental illness is

Table 1. Attitudes and perceptions of western interviewers (all white males) and Asian interviewees (all female) compared

Western interviewers	Asian interviewees
Eye-to-eye contact attempted.	Eye-to-eye contact is shameful between strangers; only street women do that.
Asks for articulateness in self-presentation; some show of assertiveness (ambition) requested.	I am just a student. I am not important enough to be heard. They're all experts, maybe my future teachers.
Relaxed demeanor.	I sit as demurely as possible.
Requests, "Tell me about yourself."	It's shameful to brag. I must deny how good I am. He should dig out my accomplishments if he really is sincere about knowing them.
Requests presentation of balance in candidate's strong and weak points.	What a rude question (i.e., weak points); I must not answer, for it will mean exposing me and my family to shame. I must take the risk of being rejected for failing to respond.

considered a genetic trait, another family secret not to be shared. The overwhelming respect for authority (and a therapist would be considered an authority figure to whom deference is accorded) adds an enormous complication to any therapeutic relationship.

However, there are several important positive factors that can be used to develop a productive relationship between an Asian client and a non-Asian therapist. Most communication in any group is nonverbal; a part, of course, is verbal. The Asian, like the Westerner, has a highly developed sense of the meaning in their Asian culture of nonverbal cues. This can be used in a positive way. For example, an Asian hostess always crosses the threshold *with* her guest when she wants to indicate that the person is welcome to return. To politely inform a client that he or she is expected to return is often experienced as a sincere gesture, and as assurance to Asians that, regardless of the nature of the discussion, they are welcome to return. Such statements are considered by most Western psychoanalytic therapists as too structural and invasive, for they interfere with the client's freedom of choice.

To draw out the internal dialogue, some counselors have found Rogerian methods especially useful in working with Asian clients. The client-centered approach has clear advantage for a client accustomed to authority and direction, but it may also increase anxieties and instill a sense of futility. Resistance to interpretation may be a socially defined way an Asian protects his or her integrity.

In a series of conversations on psychotherapy and Asians, counselor Kiyo Morimoto of Harvard noted:

> There is a crucial distinction related to the meaning of shame to Asians in the counseling process. The recognition of feelings in the western culture through sharing generally results in a confirmation of the legitimacy of the feeling. The sharing opens up the possibility for exploring and understanding other sources of conflict and pain.

> For an Asian however, the empathic recognition of his/her feelings by the counselor threatens the client who is already experiencing feelings of shame for needing help and of even greater anxieties at further exposure of unacceptable feelings.

Some have found the traditional counseling relationship, which is heavily dependent on the client talking about personal experiences and problems, to be less effective than a relationship in which the therapist reveals some personal problems, sanctioning through this sharing the client's vulnerability. Through sharing, a trust can be developed with the therapist, who has had a completely different orientation and value system but has experienced the same feelings, yearnings, and experiences of love, hate, fear, loneliness, etc.

To some readers this may imply that group process might be a useful mechanism for Asian clients. However, many Asians have found groups especially traumatic in themselves. To share one's problems with *one* person was shameful enough; to share with a group was overwhelming. Also, work in a group seemed to require more expression of verbal aggression than Asians find worth the emotional effort. One student described her experience in these terms: "As soon as I had convinced myself that what I had to say was 'important' or as important as everyone else's problems, the session was over..."

Any Western therapeutic process is likely to be slower even for an acculturated Asian, for the client will need to overcome resistance to the sharing of perceptions that renders the Asian vulnerable to shame. Asians must familiarize themselves with the language of the expression of innermost feelings. The therapist, in turn, must learn the acute anxieties the Asian client is feeling by just being "in therapy," and understand that verbalizing may not bring relief. In fact, it is not unusual for the Asian client to pick up nonverbal cues and hold them in an internal dialogue while talking about thoses issues the client feels the *therapist* would like to hear. Angry at the therapist for accepting these discussions as the client's innermost concerns, and frustrated that the therapist has not picked up on nonverbal cues, the Asian client often ends therapy abruptly.

In charting the goals of therapy, it is important for therapists to understand what personal change will mean to the Asian client. Therapists need to ask if they can help the Asian client switch, so that the client can use Western signals in a Western setting and Asian signals in an Asian setting. It would seem that only by helping the Asian client to understand and accept the need to develop "switching" signals according to the setting can the integrity of the individual Asian be respected and maintained.

REFERENCES

1. Chun Hoon, I. 1975. Teaching the Asian-American experience: Alternative to the neglect and racism in textbooks. *Amerasia J.* 3 (1):40–58.
2. Feagin, J. and Fujitaki, N. 1972. On assimilation of Japanese Americans. *Amerasia J.* (Feb.):13–30.
3. Kingston, M. 1976. *The woman warrior: Memoirs of a girlhood among ghosts.* Knopf, New York.
4. Kitano, H. 1976. *Japanese americans.* Prentice-Hall, Englewood Cliffs, N.J.
5. Nakane, C. 1970. *Japanese society.* University of California Press, Berkeley, Calif.
6. Pye, L. 1968. *The spirit of chinese politics: A study of authority crisis in political development.* MIT Press, Cambridge, Mass.
7. Ten Broek, J., Barnhart, E. and Matson, F. 1954. *Prejudice, war and the constitution.* University of California Press, Berkeley, Calif.
8. Weglyn, M. 1976. *Years of infamy.* William Morrow, New York.
9. Yu, E. 1977. Koreans in America: An emerging ethnic minority. *Amerasia J.* 4(1):117–131.

30

Social Work with Asian Americans

Man Kueng Ho

Asian Americans are one of the most neglected minorities in America.[1] Unlike the blacks, Chicanos, and recently the American Indians, Asian Americans have tried to maintain their social structure with a minimum of visible conflict with the host society. Historically, they have accepted much prejudice and discrimination without voicing strong protests.[2] Their cultural heritage as Asians, historical experiences in a discriminatory society, and their unique problems and concerns are relatively unknown to other Americans.

In fact, Asian Americans frequently have been described as "the most silent minority," "the quiet Americans," or "the model minority." Pei-Ngor Chen attributes such a misconception to two significant factors: the general public's tendency to stereotype ethnic groups and Asian tendencies to hide the "darker side" of their culture, as well as other cultural values militating against self-assertion and open expression of thoughts and feelings to outsiders.[3] It is unfortunate that the prevalent belief that Asian Americans are somehow immune to the effects of white discrimination has served to mask a multitude of problems, such as poverty, unemployment, physical and mental illness, educational deficiencies, and social service inadequacy and unavailability. Problems of Asian Americans and their experiences resulting from white American discrimination have been discussed elsewhere.[4] This article focuses on the

[1]The definition of an Asian American remains necessarily broad and flexible—it has traditionally included the Chinese and Japanese, and more recently the Filipino, Korean, and South Sea Islanders, especially from Guam and Samoa.

[2]Roger Daniels and Harry H. L. Kitano, *American Racism: Exploration of the Nature of Prejudice* (Englewood Cliffs, N.J.: Prentice-Hall, 1970); Gail DeVals and Karen Abbott, The Chinese Family in San Francisco, unpublished master's thesis, University of California, Berkeley, 1966; Samuel M. Lyman, *The Asian in the West* (Reno, Nev.: University of Nevada, 1970).

[3]See Pei-Ngor Chen, The Chinese Community in Los Angeles, *Social Casework,* 51:10 (December 1970).

[4]See Ford H. Kuramoto, What Do Asians Want? An Examination of Issues in Social Work Education, *Journal of Education for Social Work,* 7:3 (Fall 1971); Harry L. Kitano, ed., *Asians in America* (New York: Council on Social Work Education, 1971); Ronald A. Kimmigh, Ethnic Aspects of Schizophrenia in Hawaii, *Psychiatry,* 23:4 (1960): Pei-Ngor Chen, Samoans in California, *Social Work,* 18:2 (March 1972).

indigenous cultural influences operating among Asian Americans and social work intervention with this unique ethnic group.

SALIENT CULTURAL VALUES

Filial Piety

At the beginning of the mid-nineteenth century, the lure of the Mountain of Gold, intensified by social upheavals and natural disasters in many of the Asian countries, began drawing the excess populations of Asia to the Americas. These Asian immigrants brought with them the cultural trappings of a rigid social order in which they generally occupied the lowest position. Among the fundamental beliefs of Asian society were the doctrines of filial piety and an unquestioning respect for and deference to authority. Thus, the individual was expected to comply with familial and social authority, to the point of sacrificing his own desires and ambitions.

Parent-Child Interaction

Clearly defined roles of dominance and deference based on paternalism virtually preclude any discussion and debate in a traditional Asian family. The role of the parent is to define the law; the duty of the child is to listen and obey. Communication flows one way, from parent to child. Directive messages predominate, and exchanges are generally brief and perfunctory. Constantly battered by prohibitions and orders, the Asian child begins to see himself as an obeyer rather than a director. The second generation of Asian American families no doubt has altered considerably this traditional family structure, but the configuration of the traditional parent-child interaction is basically unchanged.[5]

Self-Control

Asians generally are taught to respect all elders and to enhance the family name by outstanding achievement in some aspect of life, such as academic or occupational success. Conversely, an individual learns quickly that dysfunctional behavior such as juvenile delinquency, unemployment, or mental illness, reflects upon the entire family. If he feels his behavior might disrupt family harmony, he is expected to restrain himself. Indeed, Asian culture values highly self-control and the inhibition of strong feelings.[6]

---

[5]Edwin O. Reischauer and John K. Fairbank, *East Asia: The Great Tradition* (Boston: Houghton Mifflin, 1960), p. 33.

[6]See Karen A. Abbott, *Harmony and Individualism* (Taipei: Oriental Cultural Service, 1970).

Shame As a Behavioral Influence

Seen from an Asian American point of view, individualism, with its emphasis on aggressive competition with those of any status, conflicts totally with traditional Asian respect for authority and filial piety toward parents and ancestors. Violation of that tradition almost inevitably leads to family tension and possible disruption. It is understandable, therefore, that if the Asian American is unable to acquiesce to the teachings and commands of family elders, he will suffer a sense of guilt and shame which colors his behavior, not only in his home but in his total society as well.

Middle Position Virtue

In the training of children, Asian parents emphasize a social norm that cultivates the virtues of the middle position, in which an individual should feel neither haughty nor unworthy. In pursuing this norm, both the child and his peer group are held responsible for his actions. For example, a teacher, in talking to the misbehaving child about a given incident, will at the same time involve the entire class, making the child's destructive behavior a class problem that needs correcting for the sake of the group.

Awareness of Social Milieu

An Asian's consciousness of the welfare of the group also is related to his acute awareness of his social milieu, characterized by social and economic limitations and immobility. Thus, he becomes highly sensitive to the opinions of his peers and allows the social nexus to define his thoughts, feelings, and actions. In the interest of social solidarity, he subordinates himself to the group, suppressing and restraining any disruptive emotions and opinions. Moreover, an Asian American's compliance with social norms, which provides him with social esteem and self-respect, is so fundamental that even differences in wealth and social status are considered no excuse for deviation.

Fatalism

Fatalism, a calm acceptance of one's situation, also pervades the Asian American culture. Constantly buffeted by nature and by political upheaval over which he clearly had no control, the original Asian immigrant adopted a philosophical detachment and resignation that allowed him to accept what he perceived to be his fate with equanimity. Instead of trying to ascertain underlying meanings in events, the Asian met life pragmatically. He became adept at making the most of existing situations rather than attempting to understand and control his environment to create his own opportunities. It is unfortunate that this adaptability, the very factor that contributed to his original success in America, would later become a serious handicap; his continuing silence could only let him fall further behind the alien American culture that encouraged, and indeed demanded, aggressiveness and outspoken individualism.

Inconspicuousness

Experiences with segments of American society which were racist further convinced the Asian immigrant of the need and value of silence and inconspicuousness. Fear of attracting attention was particularly acute among the thousands of immigrants who had come to America illegally to circumvent genocidal immigration laws designed to decimate the Asian American colonies by preventing formation of new ones and denying replacement members to established ones. If caught, these immigrants had little hope of justice; the California Supreme Court ruled in 1855 that their testimony was inadmissible as evidence.[7] Fear and distrust still linger today among the descendants of these immigrants. It is understandable why Asians are extremely reluctant to turn to governmental agencies for aid, even in cases of dire need.

IMPLICATIONS FOR SOCIAL WORK PRACTICE

In view of the potential suspicion and feelings of guilt and shame of the Asian American client who needs social services, initial social worker contacts with him require unique skills and a high level of sensitivity. Considering the Asian American client as an individual who may react differently to conflicts, and considering intra and intercultural group differences, the worker should never let stereotypes cause him to assume knowledge of the client's needs and reactions without first consulting with him.[8] Instead, an open-minded attitude usually will be a key to opening up the client to reveal and discuss his problems. The following example illustrates this point:

> The behavior of Mrs. C's son has recently been out of control. Mrs. C is a widow, an immigrant from a small village of Hong Kong, where the uncle usually assumes the role of disciplinarian when the father is absent. Without implying that Mrs. C should discipline her son, the worker simply asked her what solution she would suggest so that she would not continuously need to worry about her son's behavior. Upon realizing the unavailability of the uncle's assistance, Mrs. C suggested that she had to assume the disciplinarian role herself, for she could no longer endure the misery of continuously seeing her son disgracing her deceased husband.

---

[7]Lyman, *The Asian in the West.*

[8]See Man K. Ho, Cross-Cultural Career Counseling, *Vocational Guidance Quarterly,* 21:3 (March 1973).

An Asian American client who seeks social services is risking possible family rejection and ostracism from his own cultural group. A social worker, therefore, should ensure the confidentiality of his service. Moreover, he should capitalize on the opportunity to point out to the client the kind of strength which he possesses in seeking help and rehabilitation, and to assure him this action is congruent with keeping up his family's good name.

Being aware of an Asian American's expectation of clear role definition and pragmatic approach to problem solving, the worker can reduce client suspicion and resistance if, during the first interview, he openly relates to him the agency's services and functions, and the kind of assistance that he can expect. Further, he should be explicit in discussing his work relationship with the client, who is unaccustomed to functioning with ambiguity. Since generally it takes a great deal of change and effort for an Asian American client to become a social service recipient, the worker should not engage him prematurely in ambitious long-term services and goals. Instead, short-term service with concrete results usually is needed, at least during their first contacts. Then, through witnessing the tangible success of the worker's effort, the client can establish more trust and confidence, and engage in possible long-term services and goals. The social worker should be aware that the majority of Asian American interpersonal problems center upon family conflict and cultural marginality. As a result, treatment service which focuses on exploration of self-identity and fulfillment of self-esteem will have less meaning to the client and may actually enhance guilt feelings derived from his inability to subordinate his own desire to live harmoniously with his parents and peers.

> Mr. B is a second-generation Korean high school student who experiences difficulty in getting along with his immigrant parents who violently object to his long hair. A worker's efforts in helping him to see that his need for wearing long hair has to do with his self-identity caused him to become more depressed and silent as he began to realize that he was satisfying his self-concept at his parents' expense. He withdrew from service after the first agency visit, clearly without having successfully resolved his conflict with his parents.

In view of Asian American client reluctance to admit to problems, suspicion concerning the use of social services, and frequent handicaps in the use of the English language, it is doubtful that the current practice of utilizing confrontative techniques and approaches (such as transactional analysis and Gestalt techniques) can produce effective results in working with this client group. Instead, a directive approach, with emphasis on humanistic attitudes and concrete service, seems to work more effectively.

WORK WITH FAMILIES AND GROUPS

Since admission of problems is seen as a lack of self-control, determination, and willpower, and as a family defect, open sharing of problems in a group is intolerable for most Asian American clients. Therefore, it is doubtful that the active intervention of a single worker who employs the traditional techniques of treating the family as a unit can be effective, because clients will feel that family problems and conflicts should be resolved within the family circle.

Using a Modified Group Approach

Group work practice which conforms to the nuclear family and the extended family structure, however, can produce positive results. [9] The following example demonstrates the involvement of nonparental relatives, within the extended family structure, to achieve a modified group approach to disciplining children.

> Mr. and Mrs. T, a Samoan couple, had a great deal of difficulty in keeping their children from playing in the street. They would punish the children severely by locking them in the closet for a period of twenty-four hours if they were caught. Mrs. M, a relative of the family, discussed the situation with a social worker friend. The worker asked her to arrange a time when the T family could come to her house for tea. After the worker became acquainted with the Ts, he casually brought up the difficulty of rearing children in a strange land. The Ts became very anxious and turned to the worker for advice. The worker in turn referred them to Mrs. M, who revealed that her success in disciplining her children primarily consisted of discussing the situation with them. Times and ways had changed drastically since she was a child, and she was not sure the old way of disciplining was the best, she added.

A family treatment team consisting of a male, a female, and a child worker also can be effective in working with Asian families, as the following experience indicates:

> L.C., an American-born Chinese and a junior high school student, experienced a great many learning difficulties. He habitually skipped school, and, as a result, was unaware of his homework assignments. Both of his parents were passive individuals who were confused by and ashamed of their son's behavior. Also, they were having severe marital problems and were striving to present a facade, pretending their marriage was on solid ground and that it had nothing to do with their son's failing in school.
>
> L.C. was aware of his parents' problems and defensiveness, and took advantage of their vulnerability by indulging himself whenever he pleased. A family treatment team consisting of one male and one female therapist was

---

[9]See Man K. Ho, Outreaching Approach to Counseling with Foreign Students, *Journal of College Student Personnel*, 15:1 (January 1974); Chen C. Chang, Experiences with Group Psychotherapy in Taiwan, *International Journal of Group Psychotherapy*, 22:2 (April 1972).

quite successful in helping the parents to gain some insights into their problems and to communicate more openly and fully; attempts to resolve their son's school problem, however, were met with continuous resistance, especially from L.C. himself, who accused the treatment team of conspiring with his parents against him. With the permission of the family, a child worker, actually the same age as L.C. and a personal friend of the male therapist, was introduced as an additional member of the treatment team. When L.C. repeatedly blamed his parents' marital problems for his own problems, the child worker pointed out that his skipping school was a sign of "copping out" and that continuation of this activity would only bring him failure. "We all have problems, but we have ourselves to blame if we do not live up to our share of responsibilities," added the child worker. The child worker's intervention gradually lessened the guilt feelings of the parents, who later were able to better assume the limiting role in dealing with their son.

For treatment groups to produce therapeutic results, members are expected to confront each other openly from time to time. Such aggressive behavior, however, is looked upon as rude by Asian Americans, who are taught to respect and not to openly challenge others' views. Free participation and exchange of opinions in a group also contradict Asian values of humility and modesty.[10] "Don't be a showoff or engage in any behavior that smacks of being a braggart," is a common Asian admonition, and it is directly responsible for assigning Asian Americans silent-member roles in a group. The following dialogue explains why an Asian American prefers nonverbal participation in a group.

Mr. O was a thoughtful and resourceful member of the group, although he never volunteered his opinion without the worker's encouragement. The rest of the group members valued and listened to what he had to say. When Mr. O was asked for the reasons behind his frequent silences, he said that it is better to be quiet than to ramble on and say nothing or say something that is not well thought out; the talkative person is essentially an attention-seeking, narcissistic individual; besides, the more one talks, the more chance one would have of making mistakes by saying the wrong thing.

Group interaction requiring members to compete with each other will further alienate Asian Americans, who do not wish to be singled out as winners or as losers, both of whom are considered deviants from the Asian cultural norm. Instead, Asian American group members usually welcome participation in a group atmosphere that allows them the opportunity to share problems and help each other with them. The concept of mutual aid and reciprocity is so humanistic and so fundamental to Asian culture that group members operating in this fashion are no longer conscious of the cultural inhibitions and defenses previously prohibiting social worker intervention with their problems. Worker skill in leading a

---

[10]Royal Morales, The Filipino-Americans and Samoans, paper presented at the Los Angeles County Department of Public Social Services Executive Orientation, Affirmative Action Program, Los Angeles, California, August 17, 1970.

reciprocal group of Asian Americans is demonstrated in the following report:

> Long silences, which are usually indicative of group resistance, had plagued a group of Asian Americans. After one such silence, the worker commented that because he did not feel comfortable with the silence, he imagined the members generally felt the same way. He asked the members to identify what was happening so that more could be accomplished within the time allocated for group interaction. One member immediately said that he no longer could afford to waste time sitting in a group in which the members did nothing but stare at each other. He asked the worker if he could share with the group the reason behind his silence. Would that, he added, be answering the worker's concern? The worker thanked him and said that the members' input was most needed for the group to head in the direction that was most beneficial to all members.

A worker's application of reciprocal models or any other humanistic techniques in working with Asian Americans in groups should capitalize on the authority invested in him as a professional and as an agency representative.[11] Instead of letting the group be self-directive, the worker needs to be more assertive and structured, particularly in the beginning stages of group interaction. As the group becomes more cohesive and members become more supportive, the role of the worker should be less directive, because the true value of group process and the dynamics of the group as a whole should be able to flourish without worker manipulation. But worker inability to provide preliminary structure to the group will only enhance group member anxiety and ambiguity, unwelcome to Asian American clients.

WORK WITH ASIAN AMERICANS IN THE COMMUNITY

Asian American avoidance in dealing with conflict presents a great handicap to the community worker who employs conflict as a means for effecting social change and community development. Therefore, it is imperative that the community worker never present himself to the Asian American community as an antagonist or troublemaker. Instead, he should exercise his sincerity to impress upon them his concern and real caring for their welfare. The worker will also find that he can win support from the community if he initiates programs that are small in dimension and sure of success. Since betterment of social milieu and concern for fellowmen is an accepted element of Asian doctrine and cultural consciousness, a community worker may use this element as a leverage point

---

[11]For detailed description of reciprocal group work model, see William Schwartz, Toward a Strategy of Group Work Practice, *Social Service Review,* 36:8 (September 1962); Alan F. Klein *Effective Groupwork: An Introduction to Principle and Method* (New York: Association Press, 1972).

to mobilize collective effort in community action. The following case illustrates this point.

> At a meeting with residents who were concerned with the cleanliness and health problems of a Filipino neighborhood, the worker solicited the group's help by pointing out that, regardless of who was at fault for littering the neighborhood, the Filipinos usually were blamed. The area was identified as a Filipino neighborhood, and its physical appearance would not allow the Filipinos to deny that they were contributing to the problems. After a prolonged and heated discussion, the group finally realized that individual as well as collective efforts were needed to change the image of the neighborhood. By changing the image of the neighborhood, the group felt that each member could "save face." The collective effort to "save face" was directly responsible for a cleaner and more sanitary neighborhood.

COOPERATING WITH COMMUNITY LEADERS

A community worker should be cognizant of the power vested within the established group and family associations in the Asian community. Due to Asian American cultural tradition and social and economic immobility, leaders in Asian American communities tend to have a long history of occupying high positions, and they are usually sensitive to potential threats to their status and interests. Obviously, in working for social change it is essential that this power group, already accepted by the community, not be forgotten or bypassed. Even if the community worker is of Asian American descent, it is essential that he establish positive work relationships with and capitalize on the resources possessed by indigenous leaders; if not, he will only discover later that early winning of the leader's support, rather than alienation, would have been a shorter route to the same goals.[12] An Asian American community will rarely be persuaded by a stranger to make any social change. The change would be too much opposed to tradition and attempts at bringing it about would create uncertainty and negative reactions, all of which could be avoided by involving the community's leaders at the outset in the change efforts.

CONCLUSIONS AND IMPLICATIONS

The term "Asian American" encompasses many ethnic groups, each with intragroup differences; different individuals within each subgroup may react differently to certain conflict or crisis situations. Therefore, it is impossible for a social worker always to know exactly how to react to an Asian American client. As a result, it is necessary that the worker be willing to plead ignorance when necessary, to listen more carefully, to be less ready to come to conclusions, and to be more open to having his presup-

---

[12]Chen, The Chinese Community in Los Angeles, p. 597.

positions corrected by the client. That is, he must want to know what the situation is and must be receptive to being taught.[13] Such an unassuming humanistic attitude is the key to working with Asian Americans.

Additionally, working effectively with the Asian American requires more than merely understanding his cultural background, his American experience, and his present problems. Most importantly, the worker needs to respect him as an individual first, and as an Asian American second. A worker who assumes that traditional Asian society is "primitive" and Western self-directed society is "modern" will be less likely to respect the Asian American as an individual. Respecting an Asian American as a worthy person with cultural differences simply means recognition of the fact that "yellow is not white and white is not right."[14]

Finally, recognizing the fact that yellow is not white has many other important implications, the most obvious being that social work practice knowledge based on white culture is inadequate when applied to Asian Americans. It also implies that there is a need for social work education to incorporate Asiatic culture content in its current curriculum. For Asian American social problems to be effectively ameliorated, there is a need to educate more Asian American social workers and to provide inservice training to agency staff who are currently working with Asian Americans.

---

[13] Alfred Kadushin, The Racial Factor in the Interview, *Social Work,* 7:92 (May 1972).
[14] Kuramoto, What Do Asians Want? p. 12.

31

Asians as Individuals
The Japanese Community

Amy Iwasaki Mass

Prevalent in our society today is an image of Japanese Americans who are conveniently complacent, who are hardworking, outstanding students, and who are well-educated professionals.[1] Quiet, polite, comfortably affluent, and belonging to stable, closely knit families—these are other attributes which commonly characterize the Japanese American. Success stories praising the achievements of Japanese in this country have been seen during the past decade in such widely distributed publications as the *New York Times,* Joseph Alsop's nationally syndicated column, and *Newsweek.*[2] School personnel throughout the country speak with admiration and pride about the attitudes, manner, and performance of good Japanese students. Pediatricians in the suburbs comment on the exceptionally good health and care of their young Japanese American patients. Most people, including social workers and even Japanese Americans themselves, believe in this stereotype. Like all stereotypes, however, this one does a disservice to the individual Japanese American and hampers his freedom to be himself—to find himself, and to be seen by others in the society as an individual.

WEAKNESS OF THE STEREOTYPES

Upon closer examination of the Japanese community, we find many variations from this pat image of a successful homogeneous minority. There are poor, elderly, single Japanese men who live isolated lives in substandard rooming hotels in Little Tokyo. Alcoholism, mental illness, and retarded children are all problems found in some Japanese families.

Reprinted with permission from *Social Casework.* 1976, *57,* 195–201.Copyright Family Service Association of America.

[1]The original draft of this paper was presented at a symposium, Asians as Individuals, at the Society for Clinical Social Work Second Biennial Scientific Conference, Los Angeles, California, October 1973.

[2]Amy Tachiki, *Roots: An Asian American Reader* (Los Angeles, Calif.: Continental Graphics, 1971), p. 1.

Representing a major problem are some three to four thousand war brides who, having come to this country since World War II, now face serious marital, social, and personal adjustments. Of the 25,000 international marriages in 1960 involving Japanese wives, 80 percent ended in divorce by 1964.[3] When such marriages fail, the Japanese women are often unable to return home, having left Japan against their family's wishes; in many instances, they were disowned and now feel too ashamed to return. Now they are alone in this country and have the sole responsibility for raising racially mixed children. Not only are these children socially rejected by Japanese groups in school, but they cannot completely identify with the white, Mexican or black groups to which their fathers belong.

A considerable drug problem plagues the Japanese community; many young people are heavy drug users. A total of thirty-one Asian American deaths through drug overdose were reported in Los Angeles County in 1970, and most of these were Japanese Americans.[4]

Some Japanese American youngsters do not perform well in school, nor do many go on to college to attain the honors and excellence expected of Japanese American students. There are, too, the problem pregnancies—unwed mothers with the accompanying difficulties of raising their children. Wide gaps exist between the generations in terms of outlooks, values, and behavior. As with the rest of the population, divorces are a rising statistic in Japanese American families.

Each of the people in these "nontypical" categories believes that he is part of a small minority. He feels "haji", which is a strong, emotion-laden Japanese term for shame which connotes a sense of responsibility to the family and the Japanese community beyond the individual's personal experience of shame. The atypical Japanese American needs to put up a front, to hide what is troubling him, or as a Japanese community worker graphically stated, "to live a life in the shadows." By not owning up to who they are, these people are kept from seeking out solutions or acting early enough to obtain helpful intervention.

For too long these cultural stereotypes have kept the social work community from becoming cognizant of Japanese problems. There is a great need for help—help given with sensitivity—for awareness and understanding of cultural differences and experience. It is essential to present some background information concerning the Japanese American, his characteristics and his values, and then to discuss current problems and the implications for mental health intervention.

---

[3]Data from Reverend Kogi Sayama, Director, Japanese Community Joint Counselling Center, Los Angeles, California.

[4]Office of Youth and Community Services, City of Gardena, Drug Abuse Statistics, Gardena, California, May 16, 1972.

THE JAPANESE CHARACTER AND ITS CURRENT MANIFESTATIONS

In any discussion of Japanese Americans, it is mandatory to identify the different generational groups. Japanese are the only immigrant group in America who specify by a linguistic term each generation of descendants from the original immigrant group. Immigrants from Japan who were born and raised in Japan and later migrated to the United States between 1885 and 1924 are called "Issei"; literally translated, the term means "first generation." The children of Issei parents are called "Nisei," the "second generation," and "Sansei" are the third generation of Japanese in America. The problems of each group are sufficiently unique to warrant different approaches by the social work profession.

THE ISSEI

The Issei are the Japanese pioneers who came to America with hopes of gaining wealth and perhaps someday returning to Japan once they had made their fortune. They experienced intense racial hatred during the "Yellow Peril" days in the first decades of the 1900s. "Gaman," which connotes emotional self-restraint and the maintenance of strength and endurance in the face of hardships, was a primary value in the character of the Issei. A strong sense of family honor and esteem, requiring that one conduct oneself in a manner that will avoid ridicule or ostracism, was also highly important. These values pervaded the Issei's reactions to the situation during World War II when many Japanese Americans on the West Coast were "relocated" into concentration camps.

Today, Issei in the community are facing basic survival problems typical of most of our senior citizens—income maintenance, housing, and health care. In addition, many reflect depression that stems from feelings of alienation and isolation; from being old and dependent in a country where Japanese values of revering the aged and caring for grandparents in the same home as the younger generation no longer hold true. Moreover, most Issei do not speak English fluently, and the lack of Japanese-speaking people to communicate with in family gatherings, doctors' offices, hospitals, or in other common settings adds to their sense of loneliness and isolation.

THE NISEI

The Issei have essentially maintained their Japanese identity; despite their becoming naturalized citizens, driving on the freeways, and watching sports events and Western movies on color television, they do not think of themselves as Americans. The Nisei, on the other hand, have strong conflicts in their racial identification. When a Nisei is asked, "What are you?" his answer may be "American," "Japanese," or "Japanese American," depending on mood and circumstance. The Nisei are likely to feel defensive no matter which answer they give.

The Japanese family in America up until World War II was an intact, traditional family with prescribed roles, duties, and responsibilities. Issei parents transmitted to their children strong Japanese values of filial piety ("oyakoko") and moral obligation to others ("giri"). Social activities and contacts were mainly with other Japanese. Education was highly valued in the Japanese family, and Nisei children were encouraged to participate fully and perform with excellence in the American educational system. Nisei, who were trained to respect authority, learned about America, the land of the free where everyone is equal regardless of race, creed, or color. Nisei pledged allegiance to the American flag and were exposed to the myth that the United States is a harmonious melting pot, where any American citizen can become president, can become rich, successful, and highly educated with effort and perserverance. The Nisei were fully exposed to both Japanese and American values, and struggled with the resulting conflicts.

Despite the great American dream, however, there was strong anti-Japanese feeling on the West Coast prior to World War II. College-educated Nisei were unable to obtain professional jobs or to move freely and comfortably in non-Japanese social circles.

Impact of World War II

World War II had a tremendous impact on the character of the Nisei. They were stunned—along with the rest of the country—with the news of the Pearl Harbor attack on December 7, 1941. The ensuing weeks and months became a period of intense fear, confusion, and anxiety for the Japanese living on the West Coast. Men and women who had recent affiliations with Imperial Japan were taken by FBI agents into internment camps, and children were afraid they might wake up in the morning to find their parents gone. Pictures of Abraham Lincoln and George Washington appeared on the walls of Japanese homes in the pathetic hope that this would demonstrate loyalty to America. Japanese walked around with American flag pins and with "I am an American" pins on coat lapels. Nevertheless, curfew regulations were instituted, and if a Japanese needed to travel at night, he had to crouch in the back seat of a car driven by a non-Asian friend. The myth of making it in America quickly crumbled. The student body president of Belmont High School in Los Angeles, a Nisei, was removed from office; Japanese businessmen were forced to sell out; university students had to withdraw from school. Between March and August of 1942, more than 110,000 West Coast Japanese (over two-thirds American citizens) were removed from their homes to concentration camps under the War Relocation Authority.

Emotional self-restraint, "gaman"—the Japanese way to handle hardship—was the main psychological defense used to survive this period. The feelings of fear, rage, and helplessness were repressed, and the cooperative, obedient, "quiet American" facade was used to cope with an overtly hostile, dangerous, racist America.

The picture of the Japanese American, that young fellow with thick, black-rimmed glasses, concentrating at his desk, reading his lesson, and never making trouble, is painfully understandable in the shadow of World War II. Many have tried to explain the Nisei's manner in terms of transmitted cultural values. The quiet, self-controlled, detached manner of the Nisei has been seen as a modeling after the Samurai, who had strict control over their emotions. Following World War II, however, the Nisei did not have the pride or aggressiveness of his Samurai ancestor; his head was bent in nonverbalized shame over his Japanese ancestry. He endeavored to prove his "all-Americanness."

The so-called positive attributes of the Japanese American—docility, patience, industriousness—are characteristics developed as a defense against life in a racist society. As long as Nisei assume the qualities that gain praise from the white majority, Japanese Americans are an acceptable minority group. But the price of acceptance by accommodation is the loss of the individual's own self-acceptance and sense of self-worth. This image places an exaggerated emphasis on such surface qualities as a pleasant, nonoffensive manner, neat grooming and appearance, a good job, a nice home, a new car, and well-behaved children.

Prevalent clinical problems now being revealed in the Nisei population are psychosomatic disorders such as essential hypertension, peptic ulcers, and depression. These disorders reflect the defenses of repression, denial, and suppression so widely used by the Japanese.

THE SANSEI

The Nisei's drive to succeed, to achieve, and to prove himself as "making it" in America, has put tremendous pressure on the Sansei to excel. Nisei parents push their children to be in the top one percent of the school. Overachievers are more characteristic of this minority group than are underachievers among the black and brown minorities. Community workers agree that the extensive drug problem in the Japanese community is in large part a reaction to the tremendous pressure to be Number One. Because not everyone can be Number One, and average or even passing grades constitute insufficient performance to please parents or to fit the school's stereotyped expectation of the Japanese student, drugs offer a ready escape. The Sansei youth does not feel that there are many alternatives open to him. He has to be a high achiever or he is nothing. The use of drugs is an expression of the Sansei's despair with his situation.

One step removed from the direct experience of camp life during World War II, the Sansei generation has been able to ask questions and raise issues about the whole Japanese American experience. Influenced by the Black Awareness and Brown Power movements, Sansei young people started in the late 1960s to examine the whole question of their Asian American identity. This healthy ability to question and reexamine values has led to many grass-roots self-help organizations. It has also exposed the unresponsiveness of existing community services to the needs of the Japanese American.

IMPLICATIONS FOR MENTAL HEALTH

There are very strong negative attitudes toward mental illness in the Japanese community. The need for mental health services has always been seen as shameful. Issei, who arrived in America during the late 1800s and early 1900s were strong, highly motivated young men who came to attain material success. The values of working hard and not making trouble, as well as the idea that suffering strengthens character, are reflected in the negative Japanese attitudes toward mental problems. "I ga yowai" which means "Your guts are weak," or "Ki ga chi i sai," meaning "Your spirit is small," are Japanese idioms that describe a person with psychological problems.

Language barriers and unfamiliarity with the existing institutions in a community also prevent many needy, particularly the aged and new immigrants, from seeking services to which they are entitled. The camp experience with the War Relocation Authority has also undoubtedly affected the Japanese American's attitude toward involvement with governmental agencies.

Equally serious barriers to the delivery of services to the Japanese community are the insensitivity and ignorance of community agencies, many of which prefer to maintain the myth that Japanese Americans are successful and do not need help. The social worker who acts on the stereotype of the model Japanese and expects Japanese clients to live up to this ideal will be doing his clients a great disservice. The struggle for meaningful identity is the crux of the Asian's problem, and the social work community has a responsibility to meet this need with sensitivity and understanding.

32

Therapy for Asian Americans

Joe Yamamoto

In order that Asian Americans be more adequately provided with mental health services, it will be necessary to: (1) have a thorough educational campaign over a long period of time to help Asians overcome their negative prejudices against mental illness, (2) devise culturally relevant diagnostic techniques, and (3) have treatment consonant with the cultural backgrounds of the patients and befitting the role expectations of the patients. It is likely that even with an excellent educational campaign, appropriate diagnoses, and culturally sensitive treatment methods, the first patients we will see will be those most seriously and chronically disturbed, probably when the family feels no longer able to cope with their psychotic behavior. We hope that subsequently, through the educational campaign and also through the outreach efforts of the Asian Mental Health Clinic, Asian Americans who are not psychotic but who want relief from psychosomatic syptoms, tension, depression, or help with family or marital problems will apply.

Any consideration of therapy for Asian Americans would have to address the most important problem, namely the underutilization of mental health services by Asian Americans and Pacific Islanders. This is evident in reports from Honolulu, Seattle, and Los Angeles. In all of these cities, Asian Americans and Pacific Islanders tend to significantly underutilize mental health services. This underuse is due to a combination of the attitudes brought by Asians from their homelands, of prejudice against the mentally ill and mental health services. The fact that available mental health services are conceptualized from Western European traditions, diagnostic techniques, and therapeutic modalities also detracts. Little has been done to initiate techniques consonant with the cultural values of Asian Americans.

Presented to the 82nd Annual Convention of the National Medical Association, Los Angeles, California, July 31-August 4, 1977.

Reprinted with permission from the *Journal of the National Medical Association,* 1978, *70* (4), 267–270.

Sue and Sue in 1971[1] reported that while Asians, in general, underutilize mental health services, those who did apply were severely sick. These findings suggest that only the most seriously disturbed Asians seek help from traditional mental health facilities. Lam[2] has had similar experiences at the LAC-USC Medical Center.

Kitano[3] and Reynolds[4] reported that many of the schizophrenic Asian-American patients admitted to state mental hospitals had been nonfunctional at home for many years prior to admission to hospital. Only when the patient disturbed the family tranquility, for example, in threatening a member of the family or becoming visible as a psychotic so as to cause neighborhood concern and the family to feel shame, would the patient be presented for admission to a state hospital.

The attitudes of Asians toward the mentally ill are those of fear, rejection, and ridicule. The families are reluctant to admit the existence of a "crazy" person in the family since such an admission might affect the economic and social status of the other members of the family in the eyes of the community (e.g., chances for a good job or for a proper marriage). Another reason that mental health services are underutilized is the conflict between the prevalent and traditional values of Asian Americans and the values that are implicit in the therapeutic process. In 1973, Kunishige[5] noted that Western therapy emphasizes the individual worth of each person and self-growth towards greater maturity. The increase in self-understanding is an important goal. Patients are encouraged to be expressive of their emotions, rather than to stifle them. Therapists who have such a Western orientation may be totally unaware that the conditions of therapy and the goals of therapy may often run counter to the values of some of their patients. Asian Americans thus encounter a number of conflicts if they try to participate in the therapeutic process prescribed as a way of resolving their conflicts. In a presentation at the Asian Research and Development Center in 1976, this writer expressed the feeling that most psychotherapy is essentially a white, Anglo-Saxon, middle-class activity. As such, the therapy would not be understood or felt as culturally relevant by traditional Asian-Americans. They tend to have lower verbal facility, greater verbal inhibition, and lower tolerance for ambiguity. These traits would tend to make Asians uncomfortable in psychotherapy geared to individuals with high verbal functioning, high emotional expressiveness, and greater tolerance for ambiguity.

In addition, the unacculturated Asian has a need for a bilingual therapist and there is a shortage especially in areas of rapidly increasing population density (e.g., Los Angeles). The Korean population has increased remarkably so that there are now estimated to be 80,000 Koreans in Los Angeles, of whom perhaps 50,000 have arrived within the last five years.

BICULTURAL THERAPIST

For the Asian-American patient, the bicultural therapist will be able to more sensitively explore the questions of what does the patient want and what will best help the patient to achieve his own objectives as agreed upon with the therapist. It is believed that a bicultural therapist with a knowledge of the experiences and cultural background will be able to more sensitively explore these issues than a therapist with solely Western experience. This may be especially true of the "indirect" request for help often characteristic of Asian patients. Because the patient may be unable to directly request specific help, the therapist may have to be very careful in looking for clues as to what is indirectly apparent, or the request may be entirely overlooked.

Because of the shared cultures, the therapist will be much better able to explore the role conflicts that Asians may encounter in the greater society and also in interpersonal relationships at home. Naturally, factors such as ethnicity, acculturation, generation, class, and geographical location in the United States will have to be evaluated. All of these are relevant because the Asian roots, while similar, are not identical and the degree of acculturation will certainly change the traditional Asian values, the older generations will tend to be more traditional, those from the upper classes may have been educated sometimes with a combination of Asian and European methods, etc. The geographic location in the United States is important. If a person of Asian descent grows up in Hawaii where Asians are in the majority, the ability to have a positive sense of identity is high because the educators, the government officials, the leaders, the elite, are Asian Americans. In contrast, in mainland cities where Asians are often a tiny minority, they may grow up isolated in ghetto-like communities like Korea Town, Little Tokyo, Manila Town, or China Town.

For Asian Americans, it is important to realize that extended family ties may be much more important than among American middle-class families where the emphasis is on the nuclear family. Thus, the socialization objective among Japanese families may be for close and harmonious functioning within a family-like atmosphere, with the "family" at work also being paternalistic and providing fringe benefits of various sorts. In return the workers are expected to show diligence, loyalty, and dedication in their work. This fits the Japanese conception of mutual interdependency. Just as the whole Japanese society is family oriented, so too are the unacculturated families here in the United States. There is a tendency for the children to stay at home until the time of marriage. Thus the fact that an adult stays at home within the parental situation is not an indication per se of more than average dependency needs, this is more a cultural expression of the close family ties.

The bicultural therapist, in addition to understanding the close family ties and mutual interdependency within Asian families, will also be aware that many Asians have been socialized to communicate their needs indirectly, to show a certain hesitancy about saying how it is. In fact, in the Japanese culture, there is such a stress on behaving in a proper way with authority figures such as physicians, that even patients who are psychotically depressed will try to pull themselves together, minimize their complaints, and behave in a dignified and respectful manner.

The bicultural therapist will understand the role expectations of the patients. In most Asian societies the emphasis is on a vertical relationship. This has been well described by Nakane[6] in her description of an emphasis on superior and inferior relationships. The Western psychotherapist's assumption in conventional therapy is that the situation will be democratic and the patient will be free to express himself in a safe and confidential atmosphere. The bicultural therapist will understand that the patient expects and, depending on the degree of his/her acculturation, will respond to the therapist as an authority figure who is trying to understand what the problem is and who assumes the leadership role much as a teacher might with a pupil. The assumption of the authority role of a learned professional will be relatively frequent compared to the neutral, nonjudgmental, noncritical role assumed in Western type of therapy. The goal will thus be less often insight and much more often coping with the problems.

TREATMENT FOCUS

Because of their great feelings of shame and reluctance about psychotherapy, therapy designed for Asian Americans should be promulgated and advocated as being aimed towards the relief of the following symptoms and psychological problems: (1) tension symptoms; (2) insomnia; (3) psychosomatic complaints, including hypertension; (4) specific interpersonal problems, such as marital difficulties or family conflicts; and (5) problems of self-development, including dealing with male/female role conflict between those learned in the American schools and the expectations prevalent in the Asian-American family. This will de-emphasize mental illness and the labeling as psychotic of all who see mental health professionals.

It is important to de-emphasize psychiatric labeling in a pejorative sense. In addition to the important task of educating the community and all Asian Americans about appropriate use of mental health services, we must make efforts toward better diagnoses. We have an audiovisual version of the Psychiatric Status Schedule (PSS) of Spitzer, Endicott, and Cohen.[7] The audiovisual version with a standardized translation of the

PSS into various languages will be useful training for people who may be volunteers or non-mental health professionals, for example, nurses with relatively little mental health background. For those who have had the experience of interviewing a patient who speaks only a foreign language through an interpreter, the advantages of a standardized automated translation into different languages are quite apparent.

The PSS booklet is such that the patient can be examined in whatever language is necessary, the responses from the answer sheet can then be placed upon the English language version of the PSS, and the clinician can see what the responses are.

Although it is difficult to translate certain concepts into different languages, we believe that the method, utilizing translations which have been made by mental health professionals who are bilingual and bicultural, has much to offer in the future towards better diagnostic experiences for Asian Americans and Pacific Islanders.

As there are translations of the Minnesota Multiphasic Personality Inventory (MMPI) into Chinese, Japanese, and Korean, it would be of interest to compare the results from the PSS with those from the MMPI, including an abbreviated version.

THE TREATMENT OF ASIAN AMERICANS AND PACIFIC ISLANDERS

When treatment is considered for individuals who come from varying cultural backgrounds, it is of prime importance to consider how their cultural background may affect the role expectations of the patient and treatment techniques that are suitable. For example, careful consideration of Morita and Naikan therapy suggest that these Japanese psychotherapies have cultural roots which make them specifically relevant for Japanese patients.

Morita therapy which has roots in Zen Buddhism was originated by Professor Morita who treated patients with a neurotic syndrome of psychasthenia, shyness, and inhibition which in the Japanese is called *Shinkeishitsu*. The original method of Morita therapy was a program of treatment on a hospital ward. The patient was admitted and isolated for a period of one to two weeks. During this time he was expected to stay in bed except for very limited activities such as bathing, meals, etc. The instructions were that the patient keep a diary and that this diary would be discussed by the physician. At prescribed intervals, the physician would visit the patient to discuss the entries in the diary. The fact of isolation from other family members and society at large is a very important one in Japan. Unlike Americans, for the Japanese the whole emphasis is on the family so that all the activities are done as a unit. Indeed, after beginning school, many activities are done as a member of the school class and school group. For the rest of their lives then, the Japanese live as members of various groups whether at home, at work, or in social activities (university alumni associations, etc). The ties with these groups are so strong that by and large workers do not change from one job to another. As Lebra[8] has pointed out, there is strong emphasis on social adaptation. The concept is of mutual interdependency, for the employing company, on the other hand, does much to be protective and paternalistic toward the workers, offering health insurance, vacation facilities, bonuses twice a year, and encouraging a feeling of strong "family" ties in the work situation.[4]

Thus, the patient in Morita therapy is a part of the social context. After the week or two of isolation from other patients, professionals, and family, the physician may decide that the patient is ready to begin the second step of treatment which is a program of prescribed activities. A part of the assignment during the second phase is for the patient to be aware of being able to function and to disregard the troubling neurotic symptoms. The point being that the patient learns the value of functional capability and also learns to devalue the neurotic symptoms. Instead of being preoccupied with his neurotic suffering, the patient is encouraged to function and to focus his attention on his ability to perform. This ability to perform is a very important aspect of a culture which is achievement oriented and focuses upon each individual producing and achieving to his or her utmost abilities. The end product in Morita therapy then is a person who is able to function, has devalued his or her neurotic symptoms and, thus, subsequently will feel less troubled. The patients are told quite directly that they are not responsible for their feelings or thoughts, but that they can change what they are doing and thus function as well as possible. Again, they are confronted with the fact that what they produce is something they can change with proper attention and guidance.

In Naikan therapy, originated among prisoners, the patient is advised to sit and reflect upon his/her past life, which is divided into three-year segments. The patient is, thus, again confronted with his/her obligations to parents, teachers, peers, siblings, and society. This redevelopment of a sense of responsibility and obligation towards others is a very important part of the Japanese society for the Japanese are socialized to be aware of their obligations and how they affect others in the environment. As you can imagine, the individual who has a personality disorder may have learned to be less considerate of those around him and needs to learn to be more "Japanese" and considerate of others and aware of his responsibilities and obligations. Both Morita therapy and Naikan therapy are well related to the cultural values. Far from aiming at an individual who will be aware of his needs, wishes, feelings, and fantasies, the emphasis is upon social adaptation. Both therapies thus fit the prime objective of Japanese socialization and social adaptation and from this viewpoint, are much more consonant with the cultural backgrounds of Japanese generally.

How will this influence our treatment of Asian patients in the United States? It is quite clear that to the extent that the Asians are unacculturated and strongly influenced by their earlier socialization, therapy will have to be tailored to their cultural backgrounds. Two examples will suffice. The first concerns the concept of dependency and independency. In the United States, it is popular to assume that the objective is to be independent. Thus the emphasis in the last generation or two has been on the nuclear family and the individual as a developing self, increasing awareness, and emphasizing self fulfillment. The myth of the American cowboy, pioneering, and progressing alone on horseback and challenging all frontiers has contributed mightily towards the emphasis on individuality.

In addition, technological changes subsequent to the Industrial Revolution have also contributed towards increasing urbanization and subsequent loosening of ties among kith and kin. Some of this has happened without conscious planning or even awareness. Families are not as they used to be. Now the young mother learning to be a mother is much more dependent upon Dr. Spock or some latter-day book on infant and child care than the grandmother or aunt and uncle who once taught her how to socialize the baby and child. In addition, with the emphasis on more flexible socialization of children, there has been increasing insecurity and ambiguity about proper parenting. Thus, there is room for all sorts of authoritative dicta about how best to socialize babies and children. These two influences, the emphasis on individualism and the loosening of ties among people generally due to urbanization and the technological revolution have resulted in a picture of interpersonal relationships which is different in the United States than in most of the nations of the world.[9]

One might say that the other nations as they urbanize and become more highly technological will gradually change. For the present, the generation of patients from Asia that we shall see in the United States has been socialized in quite a different way. In general they have been taught much more respectful attitudes towards parents and authority figures. The emphasis is on mutual interdependency and not on individualism. Thus, treatment techniques may have to be tailored to these different conceptions of interpersonal relationships and family roles. The objective of therapy may not be individualism, so much as coping within a family context at home and also coping with family support in the surrounding environment. In this light, then, the patient and the patient's family may be seen much more frequently than among the average American patient population. The objective will be a family treatment approach not to find the scapegoat or the double bind, but to use the family team as a cooperating, facilitating, and restoring group aiming towards the improved functioning of the defined patient.

Another example has to do with the mental health conception of appropriate roles. The popular view that American mental health professionals have is of a democratic, relatively neutral, objective, and noncritical individual who is open, accepting, and empathic. This fits the democratic needs of American individualists when they seek therapy. However, when Asians seek help, they may be looking for much more structure. For example, in the Japanese society it would be expected that the therapist would be like a learned teacher *(Sensei)* who having learned the problem will lead the way towards the best solution. The patient and the family will be considered, but as members of this treatment team towards improved functioning. The role then will be with due acceptance of the vertical structure of society and the hierarchical relationship between the doctor and the patient and the patient's family. The authority of the doctor must be invoked at times with direct advice about what to do or what not to do.

In order to promote more accurate diagnoses, bicultural and bilingual personnel and translations of the Psychiatric Status Schedule of Spitzer, Endicott, and Cohen into Chinese (Cantonese, Seyup, and Mandarin), Japanese, and Korean are needed. Translations into Filipino, Vietnamese, and Samoan are in progress.

LITERATURE CITED

1. Sue S, Sue DW: Chinese-American personality and mental health. Amerasia J 1:36–49, 1971.
2. Lam J: personnal communication, 1977.
3. Kitano HHL: Japanese American mental illness. In Plog S, Edgerton E (eds): Changing Perspectives in Mental Illness. New York, Holt Rinehart and Winston, 1969, pp. 256–284.
4. Reynolds B: The Quiet Therapies. unpublished manuscript.
5. Kuneshige E: Cultural Factors in Counseling and Interaction. Personnel and Guidance J 51:407–412, 1973.
6. Nakane C: Japanese Society. Berkeley, University of California Press, 1970, pp. 1–151.
7. Spitzer RL, Endicott J, Cohen GM: Psychiatric Status Schedule. Evaluation Unit, Biometrics Research, New York State Department of Mental Hygiene, New York State Psychiatric Institute, Department of Psychiatry, Columbia University, New York, October 1968, pp. 1–21.
8. Lebra TS: Japanese Patterns of Behavior. Honolulu, University Press of Hawaii, 1976, pp. 1–258.
9. Anthony P: On the Boring Patient. Psychiatric News 12: July 15, 1977, pp. 18, 19, 24.

33

Identity Conflict and
Acculturation Problems
in Oriental-Americans

Vita S. Sommers

For my presentation today, I have selected two cases of Oriental-Americans from a group of similar patients with whom I have worked at the Los Angeles VA Mental Hygiene Clinic. One of these World War II veterans is an American-born Chinese; the other, a Japanese-American. They are presented: 1) to examine the interdependence and cross-influence of psychological and cultural processes in personality functioning; and 2) to demonstrate how psychocultural conflicts can be resolved.

From empirical evidence we know that psychocultural problems can be expected in many second-generation Americans. This is particularly true in those cases where the two cultures are at great variance with each other, especially with regard to family tradition and family structure. For instance, the authoritarian elements in the parent-child relationship weigh more heavily in the hierarchical climate of the Japanese or Chinese family than in the democratic traditions of the American family setting. Members of a Western culture are likely to feel it a sign of strength to rebel against tradition and parental authority, whereas, according to the Oriental culture which stresses that "one should serve one's parents as one serves heaven," strength of character is shown in *conforming* and not in *rebelling*. No wonder then that any violation of this Confucian doctrine invokes in its adherents severe conflicts.

> Chune is a 29-year-old Chinese who was born and raised in California. Obsessional thoughts and fears of death and insanity brought him into therapy.
>   When I first saw this young man I was struck by his youthful and delicate appearance. His shy and gentle look contrasted with the nature of his obsessional fears "to pierce a knife into my brother's neck," and "to bring death to my mother and to myself."

Presented at the 1959 Annual Meeting.

Reprinted with permission from the *American Journal of Orthopsychiatry*, 1960, *30*, 637–644. Copyright © 1980 by the American Orthopsychiatric Association, Inc.

Chune lost his father at the age of 2. His brother, two years his senior, took over the paternal role as a disciplinarian. When the patient was 8, his mother fell seriously ill. She returned to her family in China to secure a home for her two sons in case of her death. At the outbreak of the Sino-Japanese War, when Chune was 15, the mother sent the two boys back to the States while she herself remained in China. She was never able to rejoin her sons in this country.

Ever since Chune can remember, he had to work for "white" people. He resented the fact that he always had to "please" people. All his life he felt that white people were "superior" to Chinese. He held his feeling of inferiority responsible for his inability to relate to people. Initially in treatment, he found it equally difficult to relate to the therapist. He firmly believed, "There is no sense in talking; one can think about problems, but you don't talk about them to people." Not talking was identical for him with "not losing face." In spite of many critical feelings toward Americans, he wished he could be an American. He felt deeply ashamed of being Chinese.

When I reflected that it must have been confusing for him to have lived in two entirely different cultures, Chune felt grateful that I could understand him, for he finds it difficult to make an adjustment to either one. He feels different among Americans, and equally different among Chinese. "I feel I'm a stranger everywhere; I'm even a stranger to my mother. I feel I'm all alone in the world." He talked a great deal about the difference between American and Chinese parent-child relationships, saying, "In China, children are completely submissive to the wishes of their parents, especially to their mothers, whereas American parents seem to submit to the wishes of their children." He was envious of the "buddy-buddy relationship between American parents and children. They have more fun while Chinese children have more fear... and are trained to obey."[1] All of his life he was made to think, "Why argue with an authority if you know you cannot win?"

As therapy progressed, he became increasingly outspoken in his dislike for China. He exclaimed, "I feel everything is wrong with China." The more he verbalized feelings of shame, the more it became apparent that the shame was related to his own person. As he became aware of it, he related it primarily to his "small size" and some of his other Oriental features. He felt he didn't look like a man. To him, all Americans appeared manly, husky, and superior. Also, his poor English bothered him. He resented the fact that "even though I was born here, people call me Chinese." With a good deal of feeling, he often commented, "I wish I were white." Being white meant to him feeling accepted, secure, justified in being self-assertive; whereas being Chinese was identical with submission, discrimination and rejection. He admitted that Chinese philosophy is good, but he strongly disapproved of Chinese culture. He said, "It is weighted down by tradition. One person out of a hundred is able to read and write and my own mother is illiterate." A strong positive transference relationship stimulated fantasies such as being adopted by a white parent or wanting to marry a white girl.

During his Army service he had dated white girls only. This was the only time in his life that he was aggressive, that he didn't feel inferior. In fact, he felt very proud of himself because he was the youngest first sergeant in a mixed Army unit. He had more than 100 men under his command and was

---

[1]There is a Chinese mental illness called "Latah," which is a trancelike state marked by automatic obedience.

chosen out of 1200. He believed that it must have been his military uniform which gave him an appearance of manliness and importance, and a feeling of success. He wondered, "How come that I feel so utterly unmanly now? Do I have two personalities?"

With the aid of therapy he recognized how the uniform had given him permission to release his hostility and aggression. Also, he gradually realized how returning to a civilian's role made him once again repress his urges to fight, to hurt, and to assert himself. He came to see how this "re-repression" evoked anxiety and led him to depreciate and even hate himself. In spite of his increase in awareness of his angry and destructive feelings, Chune remained unable to bring out any kind of negative feelings, either toward his brother or his mother, or toward the therapist. Whenever this was pointed out to him, he would protect himself by saying, "How can I feel angry? My mother, my brother and you, all have done so much for me."

In working with Orientals and other members of ethnic minorities, I have frequently encountered marked transference resistance, which stems primarily from the fact that these patients try to conceal their deep feelings of hatred of a parent image or of a white authority figure because of their fear of retaliation. The idealization of, and identification with a white parent figure is then often extended to the white race as a whole, thereby intensifying already existent racial and intrapsychic conflict and distortion of transference responses. Therefore, after a year of individual therapy, Chune was placed in a therapeutic group with other members of ethnic minorities.[2]

It was only four months after he had joined the group and listened to other patients who brought out open resentment and contempt for their mothers and brothers that Chune began to drop his defenses and expose some of his negative feelings, first toward his mother and later toward his brother. Whenever he had done so in individual therapy, he used to add, "Perhaps I'm confused, I don't really understand what I'm saying." Chune told the group members how throughout his life he resented the fact that he could not be proud of his mother, who is "illiterate, eats with chopsticks and lives on husks of rice." A few sessions later he recalled that at the age of 12 he once threw a pair of scissors at his brother. Prior to this he never dared to hit his brother because of his mother's tearful pleas, "My children are all I have—I cannot understand why brothers should want to kill each other."

He told the group how he hated his brother's thriftiness. He also remembered how often he had avoided his brother's company; how on New Year's Eve he had failed to keep a date with his brother, and felt panicky when he later bumped into him on the street. "I was overwhelmed by my guilt when I looked at him and saw how lonely he felt. I thought, I'm like an

[2]"In group therapy the support and mutual acceptance of the other group members who often serve in a sibling relationship encourage 'catharsis-in-the-family'—without fear of retaliation. Apparently the siblings serve as an insulation against the fear of authority and thus lessen guilt and anxiety, reduce suspicion and lower resistance" Vita S. Sommers, *An Experiment in Group Psychotherapy with Members of Mixed Minority Groups,* Int. J. Group Psychother., 3:265, 1953.

animal, having no brain. If I had a brain, I couldn't act this way." The patient added that in the past he had never thought of himself as a hostile person; now he can see himself as he actually is.

After Chune and the other members of the group had related many similar experiences, which were associated with feelings of shame and guilt, the group was helped to understand how their own thoughts and feelings of hatred and revenge toward a family member and other people created in them a sense of unworthiness and self-hatred, and how they had projected some of these reactions onto the outer world, thinking that this was how people were judging them. In actuality this view of the outer world was largely a reflection of their own feelings about themselves. Chune was also helped to see how in the past he might have tried to suppress these feelings of hatred and aggression and might have used his race and culture as a projection defense to conceal some of his own inner conflicts from himself and others.

The more the patient reached an understanding of himself through treatment, the more accepting he became of his race and culture. His better acceptance of his Oriental background was most vividly expressed in his marriage to a Chinese girl, in the changed focus of his vocational career, and in the opening of his studio called "Oriental Design." Initially in treatment, as a student of industrial arts, he criticized China for "being weighed down by traditions; people live with furniture that is thousands of years old in design; tables are still in one and the same place in every home; beds have no springs; stoves still burn wood." He was planning to design "American furniture." In the later phase of treatment he changed his plans. Now he is designing Chinese furniture that is more suitable for the American and more functional for the Chinese home.

Summarizing briefly, we may say that this patient's problems stem from low self-esteem and self-hatred which generated from multiple sources: from his lack of basically secure and growth-inducing relationships; inability to identify with a parent figure; intense sibling rivalry and, last but not least, from the conflicting aspects of his dual cultural background. The rivalry situation appears in this case to be magnified by his brother's taking over the father's place. Thus we are led to believe that some of his feelings of discrimination have actually originated in his own home and given him the subjective impact of his intense feelings of worthlessness and difference. Obviously, these feelings were highly sharpened and magnified in later years by his having lived on the fringes of two widely different cultures. We know that the differences in the value systems of these two cultures—American and Chinese—make identity and acculturation processes much harder, Chune manifested an ardent desire to be a Caucasian. The constant discrepancy between illusion and actuality, fantasy and reality, created a constant source for frustration and brought forth strong feelings of hatred and aggressive thoughts and wishes for which his brother became the scapegoat. These hostile thoughts, in turn, produced anxiety, guilt and depressed feelings. In his guilt he experienced all kinds of retaliatory fears, which were evidenced primarily in his fear of death and insanity. In part, he tried to repress and conceal his deep feelings of aggression and hate in submissive, compliant and withdrawal attitudes, and in a constriction of affect. The war and its aftermath, especially his return to his "inferior and subservient" role as a civilian, shook up his tenuous defense against turbulent hostility and pushed him into a severe neurosis.

The next case will again indicate how culture conflict can become an integral part of neurotic problems and thus make their resolution highly difficult and complicated.

Ichiro is a 32-year-old, American-born and American-reared (nisei) veteran. He is a handsome, intelligent, highly articulate young man, married and the father of a 5-year-old boy. Ichiro represents an interesting psychocultural study by virtue of at least three aspects of his development: He was reared in the spirit of Oriental ideology, and later adopted Occidental culture; he was exposed to two religions, for his mother was educated as a Methodist, while his father remained Buddhist; he was brought up in two languages—he spoke Japanese at home and English outside. Much like the first case, he was tormented by suicidal thoughts and fears of losing his mind. After ten months in the Army he was medically discharged for bleeding ulcers. Also, like the first patient, he was in psychotherapy for a period of over three years.

Ichiro is the oldest son in a family of eight children. His parents migrated to this country and settled as farmers after the father had made numerous unsuccessful attempts to secure engineering work, for which he had been highly trained in Japan. The farmers nicknamed him "the philosopher and poet," for he thought and talked about poetry rather than potatoes, and Confucius instead of crops. The patient described his father as a harsh, volatile, opinionated person with a brilliant mind. He was feared by the patient "more than anyone and anything in the world." Ichiro considered his mother puritanical, and "warm in a distant way only."

Ichiro thinks his trouble started "way back," probably at the age of three, when he acted like a "scaredy cat" and his father, who admired "strength and fearlessness," used "shock treatment" to overcome his many fears. He thinks he reached the "peak" of his conflicts in his adolescent years. He played football at the time he had to feed the horses, or he read when he should have cleaned the stable. When his father checked up on his chores, Ichiro tried to lie or make excuses. Every so often he was "beaten to the ground" for lying. He quoted his father as saying, "If I can't handle my oldest son, how will I be able to handle the other children?" As the patient put it, "The more brutally I was treated, the more obstinate and defiant I became; and the more I feared my father, the more I hated him."

As a boy he always felt deeply ashamed of his father. He resented not only his outlandish manner, his sloppy appearance, and his poor English, but also his disregard for boyish pleasure and happiness. The father made a virtue of being different, and the more he stressed the difference, the more eager Ichiro was to overconform to American thoughts and habits. He said, "I hated everything Japanese." At an early age he decided to become an English teacher and writer. He defied his father's wish that he become an engineer.

Ichiro had no clearly defined notion of who he was or how he ought to behave. He was torn between rebellion and conformity; between a desire for freedom and fear of independence; between hate and a desire for love. Hence, it was no wonder that he finally broke down at the time of an acute "identity crisis." His lifelong struggle for psychocultural self-definition took on very disturbing reality features when in World War II he experienced conflicting loyalties as a Japanese-American soldier. Prior to Pearl Harbor, he had identified wholly with American ideals and values. After entering the military service—he served as a medical corpsman in the States—he felt "like a being from another planet with thoughts and feelings that have no use in this world." He now felt rejected by America, just as he himself had previously rejected everything related to Japan. This experience had reinforced his identity diffusion and remobilized his sense of not belonging, which left him, in the words of a poet whom he quoted, "wandering between two worlds, one dead, the other powerless to be born."

As might be expected, in the initial phase of therapy his transference feelings were markedly affected, not only by his angry feelings toward his parents, especially his father, but also by his attitude to the traditional subservient role of women in Japan. In the first five months of therapy his relationship with me was strongly colored by distrust and contempt. He called me "illogical" when I pointed to his feelings; "inscrutable" when I turned questions back to him; "a liar," when I denied that I was angry at him; "unbashful female" when I referred to sex. It was necessary *to understand both the roots of such feelings in his culture and to appreciate the special psychodynamic significance* they had for the patient. A proper evaluation of the interplay between culturally influenced attitudes and neurotic needs requires careful understanding of both.

After his distrust and anger abated and his tender feelings emerged in the treatment situation, Ichiro repeatedly questioned whether he really knew his father. "Perhaps I battled the old boy too hard. I didn't give him a chance to love me." He gradually recognized that his father might have been well-meaning and right in many ways, but that he had failed in making Ichiro understand and recognize that he was right. Obviously, his father treated him as the oldest son and the heir in the hierarchical Japanese family, rather than as a child with personal needs. This new discovery, besides many other newly gained insights, helped him realize that his feelings of resentment were mixed with a good deal of admiration for his father.

In the fourteenth month of therapy Ichiro read his first book on Japan, *The Chrysanthemum and the Sword*. He knew that these kinds of books existed but "I was never interested in learning anything about Japan." In reaction to the book he said, "Now I can see that my father has been a darn good father from the Japanese point of view. Too bad that our ideas have been rooted in two different premises. . . . No understanding was possible between my father and myself because of our cultural and language barriers—I realize I have been a wellspring of resentment." He also began to realize that he had gone "overboard" in his Americanization and that his occupational choice of being an English teacher had served as an expression of rebellion against his father's wishes, as a denial of paternal and cultural identification, and as a symbolic identification with the American culture.

Freed from his internal blocks and his crippling intrafamilial conflicts, Ichiro is now able to develop a realistic acceptance of himself, the members of his family, and his cultural heritage. He can finally relinquish his overidealized distortions of the American culture and give up the unrealistic strivings of the past. Feeling more secure in his own status, he now can afford to take a more tolerant view of his foreign parentage and reconcile some of the conflicting aspects of his dual cultural background. This fusion is expressed vividly in his modified vocational interests. He is planning to spend his Sabbatical year in Japan in order to make a survey of how English is taught in Japanese schools. Also the topic of his doctoral dissertation, which deals with the Oriental influence on American literature, is a telling evidence of the resolution of his cultural conflict.

DISCUSSION

What have these two patients taught us about the etiology of the "psychocultural" neurosis? We suggest that there are *two major sources* of the problem, both of which must be considered and dealt with if our psychotherapeutic efforts are to succeed.

We have seen that one line of development proceeds within the early home life. Where the family—irrespective of cultural membership—does not provide secure and growth-inducing parent and sibling relationships, affectional gratifications, and opportunities for adequate identifications, we might well expect neurotic disorders to begin. Both patients clearly demonstrate to us how their culture conflict, primarily their self-hatred and low self-esteem, originated in their early home and how this conflict became an integral part of their psychological problems. Hence we realize that the resolution of the culture conflict becomes as difficult and as complicated as the resolution of any neurotic problem.

The second and equally crucial determinant in the etiology of the "psychocultural" neurosis is the severe emotional conflict engendered by the impact of the *culture contrast,* particularly in terms of family tradition. Oriental emphasis on unconditional parental authority and everlasting filial piety ascribes a role and responsibility which, against the backdrop of American democratic values and ideals, hardly any second-generation child can comfortably accept and discharge. It is not surprising then that the parent or parent-substitute who is the exponent of the traditional way of life becomes the cathected target of the child's hatred and revolt. This discord again deepens the culture conflict and invokes in the adherents of the Confucian doctrine an internalized conviction of sin and feelings of guilt which lead to intense inner suffering and often to physical destruction, even suicide. In order to free these patients from their strongly punitive "cultural" superego, it becomes imperative in the therapeutic process to help them to understand the roots of such feelings in their parental culture and thus assist them to relinquish the strictness of their own superego.

It should be noted also that the factor of "cultural" superego and family mores assumes heightened significance in the relationship of *im-*

migrant parents to their children. Most immigrant parents are likely to stress more rigidly their Old World traditions in a *new* country than in their native land, to protect *themselves* in their strange and insecure environment. This, in turn, increases the defiance in the younger generation and makes them perceive their parents not only as the enemies of their personal needs and wishes, but also as the exponents of the old culture which sets them apart from those with whom they desperately seek to identify.

In closing, it is suggested that in working therapeutically with people of dual cultural background, our function as therapist is not to "acculturate" the patient to what we may conceive as appropriate values in terms of our own cultural membership. Nor should it be to promote the patient's allegiance to either culture or to seek any "preconceived synthesis of cultures." Our function should be mainly to work with the cultural material as with any other conflict-laden material in order to resolve the patient's neurosis. However, in spite of the "therapeutic neutrality," it will be helpful for the therapist to be well versed in the major aspects of the patient's culture. Finally, let me briefly summarize what the resolution of the "psychocultural" neurosis has achieved for the two patients: Freed from their culture conflict, they are no longer blinding themselves to the social reality that there can never be a *complete* solution to their problem. They never can slough off the signs of their origin, the racial characteristics which set them apart from the members of the Western world with whom they so desperately sought to identify. Nevertheless, they can now enjoy a new-found sense of belonging—a belonging with their own family and their Oriental heritage, as well as a belonging to the country of their birth and their Western culture. Through this fusion of both cultures they are gaining something unique and valuable for themselves and society that they could not have done previously by their torn allegiances. Both Chune and Ichiro have finally found their *own* identity.

34

Eliminating Cultural
Oppression in Counseling
Toward a General Theory

Derald Wing Sue

Counseling and psychotherapy are perceived by many to be "hand-maidens of the status quo," (Halleck, 1971) transmitters of society's values, and instruments of oppression (Halleck, 1971; Pine, 1972; Ruiz & Padilla, 1977; Smith, 1977; Sue & Sue, 1977b; Szasz, 1961). These perceptions seem especially applicable when various racial and ethnic minorities are discussed within the context of counseling. As a result of increasing awareness and sensitivity to these issues, there has been a proliferation of literature on counseling various Third World groups. Yet, most suggestions on counseling the culturally different suffer from two weaknesses: They fail to offer a conceptual basis for integrating culture- and race-specific forces on the self-identity of minorities, and they fail to identify differences in world view that members within a minority group may hold.

The issue of understanding a minority client's world view in counseling has not been adequately discussed or stressed. A world view may be broadly defined as how a person perceives his or her relationship to the world (nature, institutions, other people, things, etc.). World views are highly correlated with a person's cultural upbringing and life experiences (Jackson, 1975; D. W. Sue, 1975). Not only are they composed of our attitudes, values, opinions, and concepts, but they may effect how we think, make decisions, behave, and define events. For minorities in America, a strong determinant of world views is very much related to oppression and the subordinate position assigned them in society. While the intent of this article is to discuss racial and ethnic minorities, it must be kept in mind that economic and social class, religion, and sex are also interactional components of a world view. Thus, upper and lower socioeconomic class

A longer version of this article was presented at the 15th Annual Meeting of the American Psychological Association, San Francisco, August 1977.

Reprinted with permission from the *Journal of Counseling Psychology*, 1978, *25*(5), 419–428.

Asian Americans, blacks, Chicanos, or native Americans do not necessarily have identical views of the world.

The lack of a theory on cultural oppression and its relationship to the development of world views continues to foster cultural blindness within the counseling profession. Counselors tend to respond according to their own conditioned values, assumptions, and perspectives of reality without regard for other views. Counselors need to become culturally aware, to act on the basis of a critical analysis and understanding of their own conditioning, that of their clients, and the sociopolitical system of which they are a part. Without this awareness, counselors who work with the culturally different may be engaging in cultural oppression.

In this article, I would like to propose a general working theory of how race- and culture-specific factors interact in such a way as to produce people with differing world views. First, two major dimensions that are important in the development of world views will be discussed. Second, how these variables form four different psychological outlooks in life and their consequent characteristics, dynamics, and implications for counseling will be presented. Last, some conclusions and precautions will be discussed.

DIMENSIONS OF WORLD VIEWS

Locus of Control

Rotter (1966) first formulated the concept of internal-external locus of control. Internal control refers to people's belief that reinforcements are contingent upon their own actions and that people can shape their own fate. External control refers to people's belief that reinforcing events occur independently of their actions and that the future is determined more by chance and luck. Rotter conceived this dimension as measuring a generalized personality trait that operates across a number of different situations. Based upon past experience, people learn one of two outlooks; the locus of control rests with the individual, or the locus of control rests with an external force. Lefcourt (1966) and Rotter (1966, 1975) have summarized the research findings, which correlate high internality with (a) greater attempts at mastering the environment, (b) lower predisposition to anxiety, (c) higher achievement motivation, (d) greater social action involvement, and (e) placing greater value on skill-determined rewards. As can be seen, these attributes are highly valued by United States society and constitute the core features of mental health.

Early research on generalized expectancies of locus of control suggests that ethnic group members (Hsieh, Shybut, & Lotsof, 1969; Levenson, 1974; Strickland, 1973; Tulkin, 1968; Wolfgang, 1973), lower class people (Battle & Rotter, 1963; Crandall, Katkovsky, & Crandall, 1965; Garcia & Levenson, 1975; Lefcourt, 1966, Strickland, 1971), and women (Sanger & Alker, 1972) score significantly higher on the external end of the continuum. Using the internal-external dimension as a criterion of mental health would mean that minority, poor, and female clients would be viewed as possessing less desirable attributes.

Rotter's internal-external (I–E) distinction has come under severe criticism from several reseachers. Mirels (1970) feels that a strong possibility exists that externality may be a function of a person's opinions about prevailing social institutions. For example, lower-class individuals and minorities are not given an equal opportunity to obtain the material rewards in Western culture. Because of racism, blacks may be perceiving, in a realistic fashion, a discrepancy between their ability and attainment. Gurin, Gurin, Lao, & Beattie (1969), in their study, have concluded that while high-external people are less effectively motivated, perform poorly in achievement situations, and evidence greater psychological problems, this does not necessarily hold for minorities and low-income persons. Focusing on external forces may be motivationally healthy if it results from assessing one's chances for success against systematic and real external obstacles rather than unpredictable fate.

Locus of Responsibility

Another important dimension in world outlooks has been formulated from attribution theory (Jones et al., 1972) and can be legitimately referred to as *locus of responsibility*. In essence, this dimension measures the degree of responsibility or blame placed upon the individual or system. In the case of many blacks, their lower standard of living may be attributable to their personal inadequacies and shortcomings; or, the responsibility for their plight may be attributable to racial discrimination and lack of opportunities. The former orientation blames the individual, whereas the latter explanation blames the system.

The individual/system blame distinction is critical to understanding minority group perceptions and behaviors. With respect to many minorities, it seems to be correlated with collective social action, militancy, civil rights activities, racial-ethnic identity, and higher levels of mental health. For example, when the 1960s riots are studied, two dominant explanations seem to arise. The first, called the riffraff theory (person blame), explains the riots as the result of the sick-criminal elements of the society: the emotionally disturbed, deviants, communist agitators, criminals, or unassimilated migrants. These agitators are seen as peripheral to organized society and possessing no broad social or political concerns. Their frustrations and militant confrontations are seen as a part of their own *personal* failures and inadequacies.

A second explanation, referred to as the blocked-opportunity theory (system blame), views riot participants as those with high aspirations for their own lives and belief in *their ability* to achieve these goals. However, *environmental forces rather than their own personal inadequacies* prevent them from advancing in the society and bettering their condition. The theory holds that riots are the result of massive discrimination against blacks, which has frozen them out of the social, economic, and political life of America. Caplan and Paige (1968) found that more rioters than nonrioters reported experiencing job obstacles and discrimination that blocked their mobility. Further probing revealed that it was not lack of training or education that accounted for the results. Fogelson (1970) presented data in support of the thesis that the ghetto riots were manifestations of grievances within a racist society. In referring to the riots, he stated that it

> was triggered not only because the rioters issued the protest and faced the danger together but also because the rioting revealed the common fate of blacks in America. For most blacks, and particularly northern blacks, racial discrimination is a highly personal experience. They are denied jobs, refused apartments, stopped-and-searched, and declared ineducable—or so they are told—they are inexperienced, unreliable, suspicious, and culturally deprived—and not because they are black. (p.145)

A series of studies concerning characteristics of the rioters and nonrioters failed to confirm the riffraff theory (Caplan, 1970; Caplan & Paige, 1968; Forward & Williams, 1970; Turner & Wilson, 1976). In general, the following profile of those who engaged in rioting during the 1960s emerged: (a) Rioters did not differ from nonrioters in income and rate of unemployment, so they appear to have been no more poverty stricken, jobless, or lazy. (b) Those who rioted were generally better educated, so rioting cannot be attributed to the poorly educated. (c) Rioters were better integrated than nonrioters in social and political workings of the community, and thus, lack of integration into political and social institutions cannot be used as an explanation. (d) Long-term residents were more likely to riot, so rioting cannot be blamed on outside agitators or recent immigrants. (e) Rioters held more positive attitudes toward black history and culture (feelings of racial pride) and, thus, were not alienated from themselves. Caplan (1970) concluded that militants are no more socially or personally deviant than their nonmilitant counterparts. Evidence tends to indicate that they are more "healthy" along a number of traditional criteria measuring mental health.

The degree of emphasis that is placed on the individual as opposed to the system in affecting a person's behavior is important in the formation of life orientations. Such terms as *person centered* or *person blame* indicate a focus upon the individual. Those who hold a person-centered orientation (a) emphasize the understanding of a person's motivations,

values, feelings, and goals, (b) believe that success or failure is attributable to the individual's skills or personal inadequacies, and
(c) believe that there is a strong relationship between ability, effort, and
success in society. In essence, these people adhere strongly to the Protestant ethic that idealizes rugged individualism. On the other hand,
situation-centered or *system-blame* people view the sociocultural environment as more potent than the individual. Social, economic, and political
forces are powerful; success or failure is generally dependent upon the
socioeconomic system and not necessarily personal attributes.

FORMATION OF WORLD VIEWS

The two psychological orientations, locus of control (personal control)
and locus of responsibility, are independent of one another. As shown in
Figure 1, both may be placed on a continuum in such a manner that they
intersect forming four quadrants. Each quadrant represents a different
world view or orientation to life. Theoretically, then, if we know the individual's degree of internality or externality on the two loci, we could
plot them on the figure. It is my intent to describe the type of person who
falls into each quadrant and then speculate as to minorities who answer
this description. I would propose that various ethnic and racial groups are
not randomly distributed throughout the four quandrants. This seems
supported by research findings to be cited later. Because the following

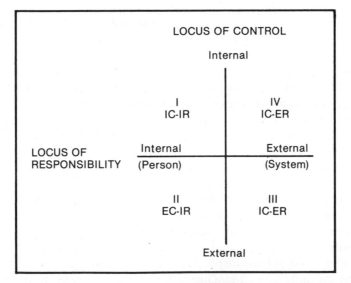

Figure 1.   Graphic representation of world views. (IC = internal locus of control; EC = external locus of control; IR = internal locus of responsibility; ER = external locus of responsibility.)

discussion will focus upon the political ramifications of the two dimensions, there is an evaluative desirable-undesirable quality to each world view.

Internal Locus of Control–Internal Locus of Responsibility

As mentioned previously, individuals high in internal personal-control (IC) believe that they are the masters of their fate and that their actions do affect the outcomes. Likewise, people high in internal locus of responsibility (IR) attribute their current status and life conditions to their own unique attributes; success is due to one's own efforts, and lack of success is due to one's shortcomings or inadequacies. Perhaps the greatest exemplification of the IC–IR philosophy is United States society. Gillin (1955) described United States culture as the epitome of the individual-centered approach, which emphasizes uniqueness, independence, and self-reliance. A high value is placed on personal resources for solving all problems; self-reliance; pragmatism; individualism; status achievement through one's own effort; and power or control over others, things, animals, and forces of nature. Democratic ideals such as "equal access to opportunity," "liberty and justice for all," "God helps those who help themselves," and "fulfillment of personal destiny" all reflect this world view. The individual is held accountable for all that transpires. Constant and prolonged failure and inability to attain goals leads to symptoms of self-blame (depression, guilt, and feelings of inadequacy). Most white, middle-class members would fall within this quadrant.

It becomes obvious that Western approaches to counseling occupy the quadrant represented by IC–IR characteristics. Most counselors are of the opinion that people must take major responsibility for their own actions and can improve their lot in life through their own efforts. The epitome of this line of thought is represented by the numerous self-help approaches currently in vogue in our field. Avis and Stewart (1976) point out that a person-centered problem definition has characterized counseling. Definitions of mental health, the assumptions of vocational guidance, and most counseling theories stress the uniqueness and importance of the individual. As a result, the onus of responsibility for change in counseling tends to rest on the person. It reinforces a social myth about a person's ability to control his or her own fate by rewarding the members of the middle class who have "made it on their own" and increases complacency about those who have not made it on their own.

Clients who occupy this quadrant tend to be white, middle-class counselees, to whom such approaches might be entirely appropriate. In working with clients from different cultures, however, such an approach might be inappropriate. Diaz-Guerrero (1977), in his attempt to build a Mexican psychology, presents much data on how Mexicans and Americans differ with respect to their views of life. To be actively self-assertive is more characteristic of Anglo-Saxon sociocultural premises than of the Mexican. Indeed, to be actively self-assertive in Mexican socioculture clinically forecasts adjustment difficulties. Counselors with a quadrant I orientation are often so culturally encapsulated that they are unable to understand their minority client's world views. Thus, the damage of cultural oppression in counseling becomes an ever-present threat.

Caplan and Nelson (1973), in discussing the causal attribution of social problems, state that Western society tends to hold individuals responsible for their problems. Such an approach has the effect of labeling that segment of the population (racial and ethnic minorities) that differs in thought and behavior from the larger society as deviant. Defining the problem as residing in the person enables society to ignore situationally relevant factors and to protect and preserve social institutions and belief systems. Counselors who hold a different world view are most likely to impute negative traits to clients. Constructs that are used to judge normality and health may be inadvertently applied. For example, an IC–IR counselor needs to consider the possibility that the individual/system blame continuum may have a differing meaning for minority groups. In the face of severe prejudice and discrimination, an internal response (acceptance of blame for one's failure) by minorities might be considered extreme and self-punishing.

External Locus of Control (EC)–Internal Locus of Responsibility (IR)

Individuals who fall into this quadrant are most likely to accept the dominant culture's definition for self-responsibility but to have very little real control over how they are defined by others. With respect to the culturally different, the term *marginal man* (person) was first coined by Stonequist (1935) to describe a person who finds himself or herself living on the margins of two cultures and not fully accommodated to either. Although there is nothing inherently pathological about bicultural membership, Jones (1972) feels that Western society has practiced a form of cultural racism by imposing its standards, beliefs, and ways of behaving (IC–IR world view) into minority groups. Marginal individuals deny the existence of racism; believe that the plight of their own people is due to laziness, stupidity, and a clinging to outdated traditions; reject their own cultural heritage and believe that their ethnicity represents a handicap in Western society; evidence racial self-hatred; accept white social, cultural, and institutional standards; perceive physical features of white men and women as an exemplification of beauty; and are powerless to control their sense of self-worth because approval must come from an external source. As a result, they are high in person focus and external control.

The key issue here is the dominant-subordinate relationship between two different cultures (Brody, 1964; Clark & Clark, 1947; Derbyshire & Brody, 1964; Freire, 1970; Jackson, 1975; Sue & Sue, 1977a). It is reasonable to believe that members of one cultural group tend to adjust themselves to the group that possesses greater prestige and power to avoid inferiority feelings. Yet, it is exactly this act that creates ambivalence in the minority individual. The pressures for assimilation and acculturation (melting pot theory) are strong, creating possible culture conflicts. Jones (1972) refers to such dynamics as cultural racism: (a) belief in the superiority of one group's cultural heritage, its language, traditions, arts, crafts, and ways of behaving (white) over all others; (b) a belief in the inferiority of all other lifestyles (nonwhite); and (c) the power to impose such standards onto the less powerful group. The phenomenon of marginality and racial self-hatred comes directly from this dominant-subordinate relationship. If, however, the relationship is one of equality and acceptance, biculturalism and all its positive ramifications might result.

The psychological dynamics for the EC–IR minority client are likely to reflect his or her marginal and self-hate status. For example, white counselors might be perceived as more competent and preferred than counselors of the client's own race. To EC–IR minority clients, focusing on feelings may be very threatening, since it ultimately may reveal the presence of self-hate and the realization that they cannot escape from their own racial and cultural heritage. A culturally encapsulated white counselor who does not understand the sociopolitical dynamics of the client's concerns may unwittingly perpetuate the conflict. For example, the client's preference for a white counselor coupled with the counselor's implicit belief in the values of United States culture becomes a barrier to successive and effective counseling. A culturally sensitive counselor needs to (a) help the client understand the particular dominant-subordinate political forces that have created this dilemma and (b) help the client to distinguish between positive attempts to acculturate and a negative rejection of one's own cultural values.

External Locus of Control (EC)–External Locus of Responsibility (ER)

A person high in system blame and external control feels that there is very little one can do in the face of such severe external obstacles as prejudice and discrimination. In essence, the EC response might be a manifestation of having given up or an attempt to placate those in power. In the former, individuals internalize their impotence even though they are aware of the external basis of their plight. In its extreme form, oppression may result in a form of learned helplessness (Seligman, 1975). Seligman believes that humans exposed to helplessness (underemployment, unemployment, poor quality of education, poor housing) via prejudice and discrimination may exhibit passivity and apathy (poor motivation), may fail to learn that there are events that can be controlled (cognitive disruption), and may show anxiety and depression (emotional disturbance). When minorities learn that their responses have minimal effects upon the environment, a phenomenon results that can best be described as an expectation of helplessness. People's susceptibility to helplessness depends on their experience with controlling the environment. In the face of continued racism, many may simply give up in their attempts to achieve personal goals.

The dynamics of the placater, however, are not related to the giving-up response. Rather, social forces in the form of prejudice and discrimination are seen as too powerful to combat at that particular time. The best one can hope to do is to suffer the inequities in silence for fear of retaliation. *Don't rock the boat, keep a low profile,* and *survival at all costs* are phrases that describe this mode of adjustment. Life is viewed as relatively fixed with nothing much the individual can do. Passivity in the face of oppression is the primary reaction of the placater.

Smith (1977) notes that slavery was one of the most important factors shaping the social-psychological functioning of black Americans. Interpersonal relations between whites and blacks were highly structured, placing blacks in a subservient and inferior role. Those who broke the rules or who did not show proper deferential behavior were severely punished. The spirits, however, of most blacks were not broken. Conformance to white rules and regulations was dictated by the need to survive in an oppressive environment. Direct expressions of anger and resentment were dangerous, but indirect expressions were frequently seen.

EC–ER black clients are very likely to see the white counselor as symbolic of any other black-white relations. They are likely to show "proper" deferential behavior and to not take seriously admonitions by the counselor that they are the masters of their own fate. As a result, an IC–IR counselor may perceive the culturally different client as lacking in courage, lacking in ego strength, and being passive. A culturally effective counselor, however, would realize the bases of these adaptations. Unlike EC–IR clients, EC–ER individuals do understand the political forces that have subjugated their existence. The most helpful approach on the part of the counselor would be (a) to teach the clients new coping strategies, (b) to have them experience successes, and (c) to validate who and what they represent.

Internal Locus of Control (IC)–External Locus of Responsibility (ER)

Individuals who score high in internal control and system focus believe in their ability to shape events in their own life if given a chance. They do not accept the fact that their present state is due to their own inherent weakness. However, they also realistically perceive that external barriers of discrimination, prejudice, and exploitation block their paths to successful attainment of goals. Recall that the IC dimension was correlated with greater feelings of personal efficacy, higher aspirations, and the like, and that ER individuals were more prone to collective action in the social arena. Gurin et al. (1969) cite research findings that indicate that blacks who were external (blame system) in locus of responsibility (a) more often aspired to nontraditional occupations, (b) were more in favor of group rather than individual action for dealing with discrimination, (c) engaged in more civil rights activities, and (d) exhibited more innovative, coping behavior. This finding supports the previous statement that locus of responsibility is a good predictor of innovative social action behavior. If so, we would expect that IC-ER people would be more likely to participate in civil rights activities and to stress militancy and racial identity. Thus, a strong case can be made on the basis of previously cited research that the ghetto rioters can be characterized as having an IC-ER world view; for example, the recognition that ghetto existence is a result of racism and not some inherent weakness coupled with the rioters' belief in their ability to control events in their own lives made a situation ripe for the venting of frustration and anger. A number of studies support the contention that those who rioted had an increased sense of personal effectiveness and control (Abeles, 1976; Caplan, 1970; Caplan & Paige, 1968; Forward & Williams, 1970; Gore & Rotter, 1963; Marx, 1976).

There is much evidence indicating that minority groups are becoming increasingly conscious of their own racial and cultural identity as it relates to oppression in United States society (Fogelson, 1970; D. W. Sue, 1975; Turner & Wilson, 1976). If so, it is also probable that more and more minorities are most likely to hold an IC-ER world view. Thus, counselors who work with the culturally different will increasingly be exposed to clients with an IC-ER world view. And, in many respects, they pose the most difficult problems for the IC-IR white counselor. Challenges to the counselor's credibility and trustworthiness are likely to be raised by these clients. The counselor is likely to be seen as a part of the establishment that has oppressed minorities. Self-disclosure on the part of the client is not likely to come quickly, and more than any other world view, clients with an IC-ER orientation are likely to play a much more active part in the counseling process and to demand action from the counselor.

The theory proposed here predicts several things about the differences between IC-IR and IC-ER world views in counseling. First, these two world views may dictate how a counselor and client define problems and how they use and are receptive to different styles of counseling. For example, IC-IR people will tend to see the problem as residing in the person, whereas IC-ER people will see the problem as external to the individual. Furthermore, IC-ER counselors may use and are most receptive to counseling skills, styles, or approaches that are action oriented. This is in contrast to IC-IR counselors, who may be more nondirective in their interaction with clients. Two particular studies seem to bear out these predictions.

Ivey (1977) cites the example of a study conducted by one of his doctoral students who compared black and white counselor trainees viewing video vignettes of black and white clients. The clients presented problems related to vocational choice. To a question of "what would you say next?", white males tended to *ask questions,* white females tended to *reflect feelings* and to *paraphrase,* and blacks tended to give *advice* and *directions.* More important, blacks identified the problem as in society rather than the individual, whereas whites tended to focus more on individual. The assumption being made is that the blacks in this study are most likely IC-ER counselor trainees. A similar study conducted by Atkinson, Maruyama, & Matsui (1978) with Asian Americans also revealed consistent findings. The more politically conscious Asian Americans (IC-ER) rated the counselor as more credible and approachable when employing a directive (structure, advice, suggestions) rather than non-directive (reflection and paraphrase) approach.

Thus, it is highly probable that problem definitions and specific counseling skills are differentially associated with a particular world view. One of the reasons why Third World clients may prematurely terminate counseling (D. Sue, 1977) is the fact that counselors not only differ in world views but employ counseling skills inappropriate to their clients' life styles. Our next step would be to research the following question: Are there specific counseling goals, techniques, and skills best suited for a particular world view? If so, the implications for counselor training are important. First, it indicates an overwhelming need to teach trainees the importance of being able to understand and share the world views of their clients. Second, it is no longer enough to learn a limited number of counseling skills. Ivey (1977) makes a strong case for this position. The culturally effective counselor is one who is able to generate the widest repertoire of responses (verbal/nonverbal) consistent with the life-styles and values of the culturally different client. Particularly for minorities, the passive approaches of asking questions, reflecting feelings, and paraphrasing must be balanced with directive responses (giving advice and suggestions, disclosing feelings, etc.) on the part of the counselor.

CONCLUSIONS

The conceptual model presented in this article concerning world views and identity development among Third World groups is consistent with other formulations (Hall, Cross, & Freedle, 1972; Jackson, 1975; D. W. Sue, 1975). In all cases, these writers believe that cultural identity for minorities in America is intimately related to racism and oppression. Using this model in counseling culturally different clients has many practical and research implications. In addition, counselors need to understand that each world view has much to offer that is positive. While these four psychological orientations have been described in a highly evaluative manner, positive aspects of each can be found. For example, individual responsibility and achievement orientation of quadrant I, biculturalism and cultural flexibility of quadrant II, the ability to compromise and adapt to life conditions of quadrant III, and collective action and social concern of quadrant IV need not be at odds with one another. The role of the counselor may be to help the client integrate aspects of each world view that will maximize his or her effectiveness and psychological well being. Ivey (1977) calls this person the culturally effective individual. He or she is a "functional integrator" who is able to combine and integrate aspects of each world view into a harmonious union. To accomplish this goal, however, the counselor must also be able to share the world views of his or her clients. In essence, the culturally skilled counselor is also one who is a functional integrator.

Some Cautions

In closing, there are some precautions that should be exercised in using this model. First, the validity of this model has not been directly established through research. While much empirical and clinical evidence is consistent with the model, many of the assertions in this article remain at the speculative level. Second, the behavior manifestations of each quadrant have not been specifically identified. Regardless of a person's psychological orientation, I would suspect that individuals can adapt and use behaviors associated with another world view. This, indeed, is the basis of training counselors to work with the culturally different. Third, each style represents conceptual categories. In reality, although people might tend to hold one world view in preference over another, it does not negate them from holding variations of others. Most Third World people represent mixes of each rather than a pure standard. Fourth, whether this conceptual model can be applied to groups other than minorities in America has yet to be established. Last, we must remember that it is very possible for individuals from different cultural groups to be more similar in world view than those from the same culture. While race and ethnicity may be correlated with outlook in life, it is certainly not a one-to-one correspondence.

REFERENCES

Abeles, R. P. Relative deprivation, rising expectations and black militancy. *Journal of Social Issues,* 1976, *32,* 119–137.

Atkinson, D. R., Maruyama, M., & Marsui, S. Effects of counselor race and counseling approach on Asian Americans' perceptions of counselor credibility and utility. *Journal of Counseling Psychology,* 1978, *25,* 76–83.

Avis, J. P., & Stewart, L. H. College counseling: Intentions and change. *The Counseling Psychologist,* 1976, *6,* 74–77.

Battle, E.S., & Rotter, J. B. Children's feelings of personal control as related to social class and ethnic group. *Journal of Personality,* 1963, *31,* 482–490.

Brody, E. B. Color and identity conflict in young boys. *Archives of General Psychiatry,* 1964, *10,* 354–360.

Caplan, N. The new ghetto man: A review of recent empirical studies. *Journal of Social Issues,* 1970, *26,* 59–73.

Caplan, N., & Nelson, D. S. On being useful: The nature and consequences of psychological research on social problems. *American Psychologist,* 1973, *28,* 199–211.

Caplan, N. S., & Paige, J. M. A study of ghetto rioters. *Scientific American,* 1968, *219* (8), 15–21.

Clark, K. B., & Clark, M. K. Racial identification and preference in Negro children. In T. M. Newcomb & E. L. Hartley (Eds.), *Readings in social psychology.* New York: Holt, 1947.

Crandall, V. C., Katkovsky, W., & Crandall, V. J. Children's belief in their own control of reinforcements in intellectual-academic achievement situations. *Child Development,* 1965, *36,* 91–109.

Derbyshire, R. L., & Brody, E. B. Marginality, identity and behavior in the American Negro: A functional analysis. *International Journal of Social Psychiatry,* 1964, *10,* 7–13.

Diaz-Guerrero, R. A Mexican psychology. *American Psychologist,* 1977, *32,* 934–944.

Fogelson, R. M. Violence and grievances: Reflections on the 1960's riots. *Journal of Social Issues,* 1970, *26,* 141–163.

Forward, J. R., & Williams, J. R. Internal-external control and Black militancy. *Journal of Social Issues,* 1970, *26,* 75–92.

Freire, P. *Cultural action for freedom.* Cambridge, Mass.: Harvard Educational Review Press, 1970.

Garcia, C., & Levenson, H. Differences between black's and white's expectations of control by chance and powerful others. *Psychological Reports,* 1975, *37,* 563–566.

Gillin, J. National and regional cultural values in the United States. *Social Forces,* 1955, *34,* 107–113.

Gore, P. M., & Rotter, J. B. A personality correlate of social action. *Journal of Personality,* 1963, *31,* 58–64.

Gurin, P., Gurin, G., Lao, R., & Beattie, M. Internal-external control in the motivational dynamics of Negro youth. *Journal of Social Issues,* 1969, *25,* 29–54.

Hall, W. S., Cross, W. E., & Freedle, R. Stages in the development of black awareness: An exploratory investigation. In R. L. Jones (Ed.), *Black psychology.* New York: Harper & Row, 1972.

Halleck, S. L. Therapy is the handmaiden of the status quo. *Psychology Today,* April 1971, pp. 30–34; 98–100.

Hsieh, T., Shybut, J., & Lotsof, E. Internal versus external control and ethnic group membership: A cross-cultural comparison. *Journal of Consulting and Clinical Psychology,* 1969, *33,* 122–124.

Ivey, A. Toward a definition of the culturally effective counselor. *Personnel and Guidance Journal,* 1977, *55,* 296–302.

Jackson, B. Black identity development. *Journal of Educational Diversity,* 1975, *2,* 19–25.

Jones, E. E., et al. (Eds.). *Attribution: Perceiving the causes of behavior.* Morristown, N.J.: General Learning Press, 1972.

Jones, J. M. *Prejudice and racism*. Reading, Mass.: Addison-Wesley, 1972.

Lefcourt, H. Internal versus external control of reinforcement: A review. *Psychological Bulletin*, 1966, *65*, 206–220.

Levenson, H. Activism and powerful others. *Journal of Personality Assessment*, 1974, *38*, 377–383.

Marx, G. T. *Protest and prejudice: A study of belief in the black community*. New York: Harper & Row, 1976.

Mirels, H. L. Dimensions of internal versus external control. *Journal of Consulting and Clinical Psychology*, 1970, *34*, 226–228.

Pine, G. J. Counseling minority groups: A review of the literature. *Counseling and Values*, 1972, *17*, 35–44.

Rotter, J. B. Generalized expectancies for internal versus external control of reinforcement. *Psychological Monographs*, 1966. *80* (1, Whole No. 609.

Rotter, J. B. Some problems and misconceptions related to the construct of internal versus external control of reinforcement. *Journal of Consulting and Clinical Psychology*, 1975, *43*, 56–67.

Ruiz, R. A., & Padilla, A. M. Counseling Latinos. *Personnel and Guidance Journal*, 1977, *55*, 401–408.

Sanger, S. P., & Alker, H. A. Dimensions of internal-external locus of control and the women's liberation movement. *Journal of Social Issues*, 1972, *28*, 115–129.

Seligman, M. E. P. *Helplessness: On depression development and death*. San Francisco: Freeman, 1975.

Smith, E. J. Counseling black individuals: Some stereotypes. *Personnel and Guidance Journal*, 1977, *55*, 390–396.

Stonequist, E. The problem of the marginal man. *American Journal of Sociology*, 1935, *41*, 1–12.

Strickland, B. R. Aspiration responses among Negro and white adolescents. *Journal of Personality and Social Psychology*, 1971, *19*, 315–320.

Strickland, B. R. Delay of gratification and internal locus of control in children. *Journal of Consulting and Clinical Psychology*, 1973, *40*, 338.

Sue, D. Counseling the culturally different: A conceptual analysis. *Personnel and Guidance Journal*, 1977, *55*, 422–426.

Sue, D. W. Asian Americans: Social-psychological forces affecting their life styles. In S. Picou & R. Campbell (Eds.), *Career behavior in special groups*. Columbus, Ohio: Charles E. Merrill, 1975.

Sue, D. W., & Sue, D. Barriers to effective cross-cultural counseling. *Journal of Counseling Psychology*, 1977, *24*, 420–429. (a)

Sue, D. W., & Sue, D. Ethnic minorities: Failures and responsibilities of the social sciences. *Journal of Non-White Concerns in Personnel and Guidance*, 1977, *5*, 99–106. (b)

Szasz, T. S. *The myth of mental illness*. New York: Hoeber-Harper, 1961.

Tulkin, S. R. Race, class, family and school achievement. *Journal of Personality and Social Psychology*, 1968, *9*, 31–37.

Turner, C. B., & Wilson, W. J. Dimension of racial ideology: A study of urban black attitudes. *Journal of Social Issues*, 1976, *32*, 139–152.

Wolfgang, A. Cross-cultural comparison of locus of control, optimism toward the future, and time horizon among Italian, Italo-Canadian, and new Canadian youth. *Proceedings of the 81st Annual Convention of the American Psychological Association*, 1973, *8*, 299–300.

Epilogue

One paradox of the last 20 years has been the creation of human services for minority persons that have been insufficiently utilized. Some consequences of underutilization have been resentment on the part of service providers, reinforcement of existing societal prejudices, and further alienation of minority persons as a result of feeling that the system continues to be unresponsive to their needs. The issue of the adequacy of the services or the manner of service delivery has only infrequently been raised. This book has presented cogent reasons for underutilization of services from within the cultures of minority persons and suggests some of the means for providing adequate services for these persons.

Middle-class, white service providers have assumed that at heart persons who are ostensibly different as a result of skin color, ethnic origin, social class, or poverty are, in fact, like themselves in all important respects except perhaps opportunity. The expectation is that the perception of whatever is real and meaningful is inevitably shared. As a result of this belief in a shared and consensual reality, mere exposure to services should suffice to relieve individual suffering and remediate some social ills experienced by minority persons. However, minority persons differ on the basis of values, beliefs, and behaviors. What is accepted without question as a reasonable basis for the good life and what is perceived as real and hence of tangible consequence in the attempt to invest acts and lives with meaning is culture-specific.

Several dimensions of cultural difference between these groups and middle-class, white Americans are apparent in these readings and will be reiterated here. These differences include the meaning of emotional distress, the manner in which a world view shapes feelings and perceptions about the self and society, and the function and importance of the family. These dimensions of difference affect the choice and training of service providers and are complicated by the extent of contact with the dominant culture and the degree to which mainstream values are accepted.

The question of what constitutes emotional distress is not to be answered by citing similar cross-cultural incidence or prevalence rates for symptoms or clusters of symptoms associated with emotional distress. Such data simply acknowledge that we are all human and able to express the consequences of distress in relatively uniform physiological and/or behavioral expressions. The meaning of these symptoms within the personal experience and the cultural milieu is overlooked by such statistics. And we cannot infer that similar symptoms merit similar interventions in different cultures.

All four of these minority groups differ from most white, middle-class persons in world view. They typically experience less personal power, feel less control over their own lives, and they may also feel that they should not be directly responsible for themselves or experience greater control over their own lives. Such world view differences suggest that many current mental health and rehabilitation practices requiring responsibility, initiative, and personal involvement for their success simply will not make sense to many minority persons.

All of these groups have some notion of extended family structure that includes a much wider range of potential influence and power over individual lives than would be acceptable for middle-class, white Americans. This is such an outstanding difference that it is even reflected in our personality theories. Among contemporary personality theorists only F. L. K. Hsu recognizes a concept of psychosocial homeostasis and assumes that it is affective involvement rather than cognitive organization that is basic to meaningful human existence (1971). More specifically, the idea of Jen or personage emphasizes individual transactions with other human beings particularly with an extended family wherein intimacy without defensiveness provides a context for full expression of feelings.

White, middle-class Americans do not often possess this family context for the discovery of personal humanity and search within themselves or in impersonal human encounters for such nourishment. The core belief of middle-class, white America in autonomy, or immanent self-sufficiency, has never been a major component of the heritage of these minority groups. When the relative absence of genuine power to control their own lives is coupled with ascription of such power to a larger social unit, it is no wonder that interventions will fail whenever they require actual individual power as well as sanctions for use of such powers. Interventions that make use of the extended family and of mutual, peer self-help, especially in natural settings, are more likely to be accepted.

The person who provides services is also important to minority persons. If the service provider is a stranger who does not speak the language or know the social etiquette that is culturally appropriate for human relationships, particularly helping relationships, there is little likelihood that contact, communication, or meaningful interface will occur. The recognition, acceptance, and collaboration with indigenous healers is mandatory, especially for those conditions that transcend the boundaries of white, middle-class belief systems. For examples, soul loss, spirit intrusion, talking with God, and emotionally-laden trance-like states.

It is also feasible to train persons from the majority culture to accept cultural differences, but we should not presume that this can be accomplished solely by information and education. In addition, it is also necessary to provide culture-relevant knowledge, language skills, and an experiential basis for understanding the implications of this formal education. By sharing the living circumstances and lifestyles of minority persons on a day-to-day basis over an extended period of time, education can become translated into human contact and respect for values that are different. Learning to see behavior in a cultural context is one outcome of these experiences. Another outcome is that the impact of white society on minority persons—racism and discrimination—should become apparent. Finally, intervention techniques that are culturally-relevant have to be incorporated into the training of these service providers.

The immense difficulty of providing such training and experience to middle-class, white persons suggests that the recruitment and training of minority persons should be a primary goal. The training of these minority persons for helping roles, however, has to be in culturally-appropriate techniques which may be applied within a context of values, settings, and other persons that is meaningful to the client.

One final issue concerns the extent of contact with middle-class, white society and the reactions of minority persons to that contact. We need to recognize that some minority persons actively seek such contact and will try to adopt the values of the dominant culture. Others by being segregated and alienated from the dominant culture remain ensconced in isolated living environments wherein they cling to traditional values. Even more frequent than this resolution, however, will be a pantraditional lifestyle that actively fosters a resynthesis of traditional values with the glue of pride, self-respect, and personal integrity. The identification of a minority person—client or human service provider—with any one of these reactions to middle-class, white America requires different human service and training responses.

This book attempts to make clear by example that these matters are not simple. We can learn from our failures to provide relevant services for minority persons to stop giving lip-service to our democratic ideals. We can begin to foster services, service delivery paradigms, and training programs that are compatible with the realities experienced by minority persons only by a reduction in the arrogance of our presumption that "we" know what is best for "them."

REFERENCE

Hsu, F. L. K. Psychosocial homeostasis and zen: Conceptual tools for advancing psychological anthropology. *American Anthropologist,* 1971, *73*(1), 23–44.

Index

Acculturation process, dynamics of, and essential values among Plains Indians, 8–11
Achievement, among Chicanos, psychotherapy and, 277
Advocacy for Indian handicapped children, 52–53
Affective approach of Chicanos, psychotherapy and, 266–267
Afro-Americans, 101–178
  behavior of, deficit hypothesis of, 117
  counseling of, see Counseling of Blacks
  ecology of, 105–111
  environment of
    economics and, 110
    overcrowding in, 107–108
    pollutants in, 106–107
  health problems of, 108–109
  life expectancy of, 109
  morbidity among, 108–109
  perspective of, in counseling, 115–133
  population implosion among, 109
  psychotherapy of, 166
  social-psychological functioning of, slavery and, 347
  struggle for recognition of, 116–125
  unemployment among, 110
  whites and, consultation and relationships between, 165–167
Age, respect for, in Papago culture, 89
Aggression, intragroup, among Cheyenne
  cultural deterioration and, 66
  taboo against, 65–66
Alcoholism, among Cheyenne, cultural deterioration and, 66, 69

American Indians, see Native Americans
Anomic depression, traditional, treatment of, 23–24
Asian Americans, 283–350, see also Japanese
  acculturation problems of, 331–338
  awareness of, of social milieu, 309
  barriers to assimilation of, 301
  counseling of, 295–306
    eliminating cultural oppression in, 339–350
    cultural norms of, 301–302
    psychotherapy and, 304–306
  cultural values of, 308–310
    implications of, for social work, 310–311
  educational attainment of, 288
  family and, 302
  fatalism of, 309–310
  filial piety of, 308
  ghetto problems of, 290
  group therapy and, 305–306, 312–314
  in Hawaii, 296–298
  identity conflict in, 331–338
  immigration policies for, 296–297
  inconspicuousness of, 310
  as individuals, 317–322, see also Japanese community
  intermarriages involving, 289, 290
  lack of assertiveness of, 301
  legislation against, 299
  median family income of, 288
  middle position, virtue of, 309
  as minority group, 287–293
  oppressed image of, 290–293
  parent-child interaction among, 308
  psychocultural conflict and, 331–338

Asian Americans—*continued*
  poverty among, 291
  psychological status of, 289–290,
    291–292
  racism and, 292, 299–300
  self-control of, 308
  shame and, 301, 302–306, 309, 318
  social work with, 307–316, *see also*
    Social work with Asian Ameri-
    cans
  as sojourners, 296–297
  success image of, 288–290
  therapy for, 323–330
Authority, respect for, in Asian culture, 305, 308

Bicultural Chippewa families, 60
  social casework and, 59
Bith Haa model for Papago tribal
  health programs, 80–82
Black ghetto, pollutants in, 106–107
Blacks, *see* Afro-Americans
Block-opportunity theory of racial
  riots, 342
Bureau of Indian Affairs and P.L. 94-
  142, 47–48, 49–50
Burial practices of Native Americans,
  97–98

Catholicism in Hispanic American
  culture, 218–219
Cheyenne Indians
  obstacles to assimilation of, into
    white man's world, 67
  resolving social disruption among,
    69
  suicide among, 65–69
    prevention of, 68–69
    reasons for, 66–67
Chicanos, *see also* Hispanic Americans
  as monolithic culture, 275–276
  psychotherapy with
    balance between formality and
      personalized attention in,
      270–272
    coping with passivity in, 272–274
    diagnostic errors in, 269–270
    family orientation and, 277–278
    machismo and, 274–275

reduced need for competition
  and, 277
reduced need for individual
  achievement and, 277
sexual dichotomy and, 278–279
suitability of, 266–267
therapist's ethnocentricity and,
  268–269
uncomfortable themes for therapist in, 276–279
Chicano child
  career choice option expansion in,
    241
  counseling of, 239–244, *see also*
    Counseling of Chicano child
Chicano family, description of,
  239–240
Chippewa families, 60
  social casework and, 59
Climate control in black environment,
  108
Communication
  in mental health services for
    Latinos, 219–221
  nonverbal, in Asian culture, 305
  as obstacle to assimilation of Chey-
    enne, 67
  verbal, paucity of, in Papago cul-
    ture, 89
Community, social work with Asian
  Americans in, 314–315
Community map approach among
  Native Americans, 74–75
Competence
  instrumental, definition of, 168
  interpersonal
    definition of, 168
    interracial consultation and,
      167–168
Competition, reduced need for,
  among Chicanos, 277
Confrontation, therapeutic, with
  Papago client, 90
Consultation
  ethnic variations in, 163–178, *see*
    also Ethnic variations in con-
    sultation
  interpersonal orientation to, model
    of, 168–172
  implications of, 176–178
  vs. direct service, policy of Mental
    Health Program of Indian

Health Service on, 36–37
Coping styles, passive, of Chicanos,
    272–274
Counseling
  of Asians, 295–306
    eliminating cultural oppression
      in, 339–350
  black perspective in, 115–133
  of blacks
    alternative approaches to,
      122–125
    attitudes toward, 126–127
    black cultural approaches to,
      122–123
    color-blindness doctrine in,
      117–118
    communication in, 124–125
    course on, model, 157–161, *see
      also* Ethnic minorities, coun-
      seling course on
    deficiencies of traning program
      for, 119–120
    discrimination in, 117–118
    emphasis on strengths in,
      123–125
    failure of counselor orientation,
      127–128
    innovation in, 132
    in integrated settings, 126
    negotiation in, 118
    proposal for training programs
      in, 120–122
    racial awareness in, 131–132
    racism in, 117–118
    staff selection for, 128–130
    struggle for services in, 125–130
    stylistic dimensions of, 139–144,
      see also Stylistic dimensions of
      counseling blacks
    systemic, 122
    white therapist in, 145–154
  of Chicano child, 239–244
    bilingualism in, 242–243
    cognitive skill development in,
      240–241
    counselor's characteristics for,
      242–244
    counselor's role in, 240–242
    cultural awareness in, 243
    language skill development in,
      240–241
    personal values in, 242

    personality for, 243–244
    pride in, 242
    repertoire for, 243
    self-respect in, 242
  of ethnic minorities, course on,
    157–161
    content of, 158–160
    feedback following, 160–161
    goals of, 158
    planning for, 157–158
    student behavior following,
      160–161
  of Latinos, 187–205
    case histories of, 196–202
    recommendations for, 203–205
Countertransference in white thera-
    pist counseling blacks, 148
Cross-cultural collaboration with
    traditional Amerindian thera-
    pists, 15–24
Crowding in black environment,
    107–108
Cuban culture, folk healers in,
    211–212
Cubans, *see* Hispanic Americans
Cultural oppression in counseling,
    eliminating, 339–350
Curandero in Mexican culture,
    210–211
Curandismo in Chicano culture, psy-
    chotherapy and, 267

Delinquent adolescent, Papago, group
    therapy with, 88
Depression, anomic, traditional treat-
    ment of, 23–24
Diarrhea Control Project on Papago
    reservation, 82
Discrimination
  against Asian Americans, 292
  racial, in cultural-historical dimen-
    sion of counseling blacks,
    139–141
Dormitory, model, in Mental Health
    Program of Indian Health Ser-
    vice, 33
Dreams, use of, in working with In-
    dian clients, 73
Drug abusers, Hispanic
  case conference approach to, 230
  clique phenomenon and, 232–233

Drug abusers, Hispanic—*continued*
  creativity and, 231
  discipline and, 229
  emotional deprivation of, 227–228
  emotional expression and, 239
  environmental deprivation of,
    227–228
  family situation of, 226–227, 234
  family therapy program for,
    230–231
  frustration among, 235
  health problems of, 233
  new model of living for, 236
  nutritional needs of, 233
  perceptual deprivation of, 228
  personal property and, 232
  privacy and, 231–232
  reality orientation for, 229
  regrowing process for, 229–230,
    235–236
  treatment of, in Hispanic therapeu-
    tic community, 225–237
  value distortions of, 233
  visual orientation of, to learning,
    231
Drugs, abuse of, by Japanese Ameri-
    cans, 318, 321–322

Ecology
  black, 105–111
  definition of, 105
  white, pollution in, 105
Education for All Handicapped
    Children Act of 1975
    (P.L. 94-142), 43, 46–48
  Bureau of Indian Affairs and,
    47–48
  Secretary of the Interior and,
    47–48
  state/local education agencies and,
    47
Emotional distress, cultural differ-
    ences and, 553
Environment, definition of, 106
Ethnic minorities
  counseling, course on, 157–161, *see
    also* Counseling of ethnic
    minorities, course on
  mental health services to, recom-
    mendations for, 213–214
Ethnic variations in consultation,

    163–178
  black-white relationships and,
    165–167
  case illustration of, 172–175
  consultant-consultee interactions
    and, 175–176
  interpersonal competence and,
    167–168
  interpersonal orientation to, model
    of, 168–172
  implications of, 176–178
  literature review on, 164–165
Eurocentric fallacy, shamanic behav-
    ior as, 18–19
Eye contact, avoidance of, in Papago
    culture, 89, 90

Family
  Asian American, social work with,
    312–314
  in Asian culture, 302
  Chicano, description of, 239–240
  orientation toward, prolonged psy-
    chotherapy and, 277–278
  significance of, cultural differences
    and, 354
Family behavior of urban American
    Indians, 55–63, *see also* Urban
    American Indians
Fatalism in Asian culture, 309–310
Feasts, traditional, in family network
    dynamics of American Indians,
    61–62
Federal mandates for handicapped,
    American Indian children and,
    43–53
Feelings, expression of, in Asian cul-
    ture, 303–306
Filial piety in Asian culture, 308
Folk healers, Latino, 207–214
  in Chicano culture, 267
  communications of, with clients,
    compared with psychiatrists,
    219–221
  in Cuban culture, 211–212
  factors causing use of, 222–223
  in Mexican culture, 210–211
  in mental health services
    community, 217–223
    to ethnic minorities, 213–214
  modus operandi of, 220–221

overview of, 208–209
in Puerto Rican culture, 209–210
relating to patient's symptomatol-
    ogy, compared with psychia-
    trist, 222
utilization of, 212–213
Foster Parents Program, Hispanic,
    245–248
assessment of foster homes by, 246
recruitment of foster homes by, 246
support services for, 247–248
training of foster families by,
    246–247

Ghetto, black, pollutants in, 106–107
Goals, individual, in counseling
    Blacks, 144
Grandparents in urban American
    Indian family, 58
"Great white father syndrome" of
    white therapist counseling
    blacks, 150
Grief, language of, 98
Grief counseling with Native Ameri-
    cans, 95–99
techniques for, 98–99
Group therapy for Asian Americans,
    305–306, 312
modified, for family, 312–314
Guilt feelings of white therapist coun-
    seling blacks, 148–149

Handicapped, federal mandates for,
    American Indian children and,
    43–53
advocacy and, 52–53
Bureau of Indian Affairs and,
    47–48, 49–50
cooperative agreements and, 51
P.L. 94-142 and, 46–48
recruitment and training of per-
    sonnel for, 51–52
Section 504 of Vocational Rehabili-
    tation Act and, 48–49
Hawaii, Asian immigrants to, 296–298
Healing, traditional Papago, 84–85
Healing powers, Native American
    concept of, 71–73
Hispanic Americans, 183–280, see also
    Chicano

community mental health services
    for, see also Mental health ser-
    vices for Latinos
counseling of, 187–205
    case histories of, 196–202
    recommendations for, 203–205
culture of, 189–193
demogaphic characteristics of,
    187–189
drug abusing, see Drug abusers,
    Hispanic
educational status of, 188–189
employment status of, 188
as ethnic group, 218
ethnohistory of, 189–193
family interdependence of, 203
folk healers among, 207–214
foster parent program among,
    245–248, see also Foster
    Parents Program, Hispanic
geographic origins of, 187–188
mental health program for,
    251–262, see also Worcester
    Youth Guidance Center's
    Hispanic Program
self-referral of, reducing, 195–196
service utilization by, 194–195
stress among
    extrapsychic, 194
    intrapsychic, 193–194
    sources of, 193–194
use of folk healing by, factors
    causing, 222–223
Housing in Black community, 108

Identity
conflict over, in Asian Americans,
    331–338
racial, in counseling Blacks,
    140–141
Inconspicuousness in Asian culture,
    310
Indian Health Service
history of, 27–28
Mental Health Program of
    future of, 39–40
    history of, 28
    Indian leadership in, 35–36
    innovative approaches of, 33–36
    Model Dormitory Project of, 33
    organization of, 28–32

Indian Health Service—*continued*
  paraprofessionals in, 35
  policy on direct service vs.
    consultation, 36–37
  policy on racism, 37–39
  policy on traditional practices, 37
  residential treatment center of, 34
  service units of, 30–32
  services of, to Indians, 32–33
  traditional medicine and, 34
Indians, American, 1–99, *see also*
  Native Americans
Initiatory sickness of shamans, 17
Instrumental competence, definition
  of, 168
Interpersonal competence
  definition of, 168
  and interracial consultation,
    167–168
Interpersonal orientation
  to consultation, model of, 168–172
  implications of, 176–178
  definition of, 168
Intrusion, spirit, shamanic treatment
  of, 22–23
Issei, character of, 319

Japanese community, 317–322
  character of, 319
  drug problem in, 318, 321–322
  generational groups in, 319–322
  internment of, in World War II,
    299–301
  Issei in, 319
  mental health services for, 322
  mixed marriages in, failed, 318
  Nisei in, 319–321
  overachievers in, 321–322
  Sansei in, 321–322
  stereotypes of, 317
Juvenile delinquents, Papago, group
  therapy with, 88

Language
  in interracial consultation, 166
  as obstacle to assimilation of
    Cheyenne, 67
  and survival of traditional Indian
    values, 9–10
Latinos, 183–280, *see also* Hispanic
  Americans

Machismo in Chicano culture, psy-
  chotherapy and, 274–275
Marginal man, world view of,
  345–346
Medicine, traditional, in Mental
  Health Program of Indian
  Health Service, 34
Medicine man, *see also* Traditional
  Amerindian therapist
  importance of, in Papago culture,
    89
Mediums in Puerto Rican culture,
  209–210
Mental health care for Latinos, folk
  healers in, 207–214
Mental health services
  for American Indians, 27–40, *see
    also* Indian Health Service
  for Asian Americans, 322
    bicultural therapist for, 325–326
    Morita techniques of treatment
      in, 327–328
    Naikan technique of treatment
      in, 328–329
    underutilization of, 323–324
  for ethnic minorities, recommenda-
    tions for, 213–214
  for Latinos
    communication in, modes of,
      219–221
    community, role of folk healers
      in, 217–223
    folk healers in, 217–225
    patients in, cultural background
      of, 217–219
  for Native Americans, treatment
    modalities in, 71–77
  for Papago Indians, 79–94, *see also*
    Papago Psychology Service
Mental health worker, Papago, indigenous, 85–88
Mental illness, Native American view
  of, 71
Metaphysic of nature and survival of
  traditional Indian values, 10
Mexican-Americans, *see* Chicano,
  Hispanic Americans
Mexican culture, folk healers in,
  210–211
Mexicans, *see* Hispanic Americans
Migration, urban, of Native Ameri-
  cans, 95–96
Minorities

ethnic, counseling, course on,
     157–161, *see also* Counseling
     of ethnic minorities, course on
world view of, 339–350, 354
Morita therapy for Asian Americans,
     327–328

Naikan therapy for Asian Americans,
     328–329
Naming ceremony among American
     Indians, 61
Native Americans, 1–99, *see also*
     Cheyenne Indians, Chippewa
     families, Papago
  burial practices of, 97–98
  children of, handicapped, federal
     mandates and, 43–53
  education of
     background on, 44–46
     delivery systems for, 44–45
     historical development of, 45–46
     Indian Citizenship Act of 1924
        and, 45
     Johnson-O'Malley Act of 1934
        and, 45–46
  grief counseling with, 95–99
     techniques for, 98–99
  healing power concept of, 71–73
  leadership by, in Mental Health
     Program of Indian Health
     Service, 35–36
  mental health services for, 27–40,
     see also Indian Health Service
  on Papago reservation, 79–94,
     see also Papago Psychology
     Service
  treatment modalities in, 71–73
  natural helping systems of, 73–76
  of northern plains, 5–13, *see also*
     North American Plains Indians
  self-help groups among, 76–77
  stereotypes of, 96–97
  traditional therapists of, cross-
     cultural collaboration with,
     15–24
  treatment modalities with, cultural
     perspective on, 71–77
  urban, family behavior of, 55–63,
     see also Urban American
     Indians
  urban migration of, 95–96
  view of mental illness among, 76

Nature, healing power in, Native
     American concept of, 71–73
Negroes, *see* Afro-Americans
Nisei
  character of, 319–321
  impact of World War II on,
     320–321
North American Plains Indians, per-
     sistence of essential values
     among, 5–13
  contemporary assessment of, 11–13
  dynamics of acculturation process
     and, 8–11

Orientals, *see* Asian Americans
Overcrowding in black environment,
     107–108

Pacific Islanders, *see* Asian Americans
Pan-Indianism, 12–13
Pantraditional Chippewa families, 60
  social casework and, 59
Papago
  culture of, traditional psychother-
     apy adapted to, 89–91
  Psychology Service of, 79–94
  reservation community of, 83–84
  traditional healing of, 84–85
  tribal health programs of, 80–83
  tribal practices of, 80–83
  verbosity, lack of, among, 89
Papago mental health worker, indig-
     enous, 85–88
Papago Psychology Service
  non-Indian professional consultant
     to, 91–94
  training of mental health workers
     in, 85–88
Paraprofessionals in Mental Health
     Program of Indian Health
     Service, 35
Parent-child interacttion in Asian
     culture, 308
  psychocultural conflict and,
     331–338
Passive coping styles of Chicanos,
     psychotherapy and, 272–274
Paternalism
  in Asian culture, 308
  of white therapist counseling
     blacks, 150

Personalismo, 192, 202
  in Chicano culture, psychotherapy
    and, 267
Personality, stability of, and survival
    of traditional Indian values, 10
Pipe, sacred, of Plains Indians, 7–8
Pollution
  in black ecology, 106
  in white ecology, 105
Positivistic fallacy, shamanic behavior
    as, 19
Pow-wow syndrome, 12–13
Power needs of white therapist coun-
    seling blacks, 149–150
Problem-solving networks of Native
    Americans, 73–76
Psychiatrist
  communication of, with clients,
    compared with Latino folk
    healers, 219–221
  relating to patient's symptomatol-
    ogy, compared with spiritual-
    ist, 222
  and traditional Amerindian thera-
    pist, collaboration between,
    15–24
Psychocultural conflict in Asian
    Americans, 331–338
Psychological security in counseling
    blacks, 141–143
Psychological service for Papago
    community, 79–94, *see also*
    Papago Psychology Service
Psychopathology hypothesis of
    shamanic healing, 16–19
Psychotherapy
  Asian cultural norms and, 304–306
  blacks in, 166
  with Chicanos, errors in, 265–280,
    see also Chicanos, psycho-
    therapy with
  traditional, adapted to Papago
    culture, 89–91
Puerto Rican culture, folk healers in,
    209–210
Puerto Ricans, *see also* Hispanic
    Americans
  migration patterns of, 252
Purification, rites of, of Plains
    Indians, 6

Racial discrimination in cultural-
    historical dimension of coun-
    seling blacks, 139–141
Racial identity in counseling blacks,
    140–141
Racism
  Asian Americans and, 292, 299–300
  policy of Mental Health Program
    of Indian Health Service on,
    37–39
  in white therapist, 145–148
Racist attitudes, negative, and survival
    of traditional Indian values,
    10–11
Religio Perennia, 5
Religion in Hispanic American
    culture, 218–219
Reservations, Indian, isolation of,
    and survival of traditional
    values, 9
Residential treatment center in Mental
    Health Program of Indian
    Health Service, 35
Riffraff theory of racial riots, 341,
    342
Riots, racial
  blocked-opportunity theory of, 342
  riffraff theory of, 341, 342

Sansei, character of, 321–322
Santeria in Cuban culture, 211–212
Schools, reservation, elimination of
    traditional Indian values and,
    8–9
Secrecy, personal, in Papago culture,
    traditional psychotherapy and,
    89
Secretary of Interior, 47–48
Self-control in Asian culture, 308
Self-help groups in treatment of
    Native Americans, 76–77
Self-inspection in counseling blacks,
    143–144
Sexual dichotomy in Chicano culture,
    psychotherapy and, 278–279
Shaman, *see also* Traditional Amer-
    indian therapist(s)
Shamanism of Plains Indians, re-
    newed interest in, 12

Shame in Asian culture, 301, 302–306, 309, 318
Sickness
  initiatory, of shamans, 17
  soul loss, shamanic treatment of, 21–22
  spirit, of shamans, 17
Slavery
  dynamics of, in cultural-historical dimension of counseling blacks, 141–143
  in social-psychological functioning of blacks, 347
Slaves, types of, in counseling blacks, 142–143
Social conservation model, Levine's, 55–56
Social milieu, awareness of, in Asian culture, 309
Social status, respect for, in Papago culture, 89
Social work with Asian Americans, 307–316
  in community, 314–315
  cultural values and, 308–315
  in family, 312–314
Soul loss, shamanic treatment of, 21–22
Spirit dance for anomic depression, 23–24
Spirit intrusion, shamanic treatment of, 22–23
Spirit power vision of shamans, 17–18
Spirit sickness of shamans, 17
Spiritism in Puerto Rican culture, 209–210
Spiritual retreat of Plains Indians, 7
  renewed interest in, 12
Spiritualists, see Folk healers, Latino
Stress, sources of, in Latinos, 193–194
Stylistic dimensions of counseling blacks
  cultural-historical, 139–144
  psychosocial, 139–144
  scientific ideological, 139–144
Suicide among Cheyenne Indians, 65–69
  prevention of, 68–69
  reasons for, 66–67
Sun Dance rites

  of Cheyenne
    in handling aggression, 66
    prohibition of, 66
  of Plains Indians, 6–7
  renewed interest in, 12
Supernatural
  belief in
    in Hispanic American culture, 218–219
    socioeconomic success and, 222
  disease and the, in traditional Indian society, 16

Therapist, white, and black client, relationship between, 145–154
  alternatives in, 153–154
  feelings of therapist in, 145–148
  guilt in, 148–149
  interpersonal similarity in, 150–151
  power needs in, 149–150
  understanding social system and, 151–153
Time, informal orientation to, in Papago culture, 90
Traditional Amerindian therapist
  advantages of, 20
  behavior of, psychiatric classification of, 18–19
  cross-cultural collaboration with, 15–24
    obstacles to, 19–20
  current reappraisal of, 19
  definition of, 15
  modern Western therapist and, differences between, 15–16
  of Papago, 84–85
  preparation for, 20–21
  psychopathology hypothesis of, 16–19
  spirit power vision of, 17–18
  training of, in Mental Health Program of Indian Health Service, 34
  western view of, 16–17
Traditional Chippewa families, 60
  social casework and, 59
Traditional medicine in Mental Health Program of Indian Health Service, 34

Traditional Papago healing, 84–85
Traditional practices, policy of
    Mental Health Program of
    Indian Health Service on, 37

Urban American Indians, family
    behavior of, 55–63
  family network dynamics and,
    61–62
  family network hierarchy and, 58
  family structure and cultural
    behavior and, 56–58
  grandparents in, 58
  lifestyle patterns of, 58–60
Urban migration of Native Ameri-
    cans, 95–96

Value systems in counseling blacks,
    143
Values, essential
  definition of, 5
  of North American Plains Indians,
    6–8
  persistence of, 5–13
Verbosity, lack of, in Papago culture,
    89
Violence, overcrowding and, in black
    environment, 107–108
Vision quest of Plains Indians, 7
Visions, use of, in working with
    Indian clients, 73

Vocational Rehabilitation Act, Sec-
    tion 504 of, 48–49

Worcester Youth Guidance Center's
    Hispanic Program, 251–262
  case management component of,
    260–261
  clinical consultation component of,
    257–258
  clinical intervention component of,
    260–261
  community education and training
    component of, 255–257
  description of, 253–255
  funding for, 254
  program consultation component
    of, 258
  Puerto Rican migration patterns
    and, 252
  research component of, 258–260
  setting for, 251–252
World view
  definition of, 339
  determinants of, 339–340
  dimensions of, 340–343
  formation of, 343–349
  locus of control and, 340–341,
    344–349
  locus of responsibility and,
    341–343, 344–349
  of minorities, 339–350, 354
World War II, Japanese American
    internment during, 299–301